HISTORIC PHOTOS OF
OKLAHOMA

TEXT AND CAPTIONS BY LARRY JOHNSON

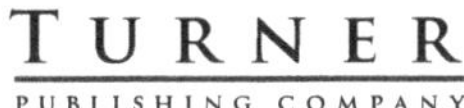

On July 4, 1889, all of Guthrie lined up to celebrate the nation's 113th birthday and to show the town's appreciation for a special visitor: Representative Bishop Walden Perkins. The Kansas congressman was called by some the "Father of Oklahoma" because of his successful attachment of the Oklahoma clause, which called for opening portions of Indian Territory to white settlement, to the Indian Appropriations bill.

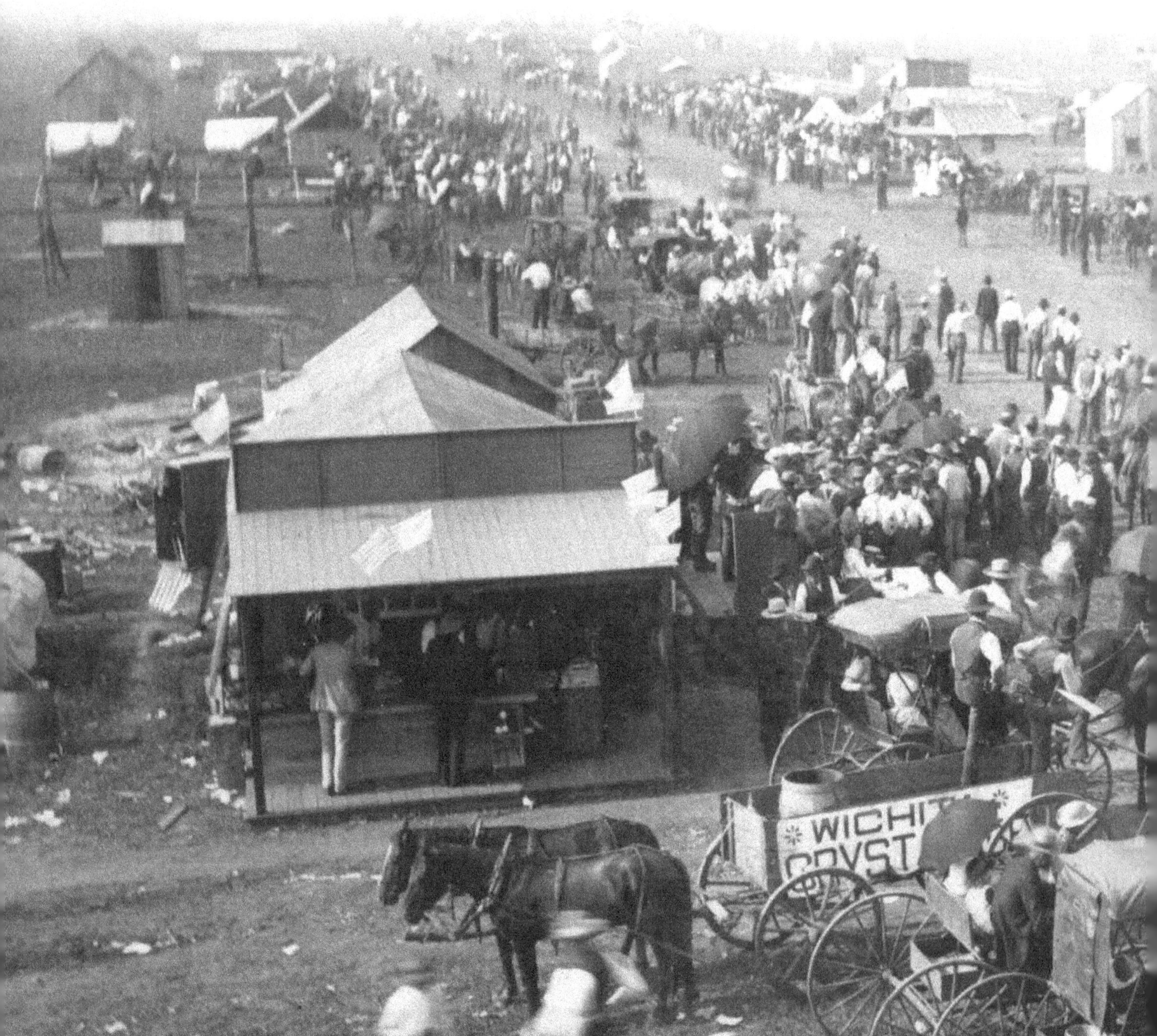

HISTORIC PHOTOS OF
OKLAHOMA

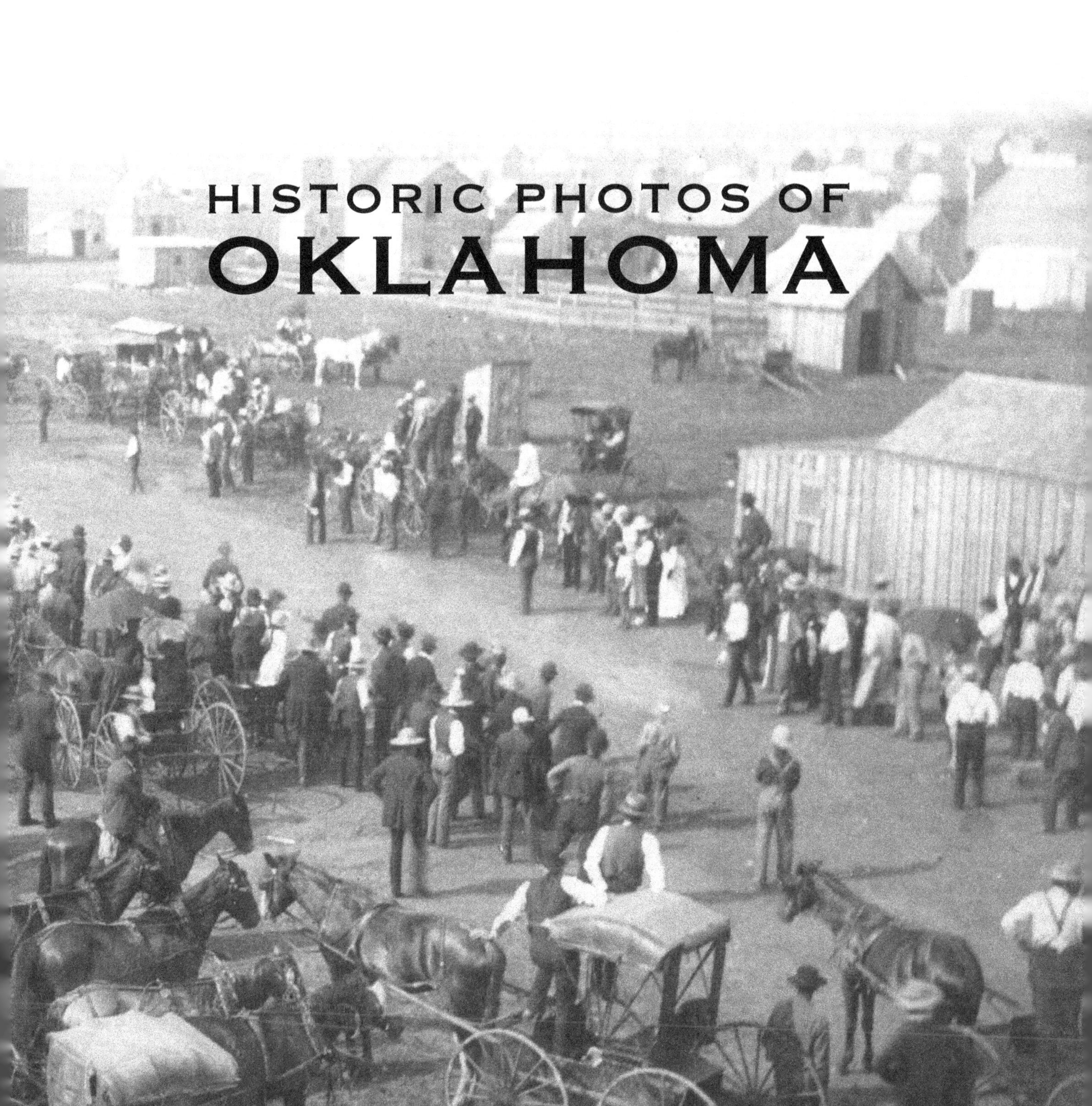

Turner Publishing Company
www.turnerpublishing.com

Historic Photos of Oklahoma

Library of Congress Control Number: 2008908518

ISBN-13: 978-1-59652-513-9

Printed in the United States of America

ISBN 978-1-68442-071-1 (hc)

Contents

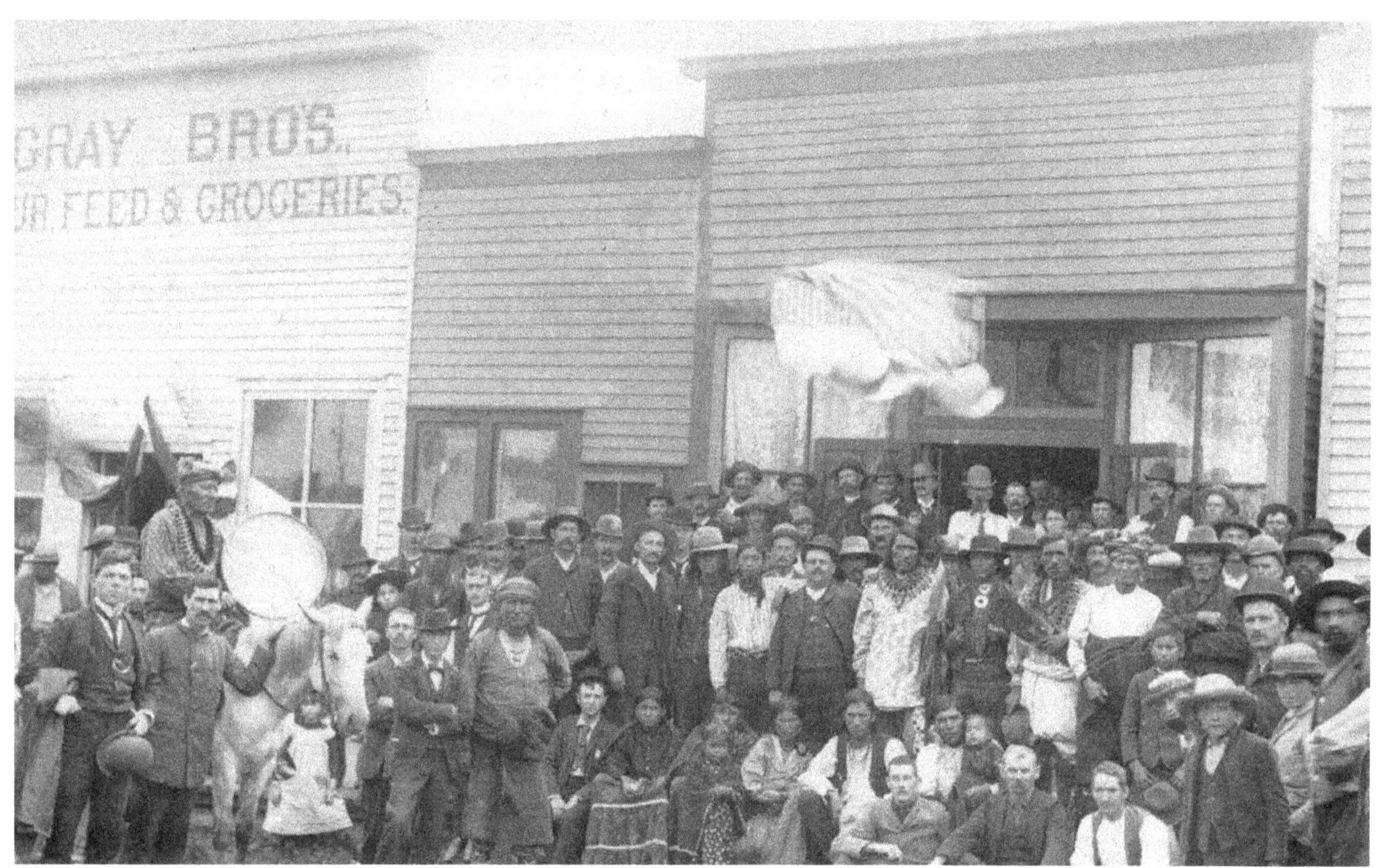

In September 1889, not long after the visit by Representative Perkins, Guthrie received a congressional delegation that had traveled west to inspect the conditions in Oklahoma. Here, Iowa Indians pose in front of Nowlan's Restaurant. They had come from their nearby reservation seeking the approval of the congressmen to unite with the Otoe tribe.

Acknowledgments

With the exception of cropping images where needed and touching up imperfections that have accrued over time, no other changes have been made to the photographs in this volume. The caliber and clarity of many photographs are limited to the technology of the day and the ability of the photographer at the time they were made.

This volume, *Historic Photos of Oklahoma,* is the result of the cooperation and efforts of many individuals, organizations, and corporations. It is with great thanks that we acknowledge the valuable contribution of the following for their generous support:

Library of Congress
Oklahoma Historical Society

Madeleine Claire, Victoria, and Jandy provided wonderful suggestions and support in the writing of the text.

Preface

In many families, the first few years of the first-born child are fully documented on film. From the first day, the photo albums begin to pile up; but as years go by, the albums get thinner, and before long the annual school photo is the only reliable photographic record of the person's childhood. So it has been with several Oklahoma towns and cities. Because of their instant birth, the first days of many Oklahoma towns are remarkably well recorded; but from later years, mostly what remain are staid real-estate photographs and views of commercial districts. As one moves into the 1950s and 1960s, the photographs available from archives begin to dwindle, dissipating further in the 1970s.

Still, Oklahoma has an excellent photographic record of life in what was then Indian Territory, before the arrival of the town builders. Photography in the late nineteenth century had become portable, affordable, and popular. By that time, the Five Civilized Tribes (Cherokee, Chickasaw, Choctaw, Muscogee [Creek], and Seminole) had been in eastern and southern Indian Territory for over 50 years. Photographs of that part of the state in that era depict the numerous missionary boarding schools in the region as well as the large homes built by the more fortunate members and leaders of the tribes.

In the west, the scene was quite different. There, images of the movable dwellings of nomadic plains tribes are contrasted against the primitive dwellings of white settlers. Photographers like Will Soule and Edward Curtis were moved by the belief that Indian Territory represented the last opportunity to capture indigenous cultures in their natural states. Although these men may not have been thoroughly knowledgeable about the cultures, they were generally earnest in their respect for the tribes, and a great debt is owed them for preserving images of these people and their lives. Likewise, lensmen such as William S. Prettyman and Andrew Forbes are remembered for their work with some of the last real working cowboys and drovers as they worked the ranchlands of the west and the panhandle.

Historic Photos of Oklahoma is not an illustrated history of Oklahoma, nor is it an attempt at a visual chronology of the state. Readers seeking photographs of famous people and landmark buildings (though there are a few) may be disappointed.

Rather, the selection of photographs here tells the story of this diverse group of people called Oklahomans as witnessed in their faces, the homes they cherished, and the streets they lived in.

Just as viewing a succession of those school photos reveals the periods of beauty and awkwardness, innocence and maturity, hardship and joy in a child's life, the reader of this book will see the tragedy of Indian removal, the exuberance of land runs, the shame of segregation, the anguish of the Depression, and the optimism for the future. In between are glimpses of how we used to live, work, and play in the forty-sixth state of the Union.

—Larry Johnson

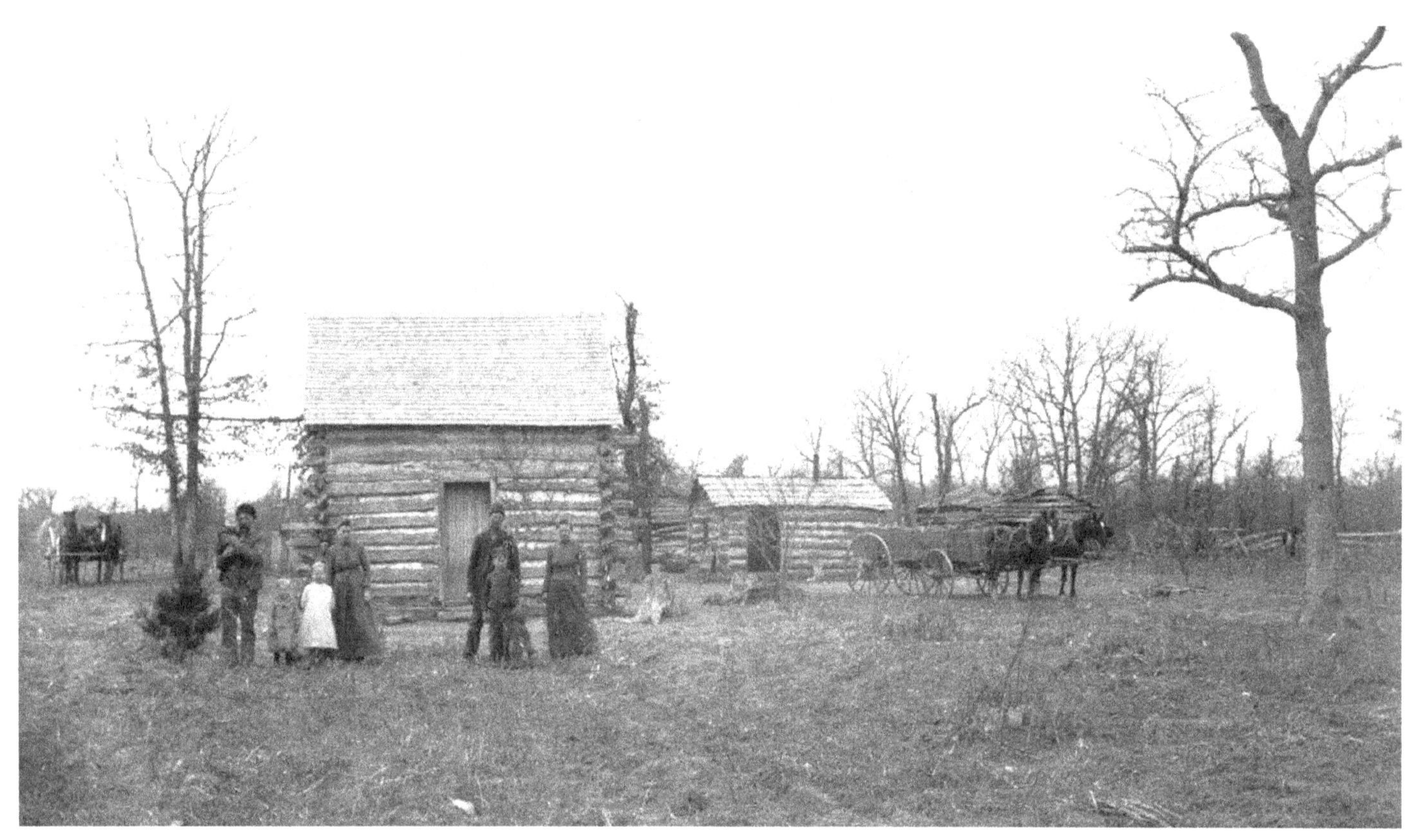

The Finley Bowen family stands outside their homestead northeast of Coyle. This photo was likely taken in the aftermath of a tornado outbreak across Kingfisher and Logan counties on May 2, 1892. Damage looks slight here, but three died in Kingfisher and several buildings were destroyed.

Way Down Yonder in the Indian Nation

(1870s–1900)

The Indian Removal Act of 1830 and the subsequent tragedy of the Trail of Tears migration define the state's early history, as the Five Civilized Tribes and, later, smaller tribes from around the United States were forced to remake their lives in Indian Territory. The five nations largely clung to the hills and timber of the south and east, preferring to lease the expansive land beyond the Cross Timbers to ranchers. Some built large plantations, while others tried to maintain traditional lives; all jealously guarded their autonomy until the Civil War forced them to make difficult choices.

Following the Civil War, during which some factions of the tribes joined the Confederacy, much of the western lands of Indian Territory were punitively stripped away and used to facilitate the removal of several plains tribes, including the Cheyenne, Arapaho, Comanche, and Kiowa. The United States Army's Fort Sill (1869) and Fort Reno (1875) represented the first permanent white settlements in the west, though ranchers from Texas and Kansas had already begun leasing and squatting on lands in the Cherokee Outlet and No-Man's Land of the panhandle.

Meanwhile, in the east, the five nations fought unsuccessfully to prevent the Missouri-Kansas-Texas Railroad (commonly known as the Katy Railroad) from piercing their homeland in order to build a route from the cattle country of Texas to markets in Kansas City. They feared, rightly, that the railroad would soon bring white settlers and the end of their autonomy. Intermarriage and the presence of outlaws and other undesirables had already caused tensions in the region.

Throughout the 1870s and 1880s, white farmers pressured the federal government to open up land in Indian Territory to white settlement. These boomers were finally successful, and in 1889 the Unassigned Lands—land in the center of the territory that had not been assigned to a particular tribe—were opened to white settlers. Within a year the western half of Indian Territory was organized into Oklahoma Territory; a series of runs and lotteries brought thousands of settlers, and hundreds of towns sprang up overnight.

The early photographs of Oklahoma reveal the abundant cultural and ecological diversity of the state as well as the many strange dualities that have been present on its land since the Louisiana Purchase: the treeless flatlands of the west and the hilly forests of the east; the plains Indians and the southeastern Indians; the outlaws and the missionaries.

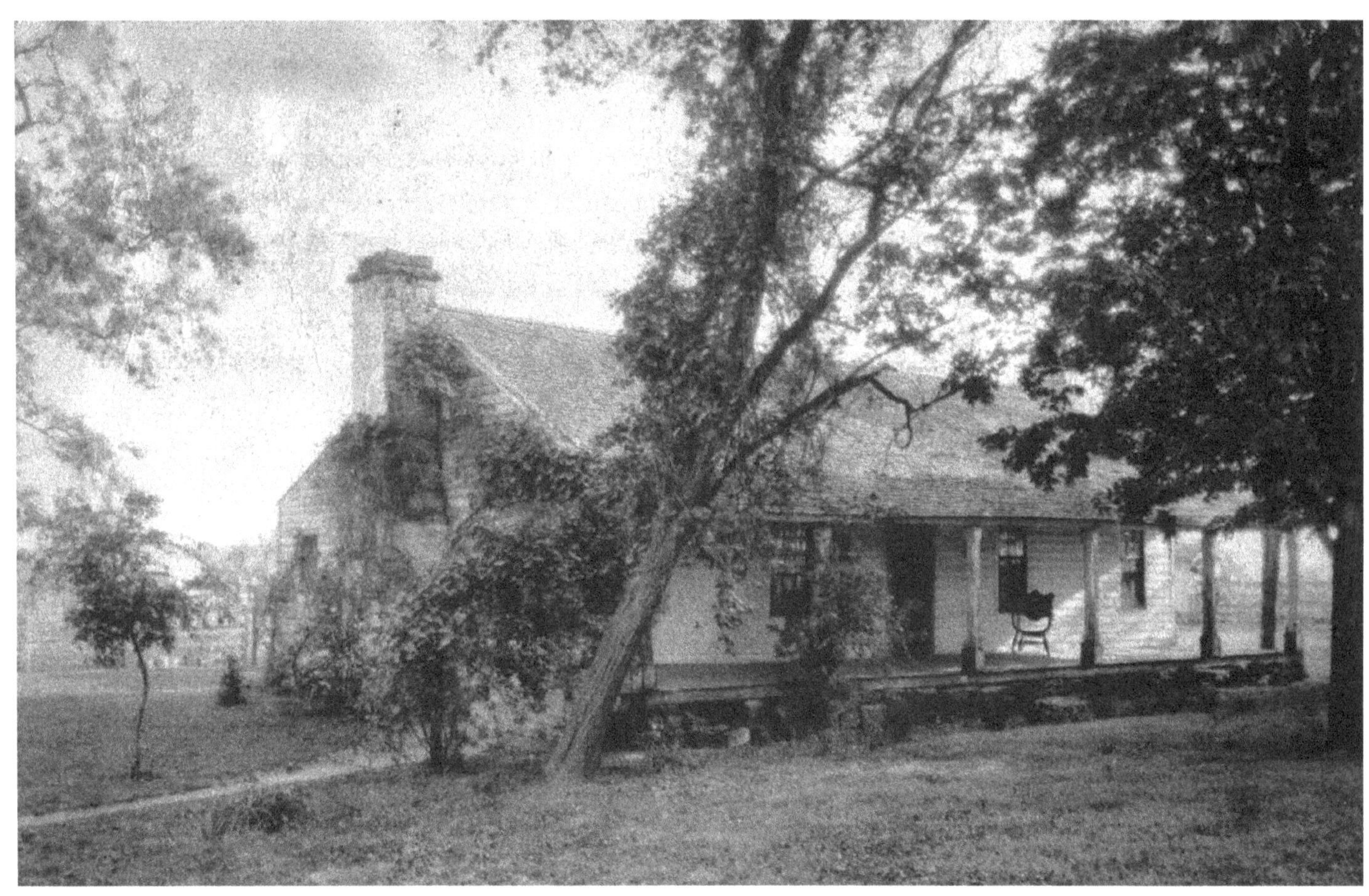

After the battle of Claremore Mound between the Osage and newly arrived Cherokee in 1817, the Army established a presence in the Three Forks area to keep the peace. The building seen here was erected in 1818 (though photographed much later) and housed officers until Fort Gibson was built nearby in 1824.

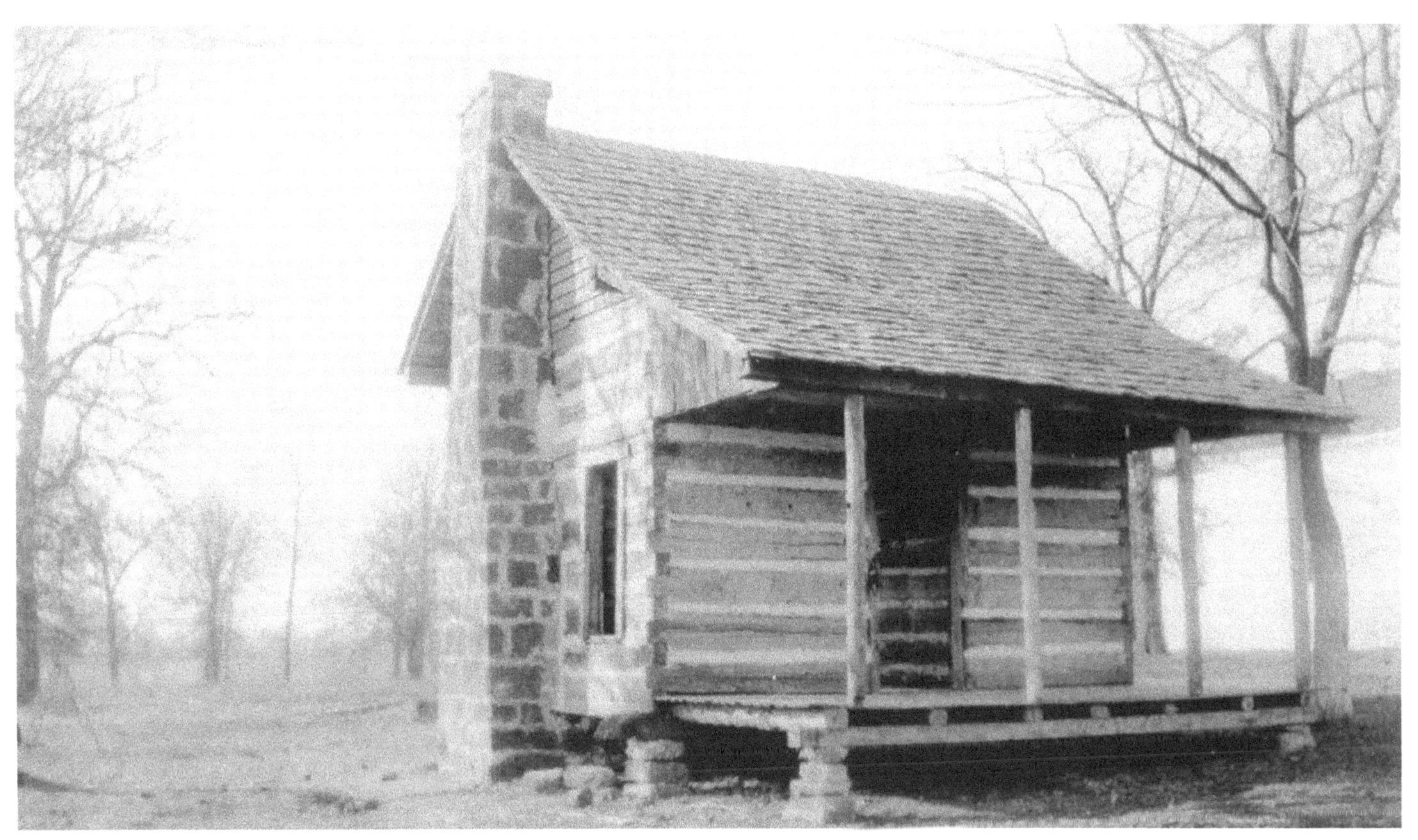

This sturdy cabin was the home of Basil LeFlore, a future Choctaw governor, in 1837. Most of the prominent LeFlore family was able to remain in Mississippi, but Basil went west during the removal and became an important political figure in the 1850s.

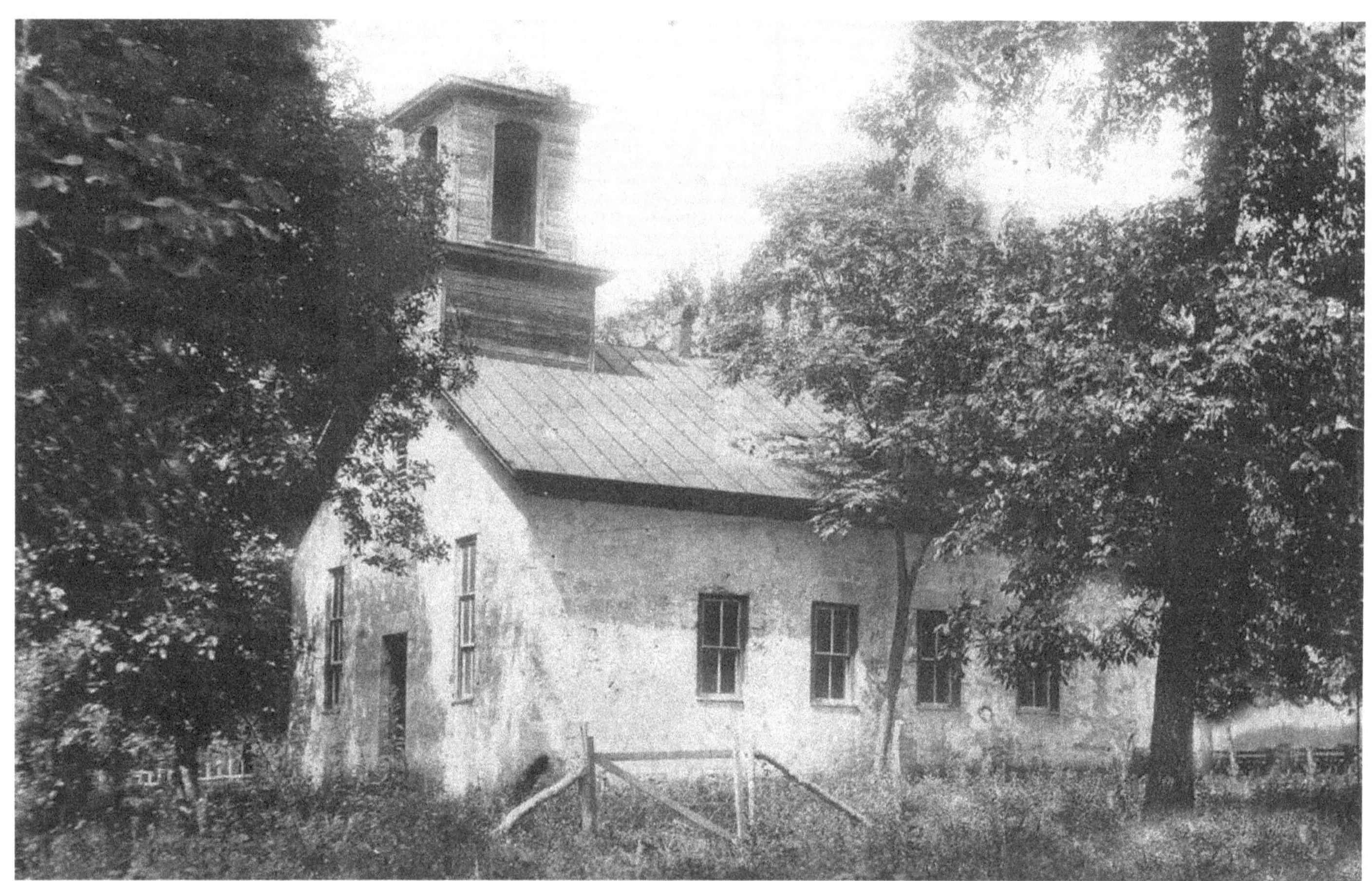

The Presbyterian missionary Alfred Wright had worked among the Choctaw in Mississippi beginning in the 1820s and resumed his work in Indian Territory after the removal. In 1846, parishioners from his Wheelock mission near Idabel built this stone church—it stands today as the oldest church in Oklahoma.

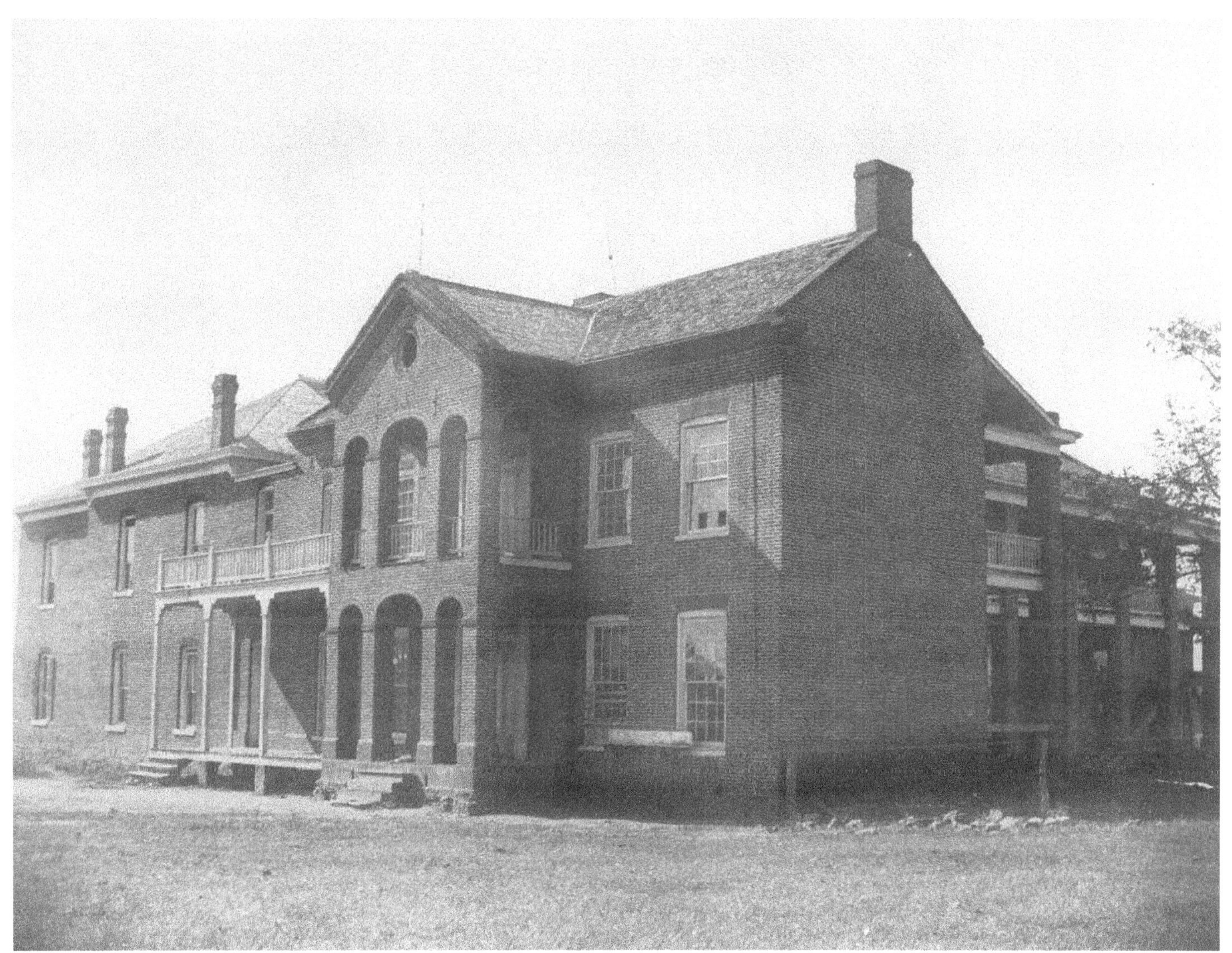

The Choctaw Nation embraced formal education, working with and even funding missionary schools. The Armstrong Academy was a boarding school for boys established near Bokchito in 1844; this structure, though photographed much later, was built only a few years after the school was founded.

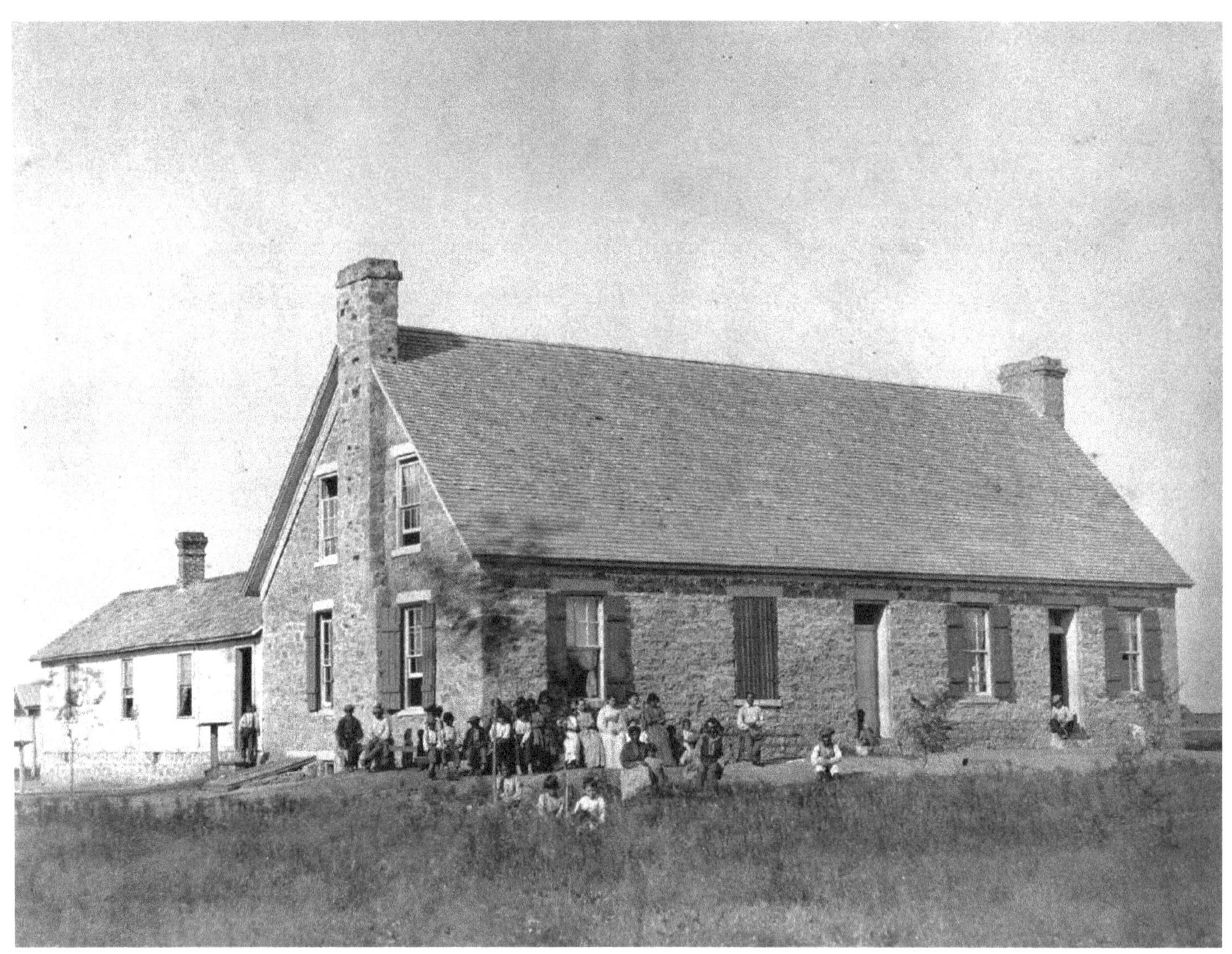

Fort Sill was established in southwestern Oklahoma in 1869 to pacify the southern plains tribes. Two miles away, the Quakers operated the Kiowa-Comanche Agency, where they constructed this school from native stone in 1871.

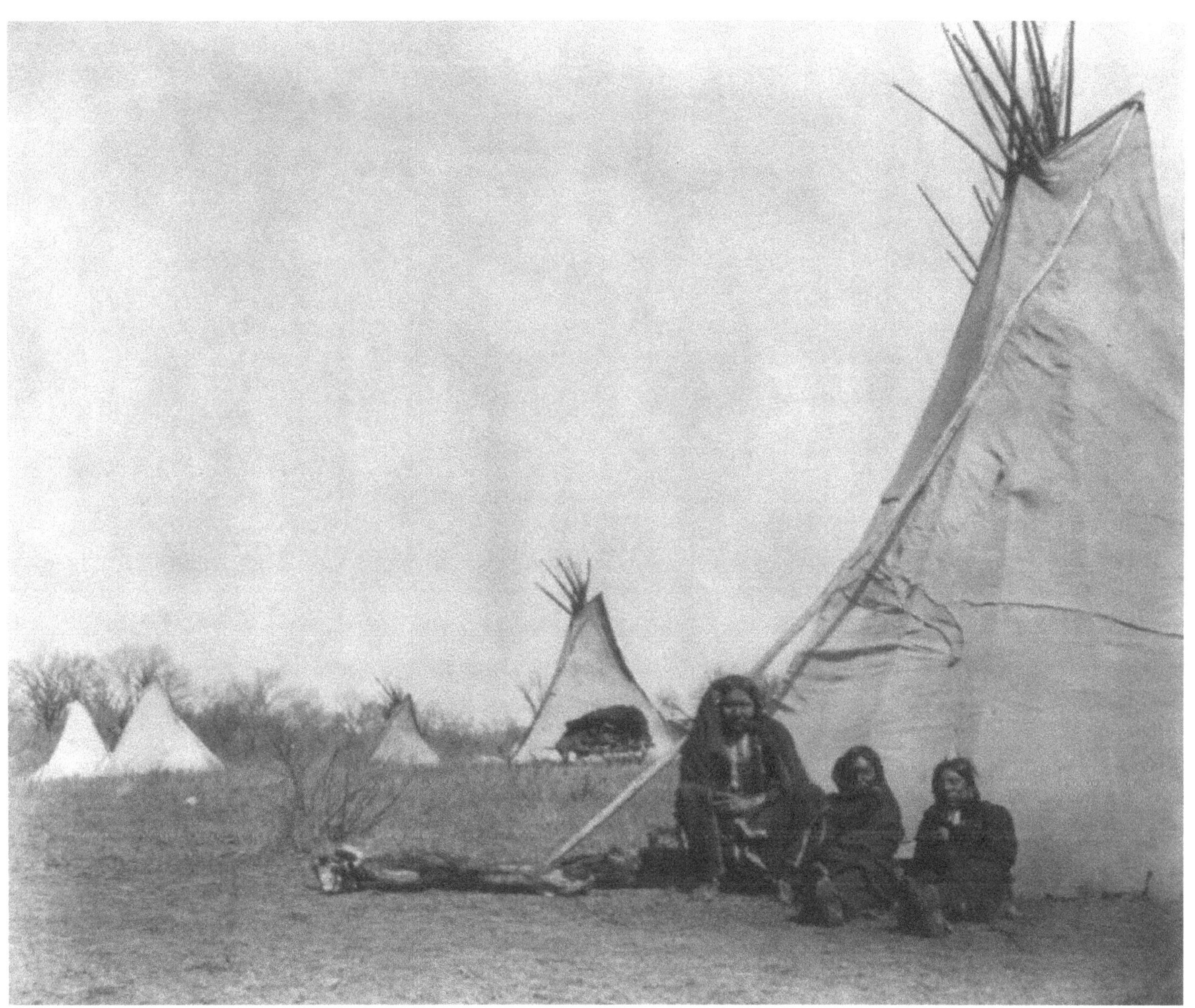

This group of Comanches encamped near Fort Sill in 1873 was likely part of the Noconee band whose chief, Horse-back, was involved in negotiations for the release of two of his captured allies: Satanta and Big Tree.

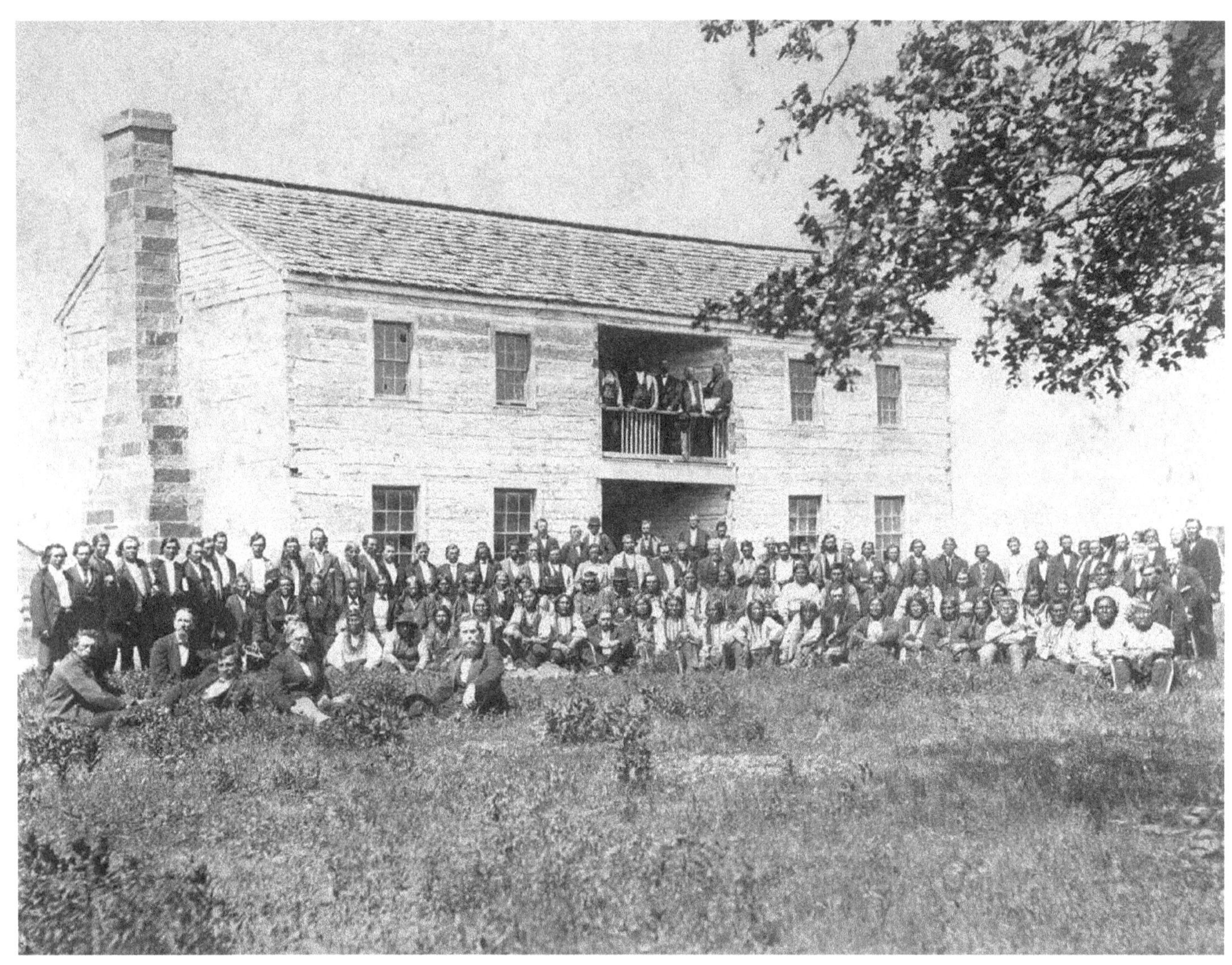

In 1875, representatives from most of the tribes in Indian Territory met at the Grand Council at the Creek Nation Courthouse in Okmulgee. Discussions centered on the possibility of an all-Indian state joining the Union, and members drafted a constitution that called for a territorial governor, U.S. courts, and a delegate to Congress.

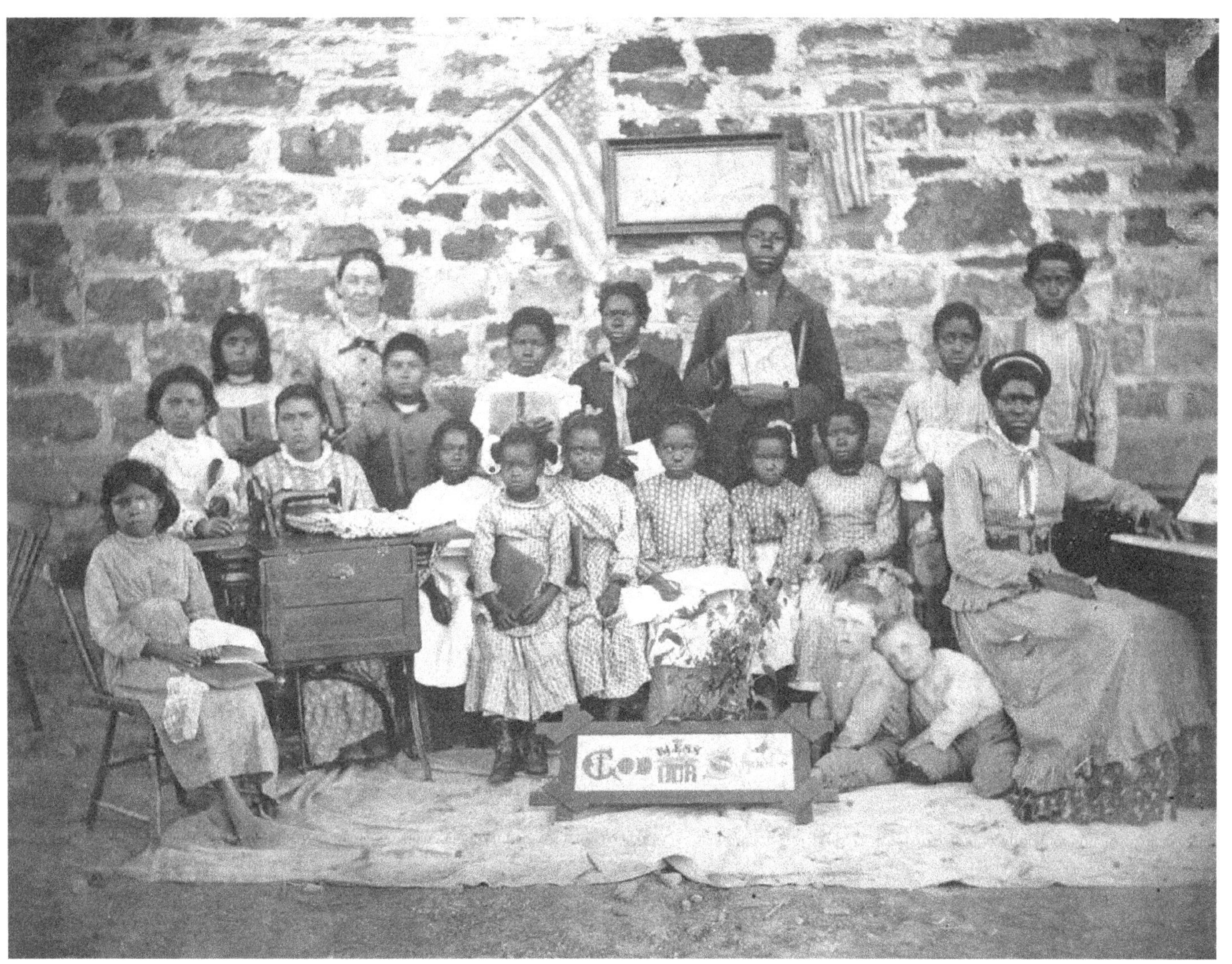

In 1880, Antoinette Constant (probably the woman standing at back-left) taught this integrated student body at the Seminole school in Wewoka. But after she defended a woman that the tribe had accused of witchcraft in a Salem-style trial, Seminole chief John Chupco declared, "Get another *ma-hi-va* (teacher)," and she was fired on the spot and not allowed to teach in Seminole country again.

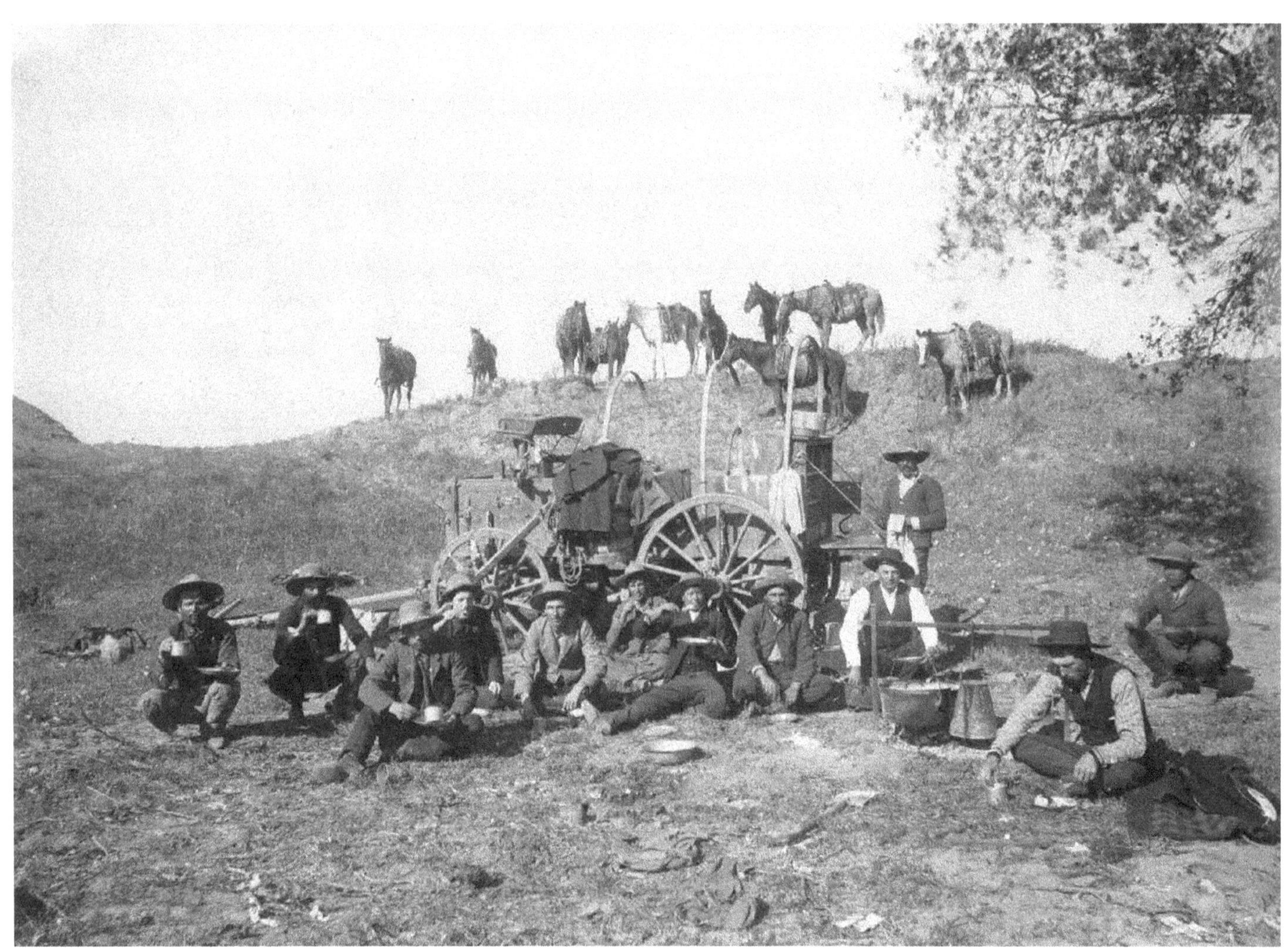

In 1887, noted photographer William S. Prettyman roamed Indian Territory living the range life of the cowboy and capturing on film the last bit of unclaimed prairie in America. Here he depicts a cowboy dinner on Ross Stratton's Turkey Creek ranch near the present site of Enid. Stratton is third from the left.

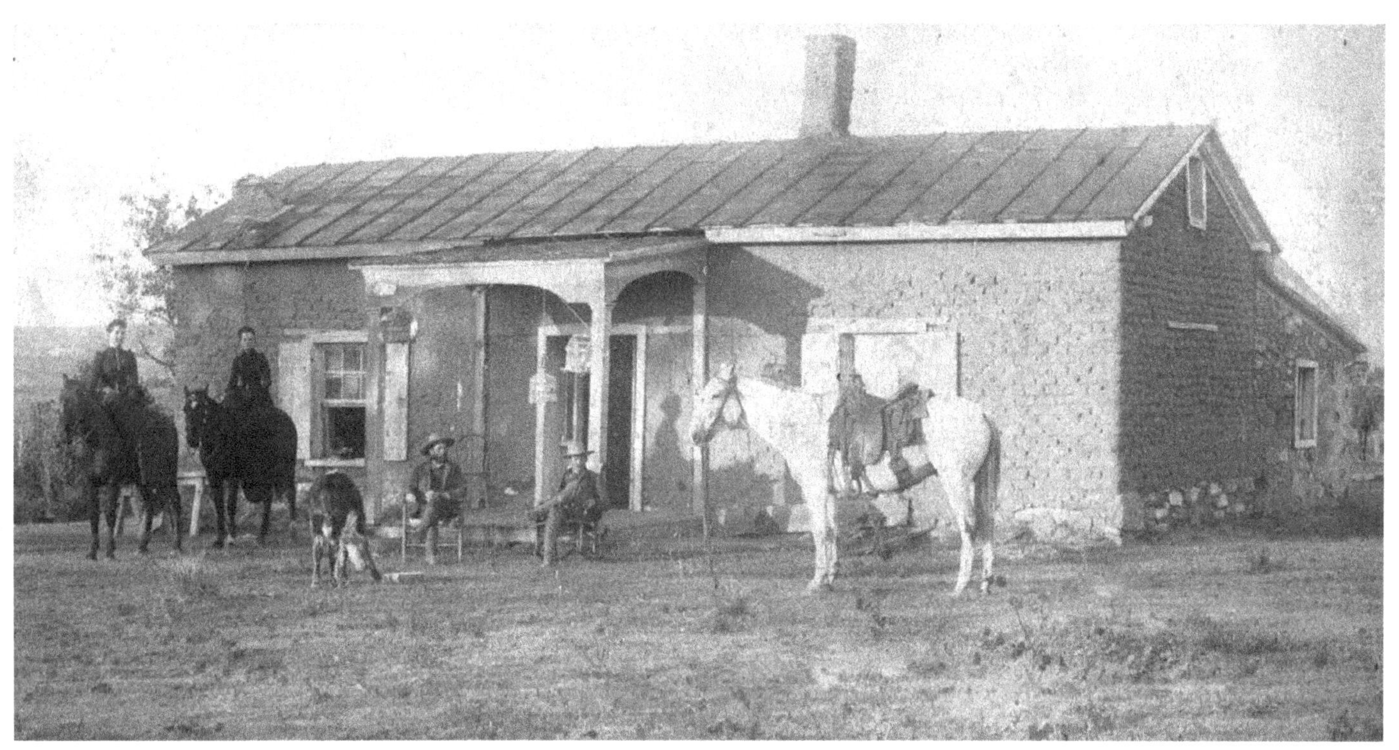

Not then attached to any state, No-Man's Land comprised miles of lucrative rangeland for cattle. Some ranchers did quite well, as seen in this photo from about 1889. Though it was a lawless land, one early rancher recalled, "The honest-to-God truth is that more people died from ennui and nostalgia than perished in outlaw combats."

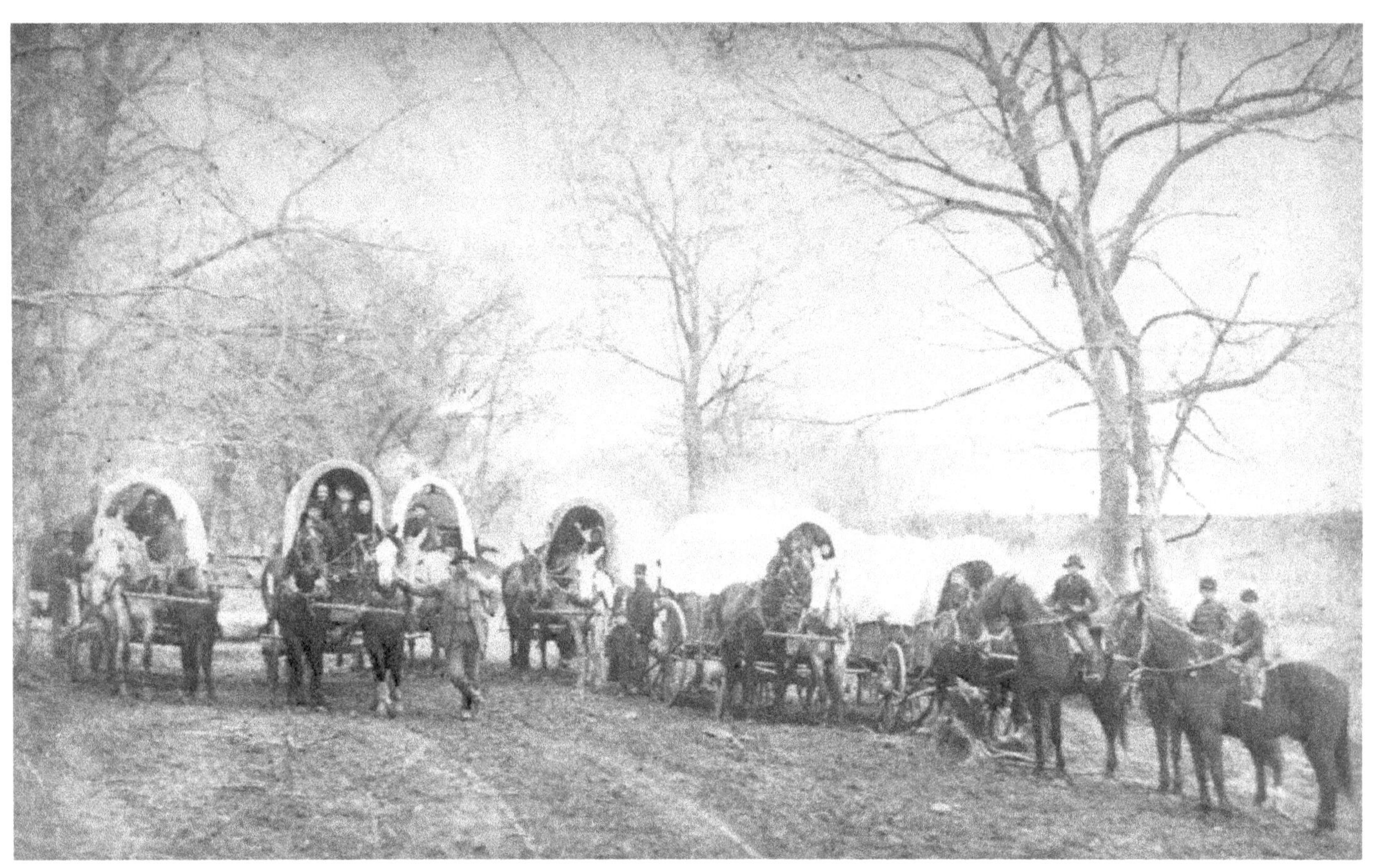

A family crosses into the Unassigned Lands at their opening, April 22, 1889. One observer in Purcell wrote that in the predawn hours of that day he saw "the ghostly forms of prairie schooners moving toward the ford a mile north of town."

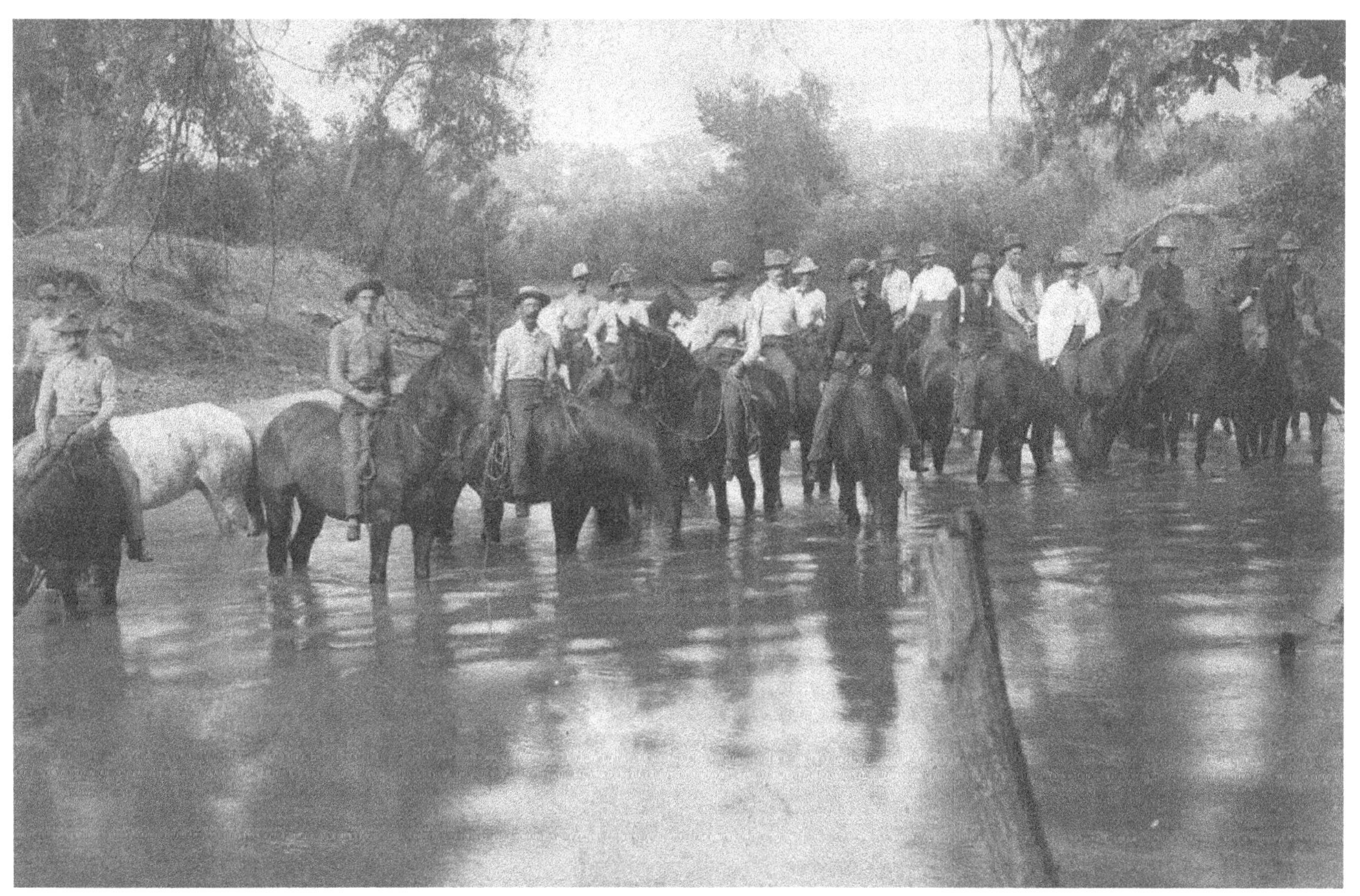

Federal troops water their horses in the Canadian River in April 1889. Several companies of soldiers made regular patrols in the days before the opening of the Unassigned Lands. Their commander, General Wesley Merritt, meant business: "They are under positive orders to keep order and quiet and they will obey at any cost."

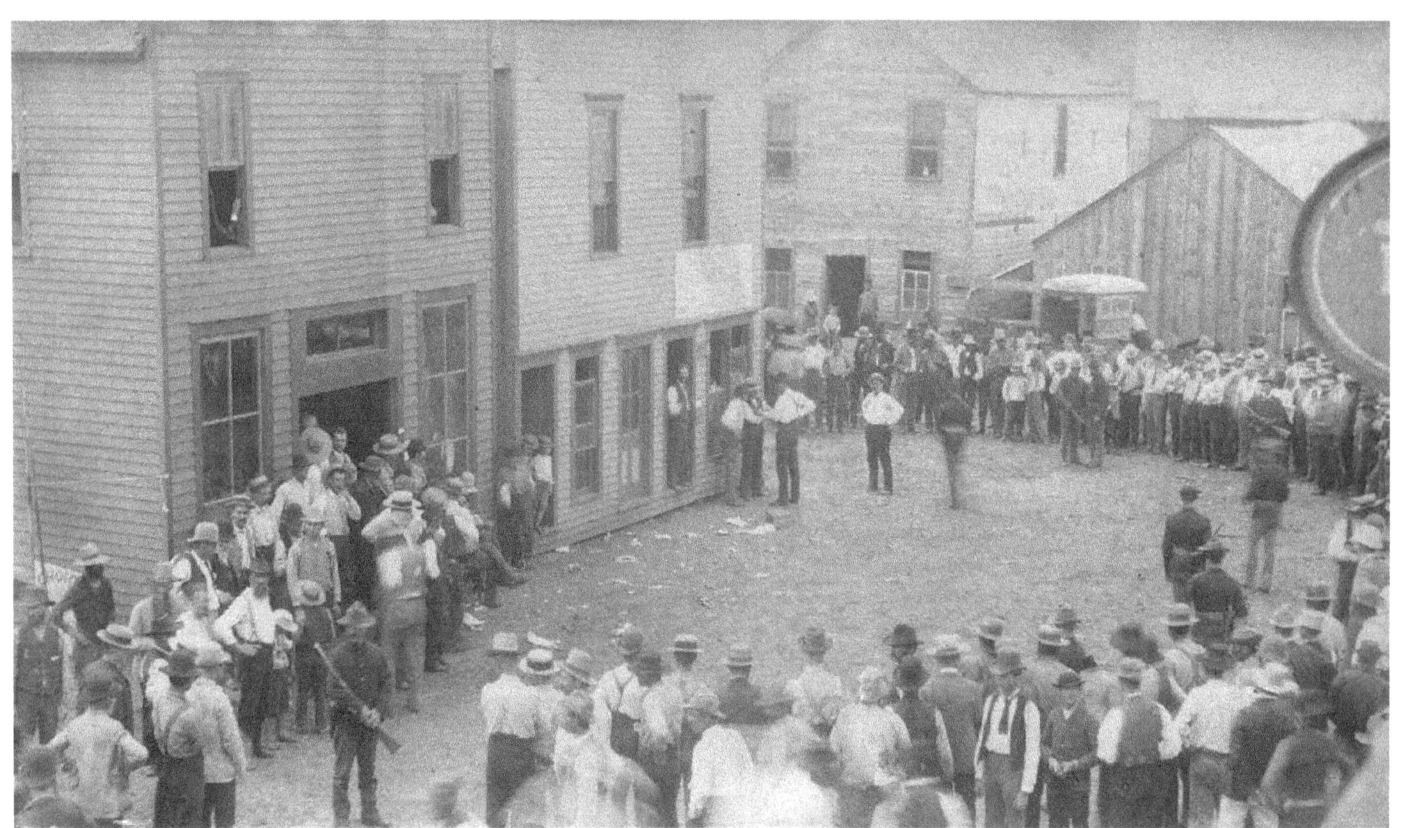

Crowds gather in Purcell in the days before the land opening of 1889. Purcell stood just a mile south of the Canadian River on the Santa Fe Railroad. On April 23 a newspaperman reported, "Yesterday it was a metropolis, to-nite it is a hamlet . . . the scenes of this hegira will never be erased from the memory of those who witnessed them."

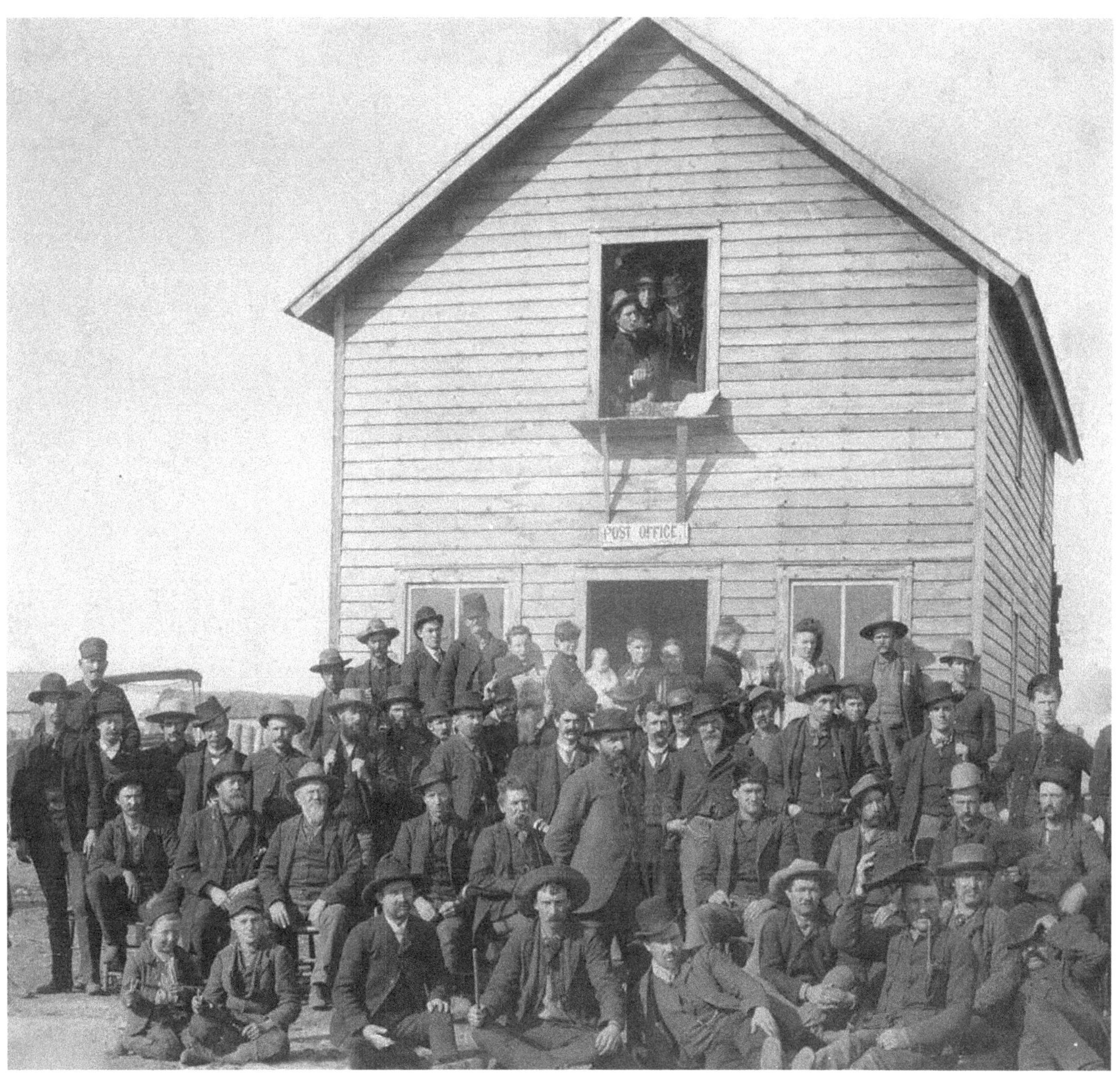

Early settlers assemble at Oklahoma City's second post office in 1889. This building was constructed on West Main across from the Santa Fe tracks about two weeks after the opening. At the time, it was the sturdiest building in town and served as a meeting place for churches, Sunday schools, the YMCA, and even Indian councils.

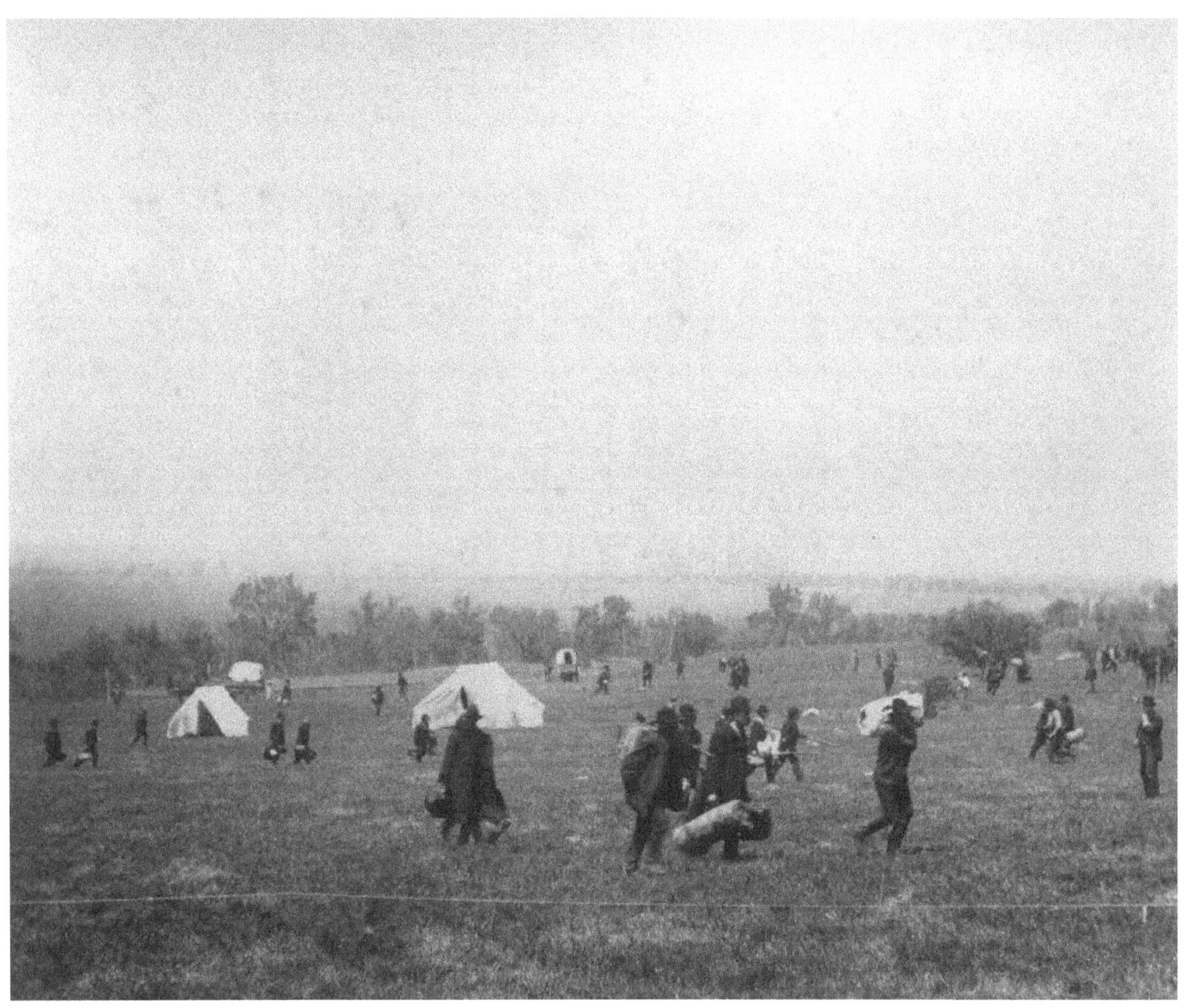

On April 22, 1889, homestead hopefuls stream across the open prairie to claim lots in what would become Guthrie. About 10,000 people settled in the new town by sundown on the first day of the land opening.

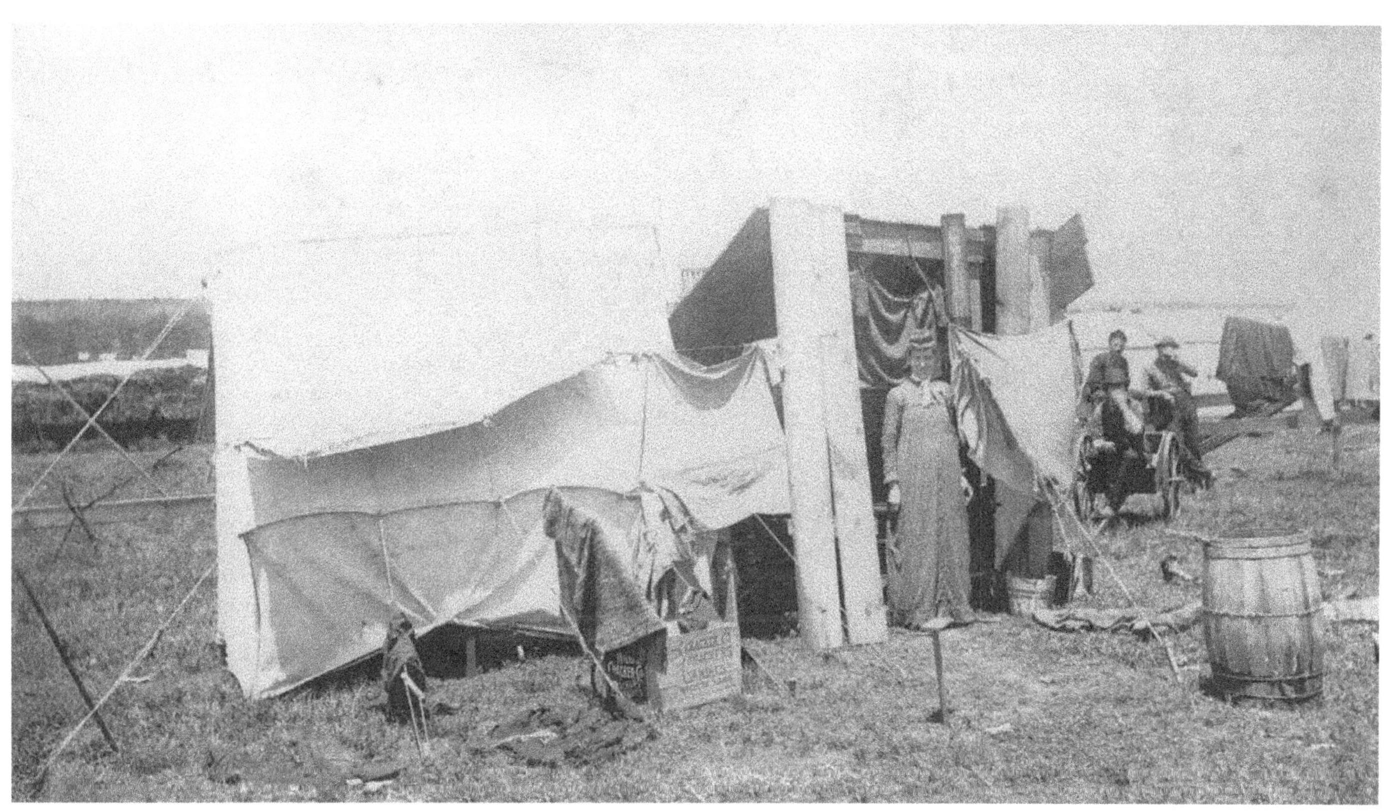

An early resident holds down a lot in Guthrie after the opening. The facts surrounding this particular settler are unknown, but it was common in the early days for women and children to occupy a claim while men made the arduous trip to the land office to file, or went in search of work to provide necessities for the family.

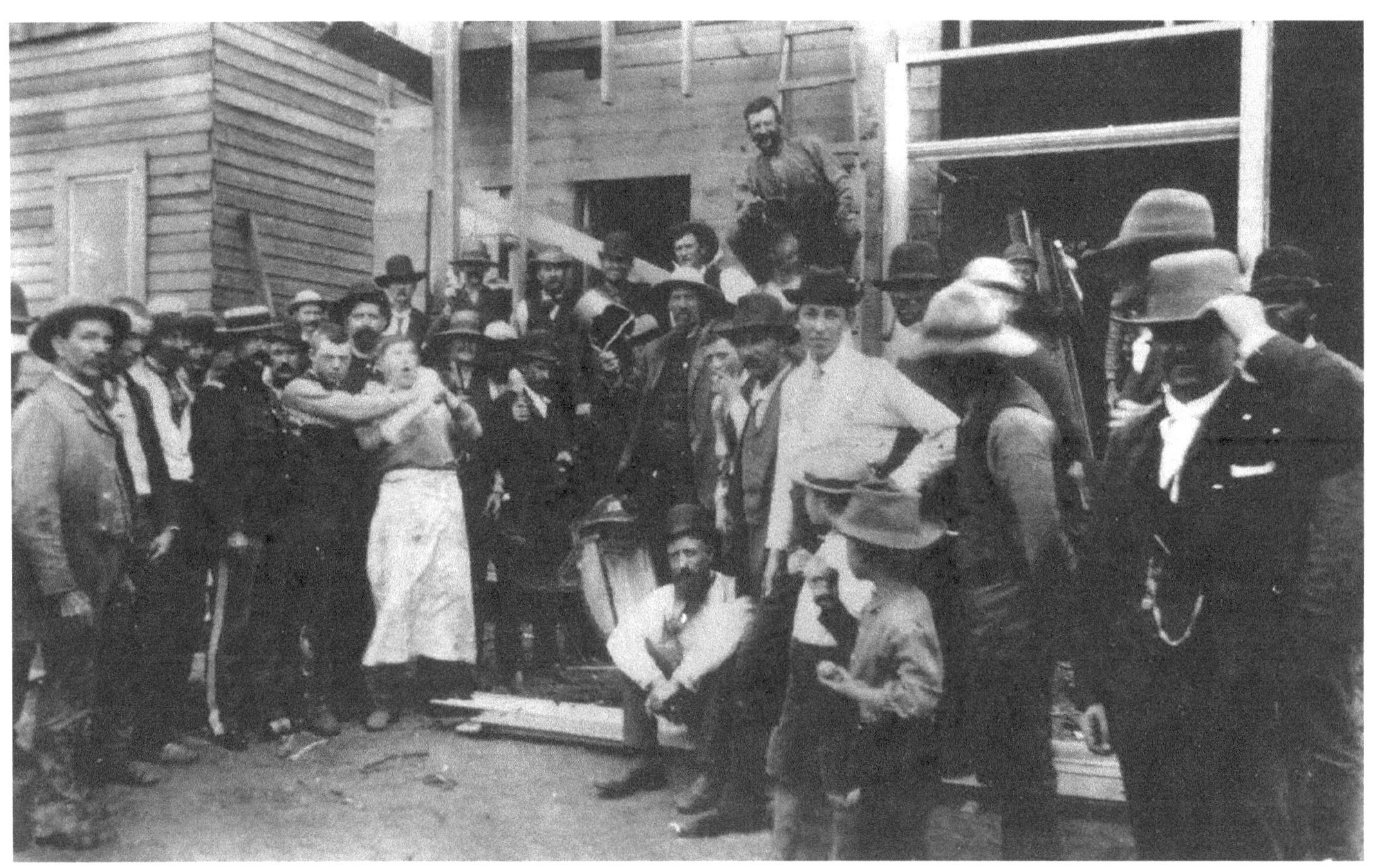

This scene in Guthrie just after the destruction of a supply of liquor by federal officials was photographed in May 1889. Contrary to public opinion, the government considered the newly opened land in Oklahoma still a part of Indian Territory, where liquor was forbidden. When Oklahoma Territory was formed in 1890, prohibition was removed.

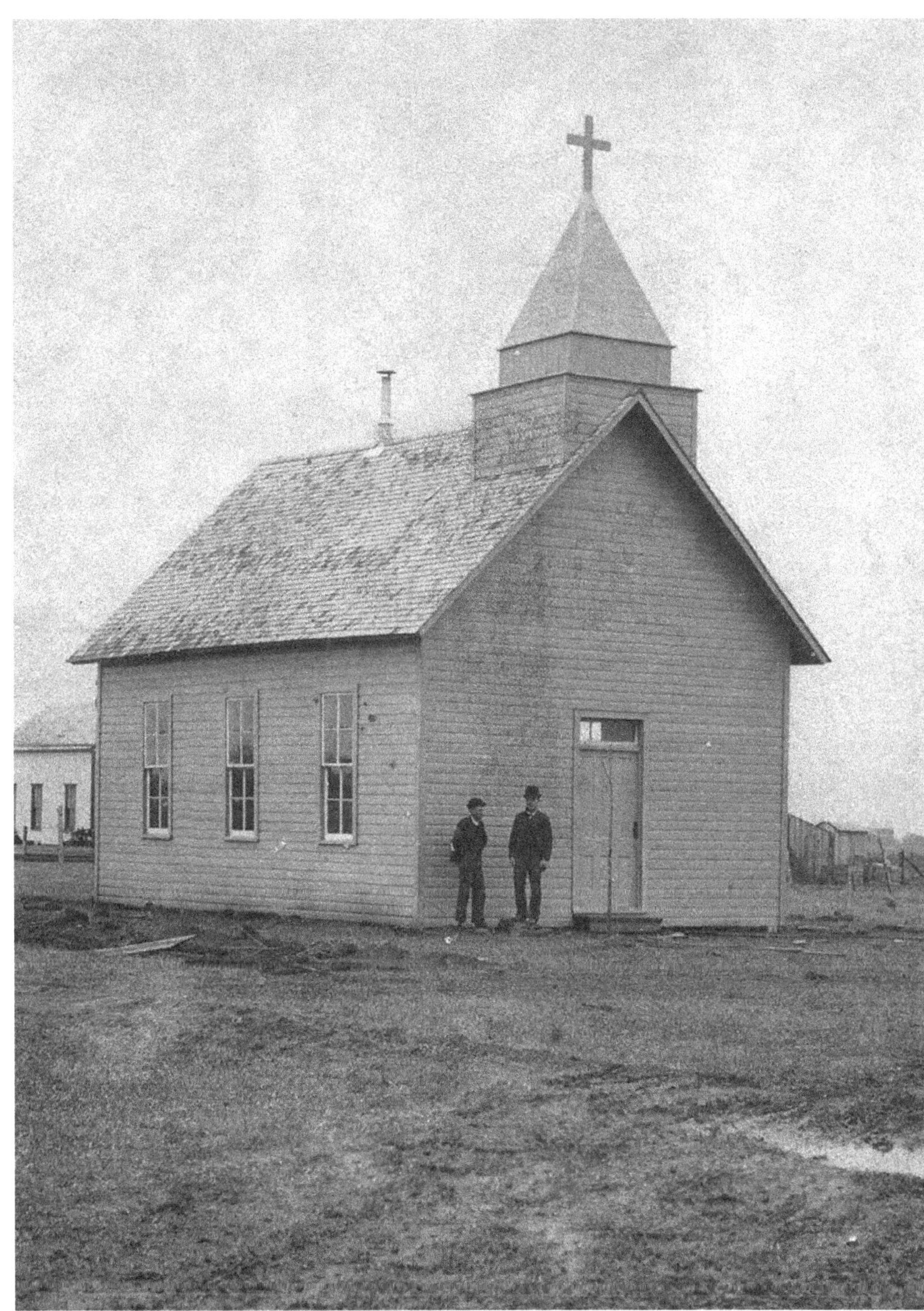

In the months before the opening, very few people were allowed to operate in the Unassigned Lands. One of those was Father Scallan, a priest from Australia. He found four Catholics living in Edmond, and on June 24, 1889, they dedicated the first church in Oklahoma—St. John the Baptist—at First and Boulevard.

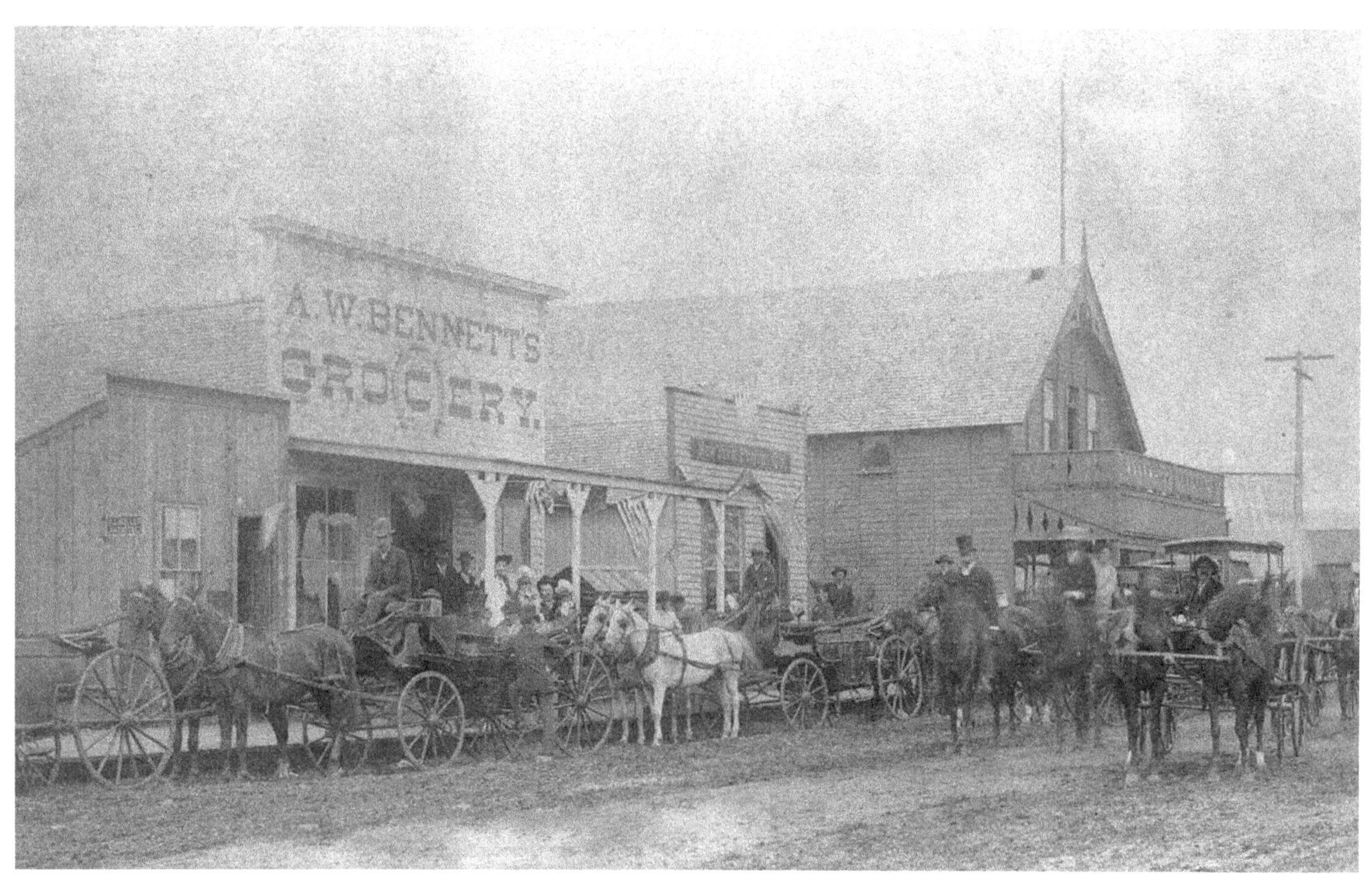

St. Louis and Kansas City newspapers reported that Guthrie provided a royal reception to six visiting congressmen in September 1889. These carriages were assembled to carry the visitors in a parade down Oklahoma Avenue—a parade that included about 3,000 of the town's 10,000 inhabitants.

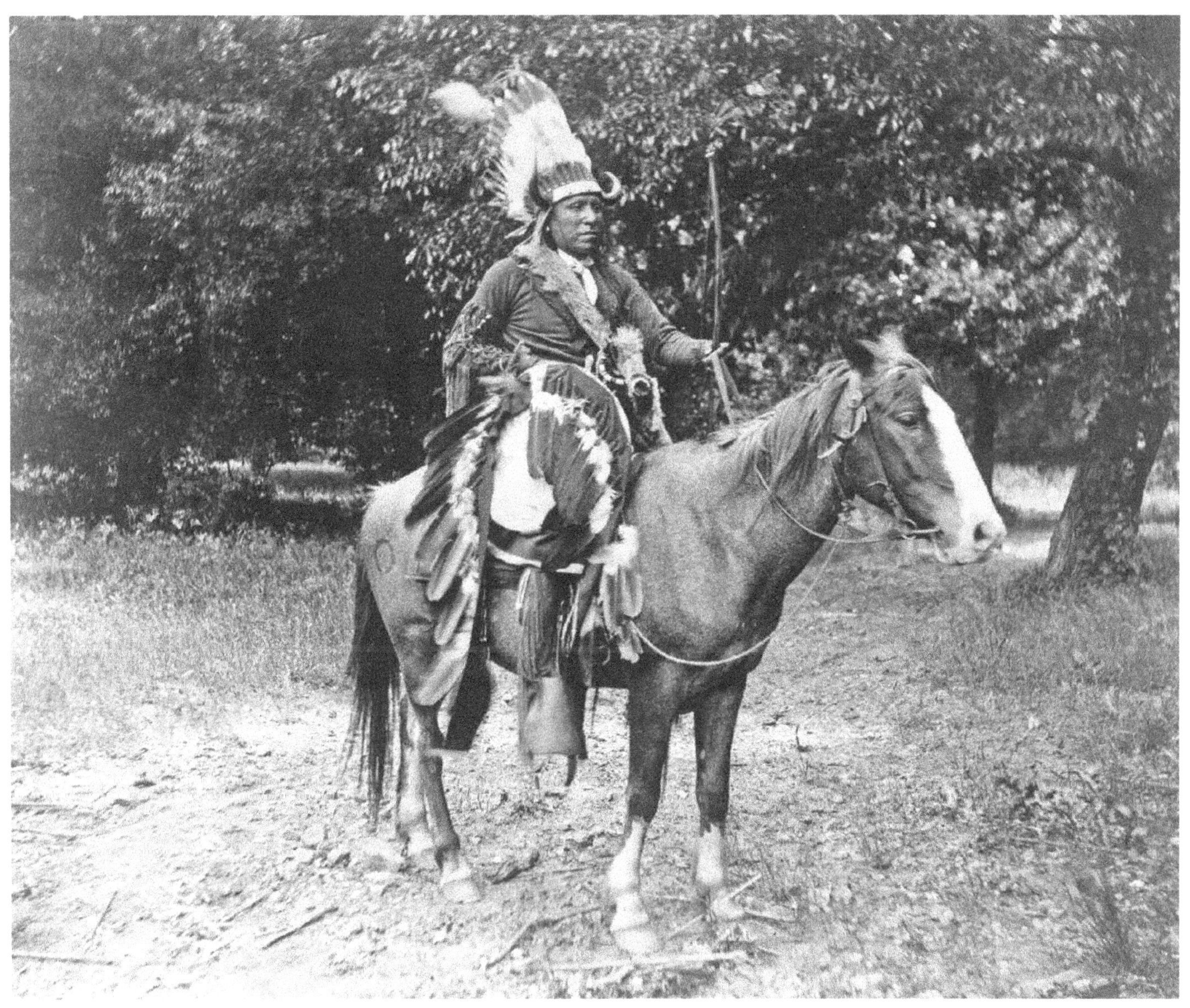

Kiowa scout Elk Tongue was photographed in full war regalia, ca. 1891. Recruited at Fort Sill in 1875, the Kiowa Scouts were later incorporated into the famed 7th Cavalry as Troop L. The scouts performed admirably and were fiercely loyal to their commander, Lieutenant Hugh L. Scott, who communicated with them in their own language.

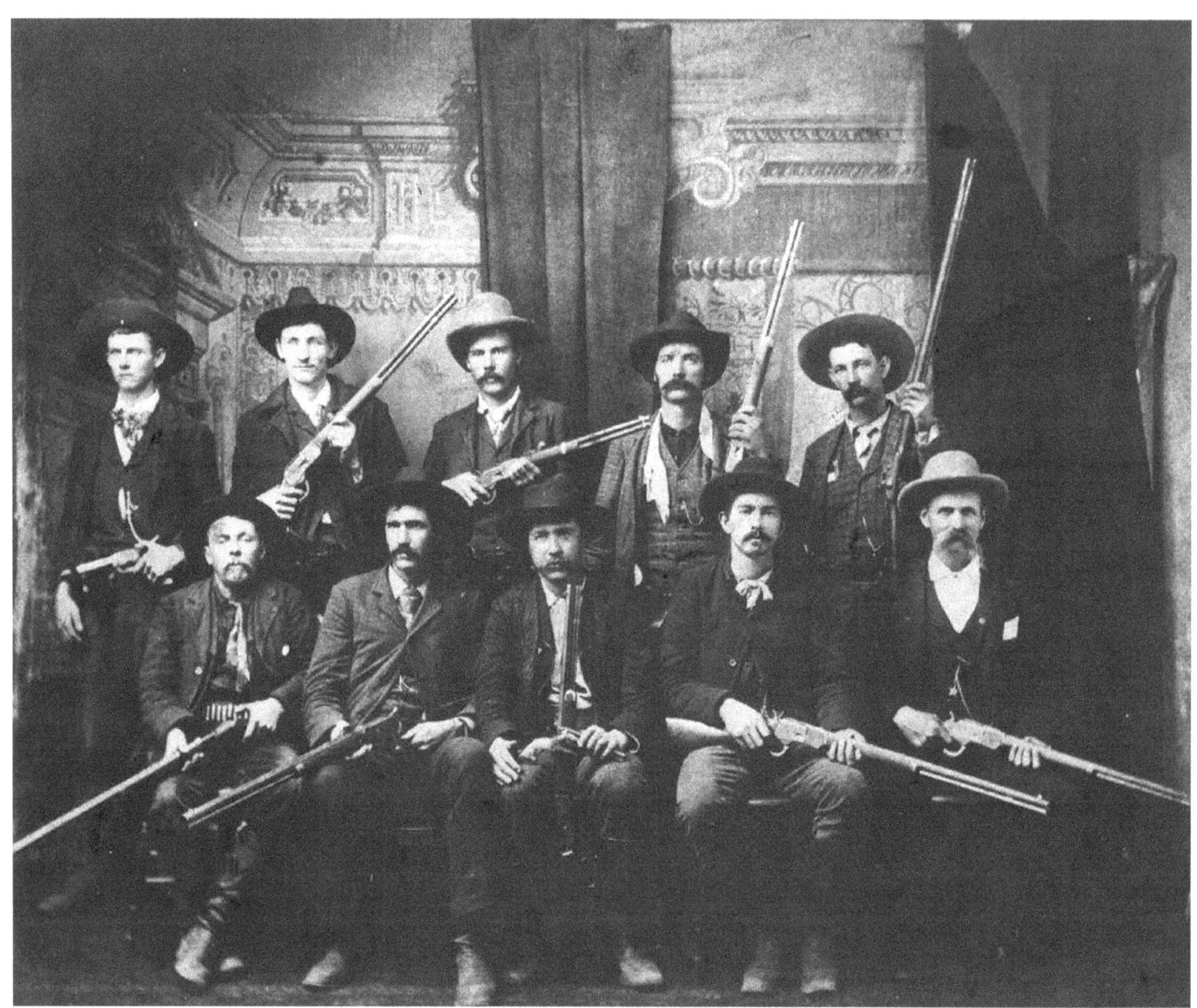

One of the more enduring controversies in Oklahoma history is that of Cherokee outlaw Ned Christie. Falsely accused of the murder of a marshal in Tahlequah, Christie went on the lam and evaded capture for five years until Marshal Paden Tolbert's posse, seen here, caught up with him in 1892, and Christie was killed in the ensuing confrontation. He was later exonerated.

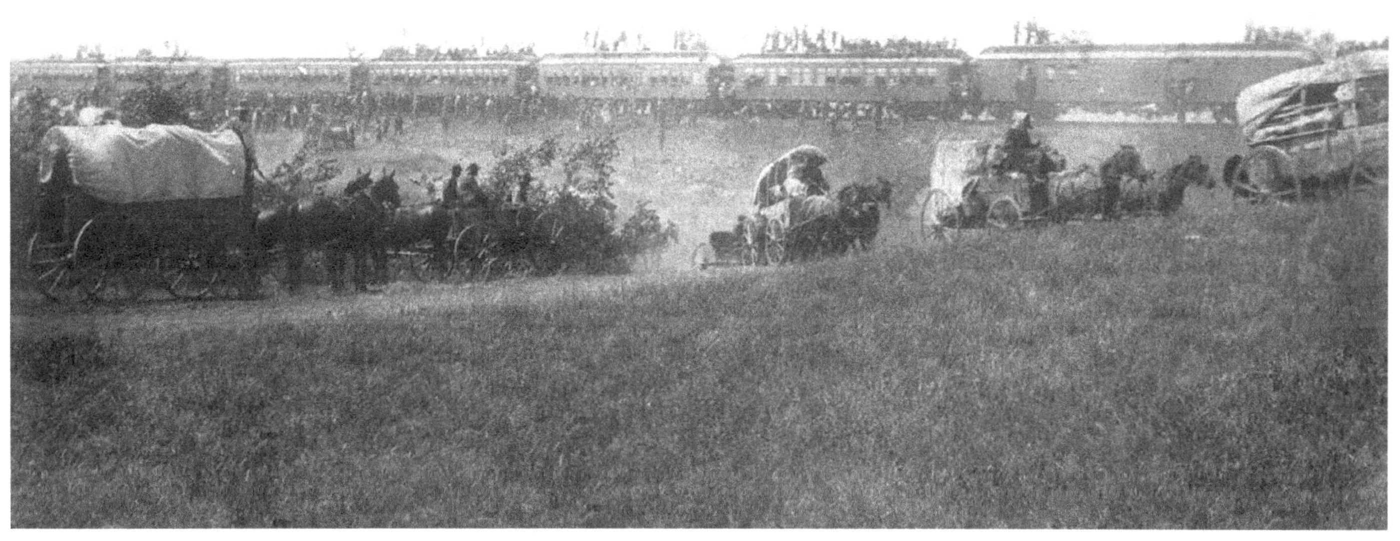

Somewhat juxtaposed to the famous "horse-race photo" of the opening of the Cherokee outlet in 1893, this photo shows some of the 25,000 people who began the land run from the line north of Orlando. Fast riders usually ran ahead in order to drive in their stakes while their families followed in the slower prairie schooners.

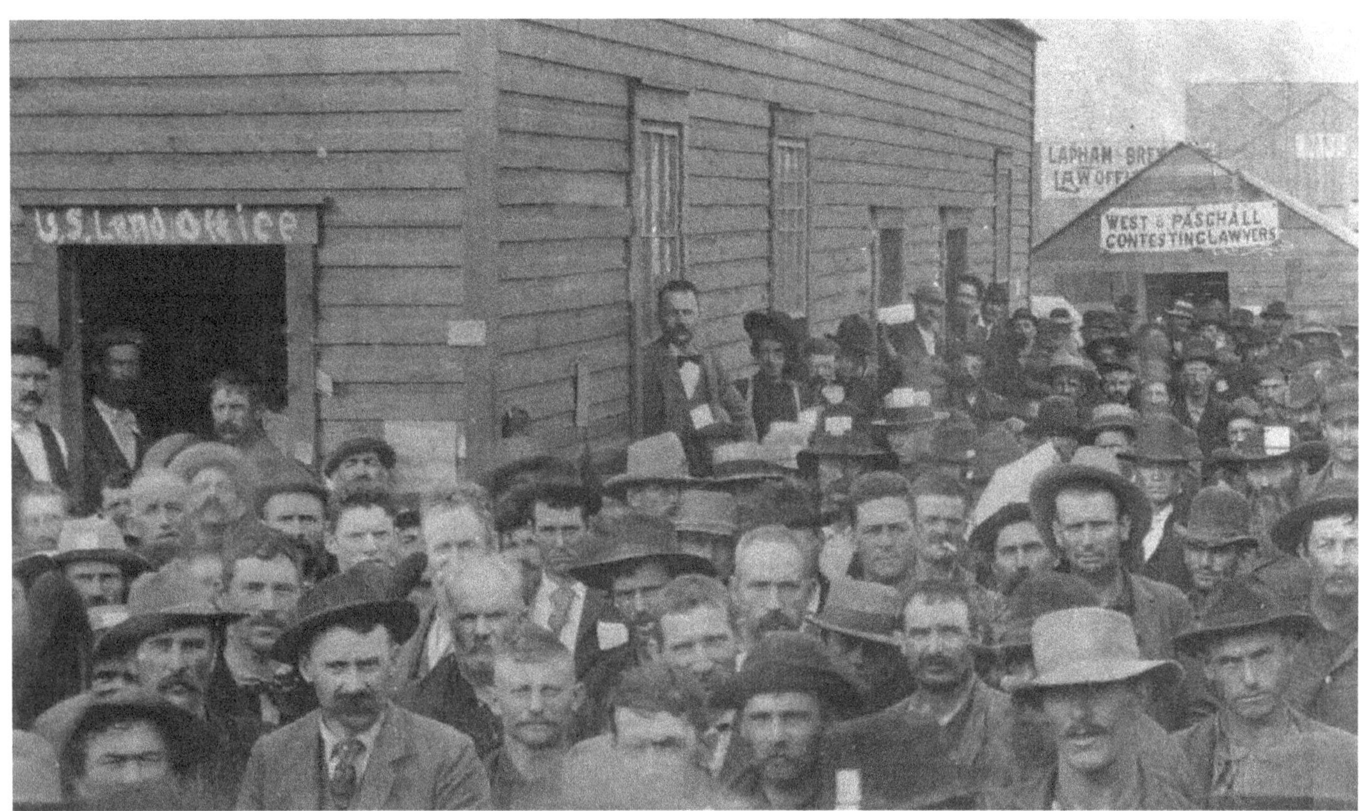

There were no smiles on the faces of this crowd waiting to file their claims at the Perry land office in September 1893. More than 100,000 people swelled the ranks of the new town, waiting in lines over a mile long. Some in line died, or fainted from sunstroke and lack of water as officials were unprepared for the sheer numbers of people making the land run.

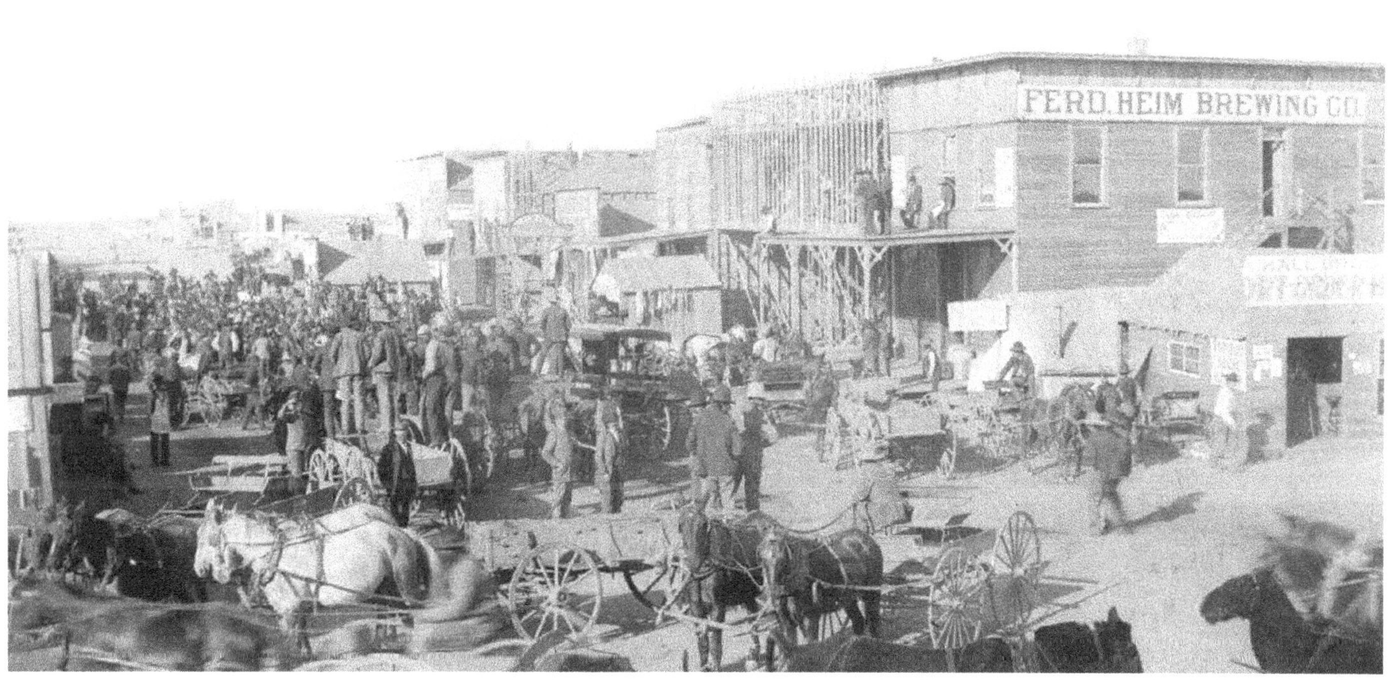

This is the view north from the corner of Sixth and C streets in Perry in October 1893. Perry quickly became the chief town in the newly opened Cherokee Outlet largely because its town lots were laid out by about 200 well-prepared sooners 15 minutes before the first settlers arrived from the starting line.

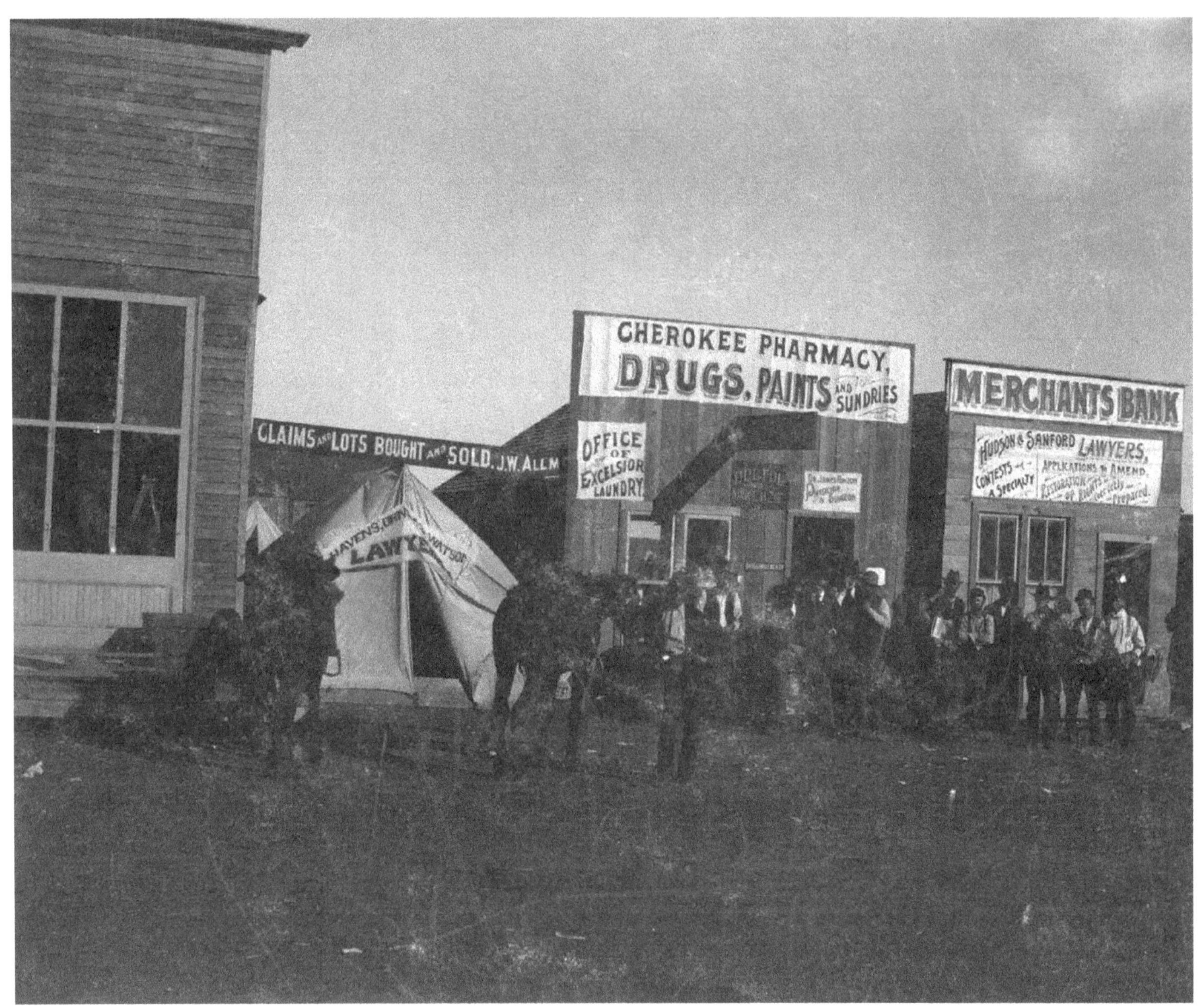

The east side of the town square, Enid, October 1893. With the possible exception of Oklahoma City, no town in Oklahoma had a more violent beginning than Enid, where railroad men, government officials, and settlers squared off in a battle over the location of the town site. By statehood, though, Enid was the fourth-largest city in Oklahoma.

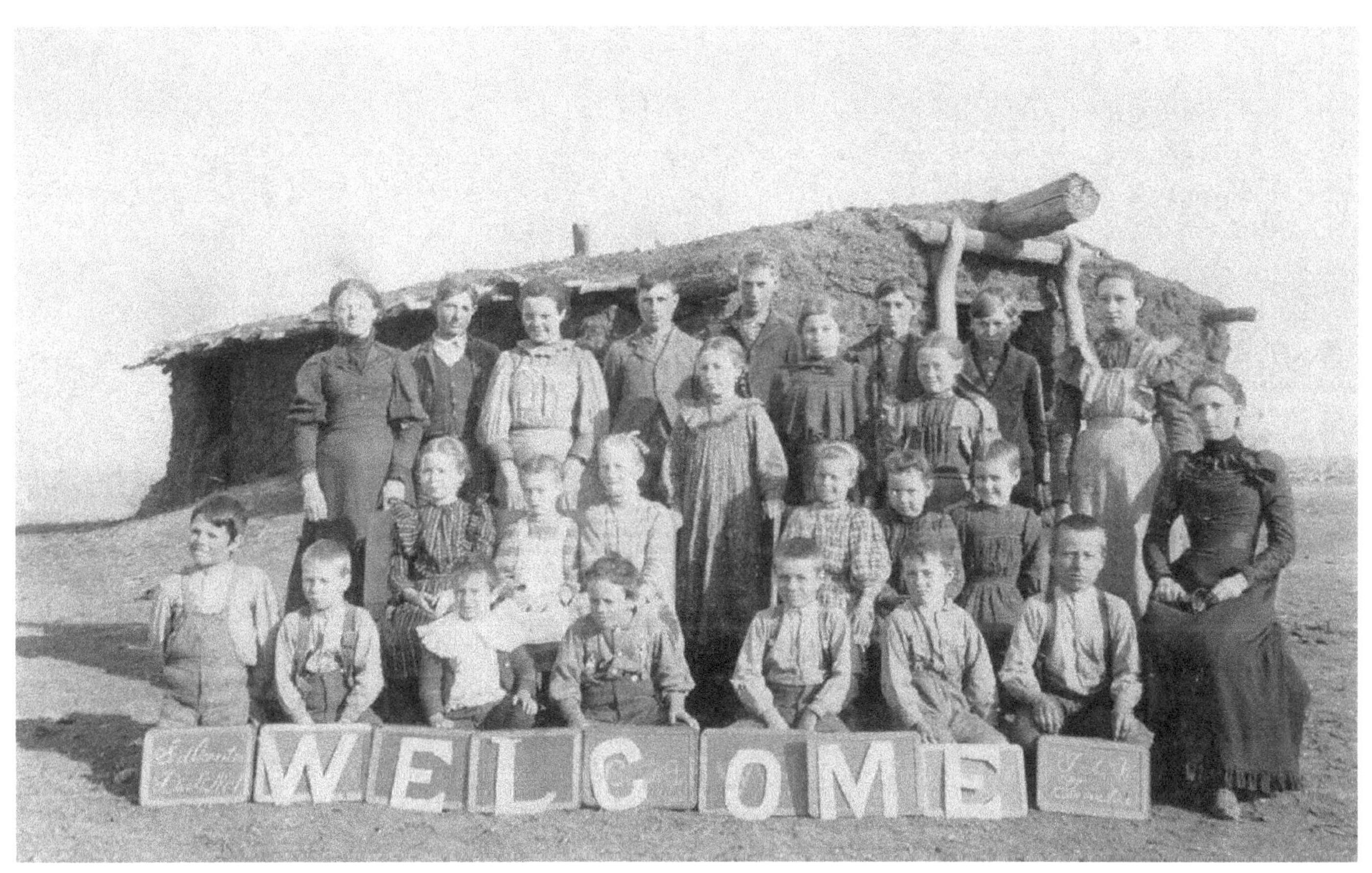

Blaine County was formed after the opening of the Cheyenne-Arapaho lands in 1892 and, as in most other areas on the treeless plain, sod structures were among the first erected in the county. The sod building seen here in 1893 was the Blaine County schoolhouse.

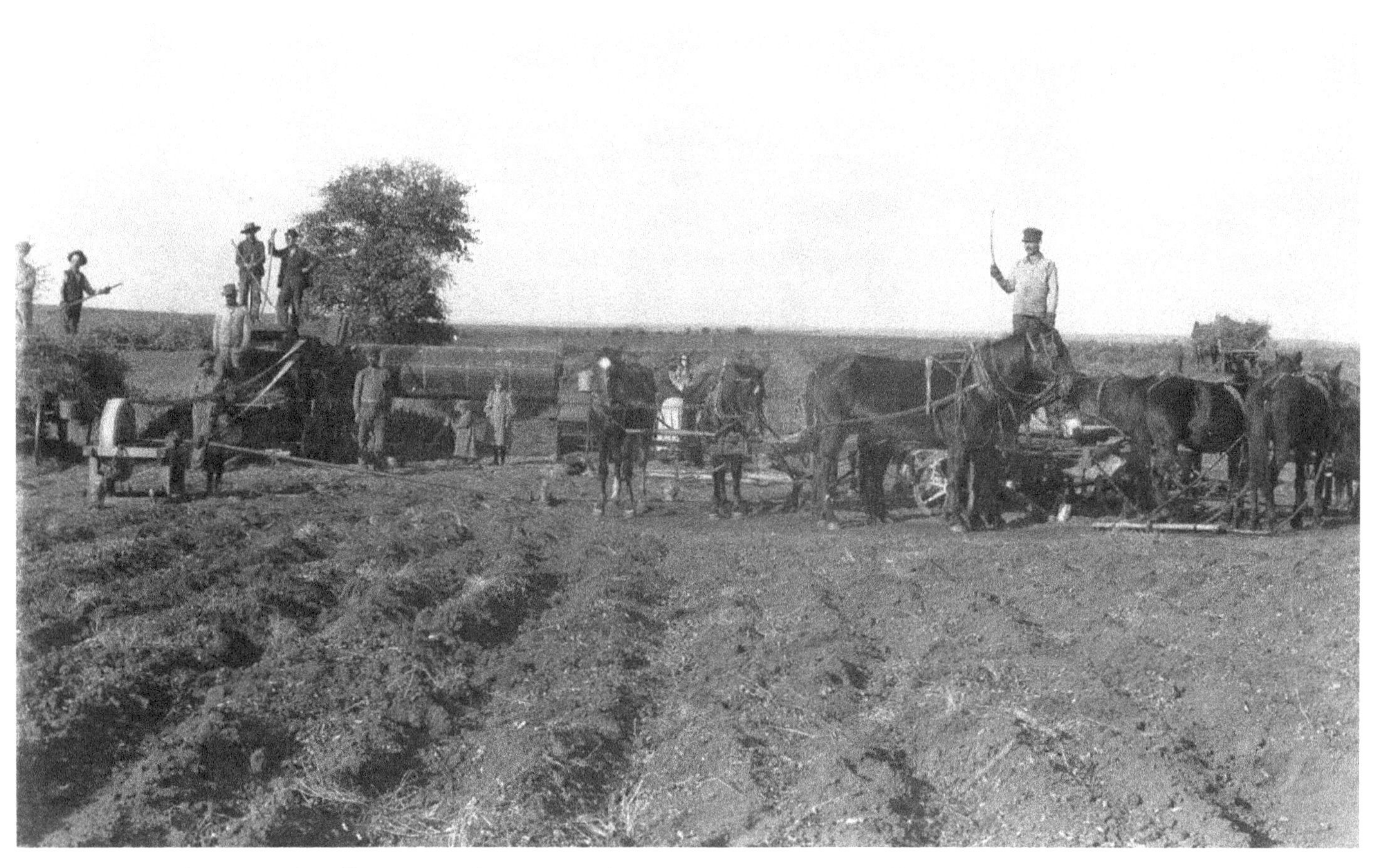

Processing threshed wheat on the Jefferson Bowen farm near Goodnight, ca. 1895. Wheat was well suited to the climate in northern and western Oklahoma, largely because it required little moisture.

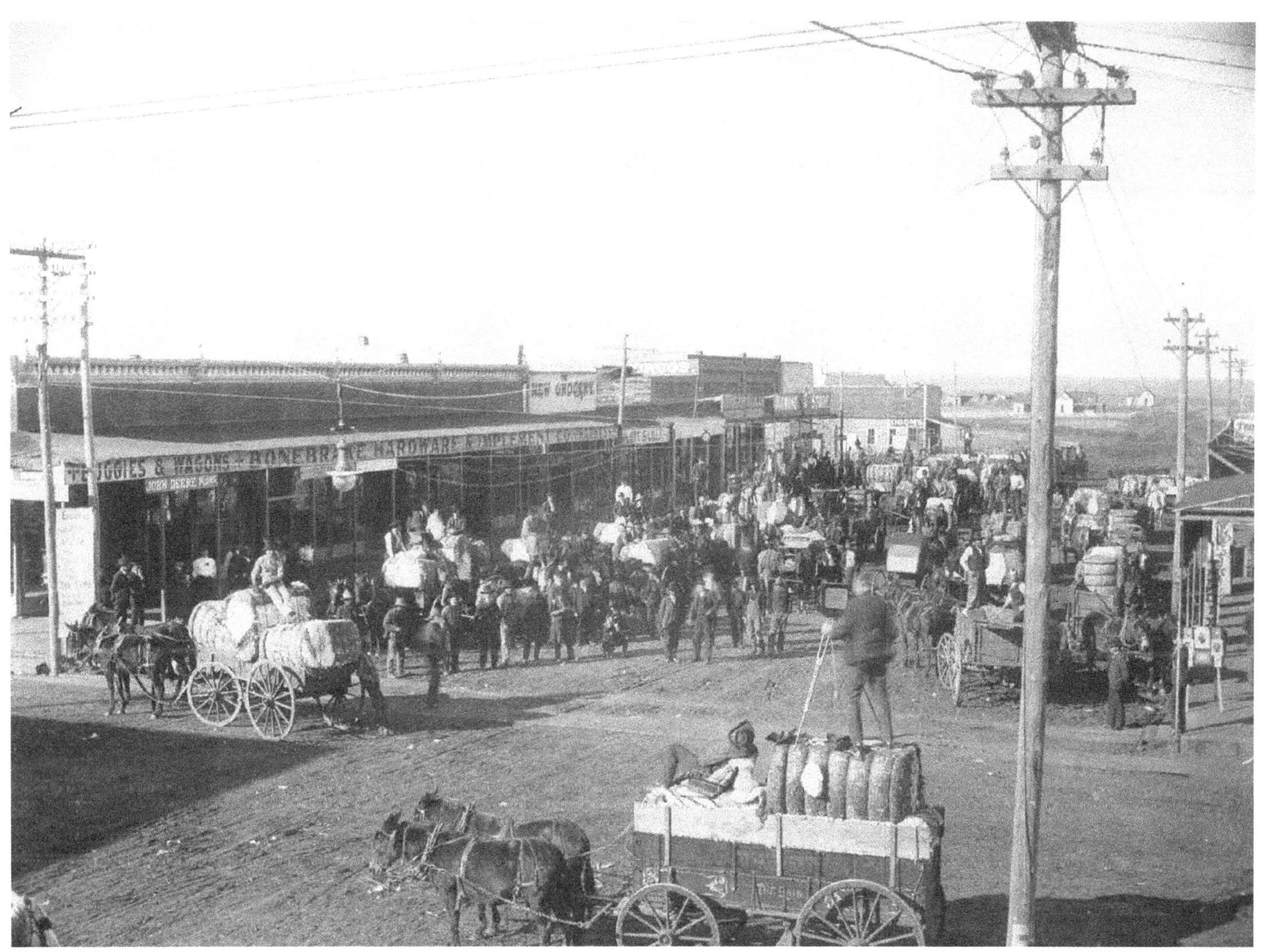

Elk City on cotton auction day, 1890s. Elk City was well situated as a major center for Oklahoma's cotton belt. By statehood, the town could boast two major rail connections, four cotton gins, and a cotton-oil mill.

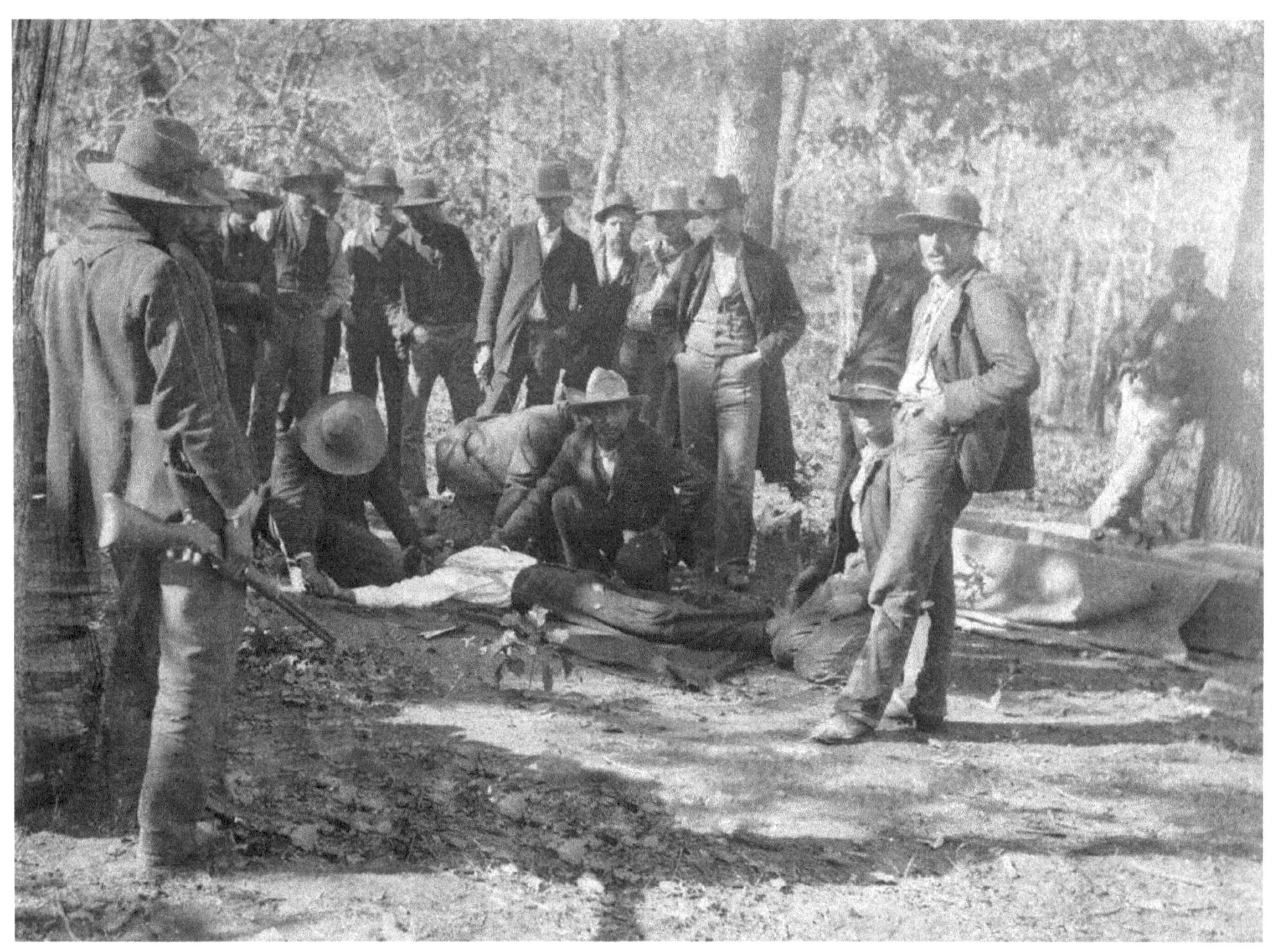

This photo was taken at the scene of the last Choctaw execution, at Wilburton, November 5, 1894. The victim was Silan Lewis, who was convicted of a political murder by the tribe and turned himself in as was tribal custom. Lewis was shot through the chest at close range and then smothered as the mournful wail of a woman arose from the creek bank.

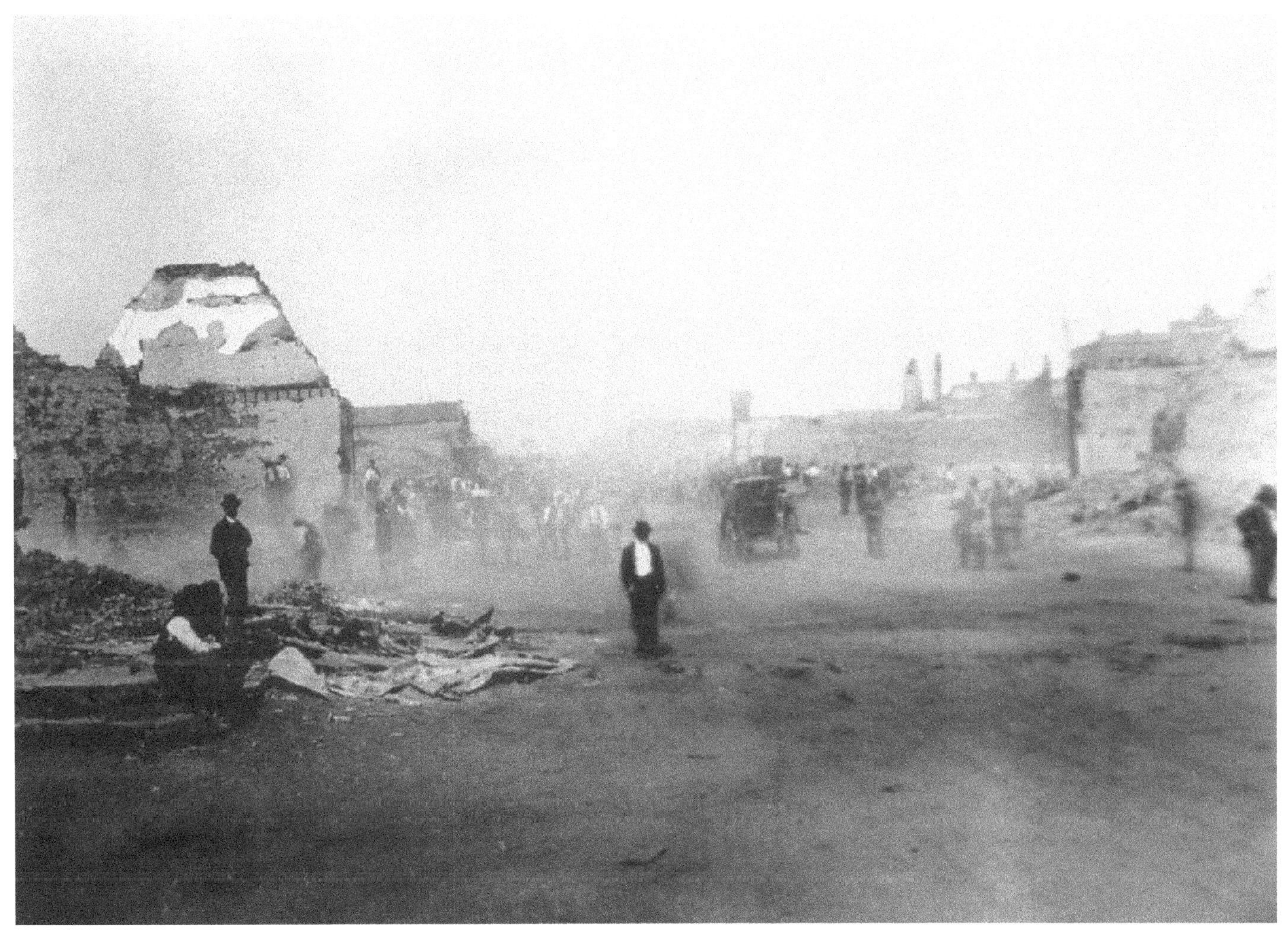

Ardmore was the largest city in Indian Territory at the time of the disastrous fire of April 19, 1895. More than 60 businesses and 150 homes were destroyed, and losses were in excess of $600,000. The town began to recover almost immediately, and a newspaper declared, "Outside aid will not be asked."

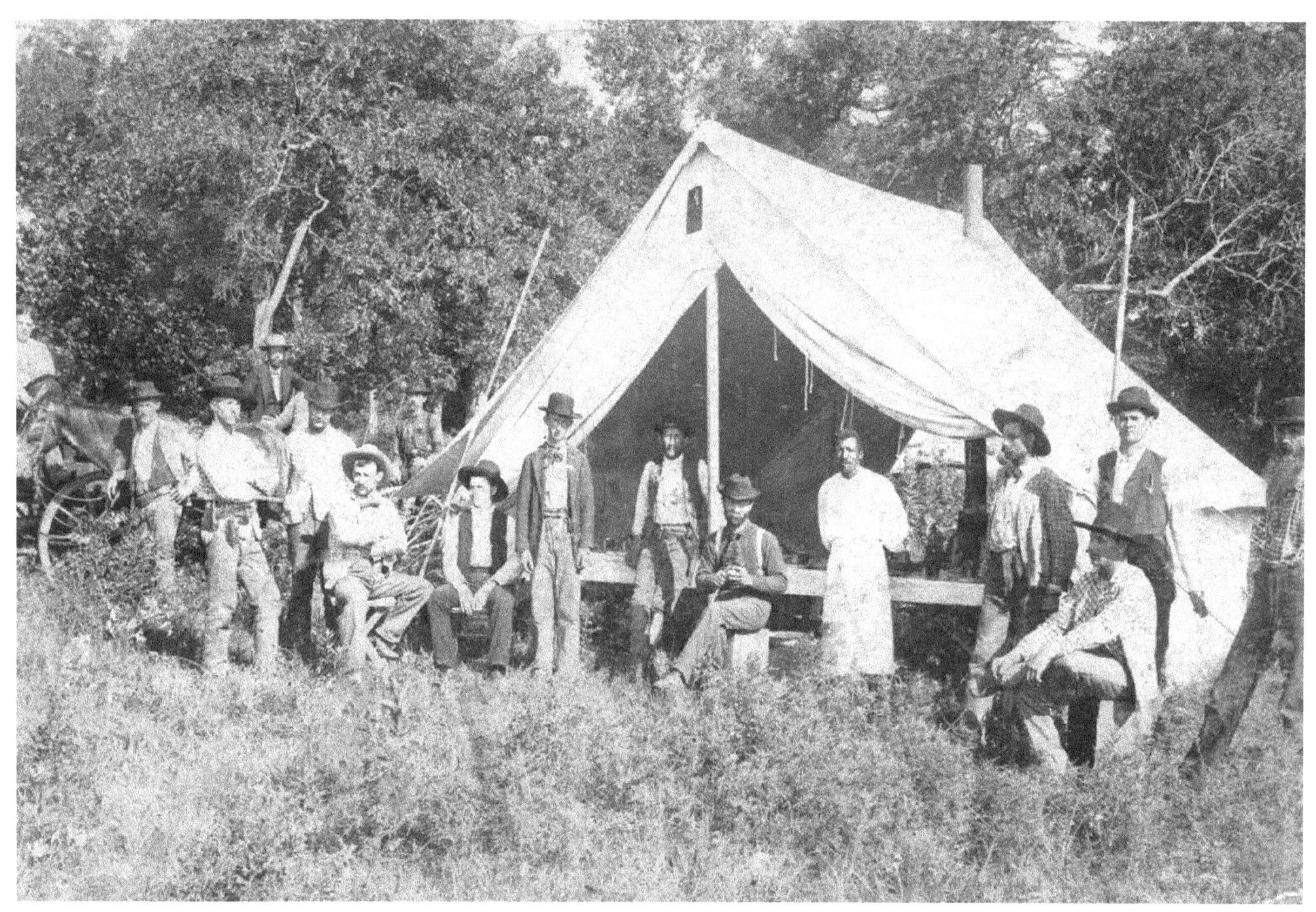

The beginning of the end of Indian Territory: a U.S. Geological Survey crew poses in camp, May 1895. The crew was responsible for surveying tribal land and dividing it into quarter-sections. These would then become allotments assigned to individual tribe members by the Dawes Commission.

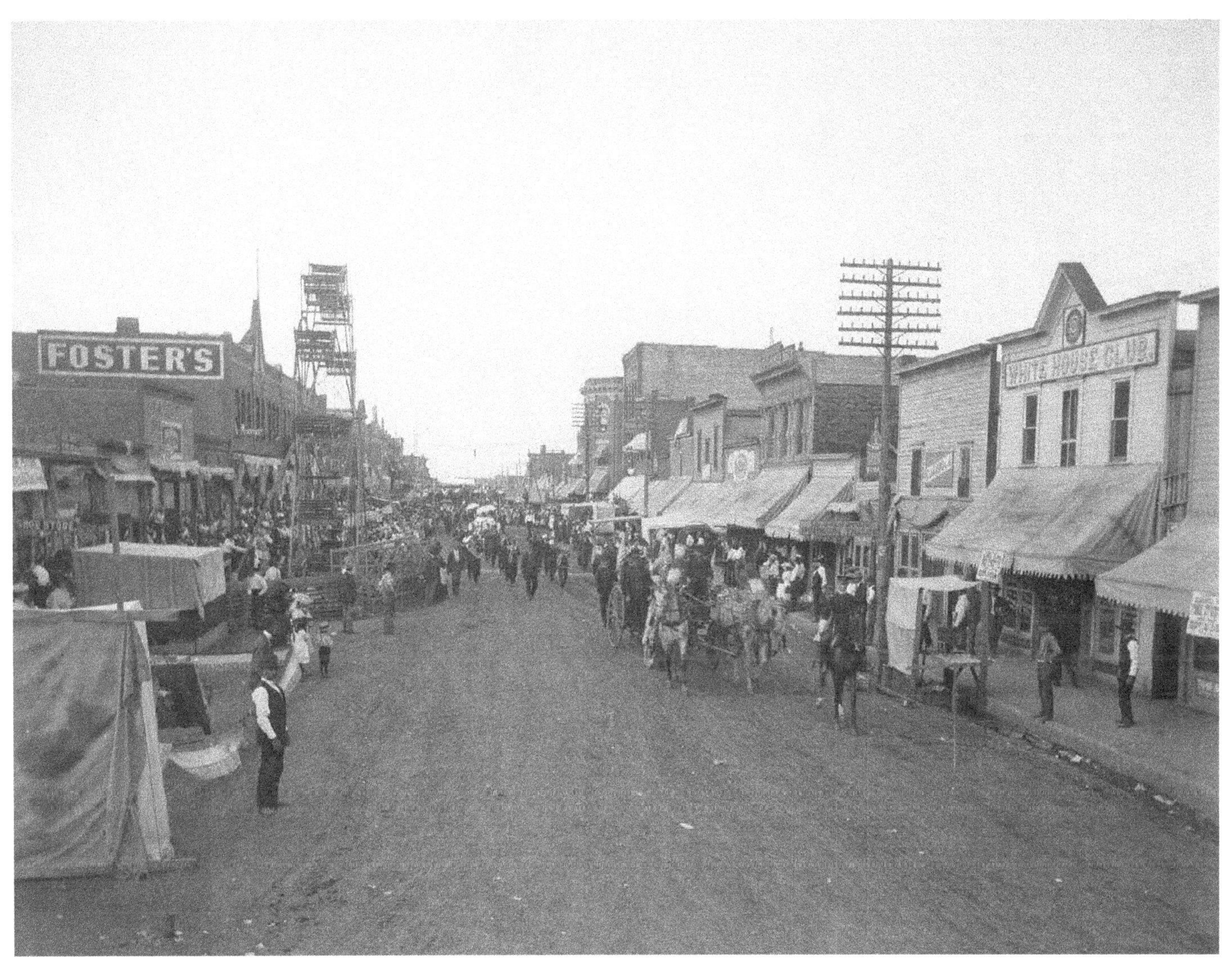

Street fair in Blackwell, ca. 1895. Blackwell was born during the Cherokee Outlet opening in 1893 and consistently prospered after the arrival of two major railroads and the discovery of oil and gas in the area.

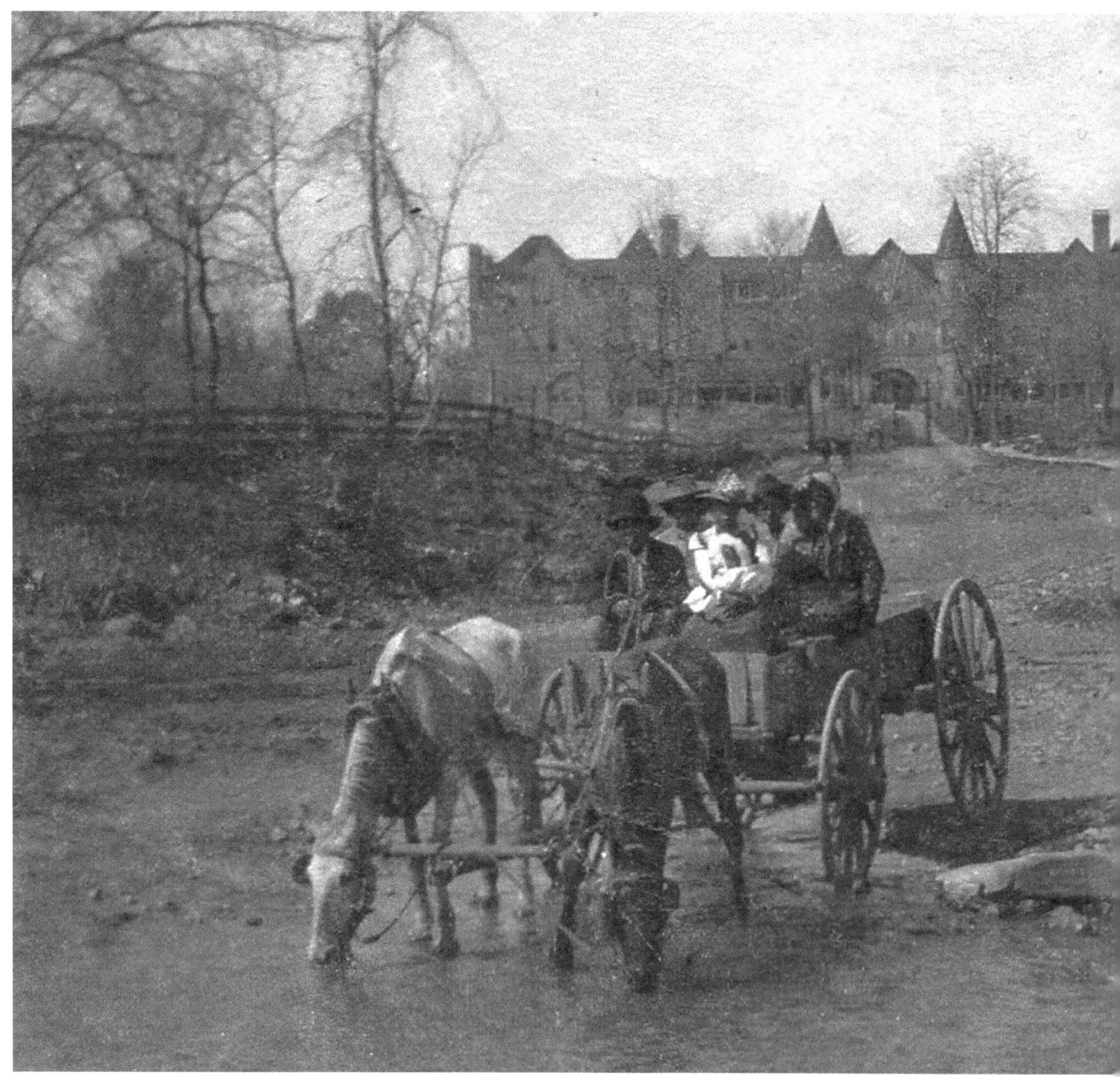

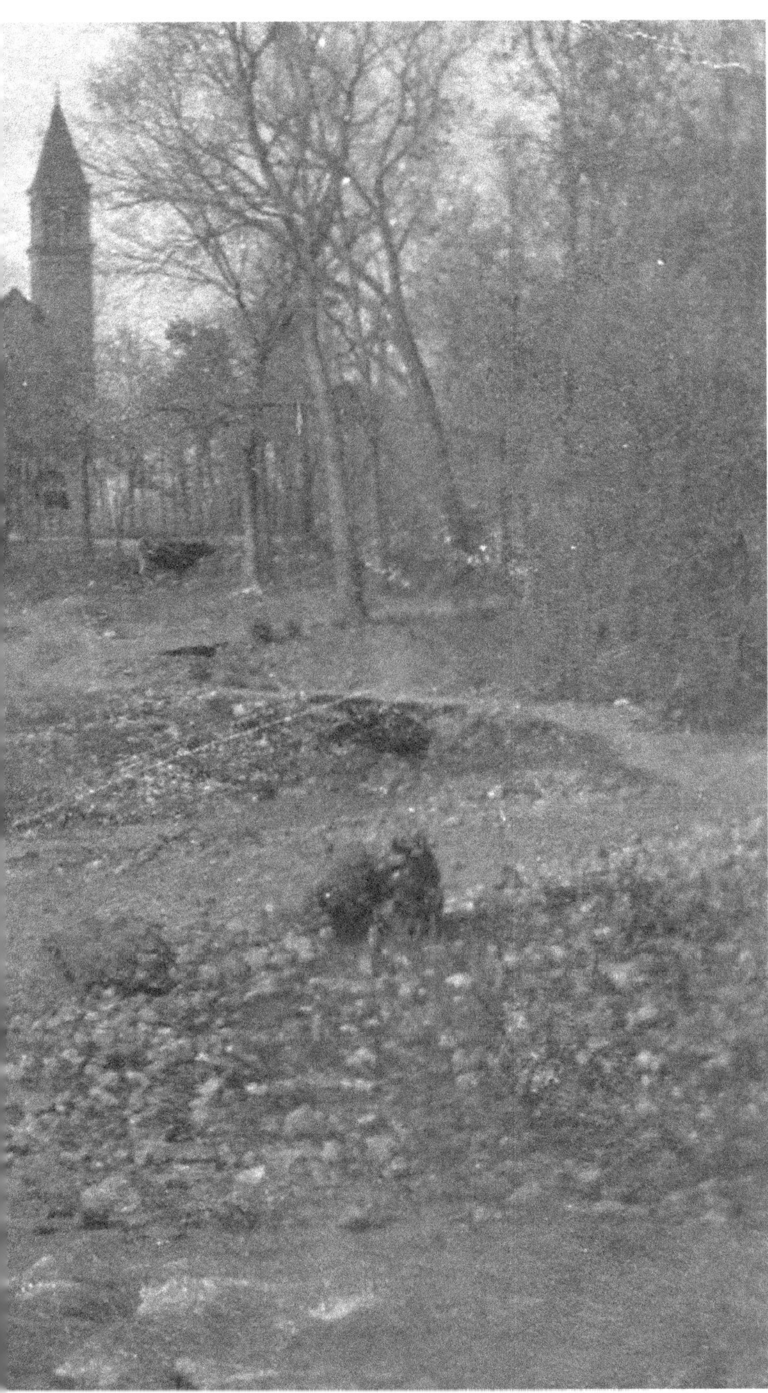

The impressive home of the Cherokee Female Seminary near Tahlequah, as seen in 1897, stood in stark contrast to the dugouts and sodhouses popping up on Oklahoma's western prairies during the land run era. The castlelike structure is still in use on the campus of Northeastern State University.

This spectacular view was captured by gutsy Oklahoma City photographer North Losey in 1898. It is unknown which tornado is depicted here, but 1898 was a particularly disastrous year for funnel clouds: the towns of Duncan and Sapulpa were nearly wiped out, and the state was even hit by a rare late-January tornado.

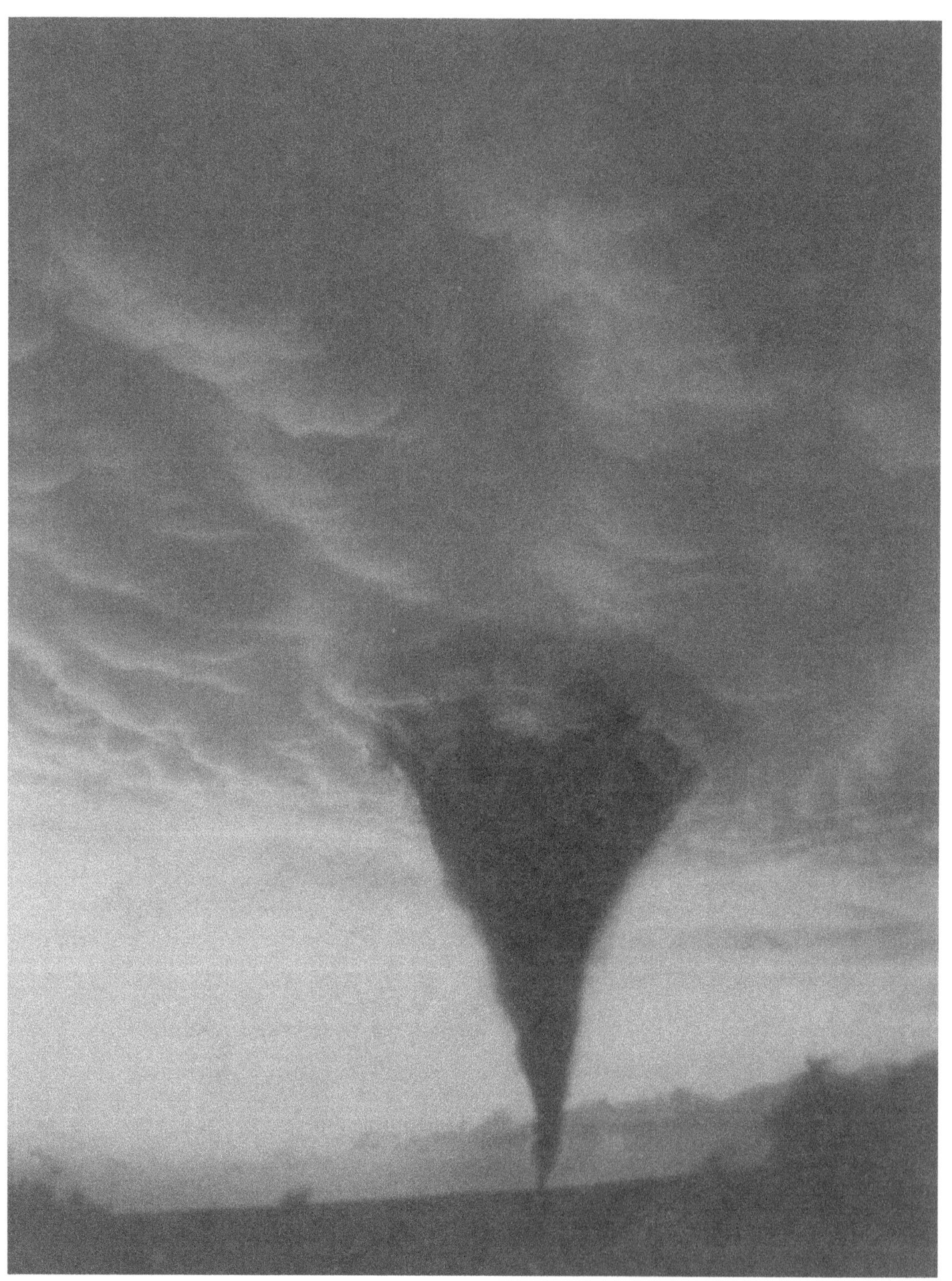

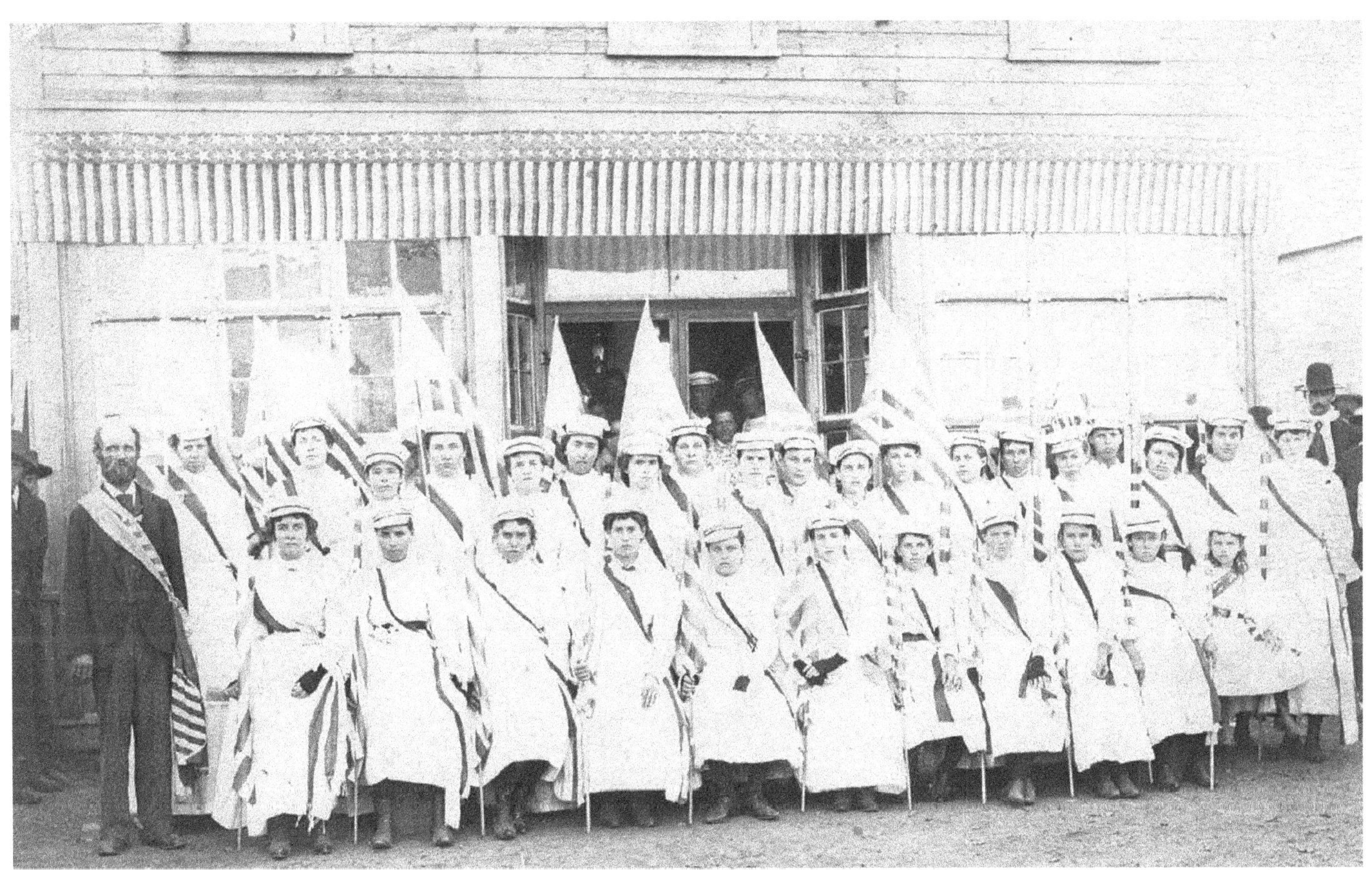

A group of girls in Augusta, Oklahoma Territory, prepare to march on July 4, 1898. The railroad bypassed Augusta by about a mile, and gradually the town drifted over to nearby Carmen. Augusta was the former home of Susanna Salter, who had been America's first female mayor, serving in Argonia, Kansas, prior to her arrival in Augusta.

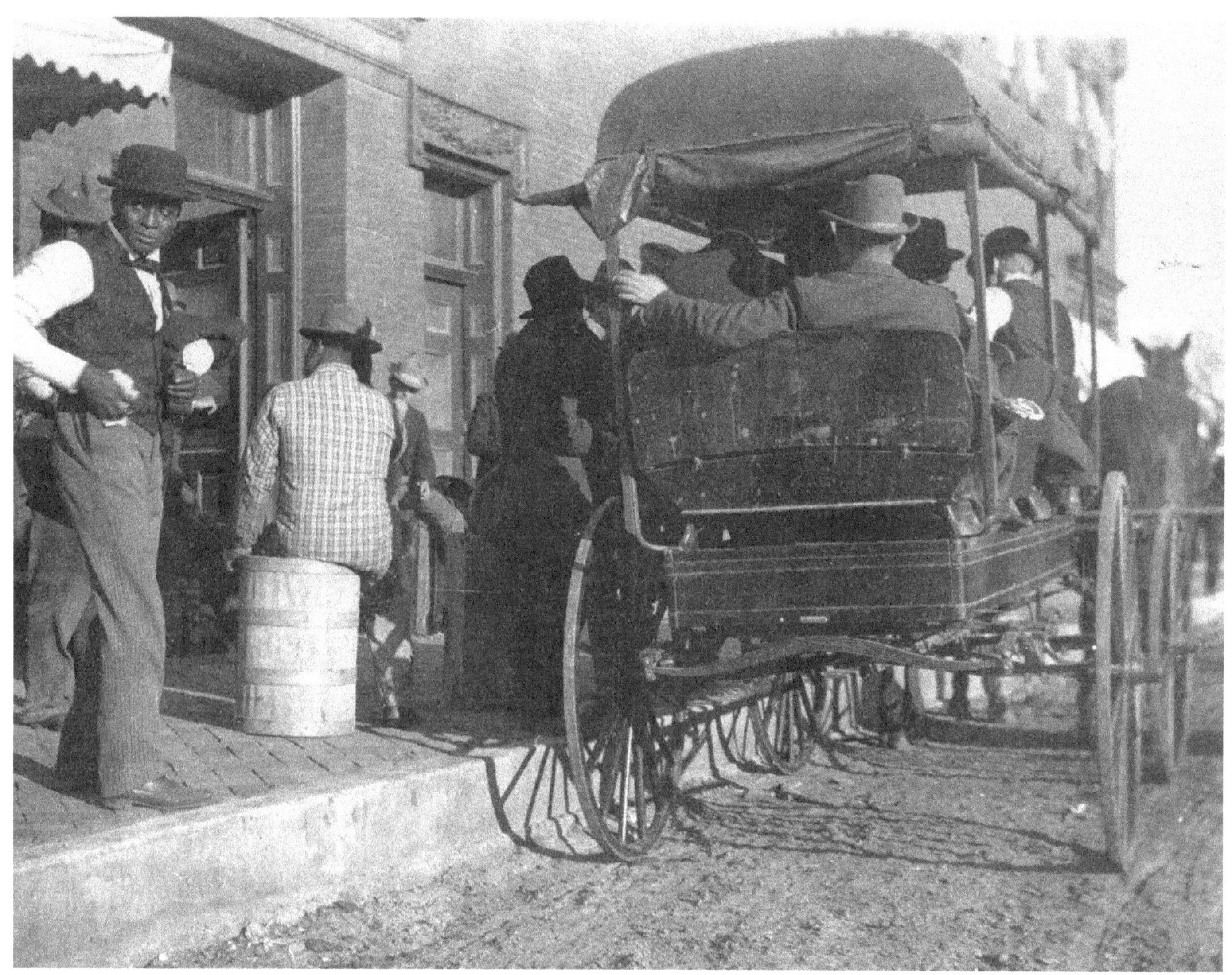

Members of the Dawes Commission departing for the field, 1899. This photo may have been made in the Creek Nation, where many freedmen had not been enrolled as tribe members due to confusion over their citizenship status. The commission made an effort to enroll as many freedmen as possible.

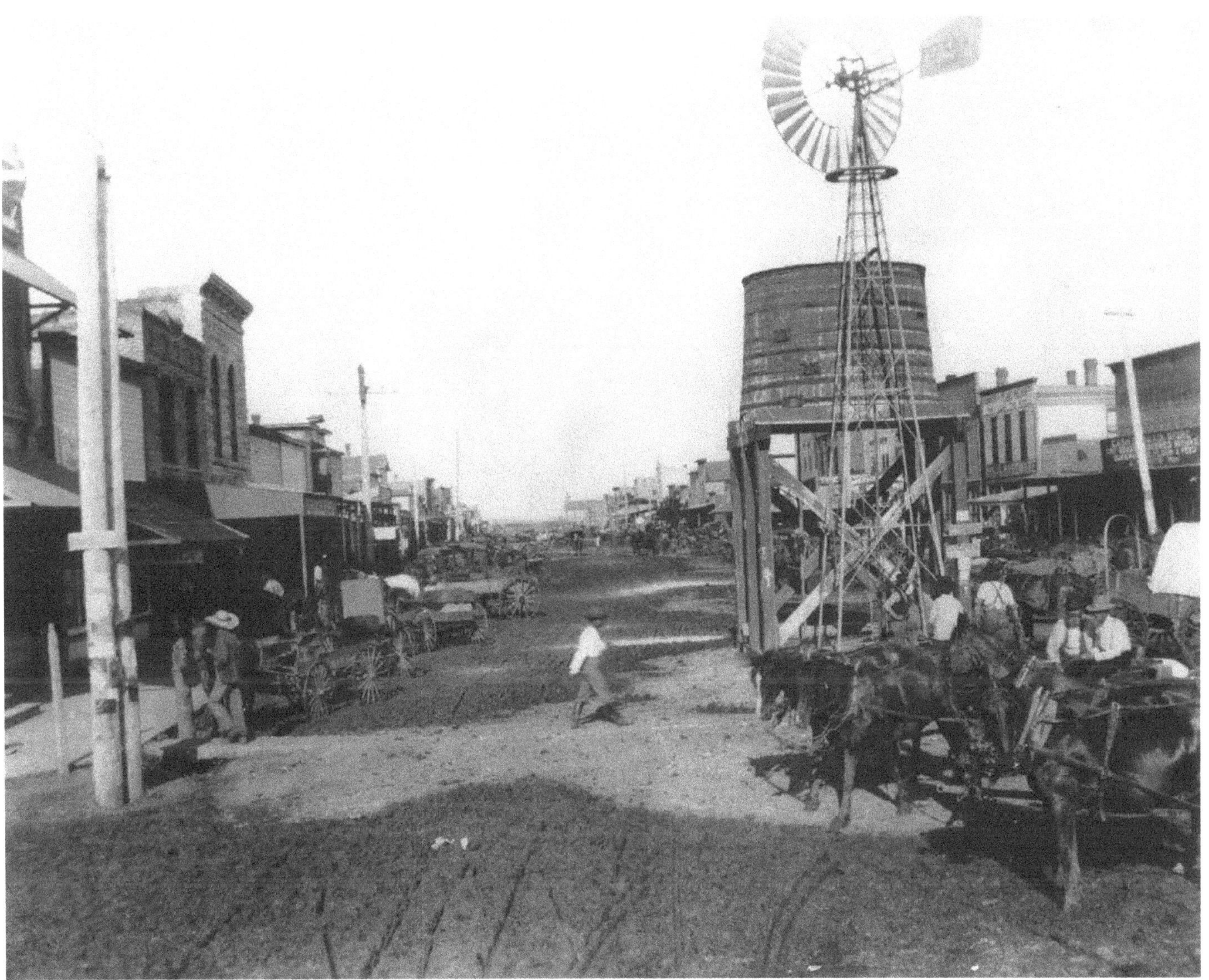

Ponca City, July 13, 1899. Like so many other northern Oklahoma towns, Ponca City was born on September 16, 1893, during the opening of the Cherokee Outlet, but the sleepy scene shown here would soon be miraculously transformed by the arrival of Marland Oil in 1911 and the opulence of the Roaring Twenties.

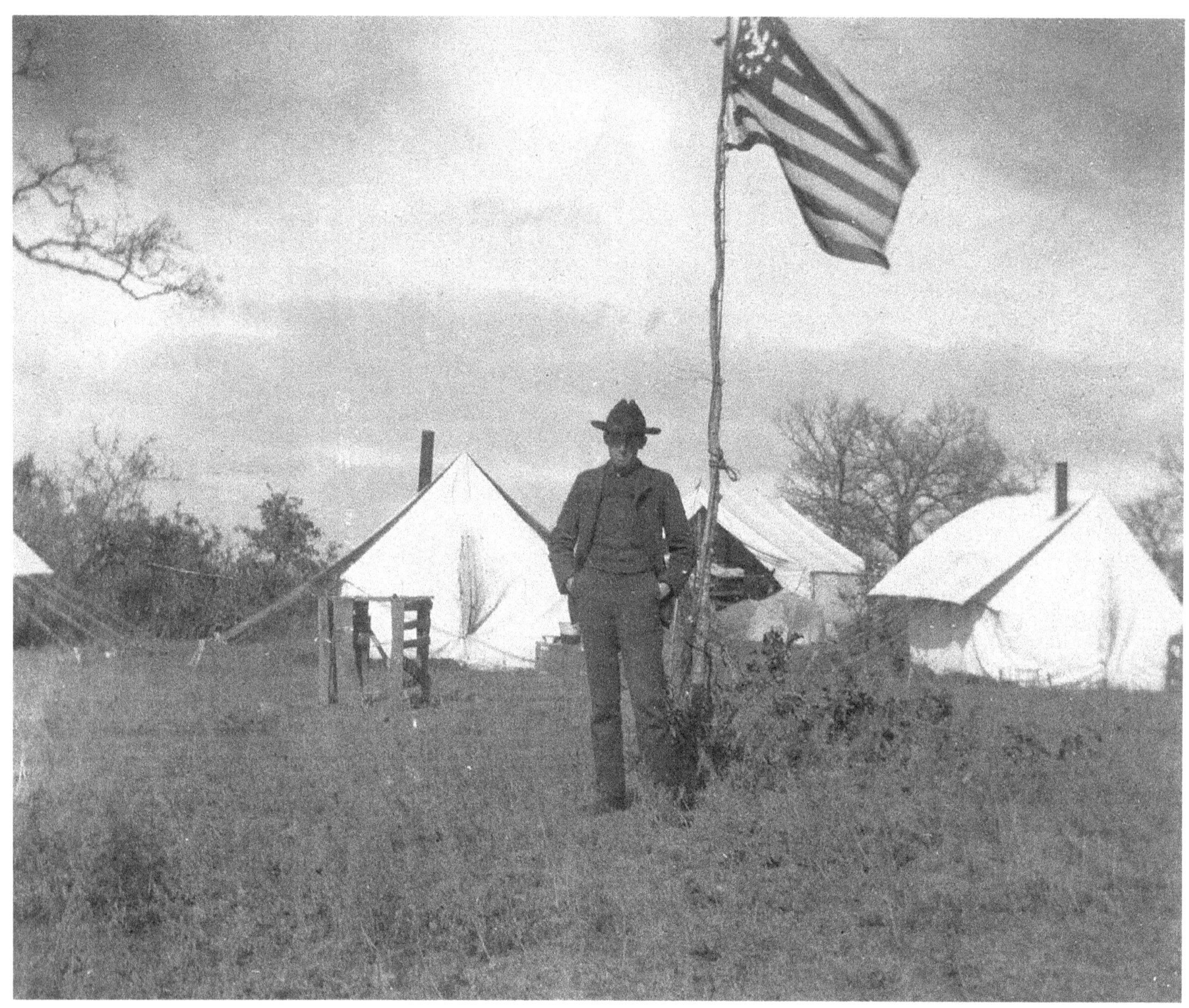

Grant Foreman in camp with the Dawes Commission, Ardmore, 1899. Foreman came to Oklahoma as a field agent for the commission but soon became a favorite son of his adopted hometown of Muskogee. In later years, he wrote tirelessly about Oklahoma history.

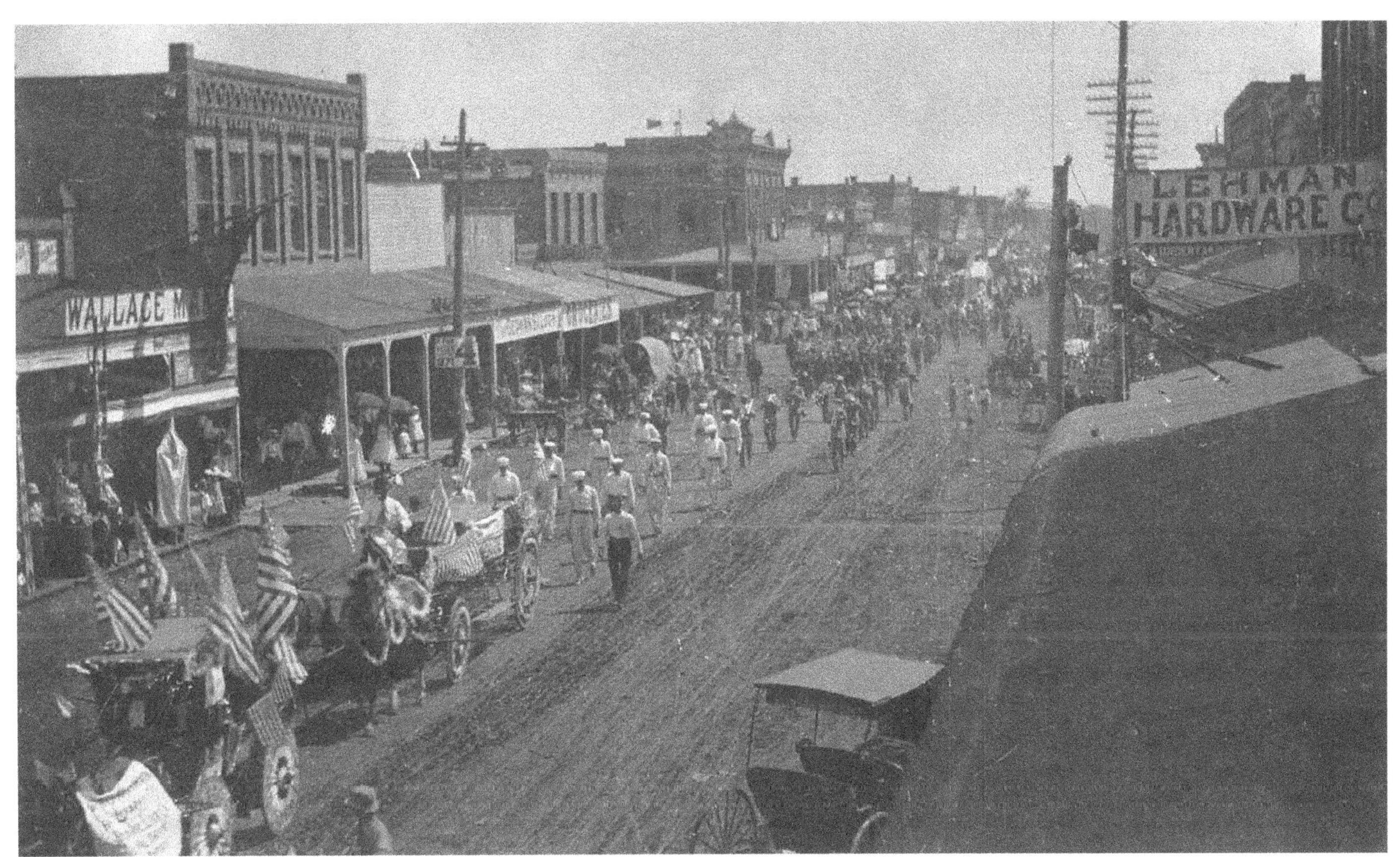

The parade during dedication of the Shawnee waterworks, September 1, 1899. The town of Shawnee arose amid several of the smaller tribes relocated to Indian Territory after the Civil War, but after its connection to Oklahoma City via the Choctaw, Oklahoma and Gulf Railroad, the town began to prosper and at times rival the future state capital.

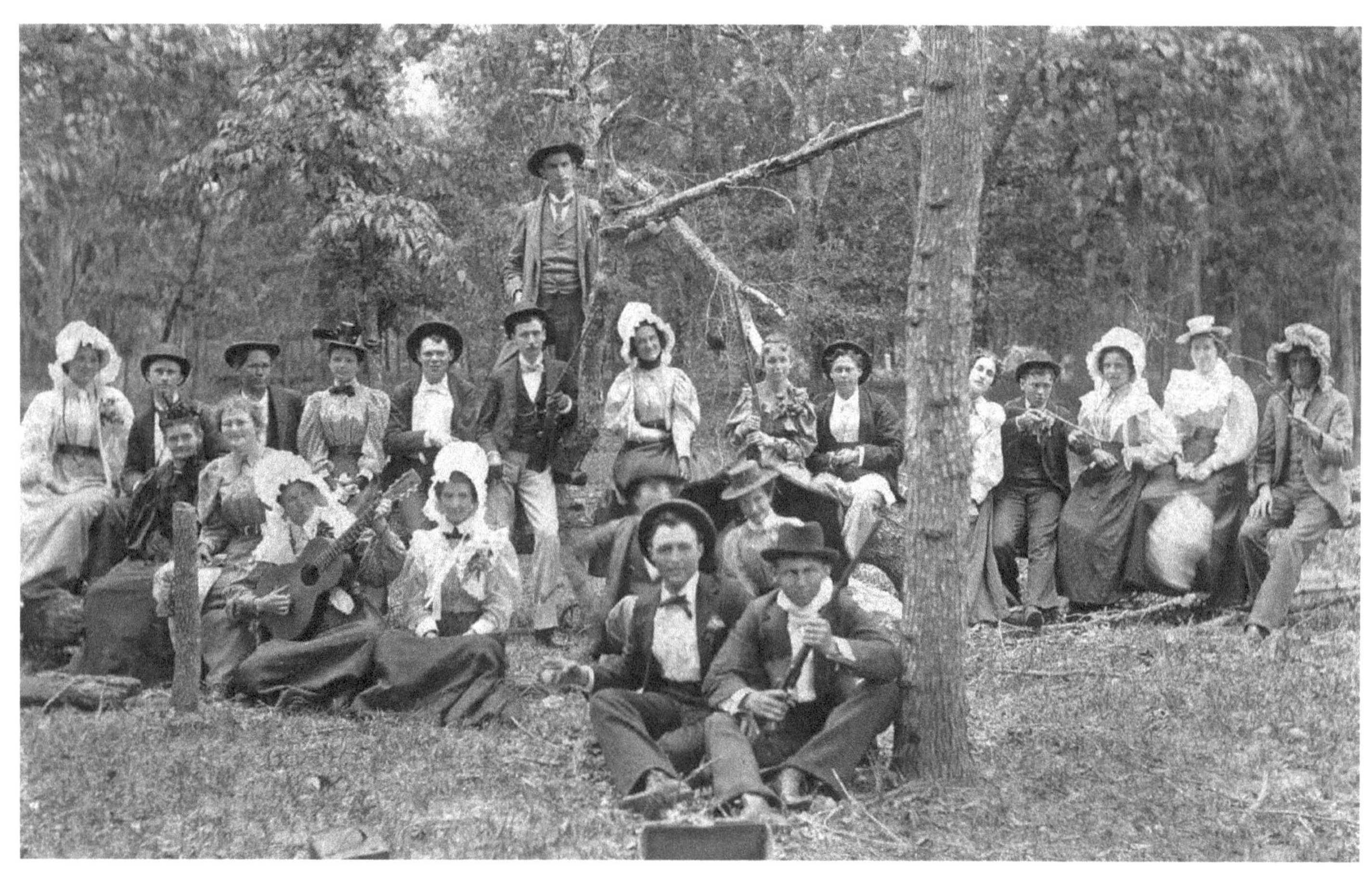
A youthful group, armed with rifles and musical instruments, take time out for a photo while frolicking in the Sulphur Springs resort area, ca. 1900.

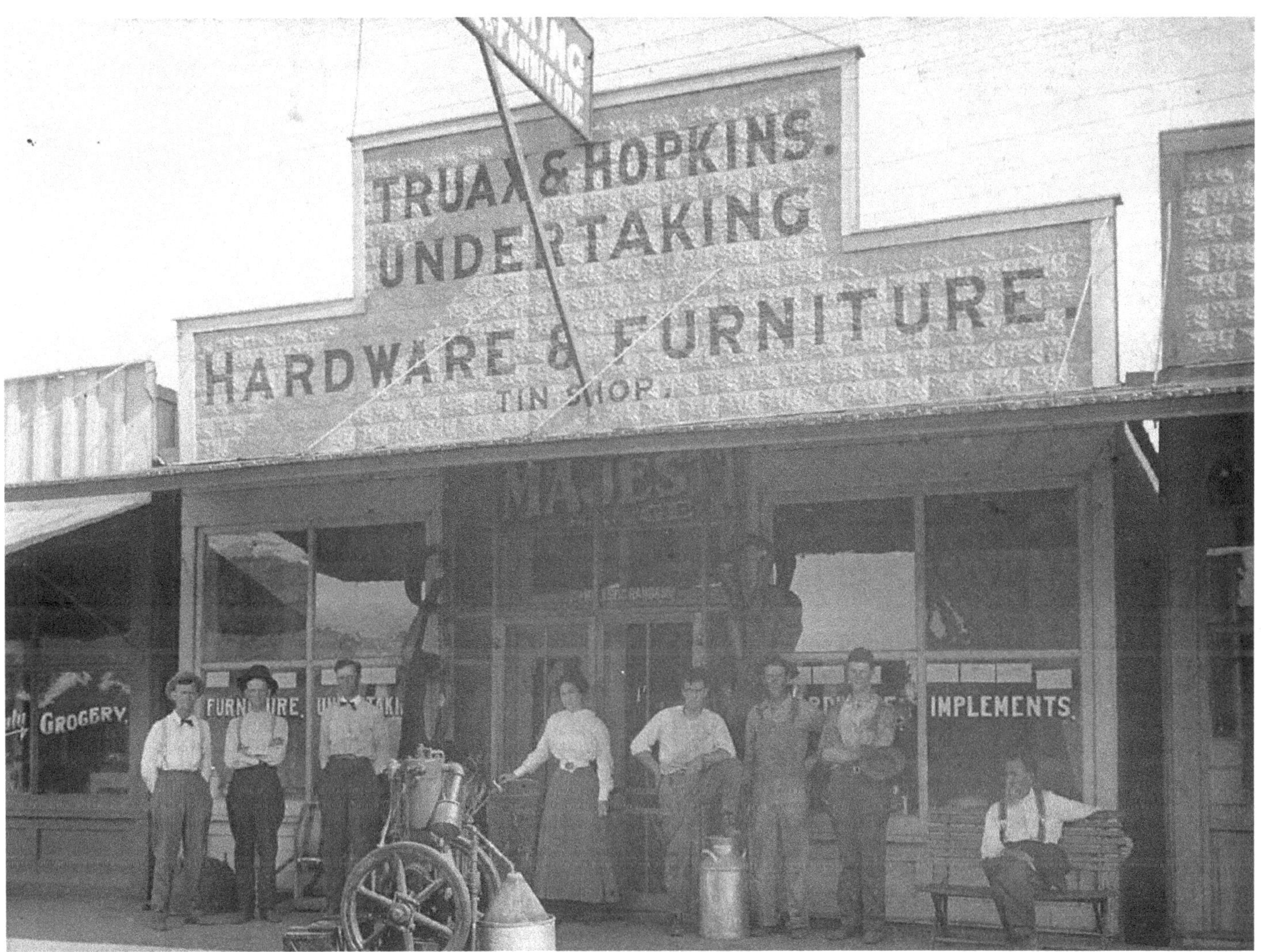

Truax & Hopkins, Beaver, ca. 1900. The remoteness of settlements in western Oklahoma often made Renaissance men of local merchants, as illustrated by this photo of the town's main street.

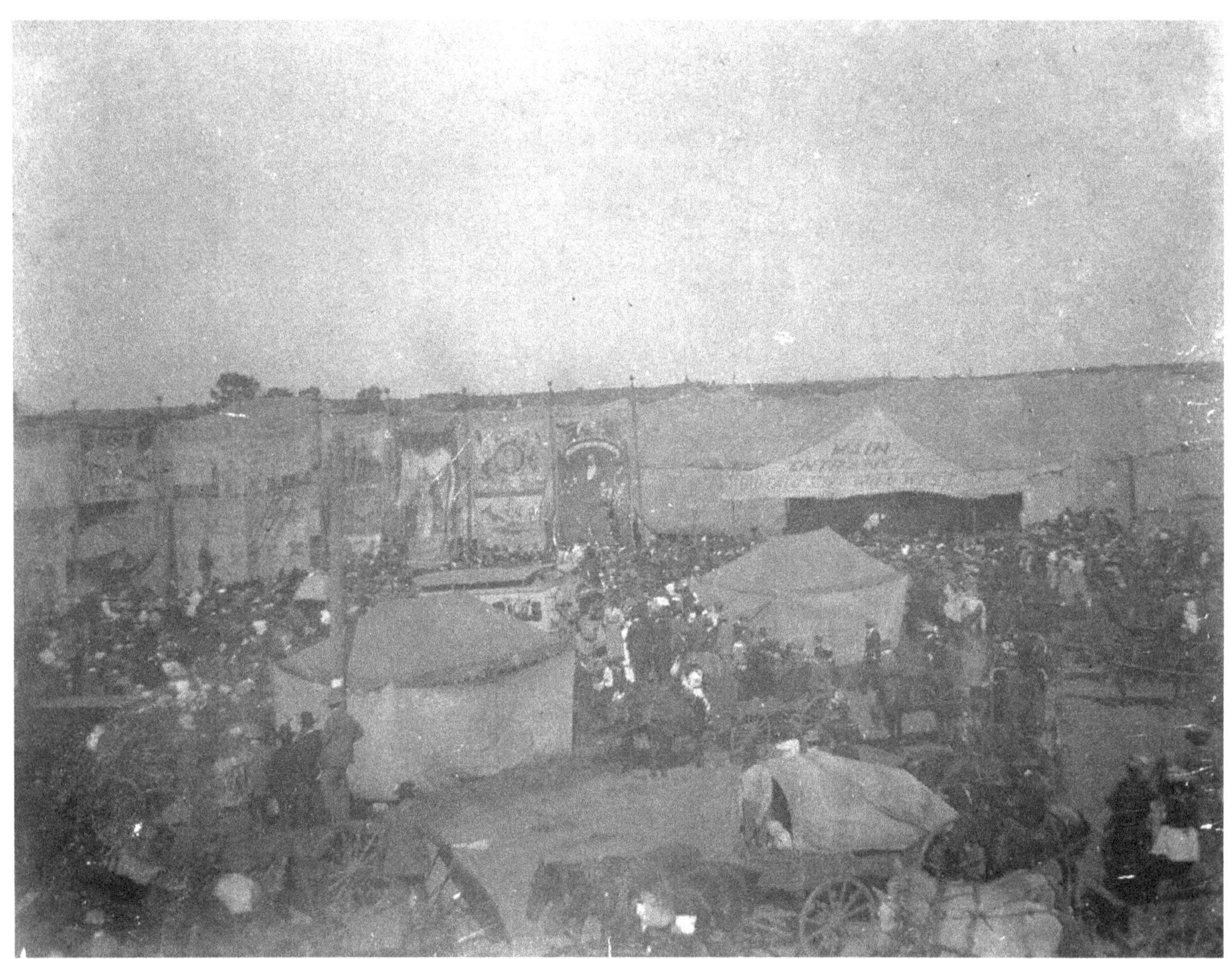

Buffalo Bill's Wild West Show encamped at Grand and Hudson, Oklahoma City, October 1900. While on a national tour, Colonel William "Buffalo Bill" Cody enjoyed a particularly friendly stop in Oklahoma City, where he had the chance to reunite with several other former Army scouts then living there.

Territory Folks Should Stick Together

(1901–1929)

Throughout the 1890s, Oklahoma Territory struggled to develop amid drought and national economic distress. But as more and more land was opened to white settlement, it became inevitable that the twin territories would one day become a state. In order to facilitate statehood, the Dawes Commission was formed to move Indian Territory from tribal land held in common to private ownership. This required painstakingly registering every member of a tribe and giving each a parcel of land. Surplus lands would be open to homesteading by any American citizen. The Dawes Commission, with the Curtis Act in 1898, abolished tribal government and placed Indian Territory under federal control, thus making possible the creation of new town sites all across Indian Territory.

This period also saw the rise of all-black towns in part of the old Creek Nation, as freedmen formed their own communities and strived for self-determination. They were often joined by black families from the Deep South who saw these towns as the Promised Land. The dream did not last, as Jim Crow segregation, white resentment, and finally the Great Depression winnowed the towns down to just a handful of residents.

The single greatest development during this period was the coming of statehood in 1907, but Oklahoma also experienced major growth in economic development. In the west this took the form of putting millions of acres under the plow to produce cotton, wheat, and broomcorn; in the east vast quantities of commodities were extracted: lead and zinc (northeast), coal (east-central), and lumber (southeast).

Of course, the money which came from these industries was but a sliver of the wealth generated throughout this period by the oil and gas industry. The first successful wells were drilled in the late 1890s, but Oklahoma was soon topping the charts in national production and stayed there for the first three decades of the twentieth century.

Many Oklahomans became wealthy overnight, and fortunes were won and lost betting on the site of the next gusher. But the heady days of the Roaring Twenties would not continue; just as the last major oil field was found in Oklahoma City, storm clouds were already brewing which would bring turbulent times for the adolescent state.

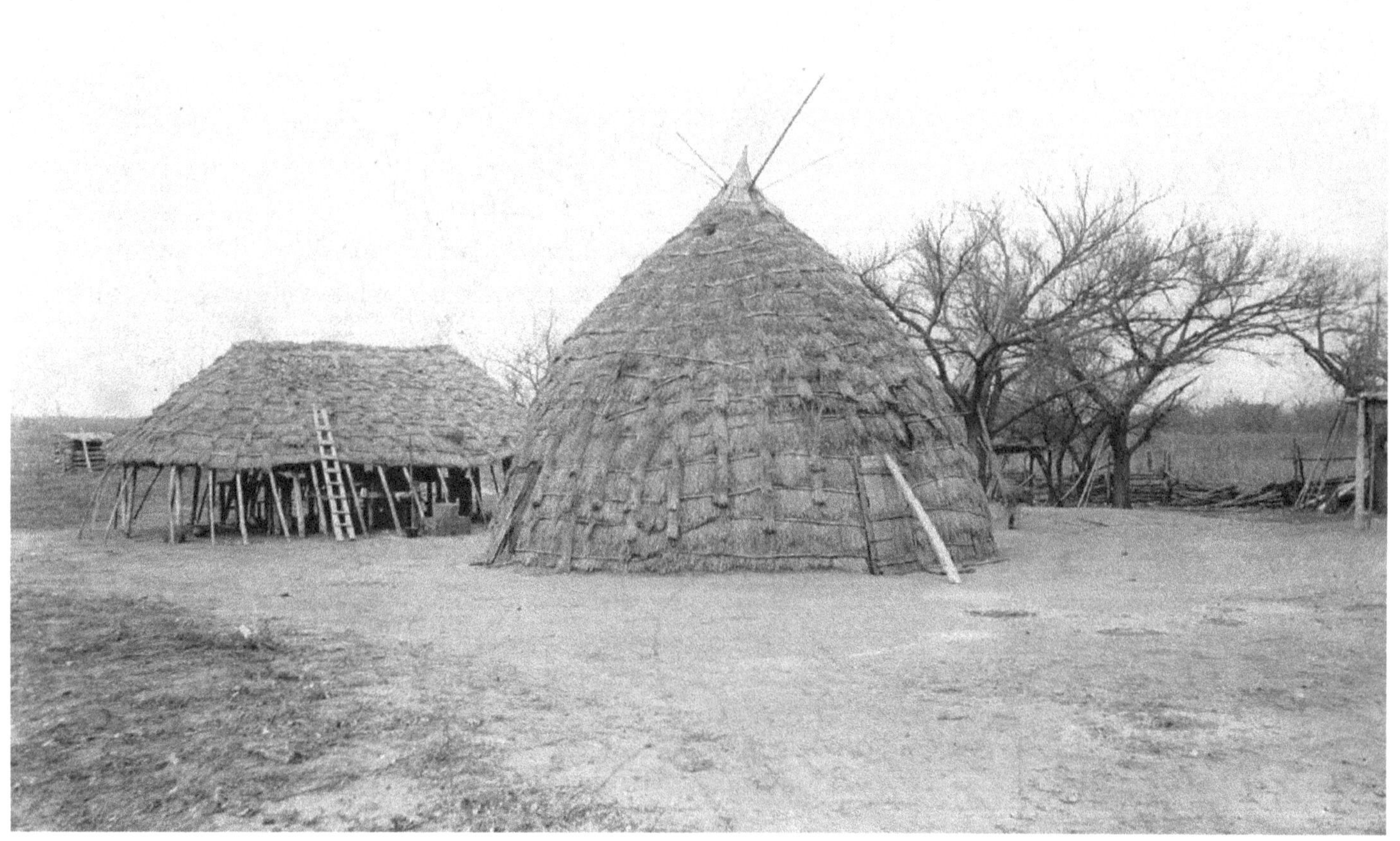

The home of Chief Tawakoni Jim is seen here near Anadarko in 1901. These wood-framed, thatched homes were typical of the Wichita and related tribes. The Wichita, although they lived among the equestrian tribes of the southern plains, practiced agriculture and were noted traders among the Spanish and French.

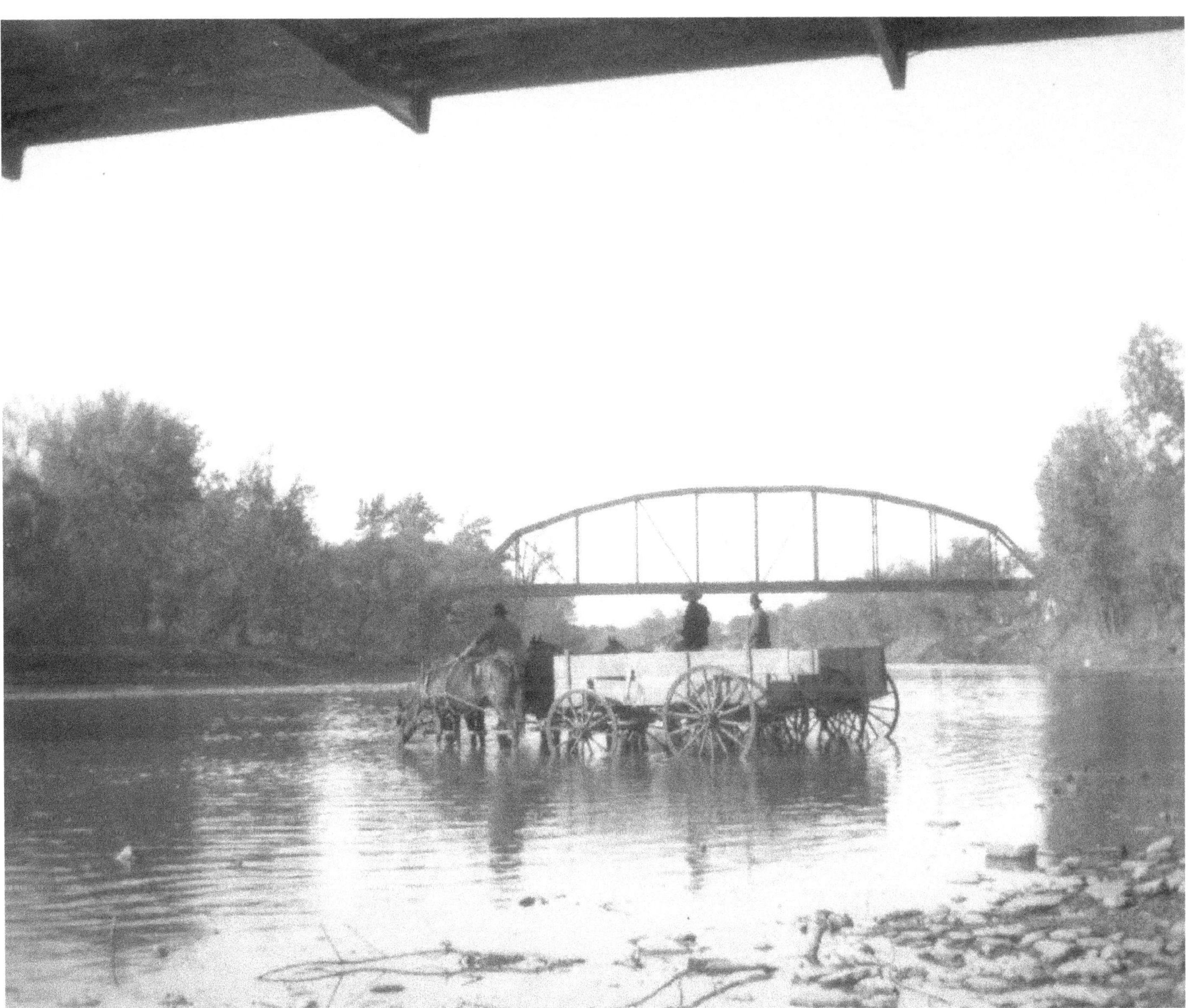

A wagon makes a treacherous ford across the Neosho River near Miami, while a bridge for the Frisco Railroad (the St. Louis and San Francisco Railroad) hangs enticingly downriver in 1901. That same year Miami succeeded in securing a nonrail bridge into the city, which may be the object at the top of the photo.

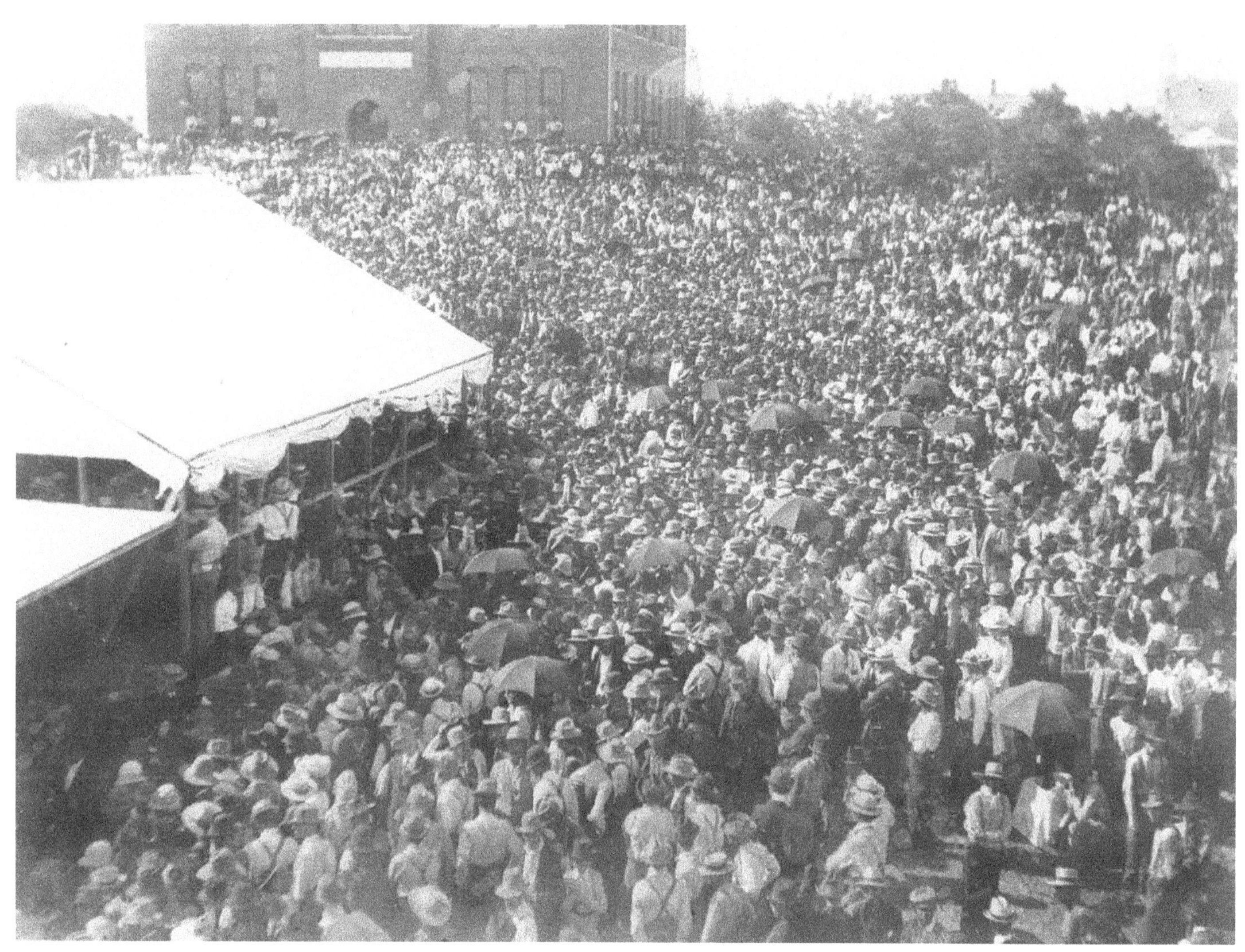

In August 1901, the Kiowa-Comanche surplus land in southwestern Oklahoma was opened to settlement. Rather than promote a chaotic land run, federal officials decided a lottery would be more orderly, so they required all home seekers to register for a chance at the 13,000 parcels of land. Over 160,000 showed up here in El Reno.

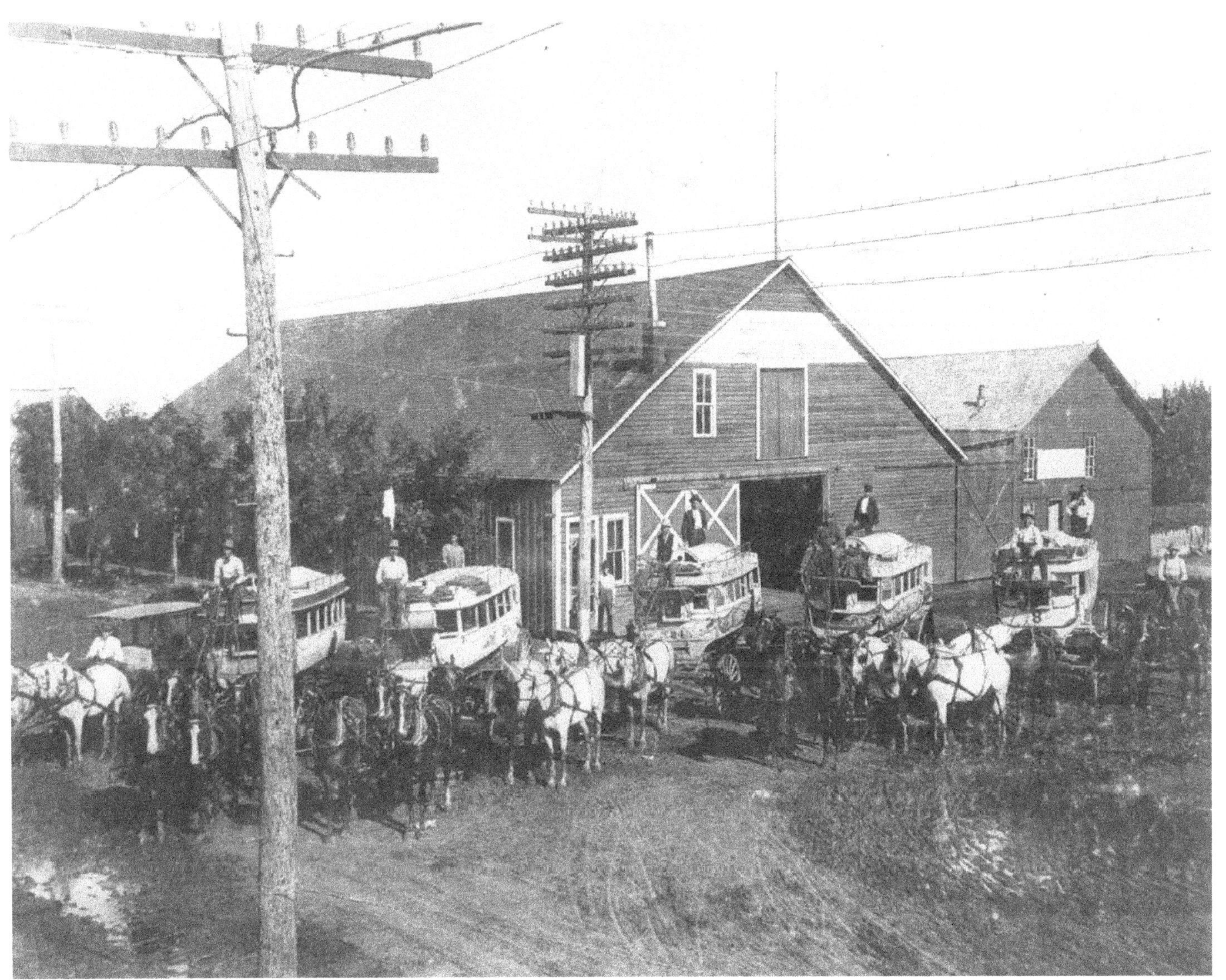

Lottery winners in the Kiowa-Comanche opening of August 1901 had the option of arriving at their claims in one of these chartered buses, seen in El Reno.

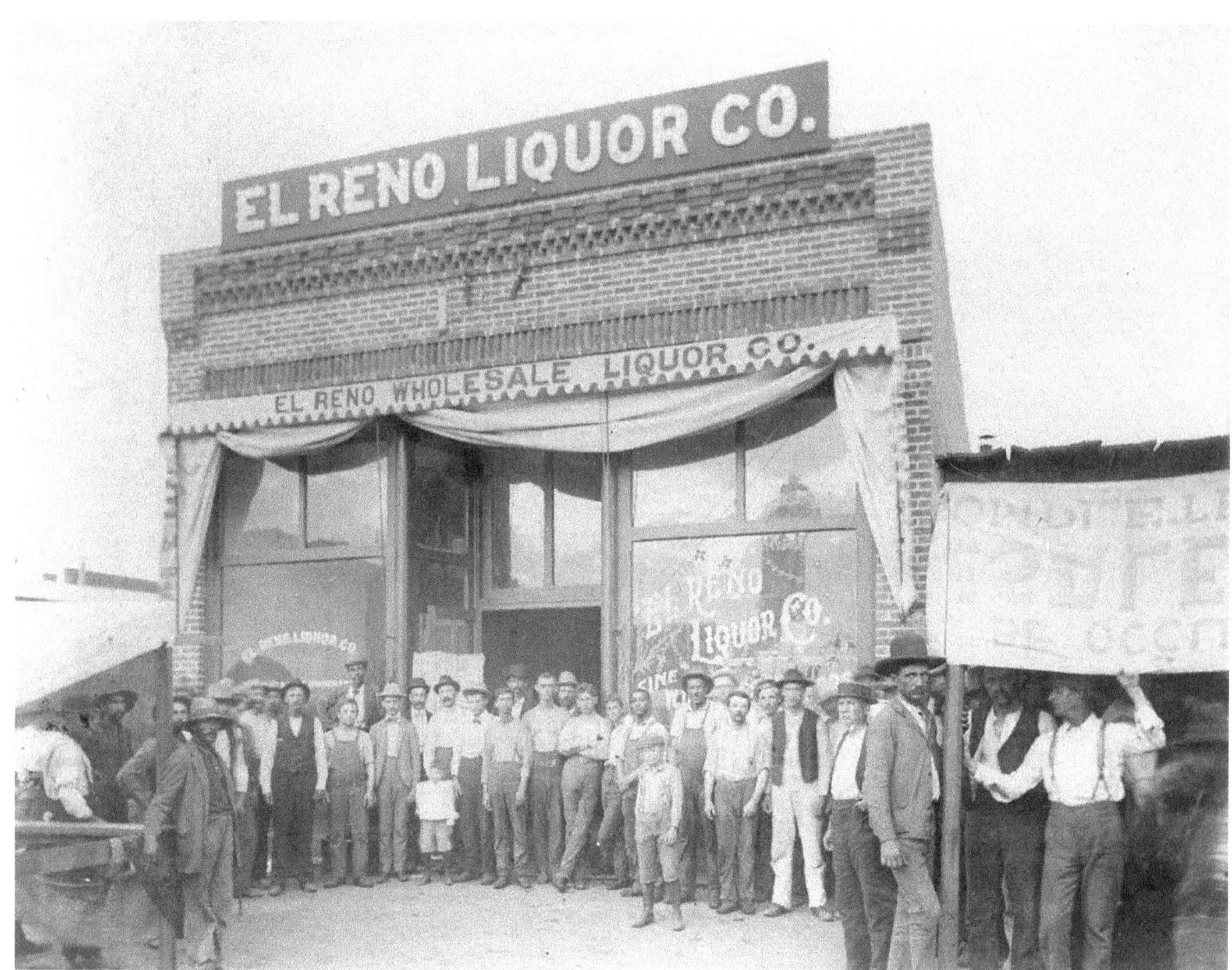

Distributors in El Reno were prepared to ply the newly wet Kiowa-Comanche lands with liquor after the opening in August 1901. Liquor sales were banned for 60 days until licenses could be issued, but the real money was made in selling water: it was going for 10¢ a vial while beer sold for 25¢ a quart.

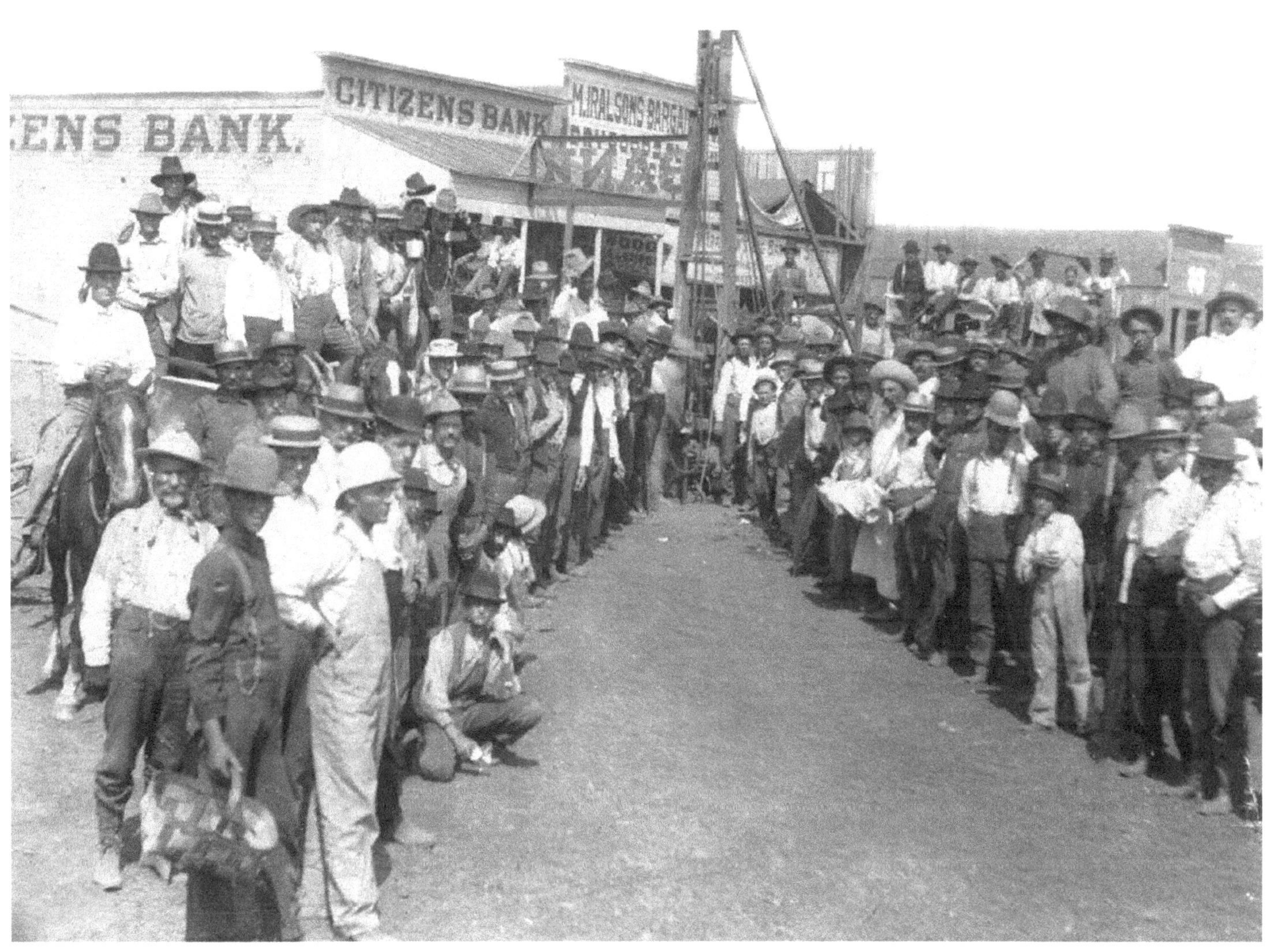

Just weeks after the new town of Lawton was established in 1901, dozens of oil companies formed to snatch up all available mineral rights. Here, a well appears in the middle of the business district. It is unknown whether this was a producing well.

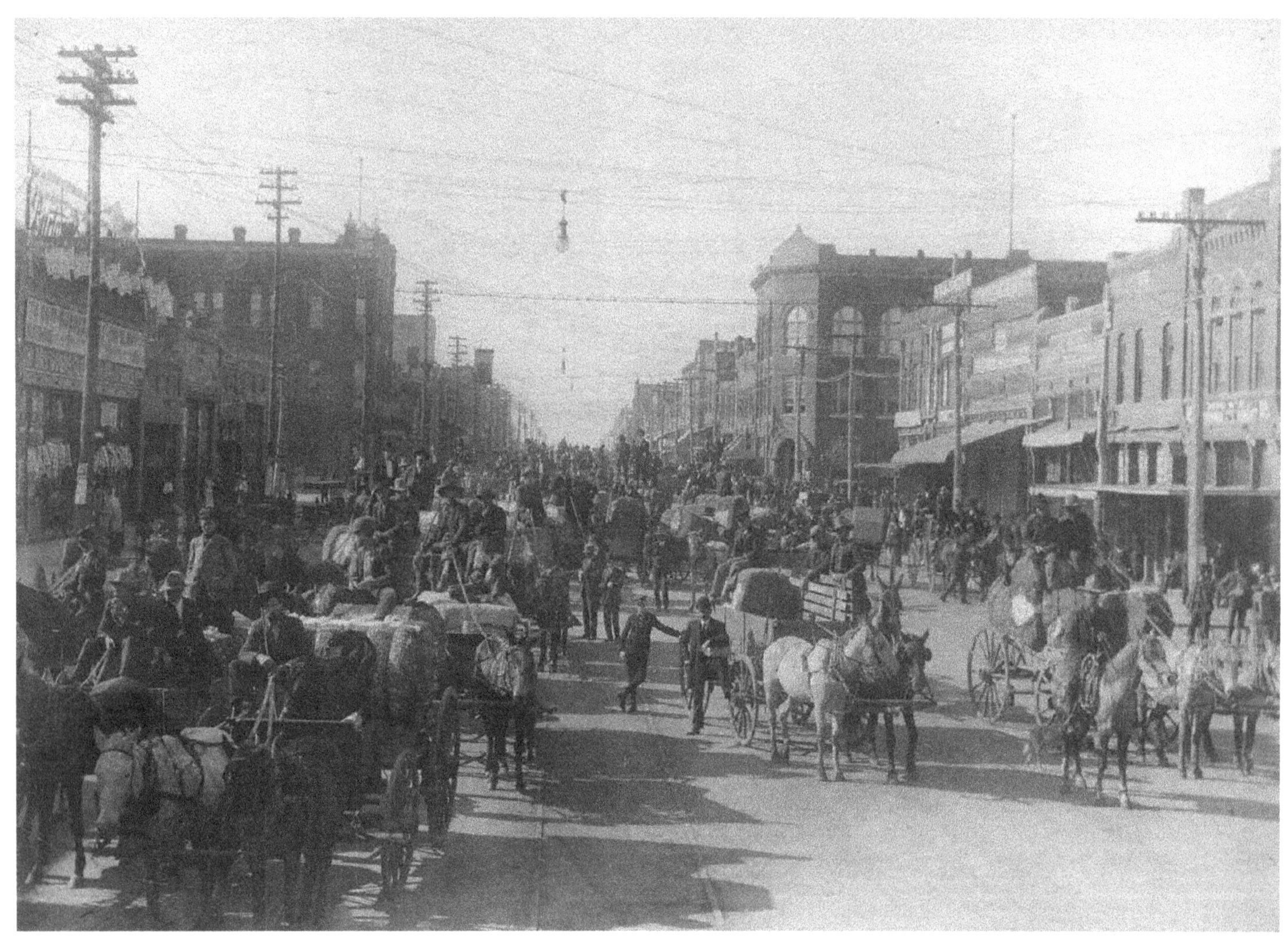

The cotton market in downtown Ardmore, 1902. Ardmore grew from a railhead for shipping cattle and cotton to a market center for the state's cotton production. One of four cotton compresses in the state was located in Ardmore, and thousands of bales of cotton made their way to U.S. and European mills from the booming town.

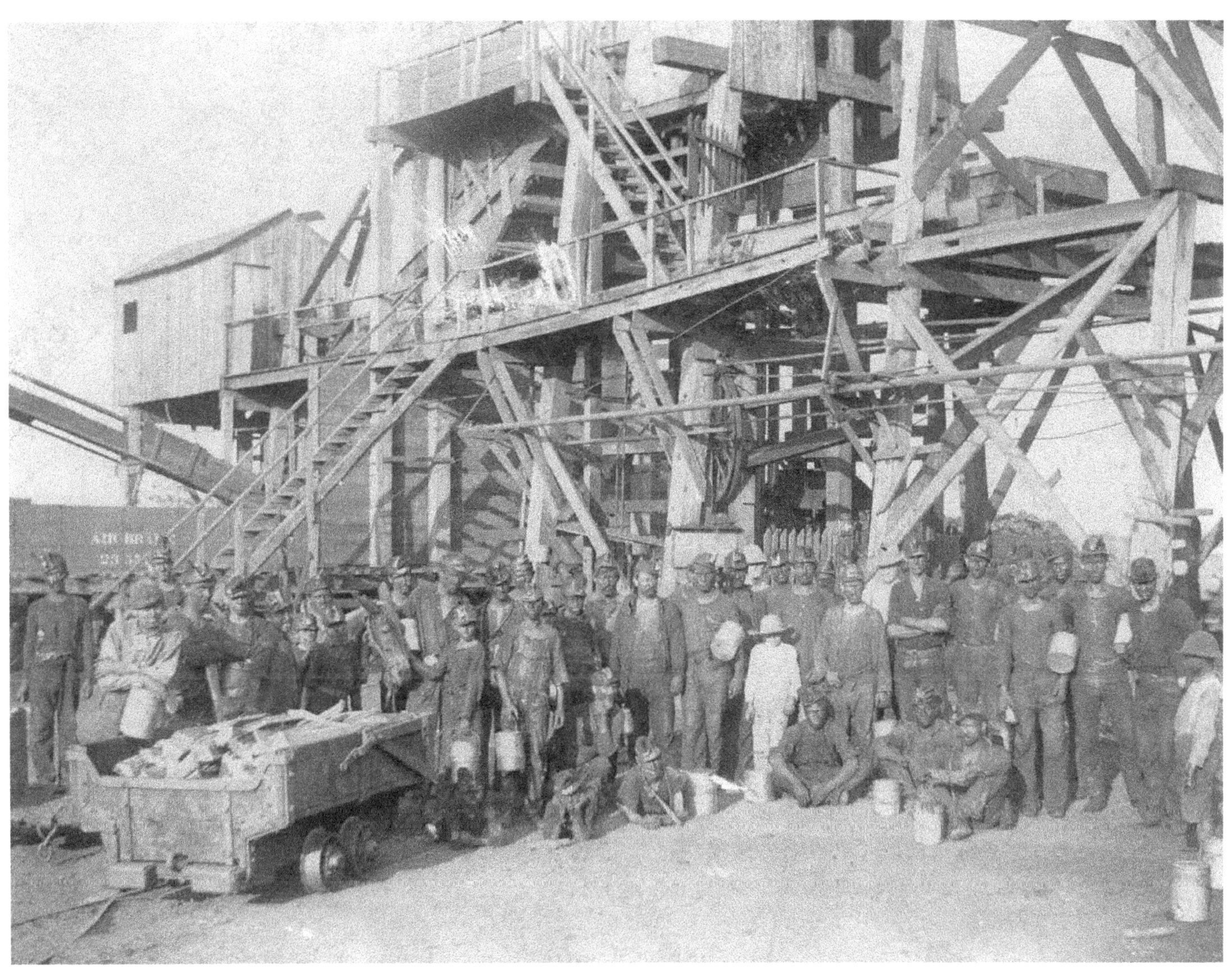

Coal mine, Wilburton, 1902. Coal mining was one of the earliest industries in Indian Territory and, by the time of this photo, was well-developed with several railroads, ready markets, and an immigrant labor force. And with minimal government regulation, the mines were some of the most dangerous in America.

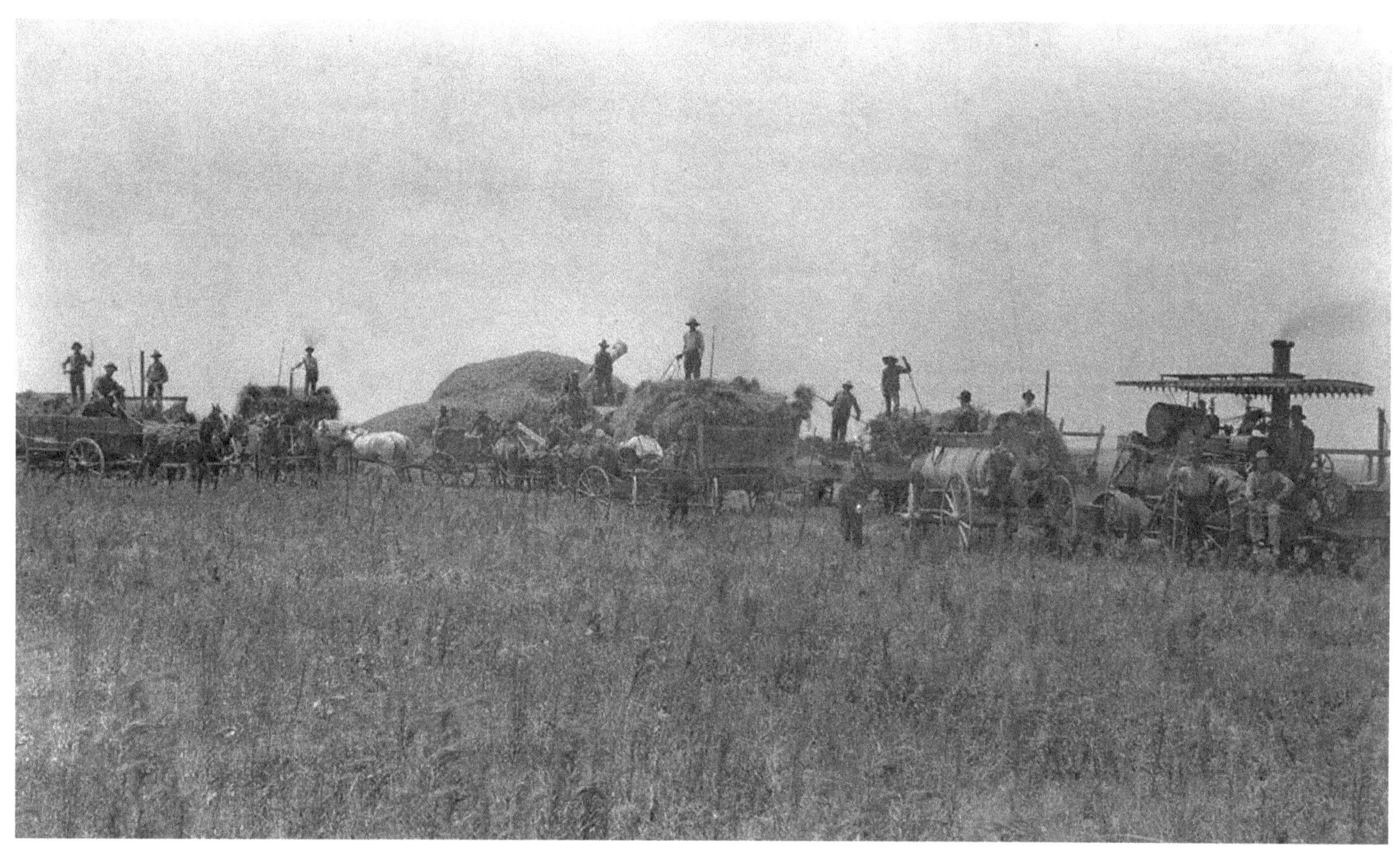

Wheat harvest near Geary, ca. 1903. Despite iconic associations of harvest with the fall season, harvest in Oklahoma comes in late spring. The wheat harvest was usually a community enterprise, and neighbor helped neighbor until the crops were all in. Mechanization would change all that, not long after the scene in this photo.

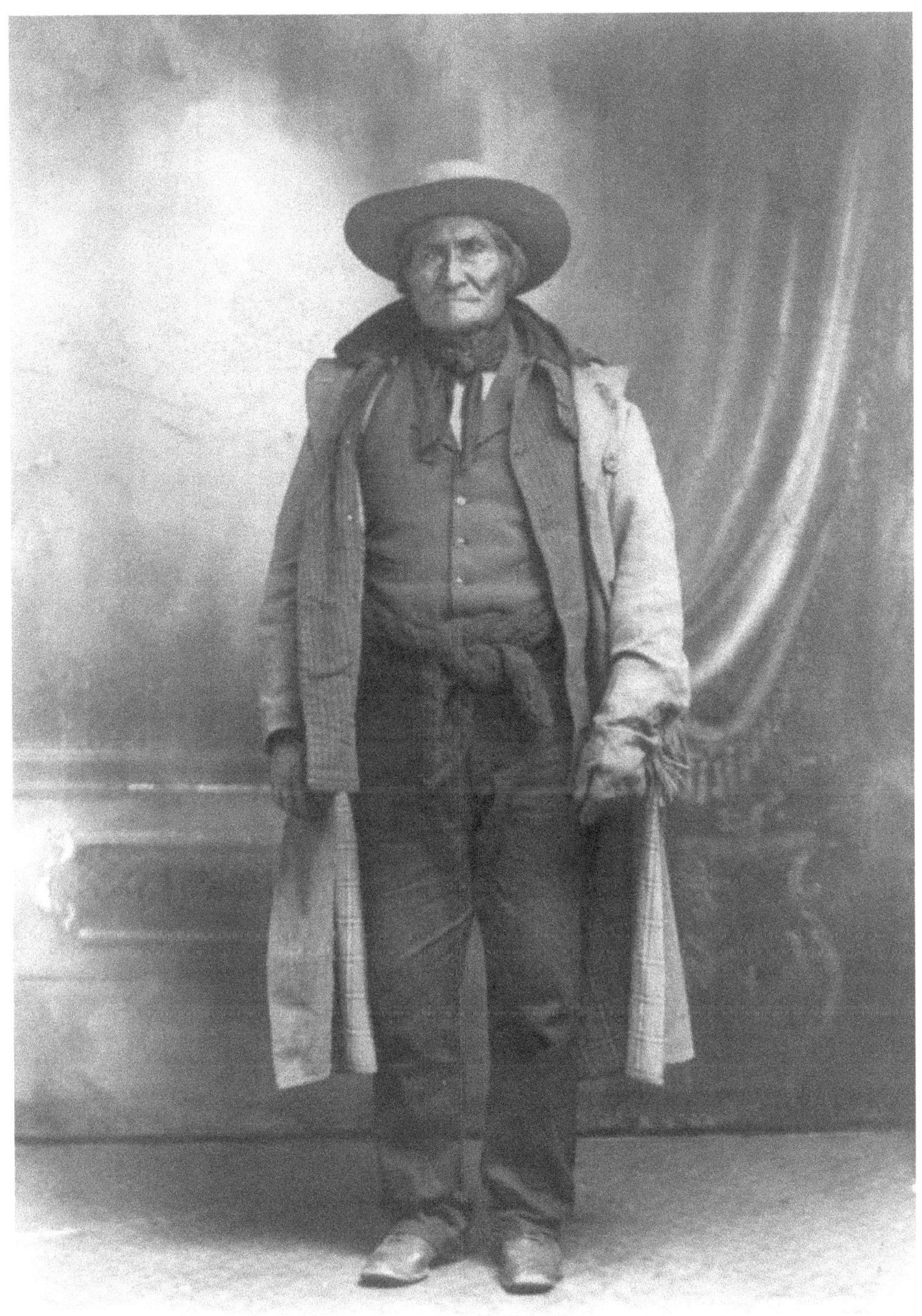

The mighty Apache leader Geronimo is pictured here in the winter of his days, Lawton, ca. 1903. Geronimo waged guerrilla warfare on Mexican and American troops in the desert Southwest for decades before his capture in 1886. He lived out his last years as a celebrity under house arrest at Fort Sill, until his death in 1909.

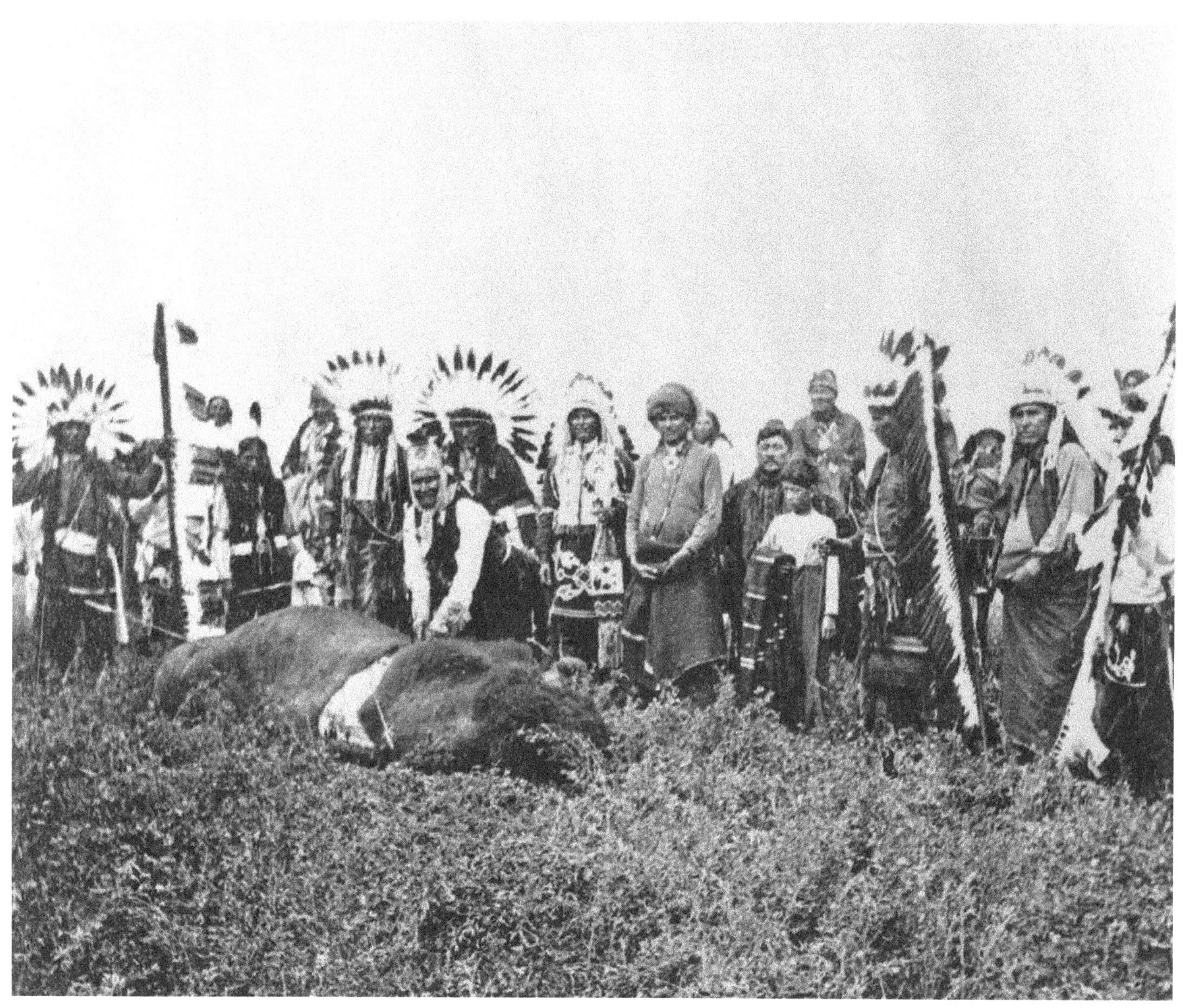

Geronimo's last buffalo hunt, June 11, 1905. Here Geronimo carves up a buffalo at a staged event (despite protestations by conservation-minded President Theodore Roosevelt) for a National Editorial Association convention at the 101 Ranch. One account has "the Apache terror" killing the beast from the front seat of a car.

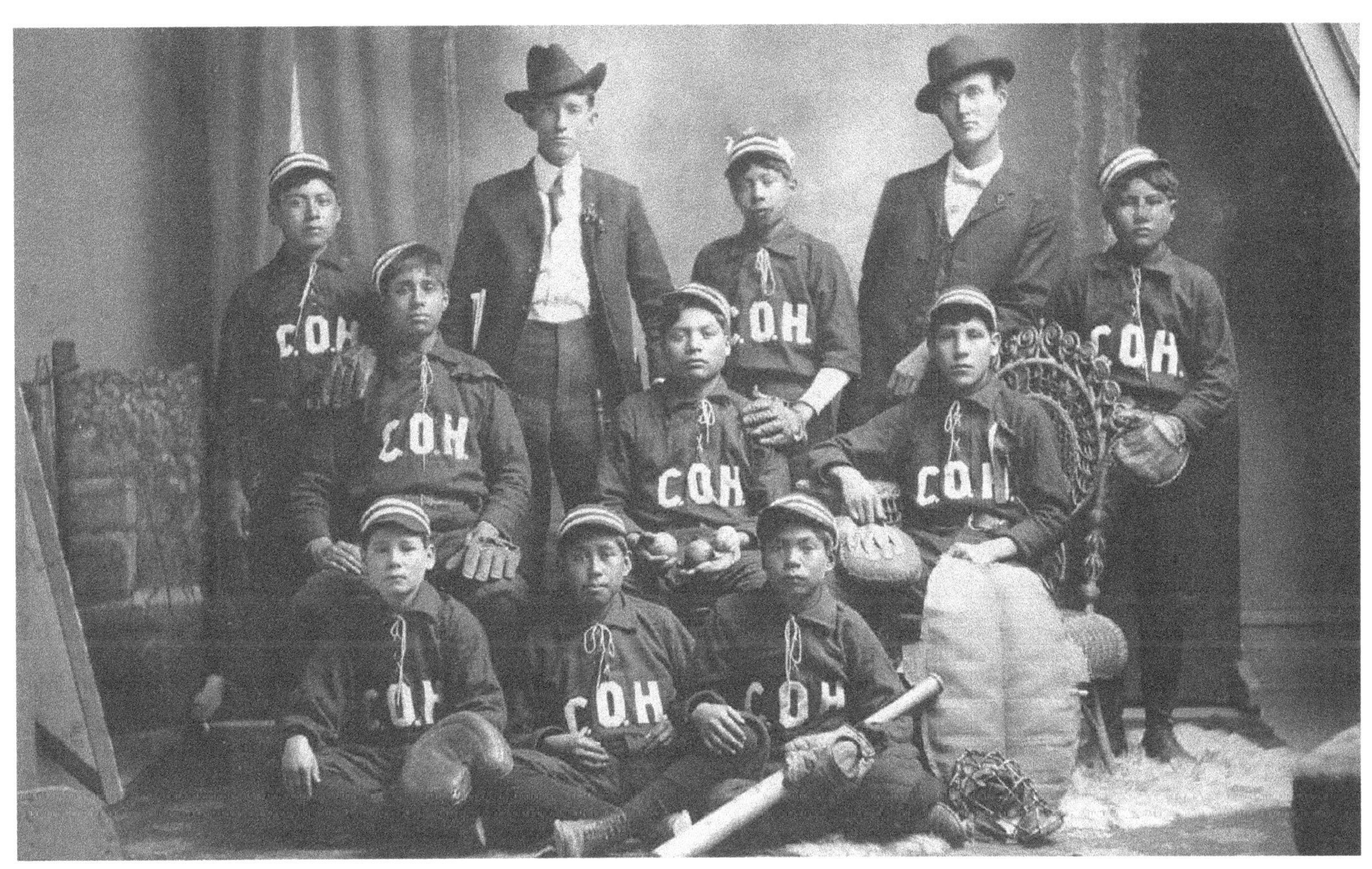

Constructive play was a new trend in education at the end of the nineteenth century and was widely adopted by the faculties of tribal boarding schools and orphans' homes in Indian Territory. The baseball teams of the Creek Orphans' Home, such as this one photographed in 1904, were quite formidable.

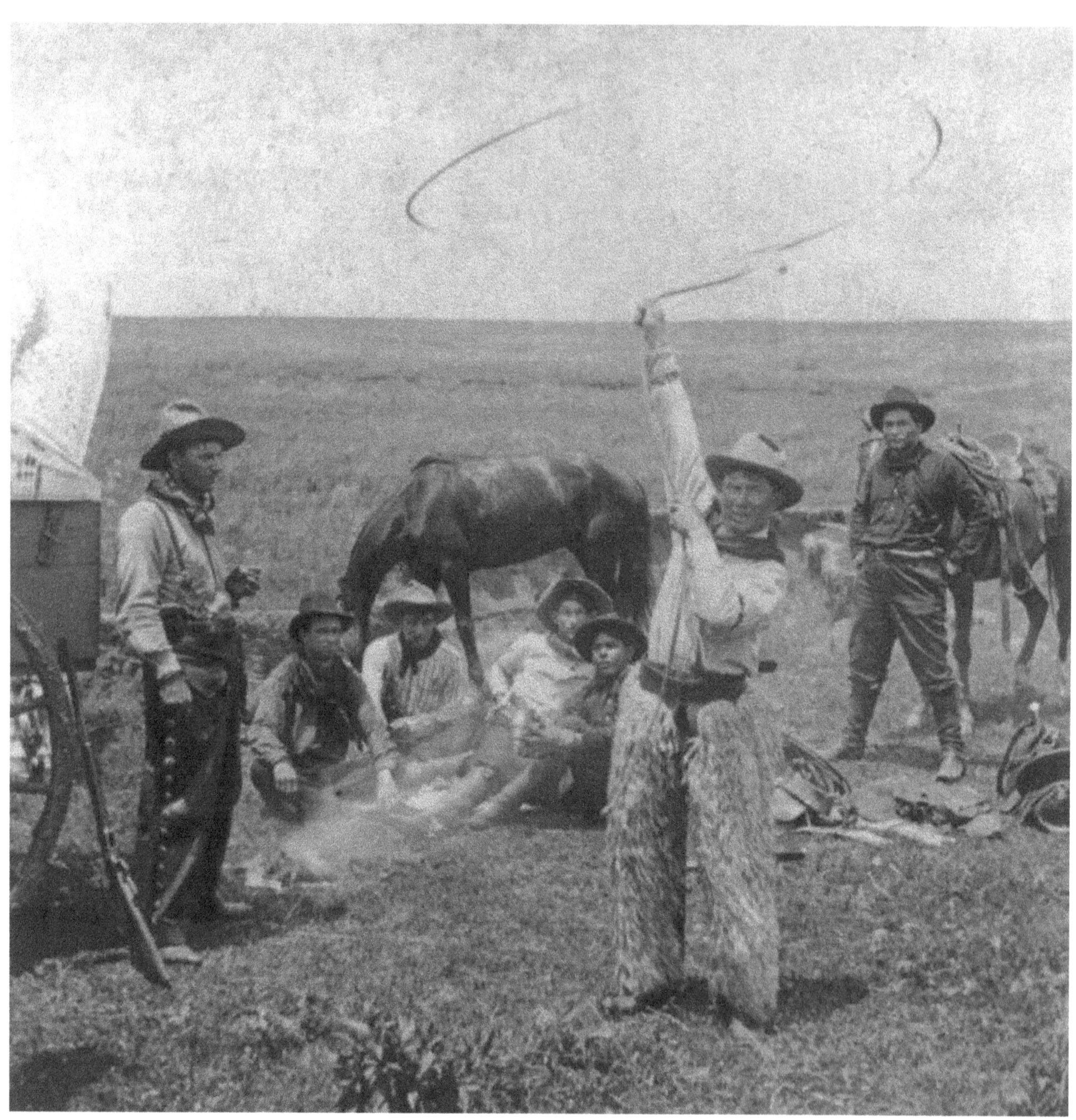

Despite the rapid settlement of Oklahoma in the two decades after the first land run, thousands of acres of ranchland remained. Times could be quite boring on the range, and storytelling, songs, and rope tricks (as seen here in 1905) helped sharpen the dull edges of life in the saddle.

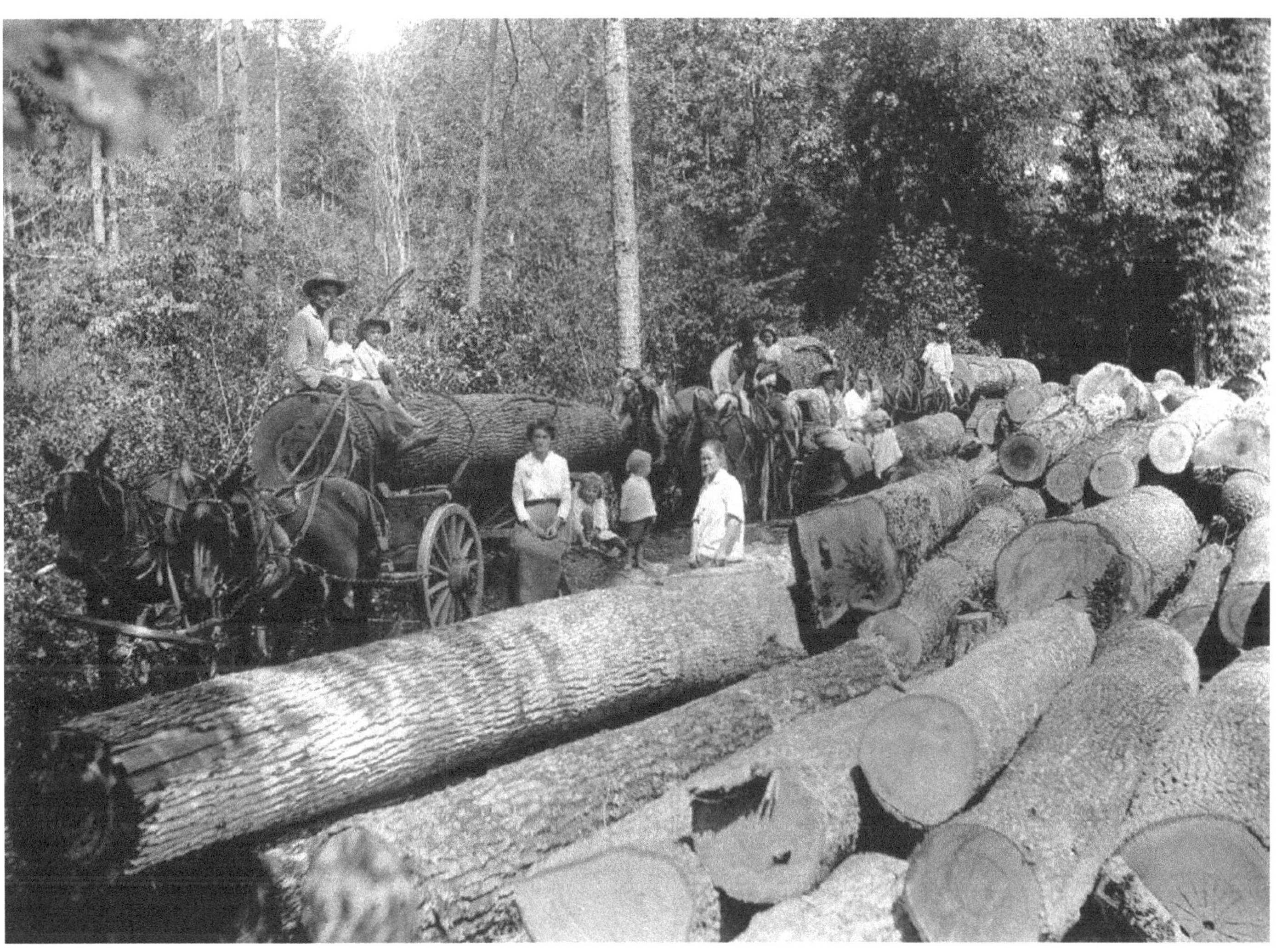

In 1906, the Choctaw Lumber Company was formed and quickly acquired near exclusive rights to millions of acres of virgin forest in the Choctaw Nation. Logs like these were hauled by mules to the company railroad and moved by rail to company mills in Broken Bow and Wright City.

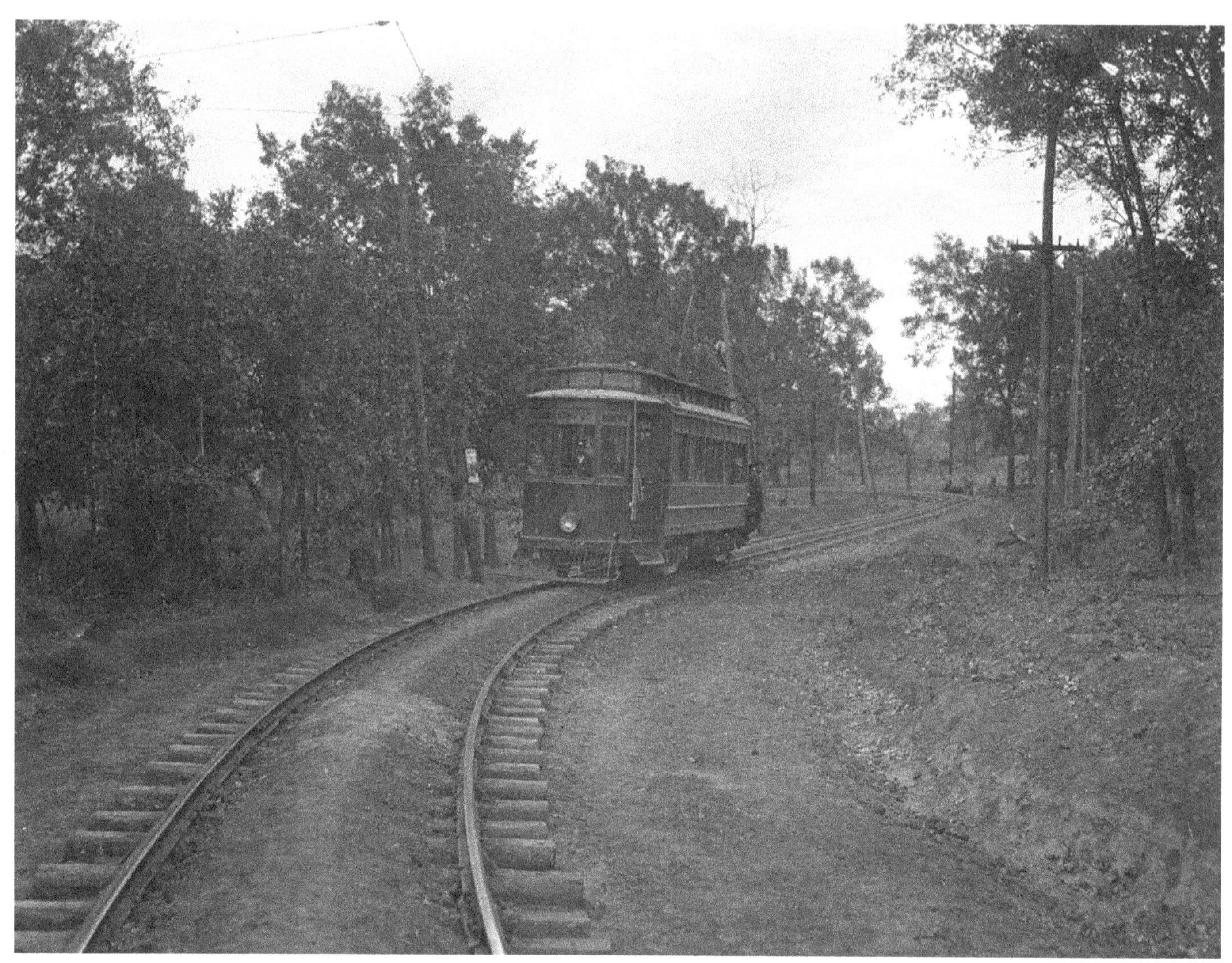

Shawnee and Tecumseh battled for decades over the location of the Pottawatomie County seat, but in 1906 the Shawnee-Tecumseh Traction Company connected the two towns and brought a measure of amicability. The trolley cars snaked through the forests between Shawnee and Tecumseh until 1932—just after Shawnee won the county seat in an election.

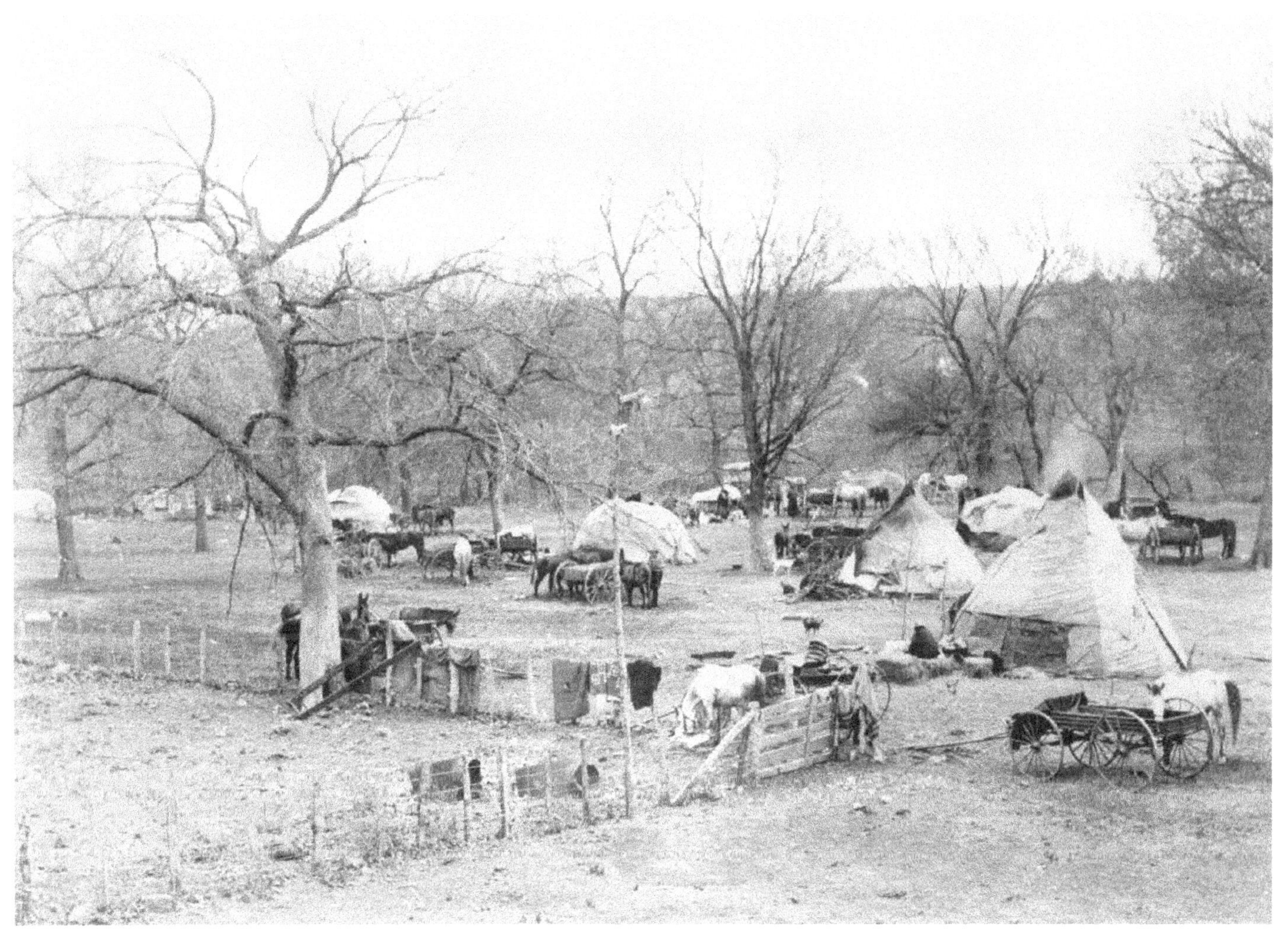

Peaceful scenes like this one in an Osage camp would vanish soon after this photo was made, as Osage tribal grazing lands were divided into private allotments in 1906, and the discovery of oil would bring challenges to the tribe's way of life.

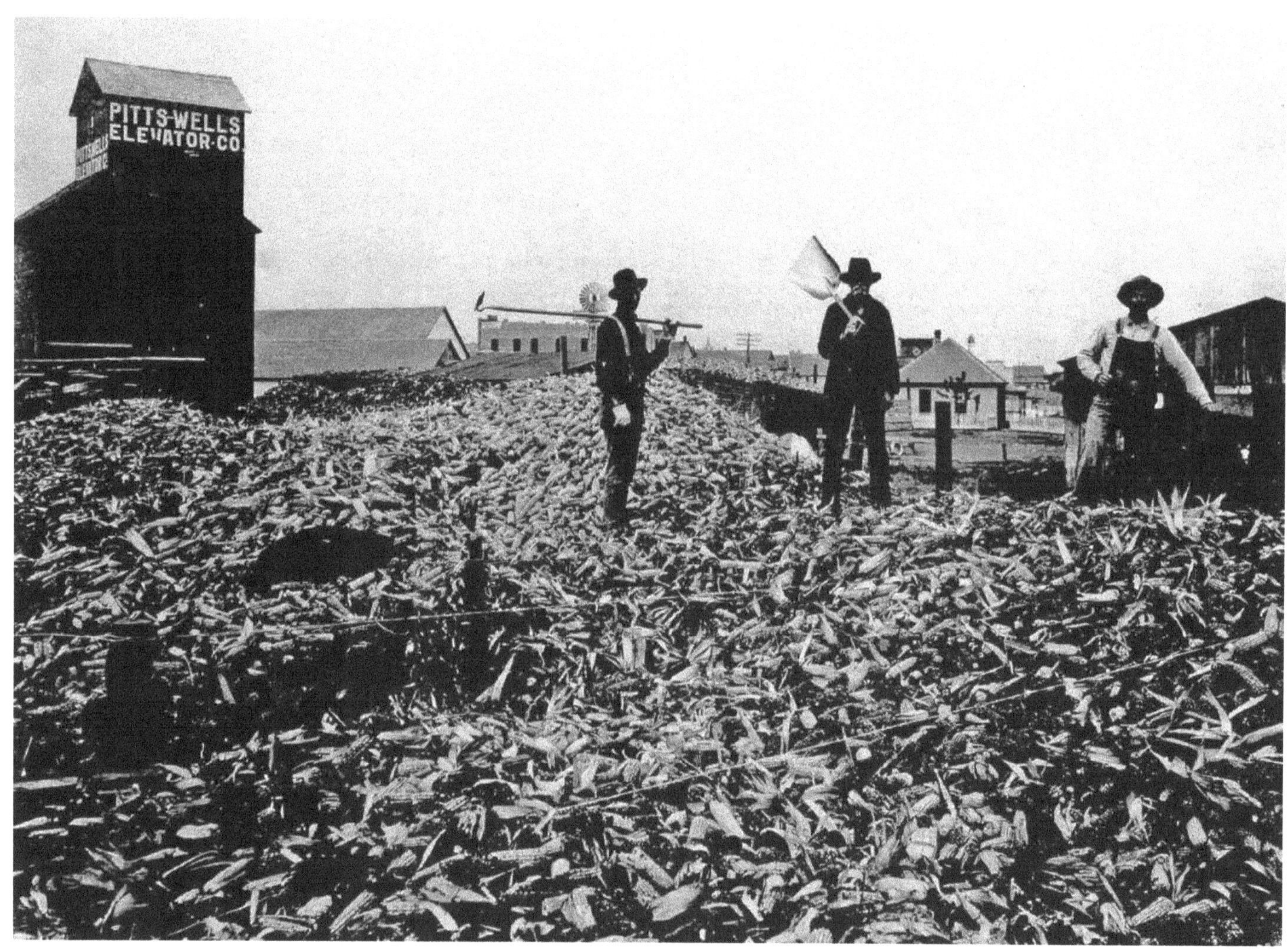

Teeming corn bins outside the Pitts-Wells grain elevator in Broken Arrow, ca. 1907. Corn was once a major cash crop in Oklahoma, until the development of large wheat farms in the west. Corn farming in Oklahoma never quite recovered from the migrations of farmers leaving the state during the Depression.

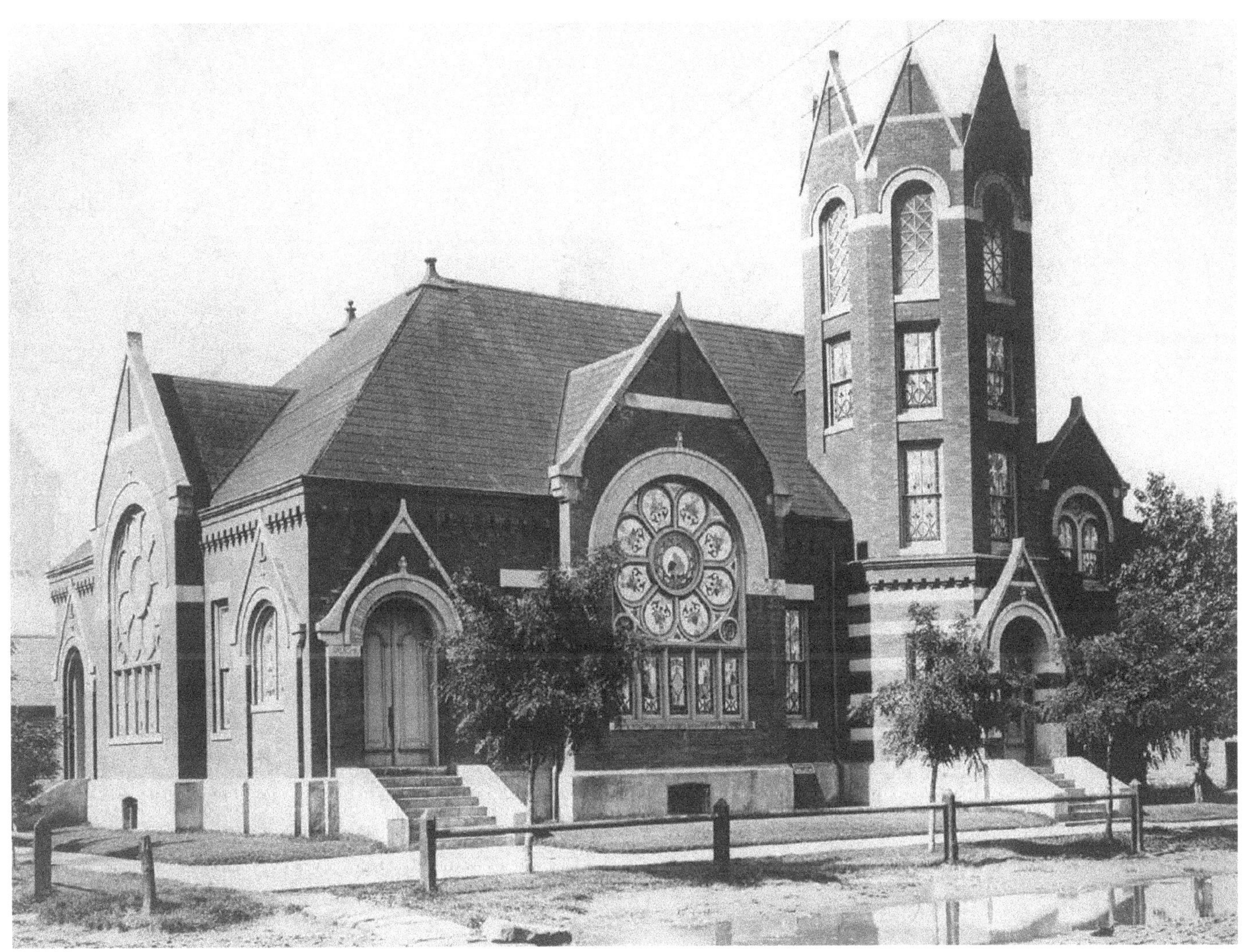

The hexagonal turret of Chickasha's First Christian Church, seen here in 1907, made the house of worship a longtime landmark at Sixth and Iowa. In later years, before its demolition, it was the home of the Church of Christ.

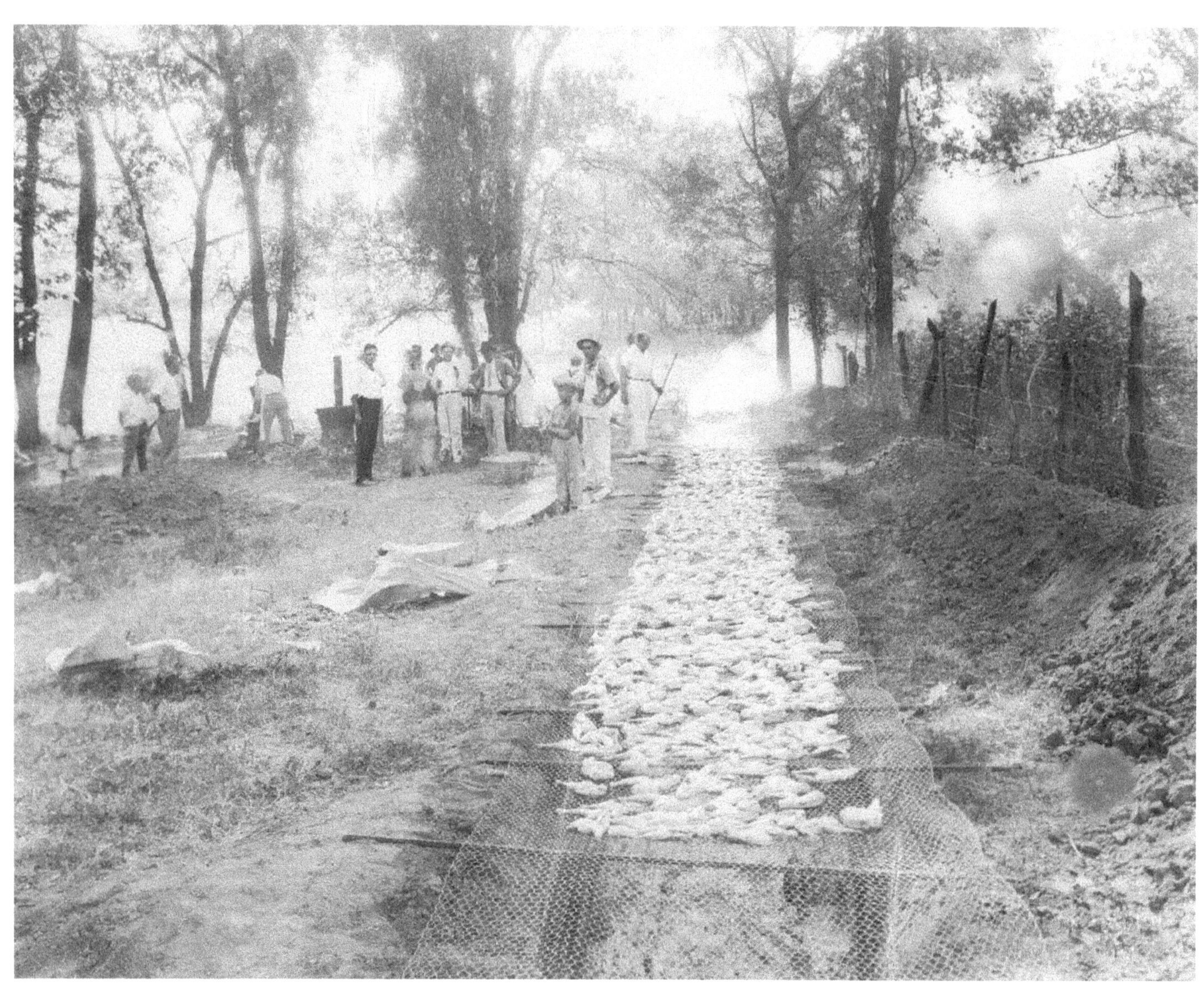

Pit-roasting chickens at a Chickasaw gathering near Ardmore.

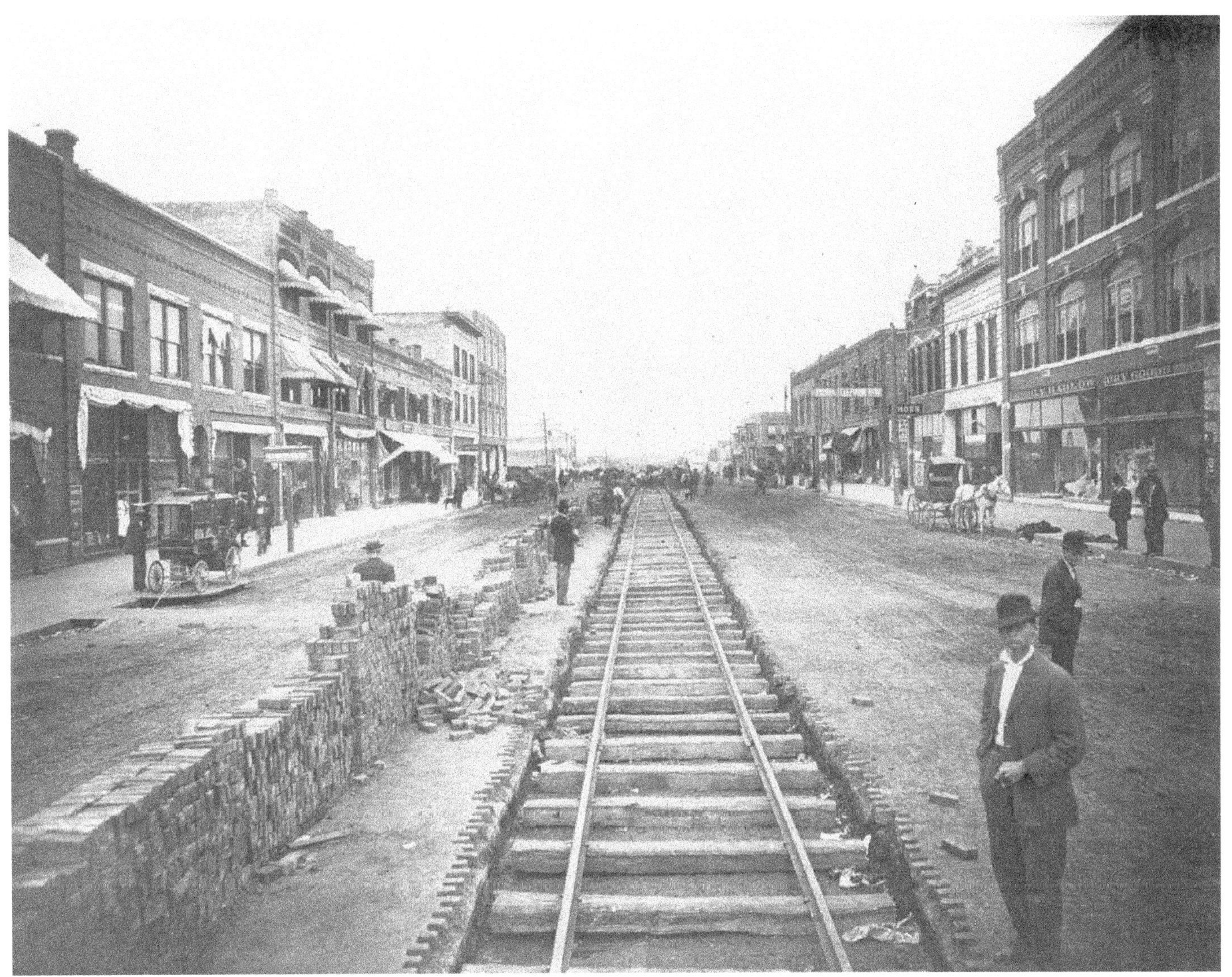

Construction of the Bartlesville Interurban Company tracks on Third Street, 1908. The interurban connected Bartlesville with the nearby industrial towns of Tuxedo and Dewey. With only 10 miles of track, the interurban couldn't keep up with Bartlesville's oil-fueled boom, and the streetcars ran for the last time in 1920.

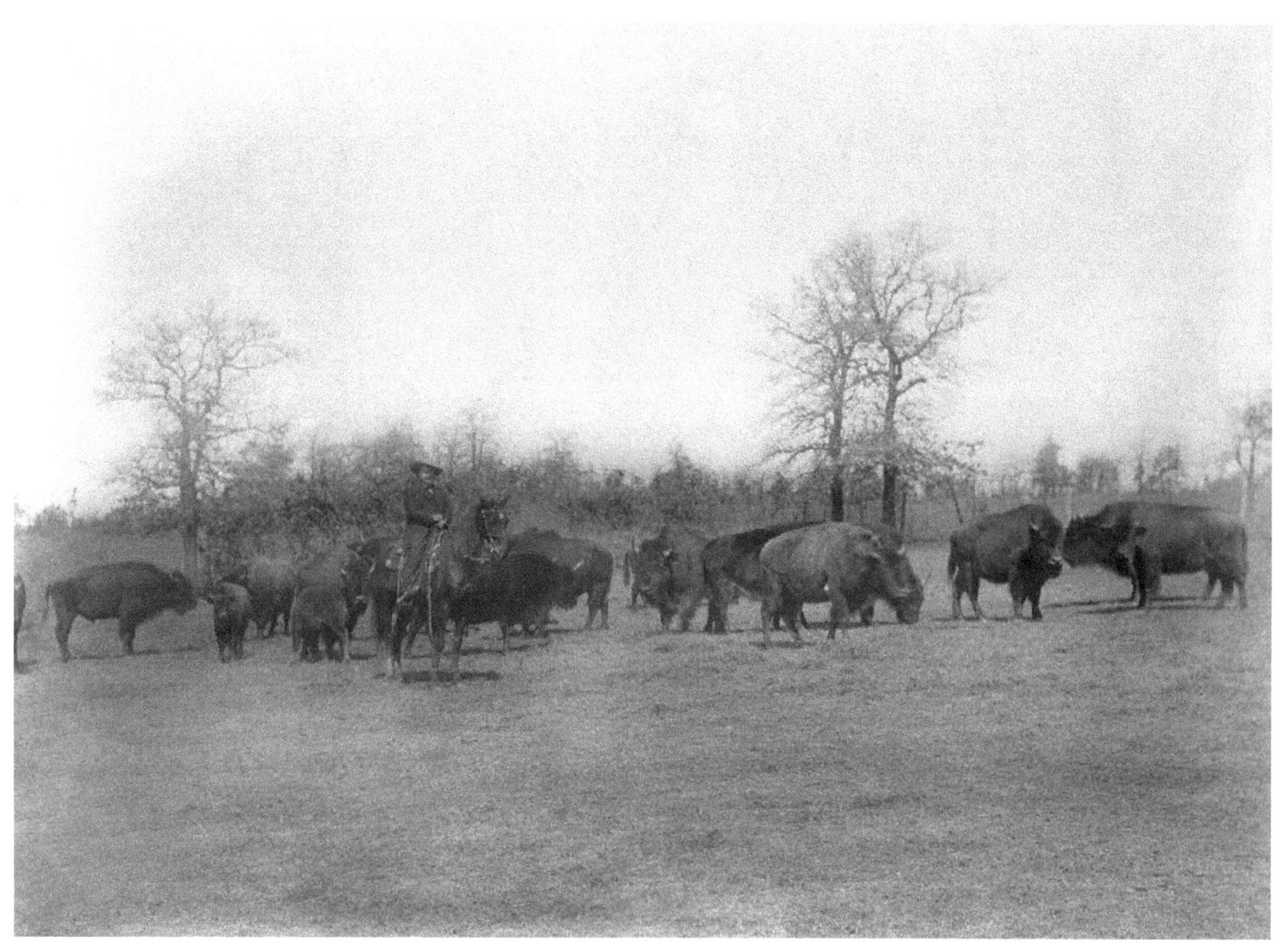

Although he once had a successful Wild West show of his own, William Gordon Lillie, known as Pawnee Bill because of his friendship with the Pawnee tribe, had joined the larger Buffalo Bill Wild West Show when this photo of him on horseback was made around 1908.

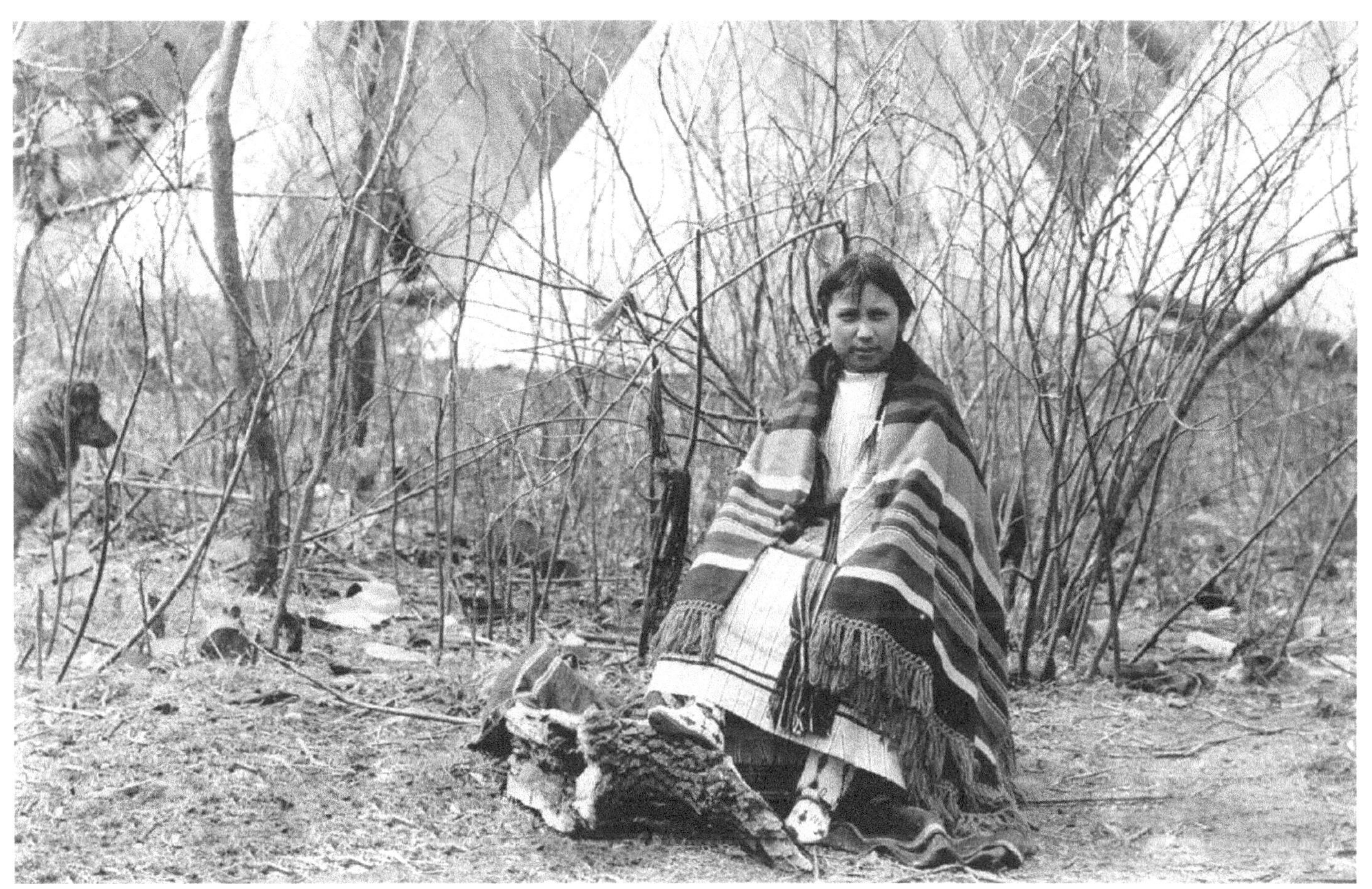

Minnie Chips is seen here in traditional Cheyenne dress, ca. 1908. She was likely a student at the United States Indian School in Canton.

Buffalo herd, probably in the Wichita Mountains Wildlife Refuge, ca. 1908. At the time, only a few dozen buffalo remained from the tens of millions that once roamed the plains. In 1905 President Theodore Roosevelt placed in the refuge a herd from which other herds grew, and today there are over 350,000 buffalo in the United States.

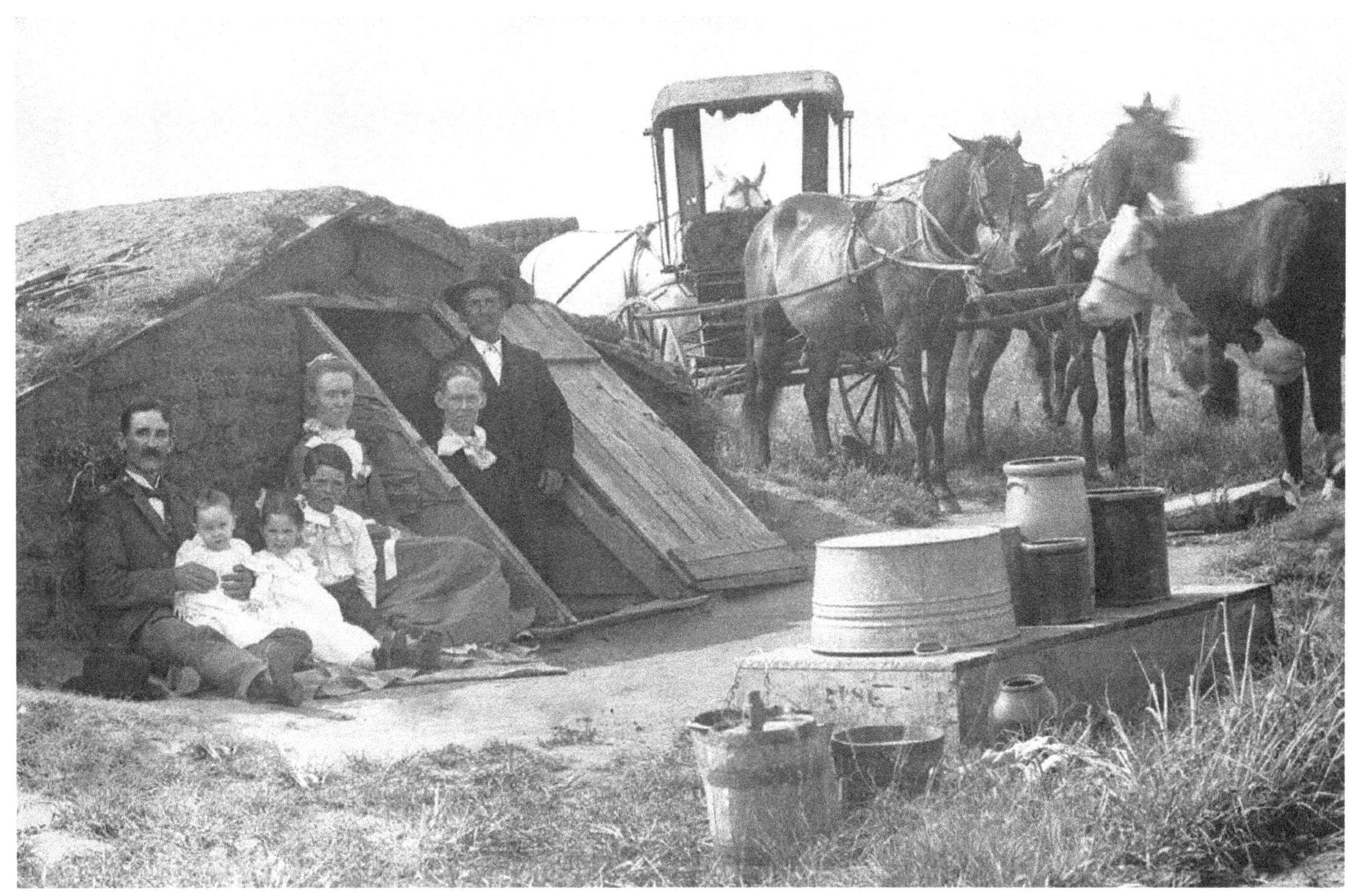

Seen here is a typical dugout in western Oklahoma, ca. 1909. A dugout was usually only a temporary housing solution, pursuant to "proving" one's claim on a homestead, to be replaced by a frame house when possible. There were many nuisances associated with living underground, including the occasional worm dangling from the ceiling.

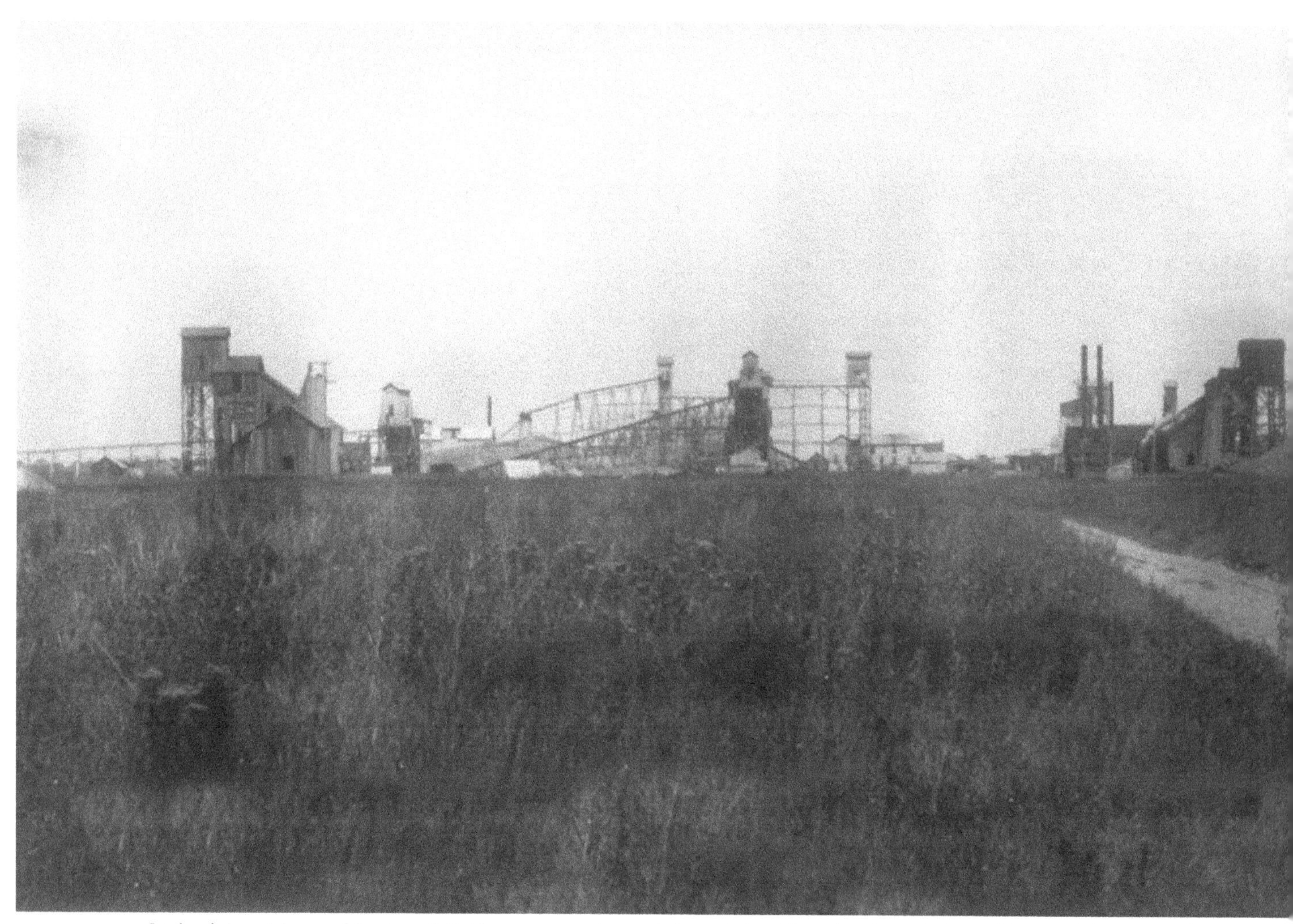

Lead and zinc mining near Miami, ca. 1909. These two minerals were vital to an industrializing America at the dawn of the twentieth century, and Ottawa County was situated atop a vast deposit. At the height of production, several hundred mines and mills were operating in the area.

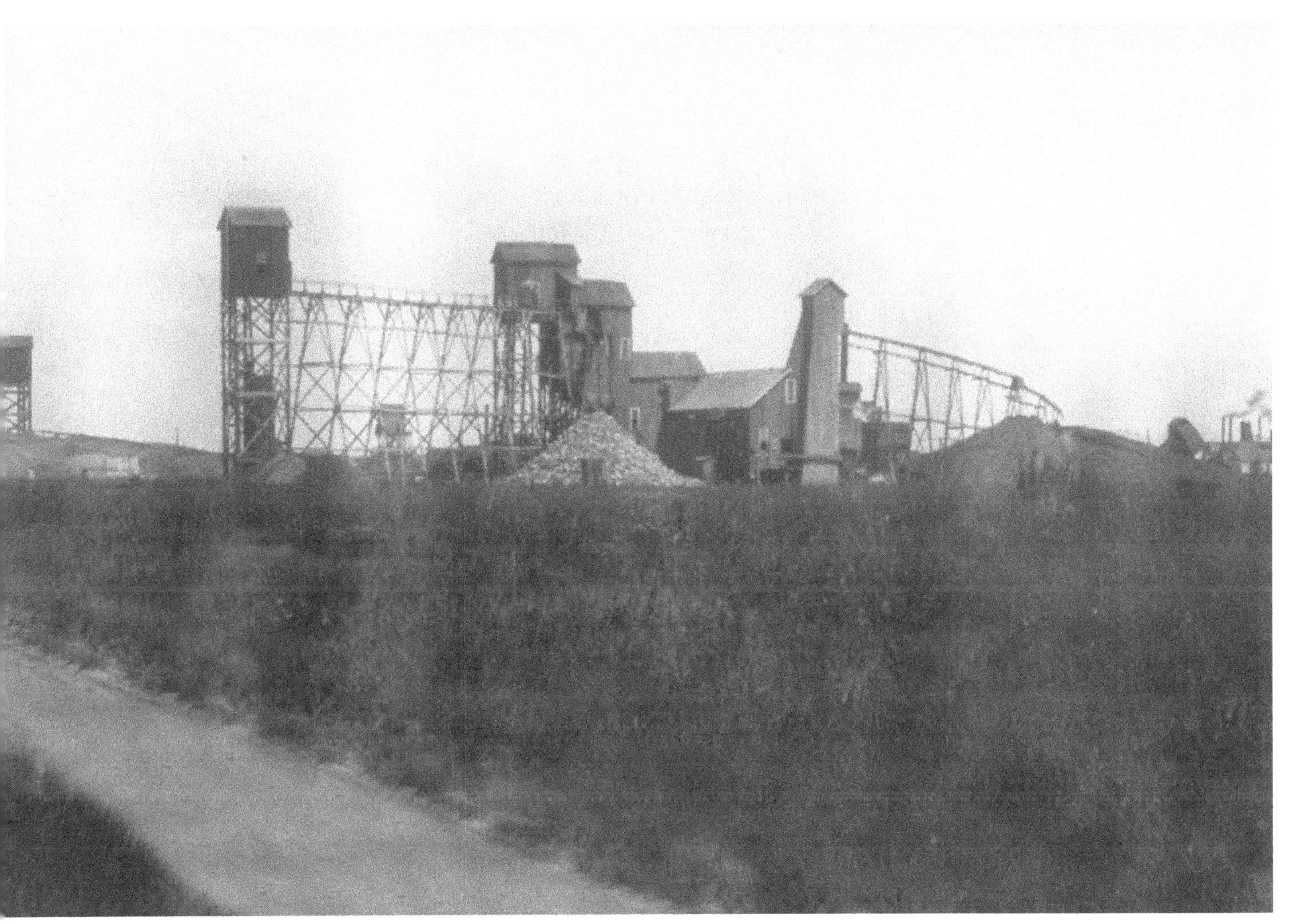

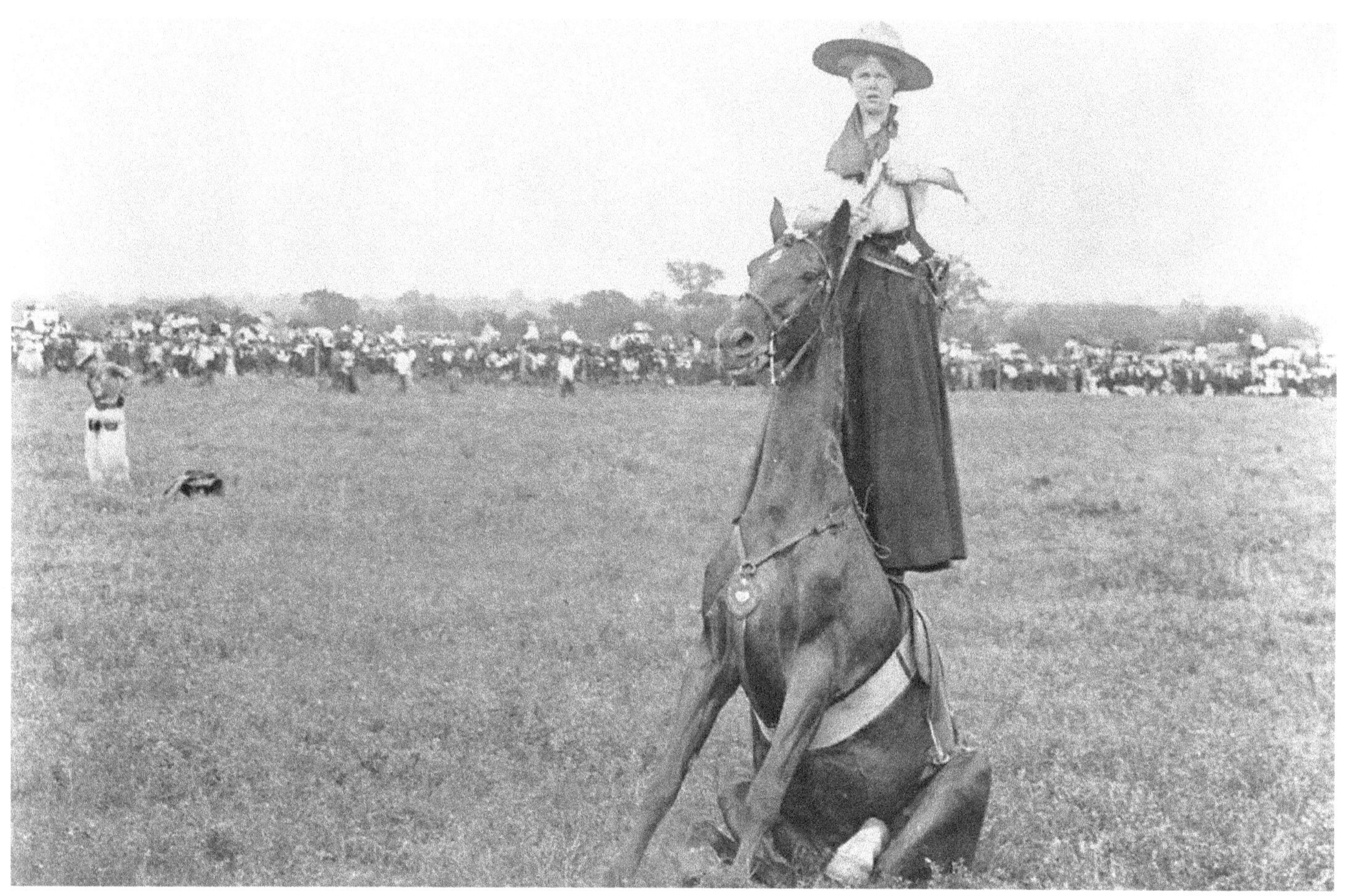

Lucille Mulhall performs at the Miller Brothers' famous 101 Ranch south of Ponca City, ca. 1909. Theodore Roosevelt called her "America's first cowgirl" after he saw her perform as a young girl at her father's ranch. She went on to a brilliant career performing riding and roping tricks in Wild West shows, but unlike Will Rogers, she never made the leap to film.

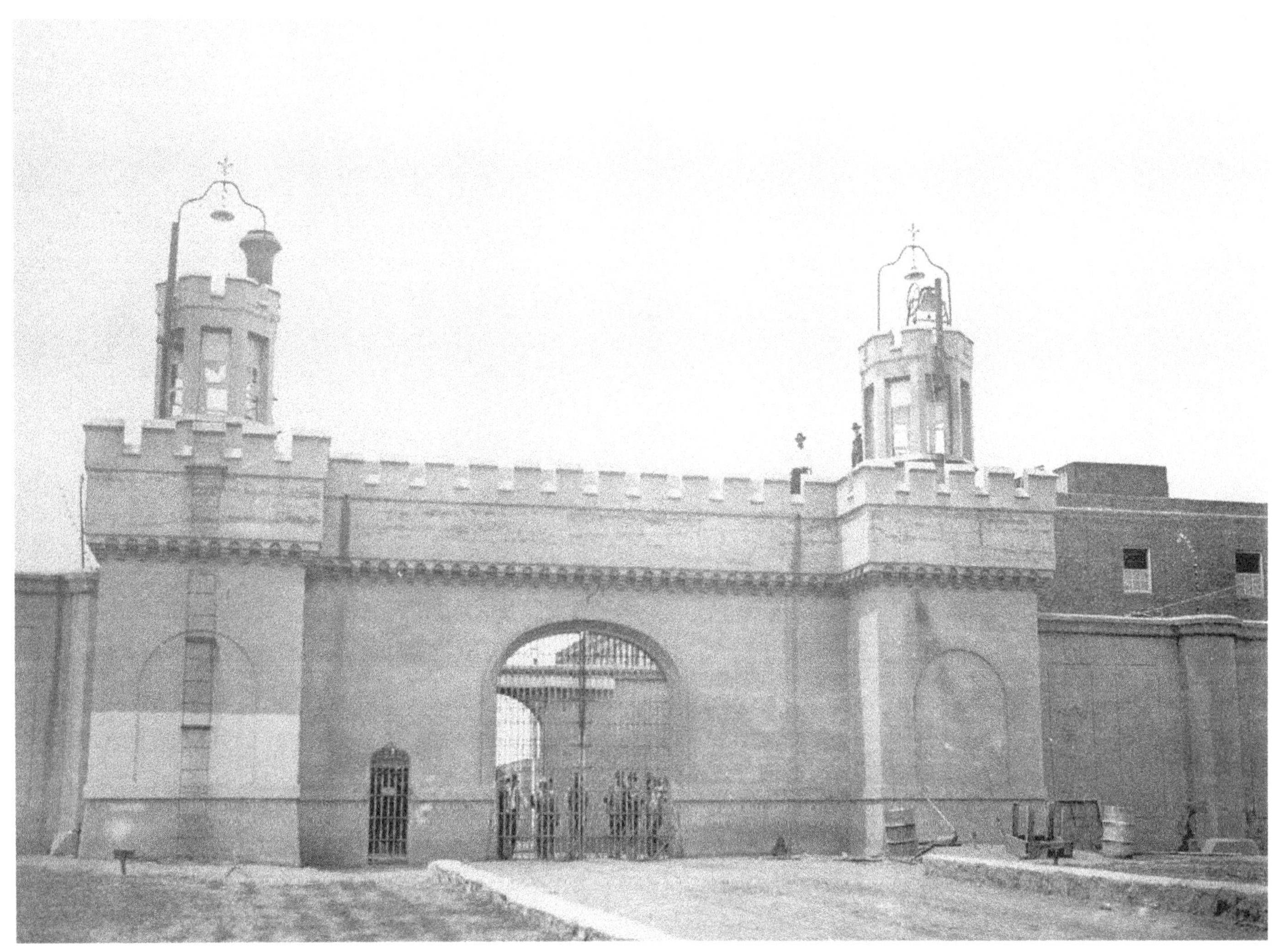

Prior to statehood, Oklahoma's criminals were housed in Kansas, but after Oklahoma's crusading commissioner of charities and corrections Kate Barnard found the conditions in Kansas appalling, appropriations were made for an Oklahoma state prison near McAlester. Here is the east gate just after its construction by convicts who were returned from Kansas in 1909.

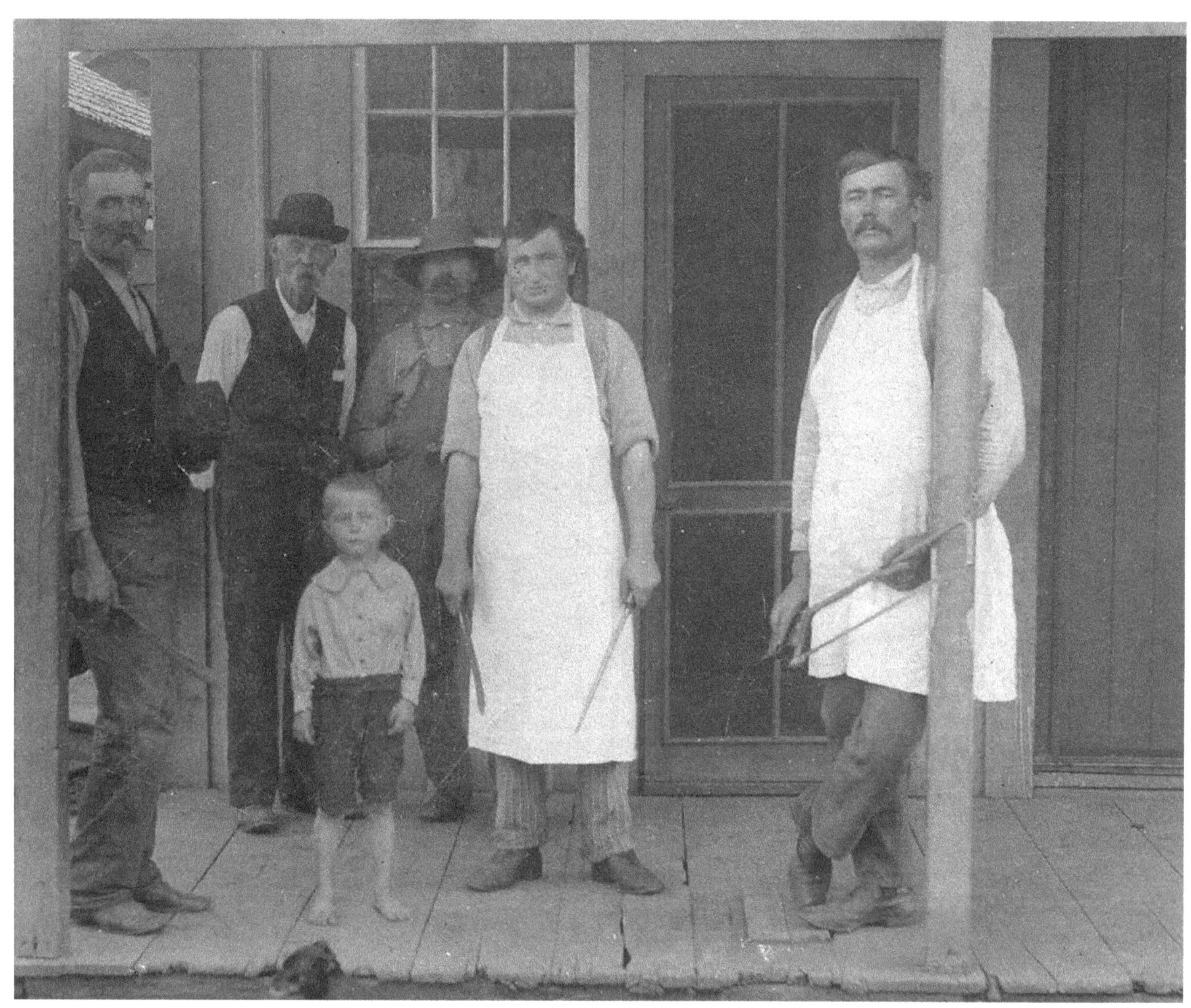

Butcher Tom Murphy and others in front of his shop, Eagle City, 1909. Eagle City had an early advantage in Blaine County because of its position on the Frisco Railroad, but when the Kansas City, Mexico and Orient Railway (later bought by the Santa Fe) built a parallel line through Longdale, Eagle City dried up.

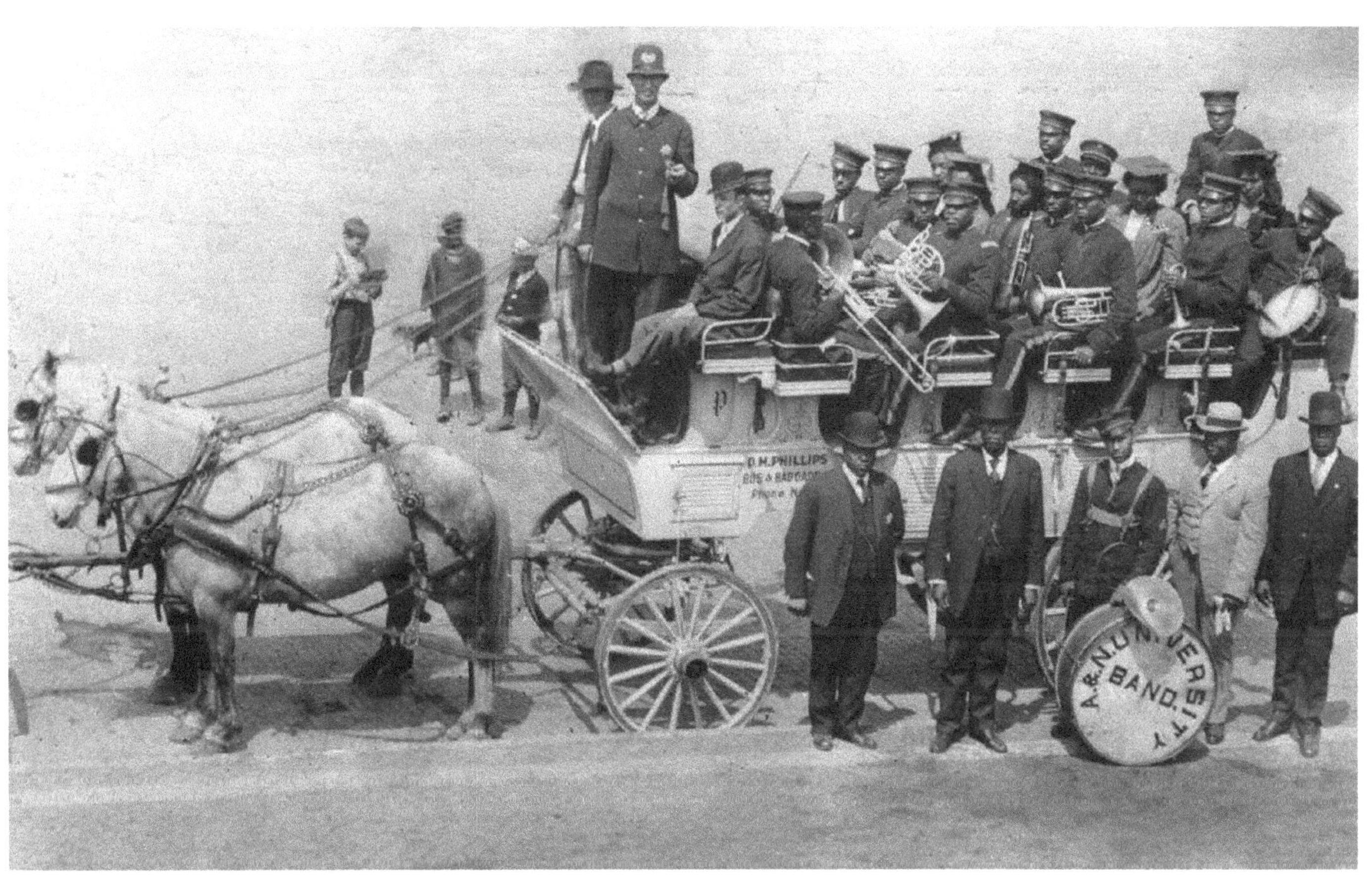

The band from the Colored Agricultural and Normal School (later Langston University) boarding a bus. This was probably part of the statewide tour the band made in the spring of 1910.

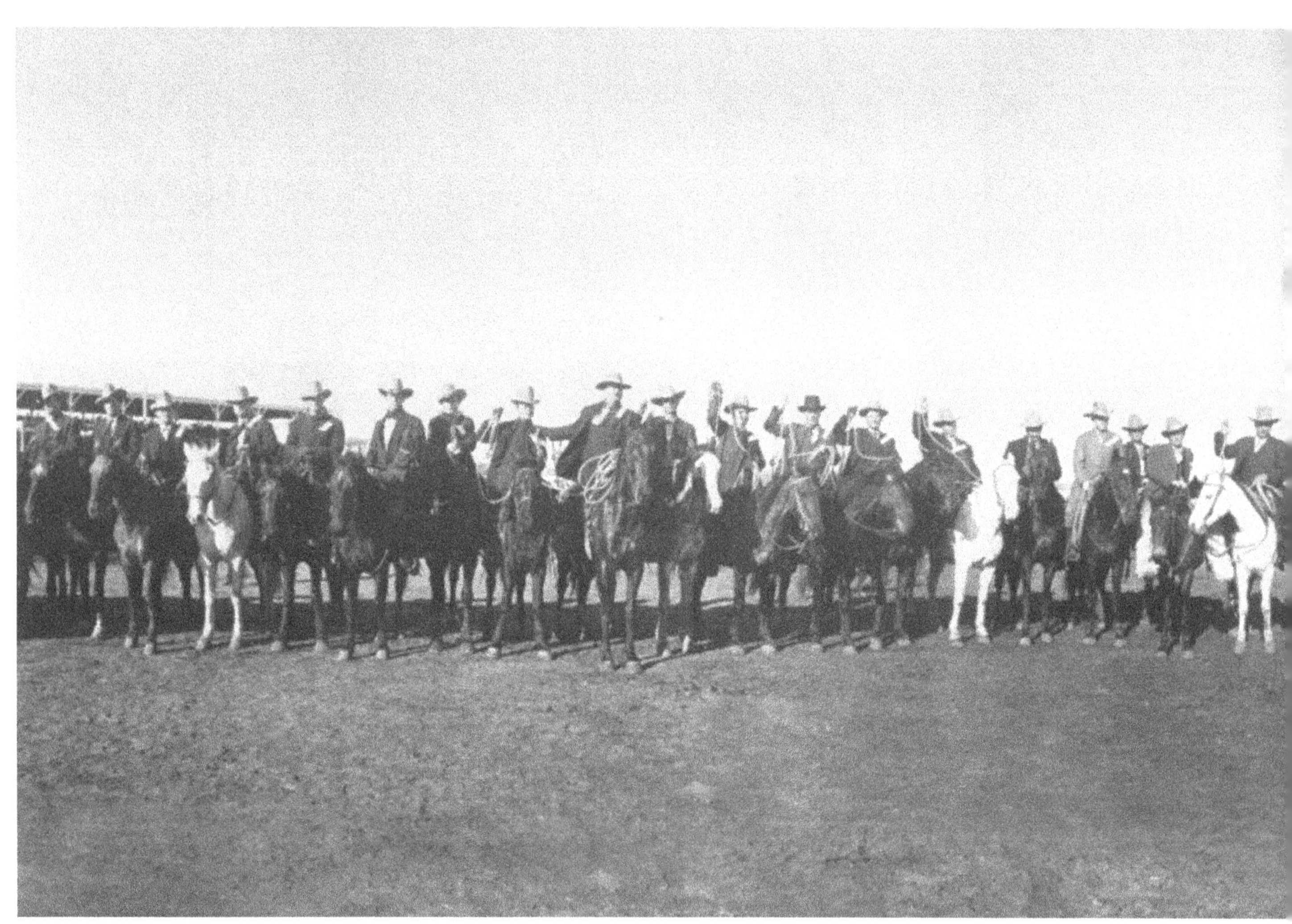

Over the New Year's holiday of 1909–1910, "Champion Roper of the World" J. Ellison Carroll sponsored a steer roping contest at the fairgrounds in Oklahoma City. Carroll defeated 300 challengers (some seen here) to win his own $1,000 prize. He also roped a steer from a moving car—which promptly got him arrested for animal cruelty.

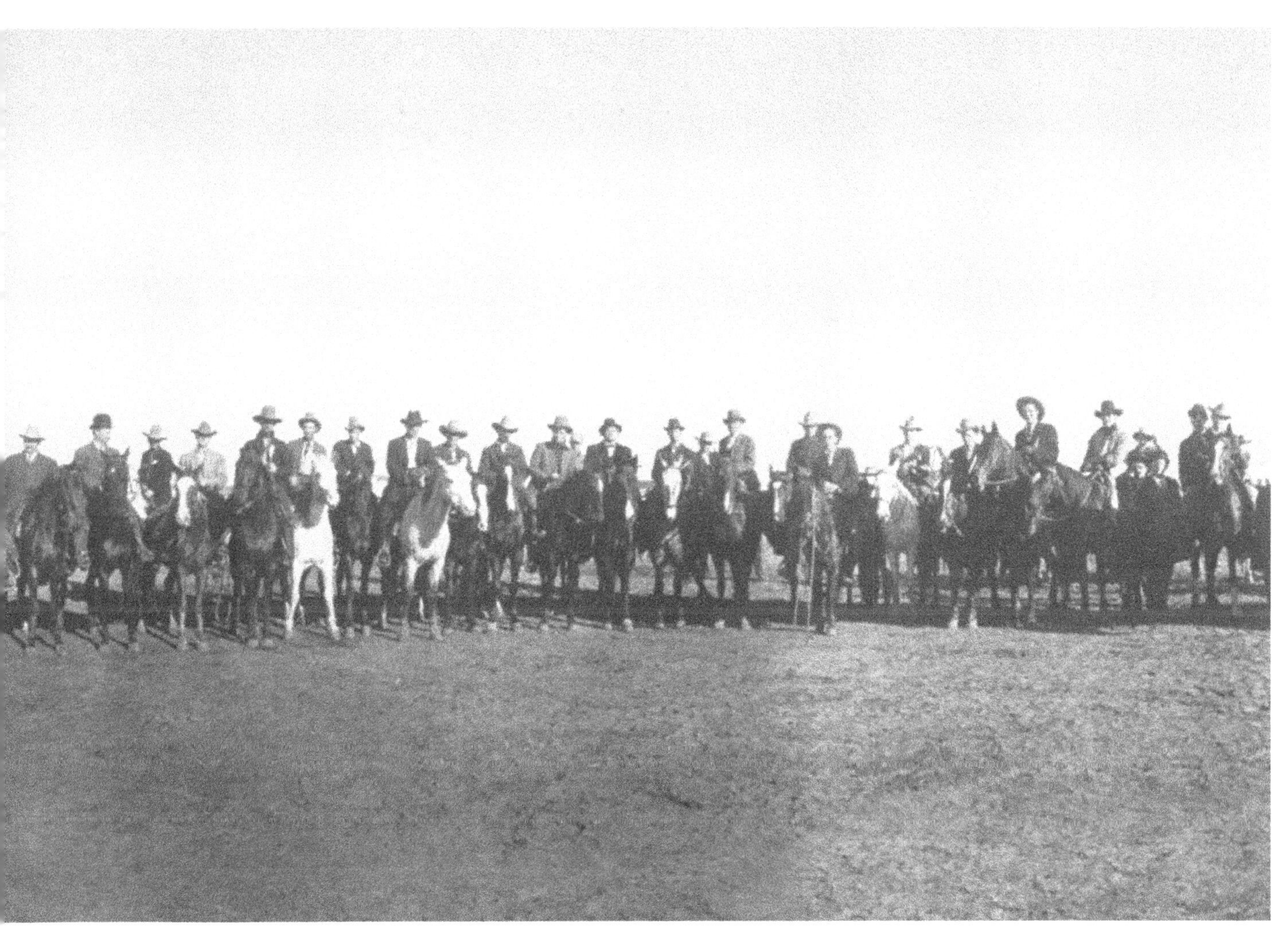

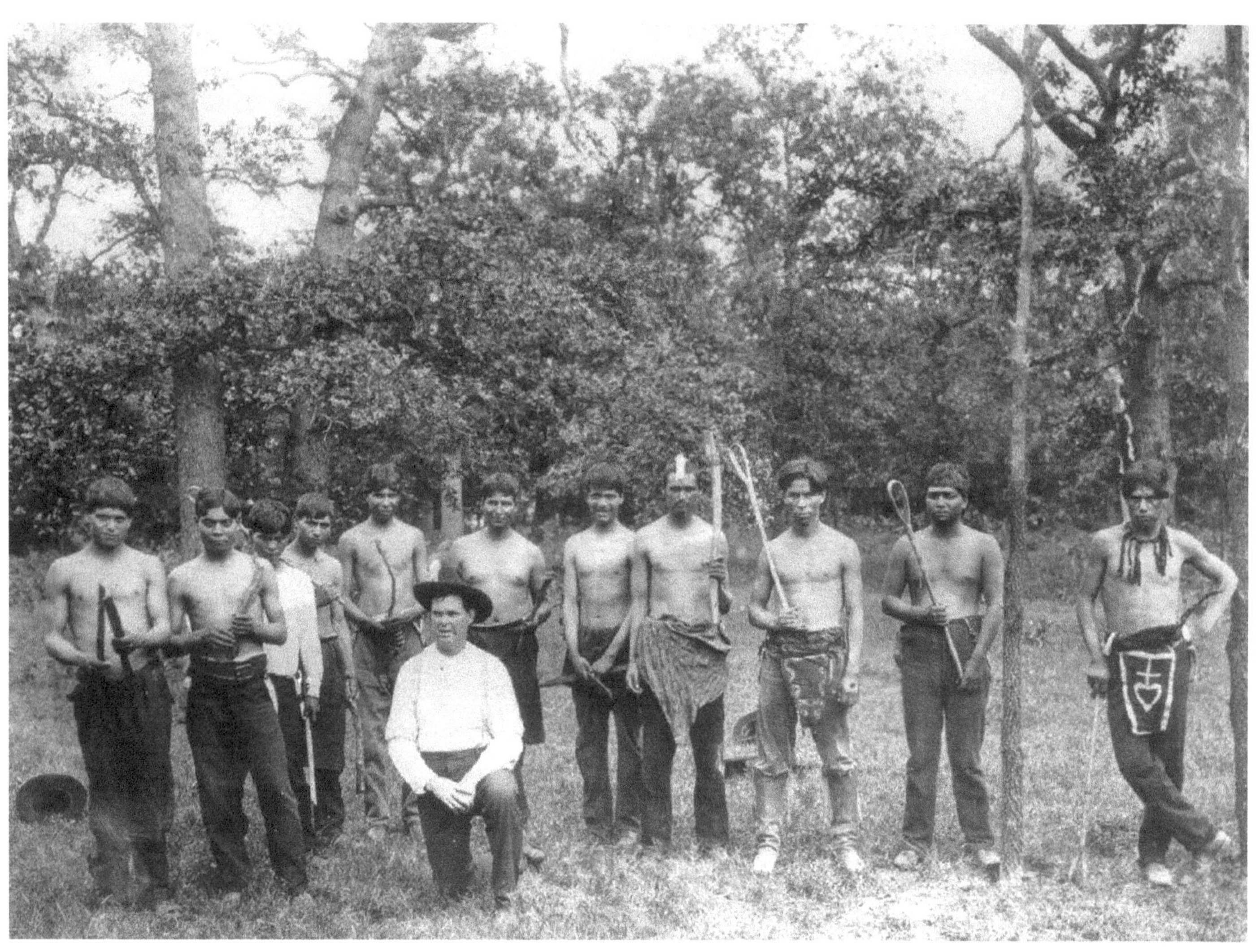

Stickball was played in some form by all of the Five Civilized Tribes. The games could be quite violent, and in ancient times opposing chiefs sometimes staged stickball games instead of waging war. Seen here is a Seminole stickball team around 1910.

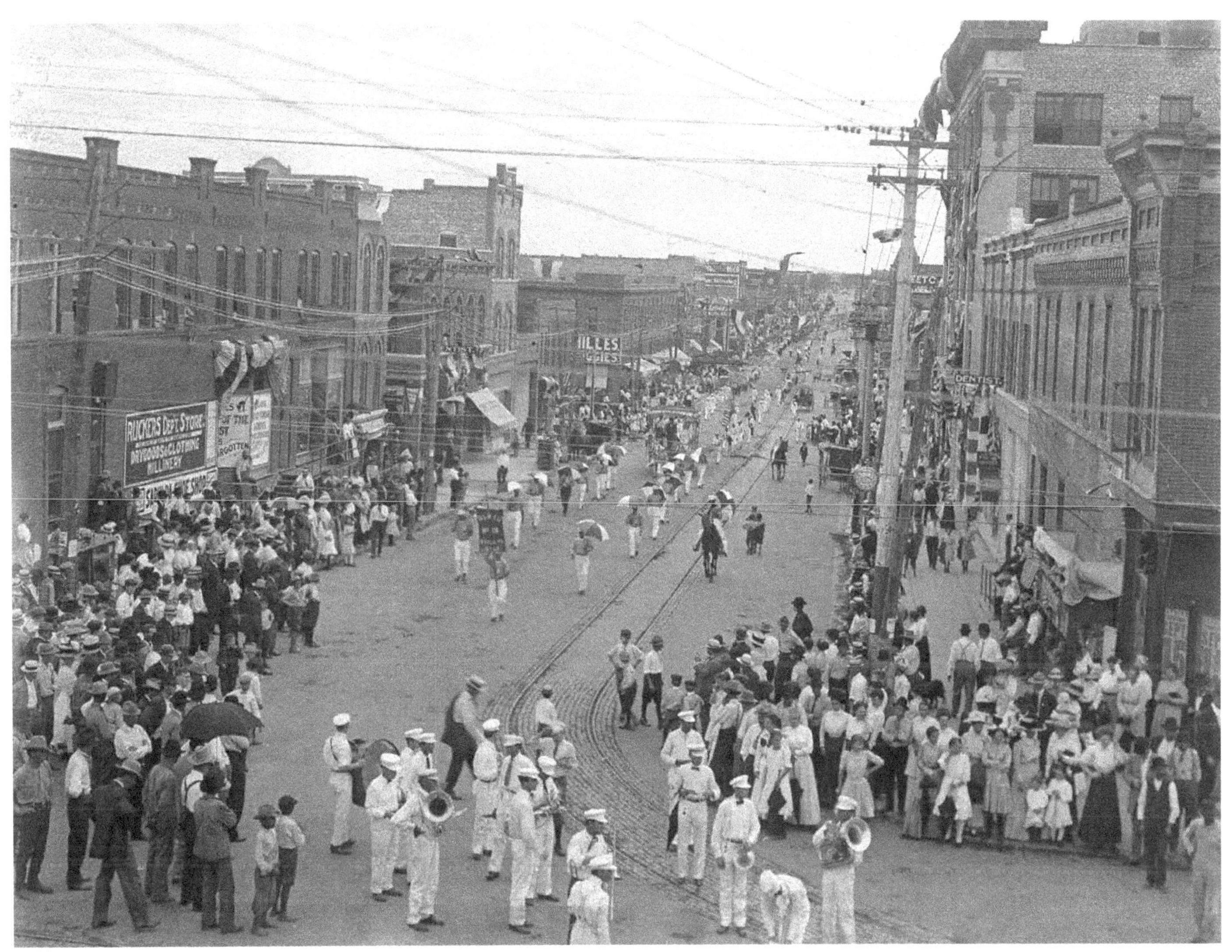

Labor Day parade, Sapulpa, 1910. The town had its beginnings in 1850 when a Creek named Sapulpa built a trading post in the area. The arrival of the Frisco Railroad in 1886 and the discovery of the Glen Pool oil field in 1905 gave Sapulpa a period of sustained growth that lasted until the Depression era.

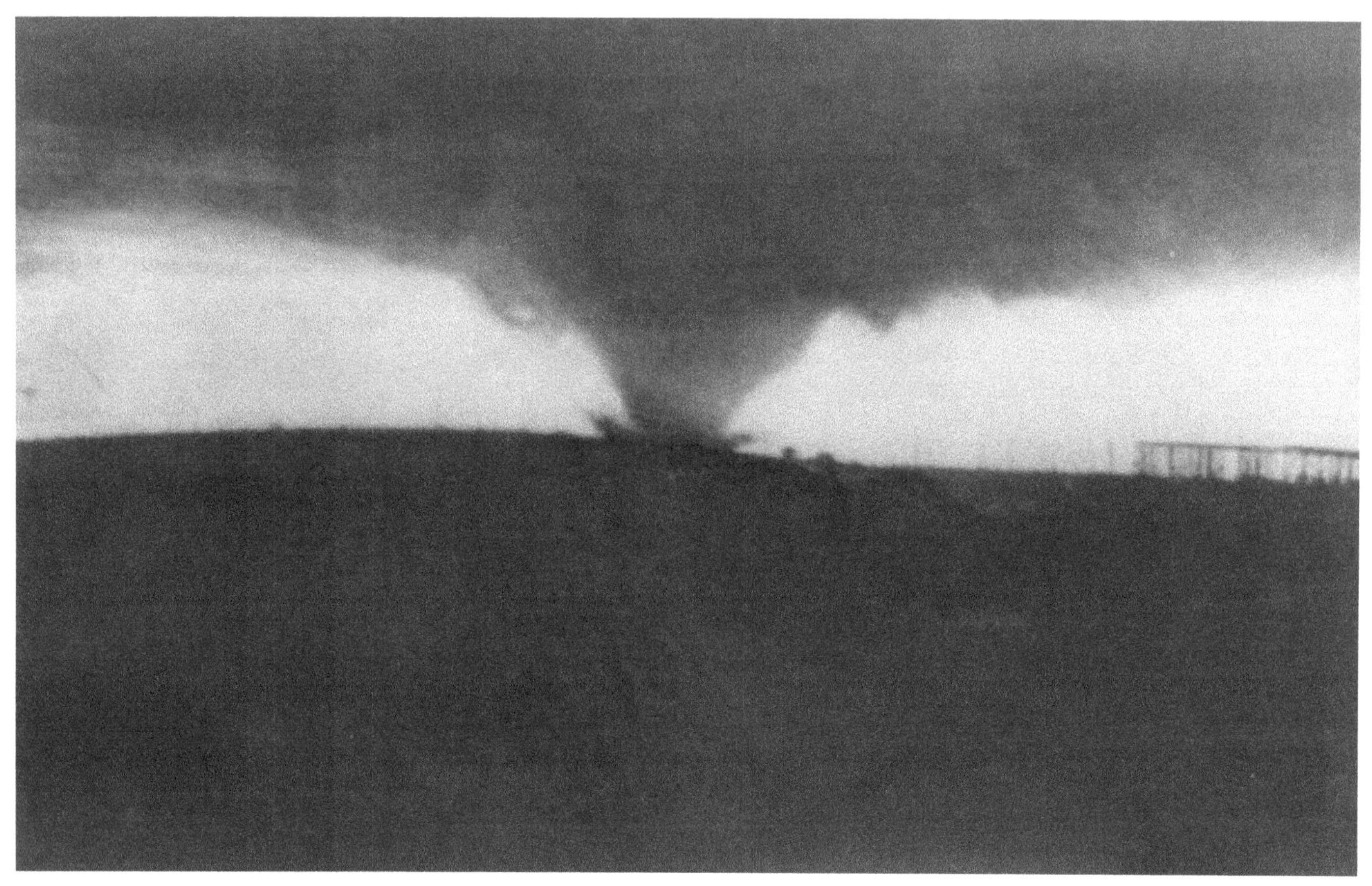

This photo is likely a view of the massive tornado that struck the west side of Ponca City on April 25, 1912. The twister killed one person, destroyed a hundred homes, mangled 14 oil derricks, and knocked down nearly all the telephone and electricity poles in the area.

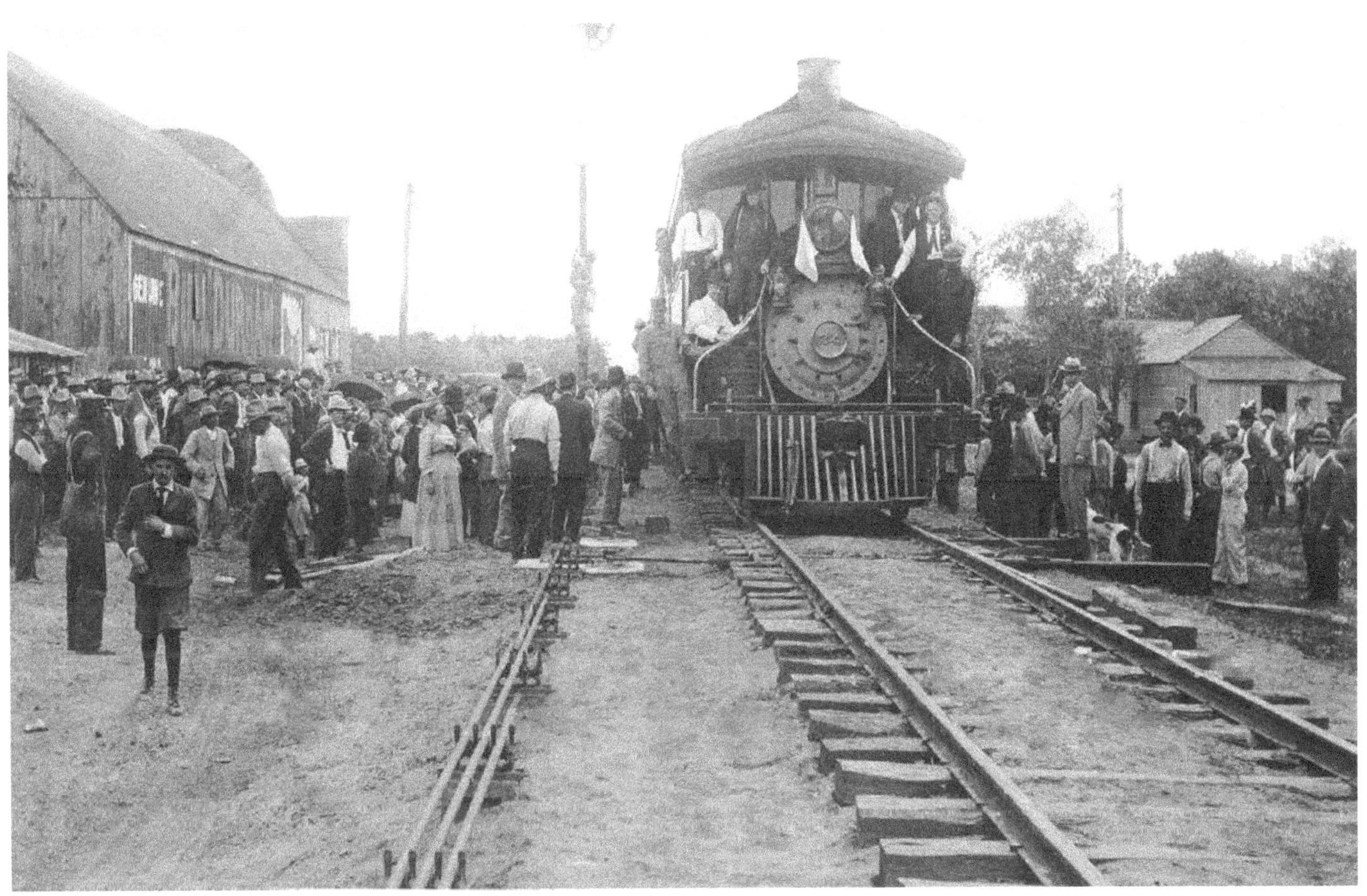

The arrival in Woodward of the first passenger train on the Wichita Falls and Northwestern Railroad, May 9, 1912. The mayor drove in a ceremonial gold spike, and citizens tossed pennies on the track for flattened souvenirs. The new route allowed northwestern Oklahomans to get to the state capital without going through Kansas.

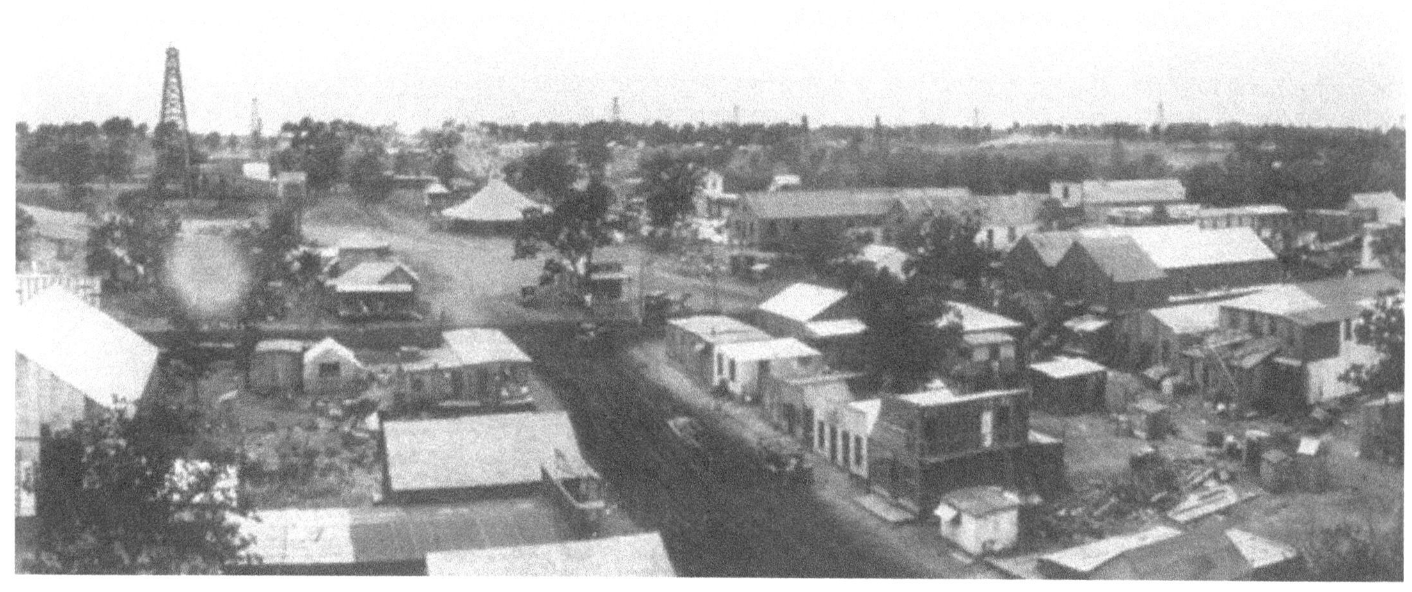

Drumright, 1914. The town was known as Ragtown early on because of the hundreds of tent dwellings that made up the oil camps of the new Cushing-Drumright Field. By the end of 1914 several substantial buildings had been erected, but this view shows a transitional period when frame structures abounded.

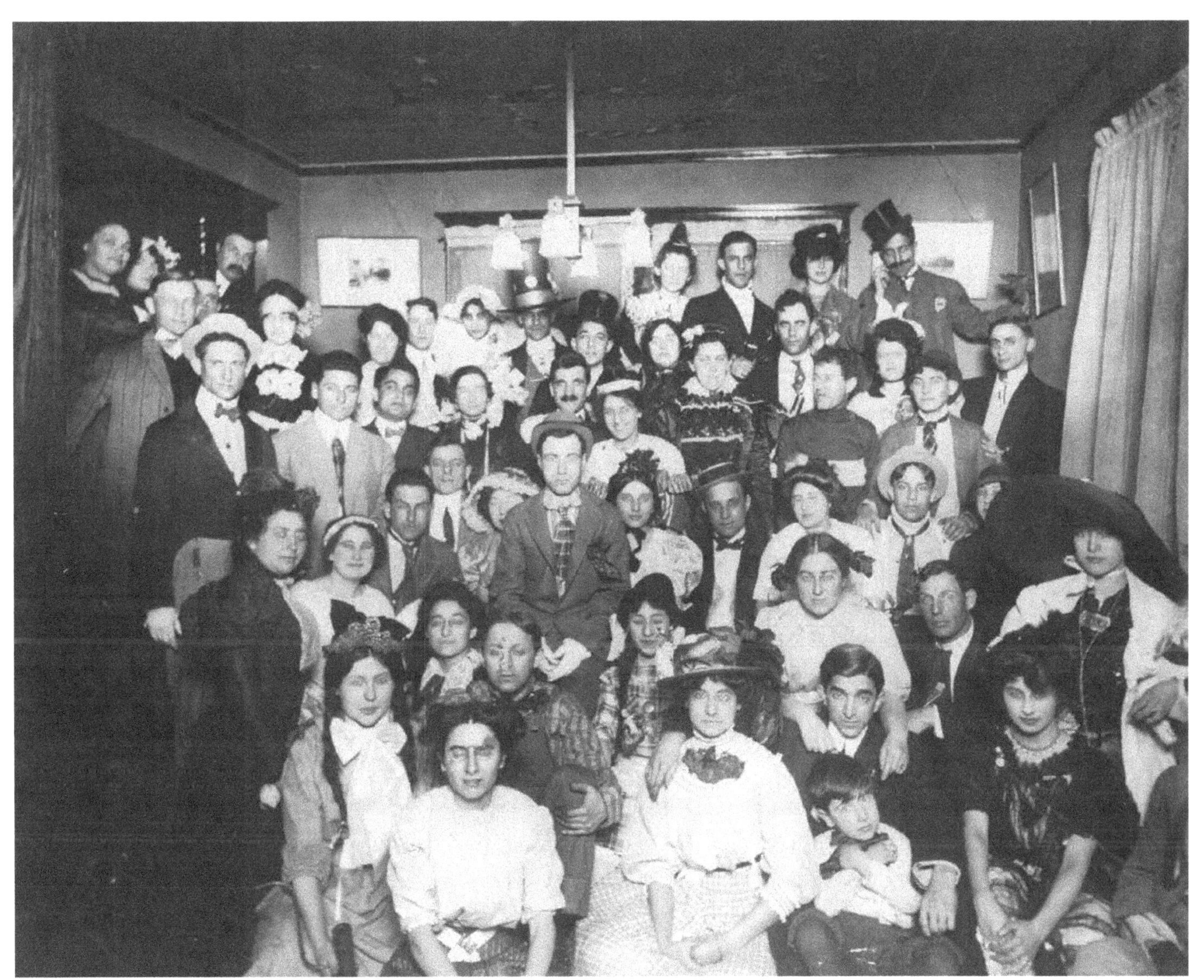

Members of Oklahoma City's Emanuel Synagogue celebrate Purim with a traditional costume party, ca. 1915.

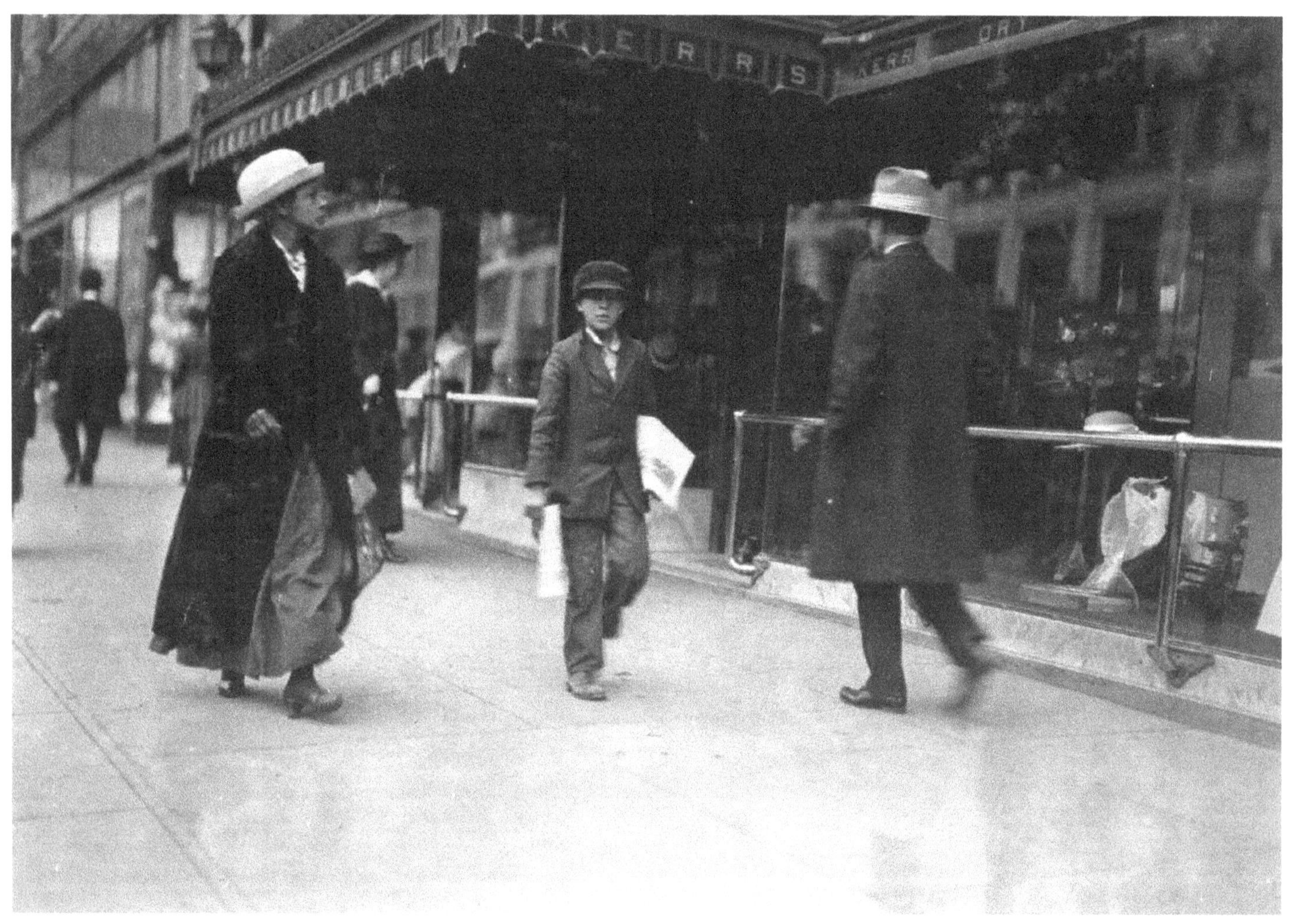

Charlie Scott was nine years old when photographed by Lewis W. Hine outside Kerr's Department Store in Oklahoma City in 1917. The newsboy admitted being truant, stating, "I dunno where the school is." Hine was an investigative photographer working for the National Child Labor Committee when he captured this and other images throughout Oklahoma in March–April 1917.

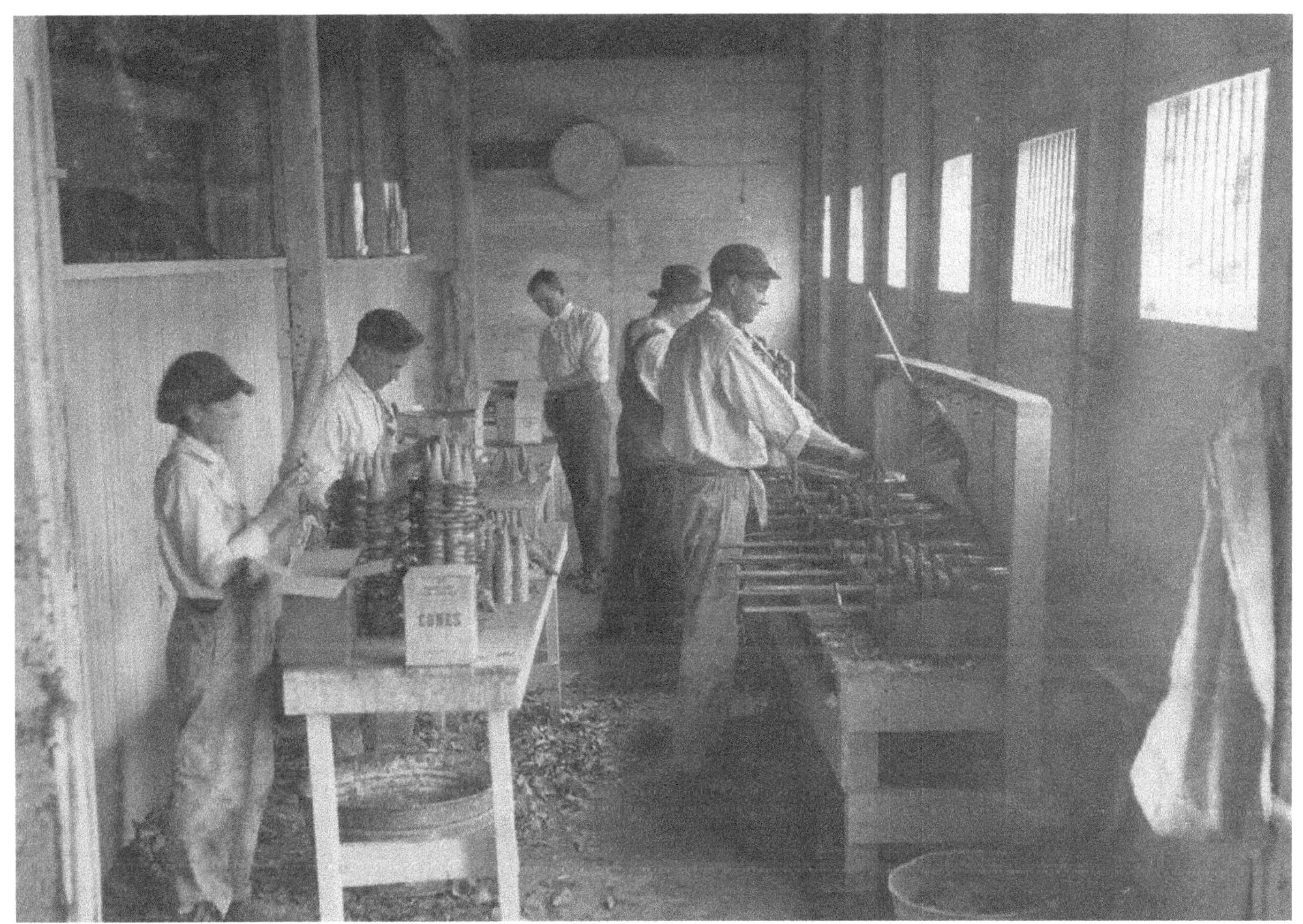

Inside the workshop of the Sanitary Ice Cream Cone Company at 116 South Dewey, Oklahoma City, April 1917. The two boys are 14 and 12 years old. Of the younger boy, his boss said, "He wasn't going to school, so I took him."

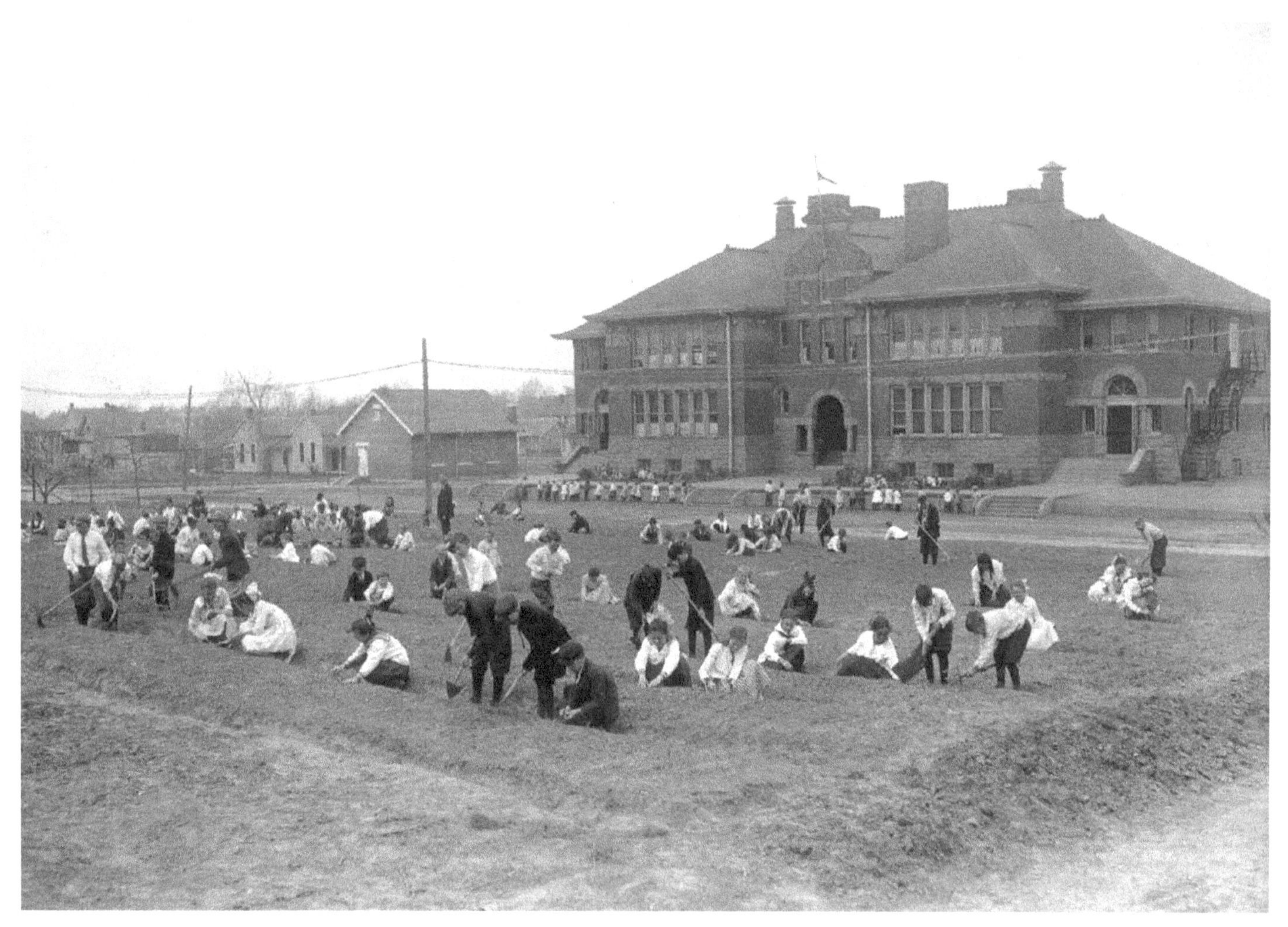

Jefferson School, Muskogee, March 1917. Jefferson served the children on Muskogee's southwest side. Here children work in the school garden.

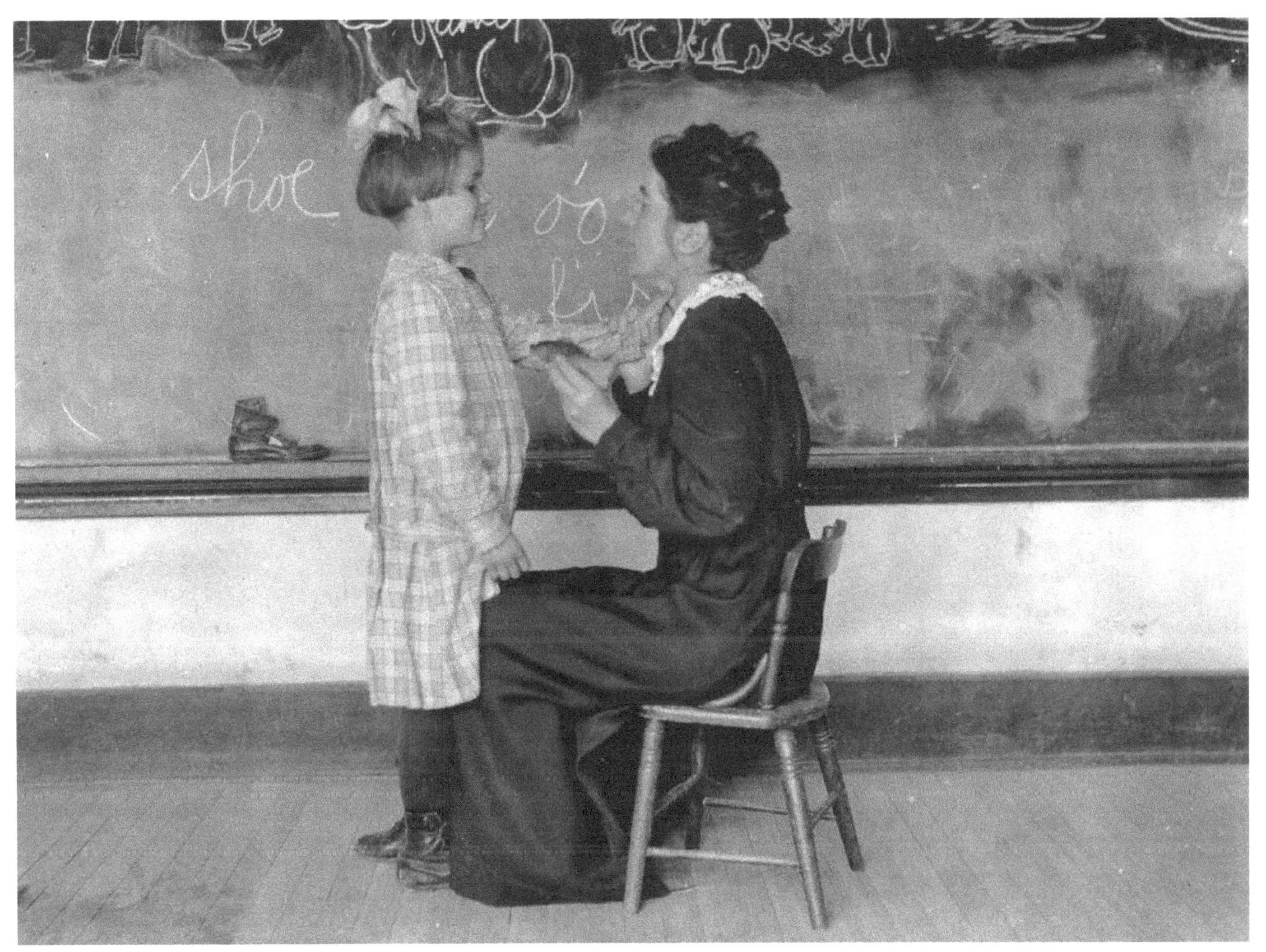

A teacher works with a young student at the Oklahoma School for Deaf Mutes near Sulphur, April 1917.

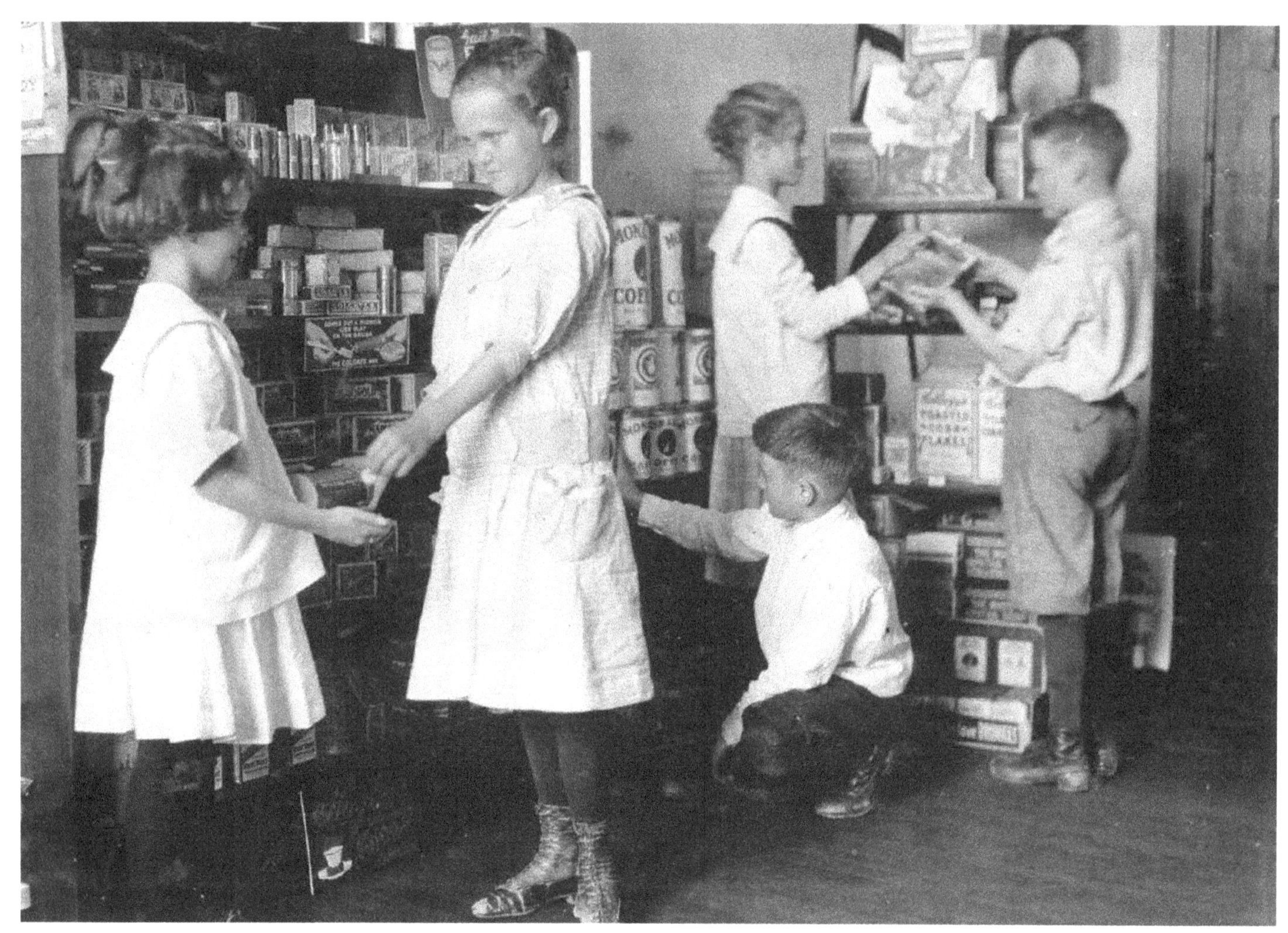

Lawton schoolchildren photographed by Lewis W. Hine in a school store, April 1917. The name of the school was not recorded, but is probably Washington School.

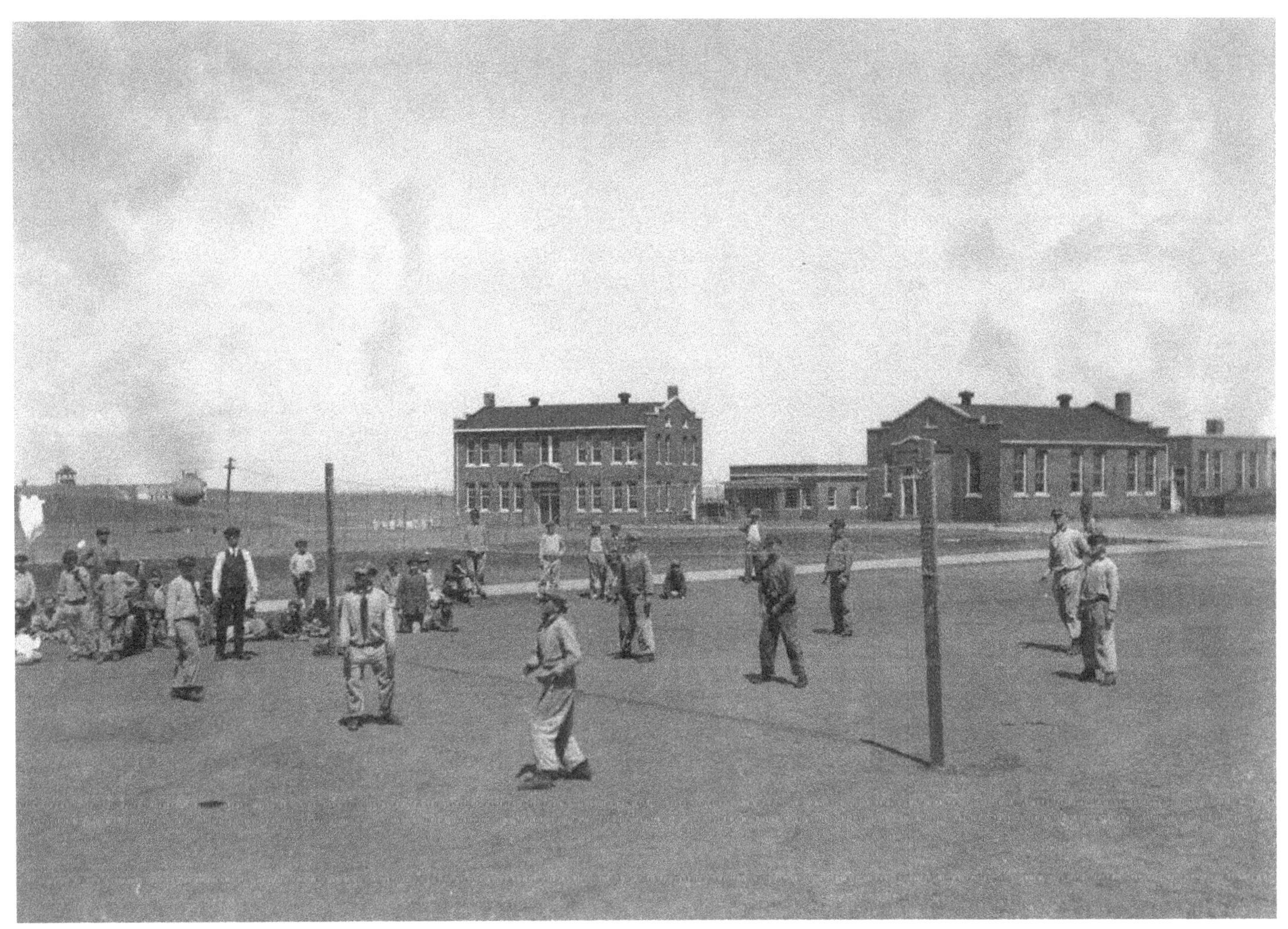

Boys playing volleyball at the Pauls Valley Training School, April 1917. Conditions appear better than state commissioner of charities Kate Barnard discovered a few years prior to this photo. She found "vicious and degenerating practices exist among the boys" and "the youths are receiving training in nothing that is useful."

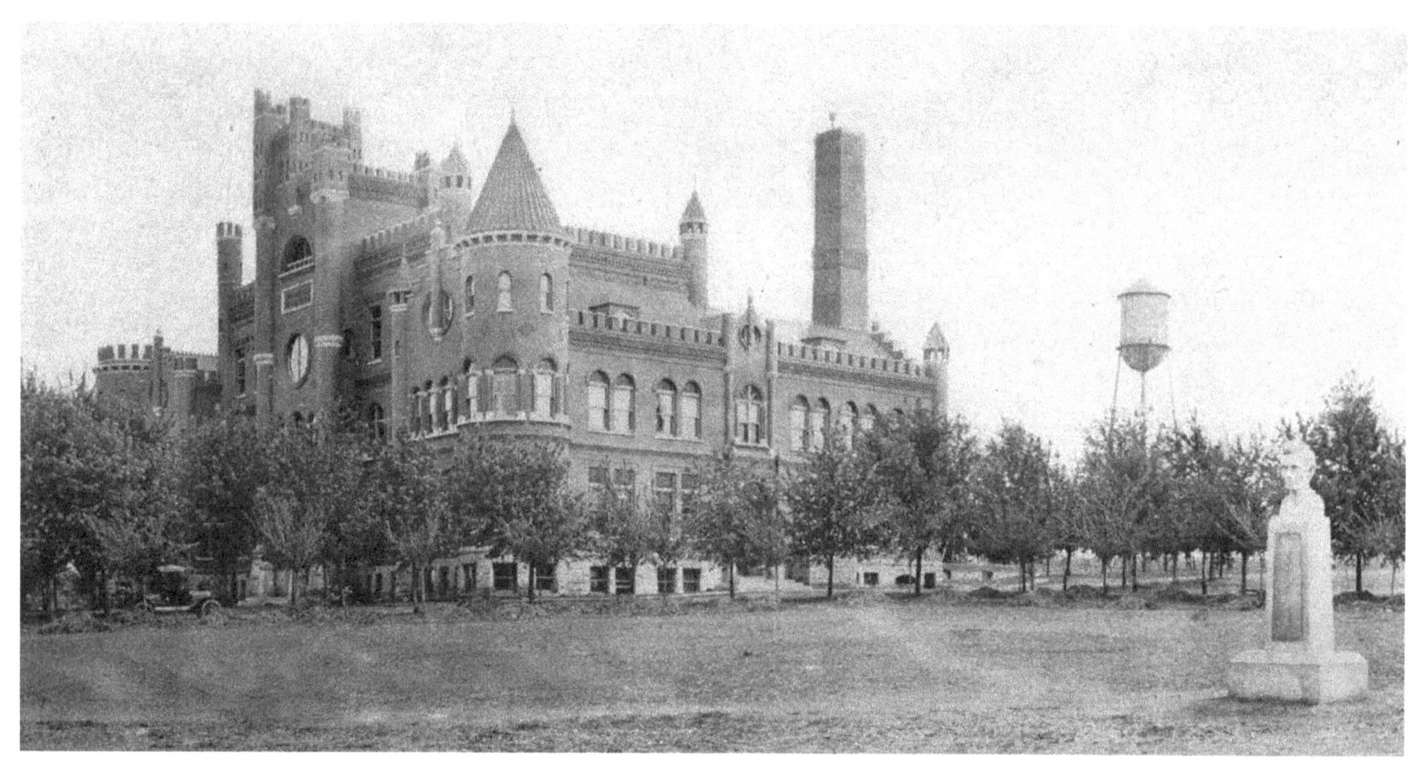

Seen here in 1918, this sprawling "Castle on the Hill" was designed by architect Joseph Foucart for the Northwestern Normal School (now Northwestern Oklahoma State University) in 1898. Though destroyed by fire in 1935, the Castle is still a revered icon of the Alva school.

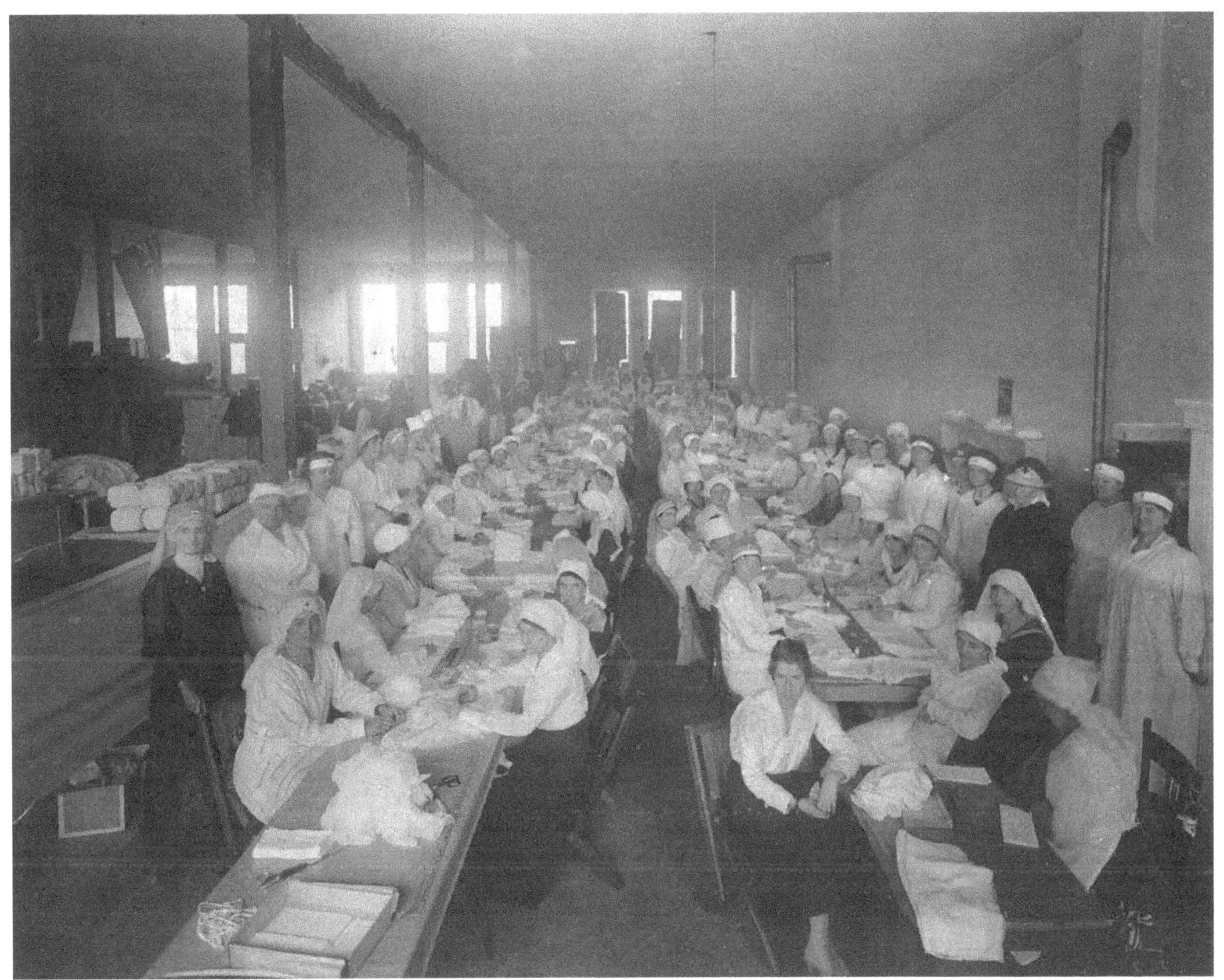

American Red Cross workers in Muskogee during World War I. Women volunteers made millions of bandages and socks for soldiers fighting the Germans, but by war's end, the volunteers were mobilized to fight an entirely different enemy: the Spanish influenza.

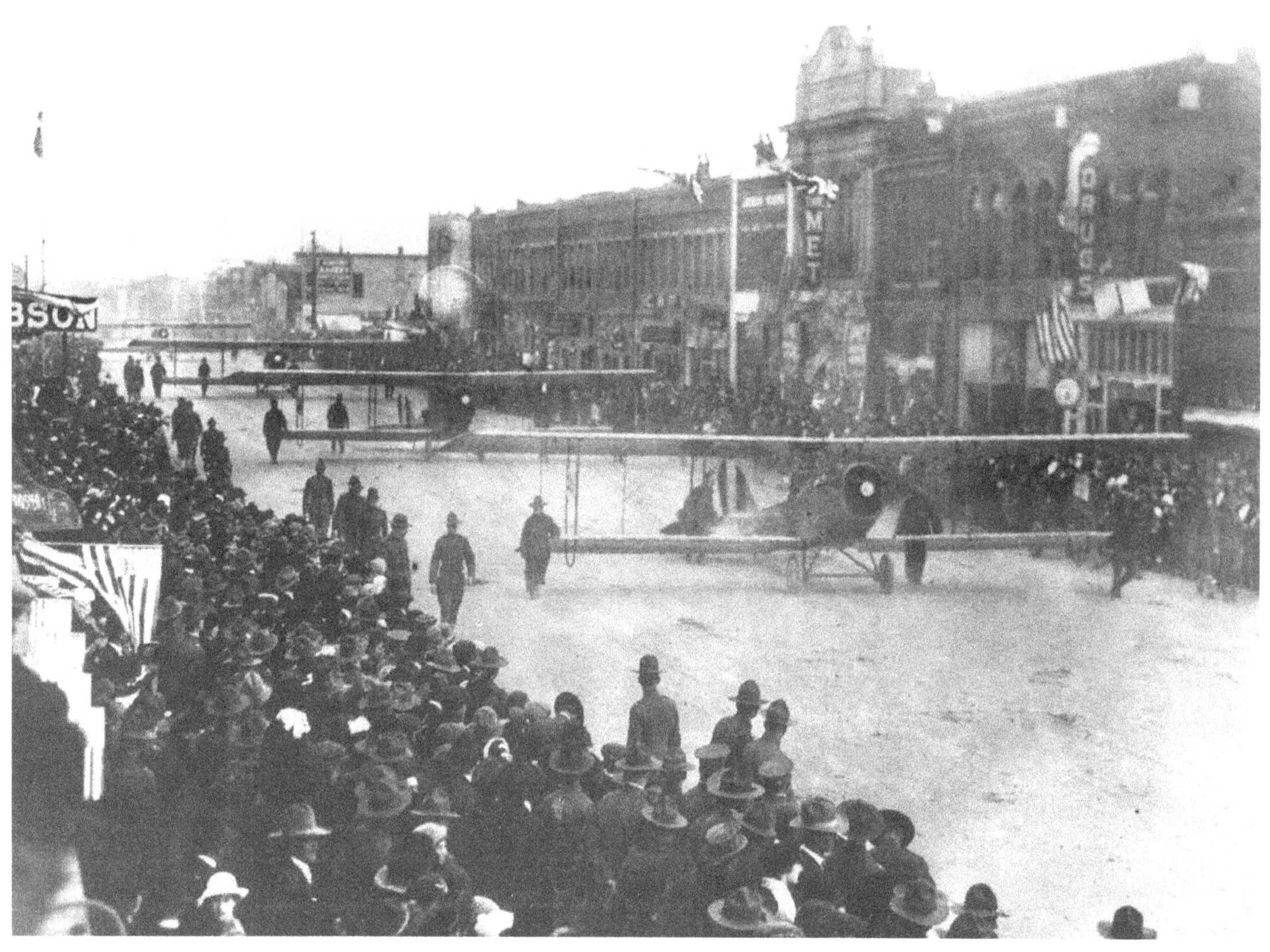

Armistice Day parade in Lawton, November 16, 1918. More than 40,000 people were on hand to celebrate the Allied victory in World War I. Included were nine regiments of artillery, six military bands, and 50 airplanes. The planes likely were from the Army's first aviation base, Post Field on the Fort Sill reservation.

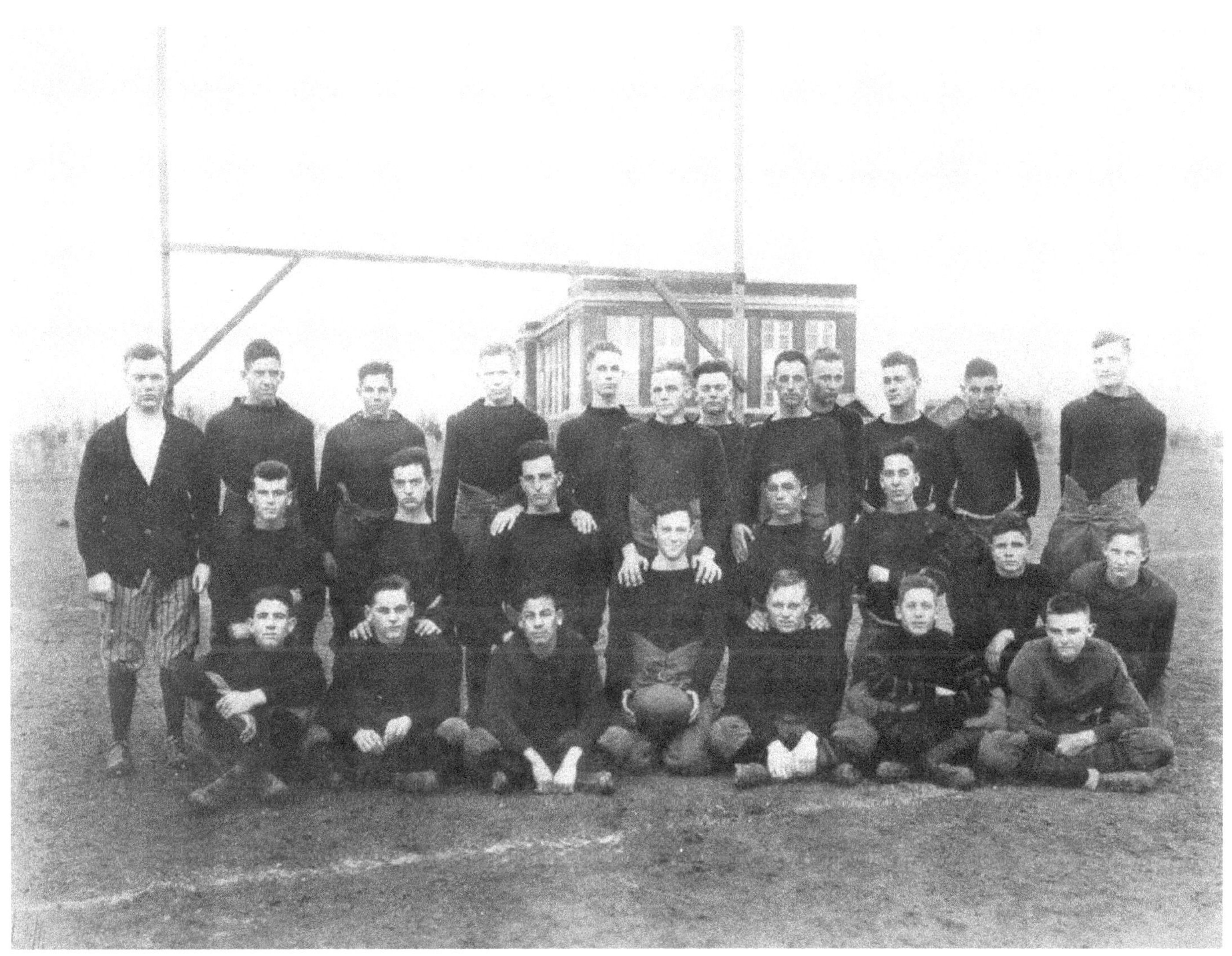

Cadets at the new Oklahoma Military Academy in Claremore line up for a team photo in 1920. The academy was a powerhouse in football in its first years of existence.

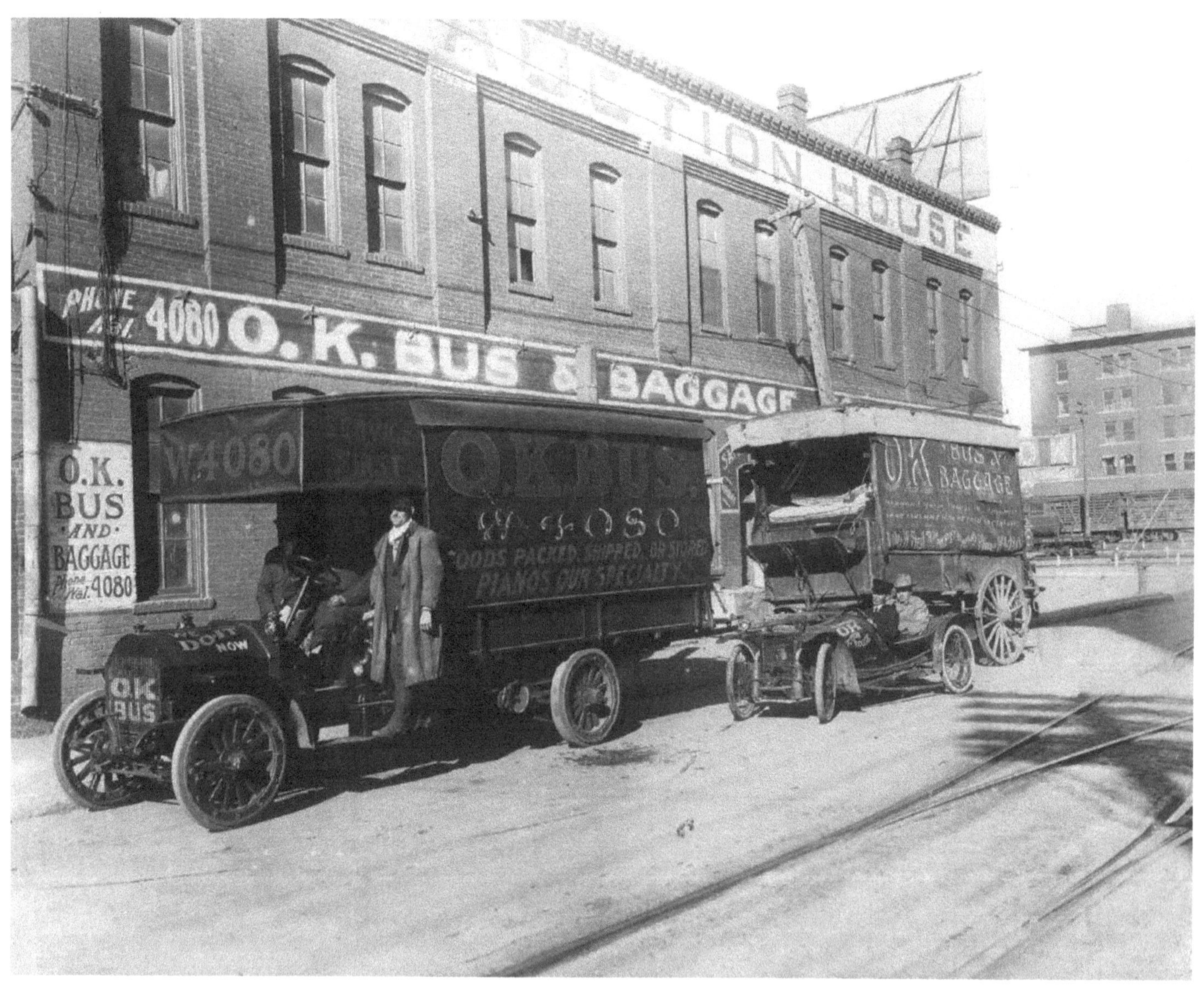

Vans of the O.K. Bus & Baggage Company at 300 West First, Oklahoma City, ca. 1920. Founded on the day Oklahoma City was established, O.K. was a fixture on city streets for decades.

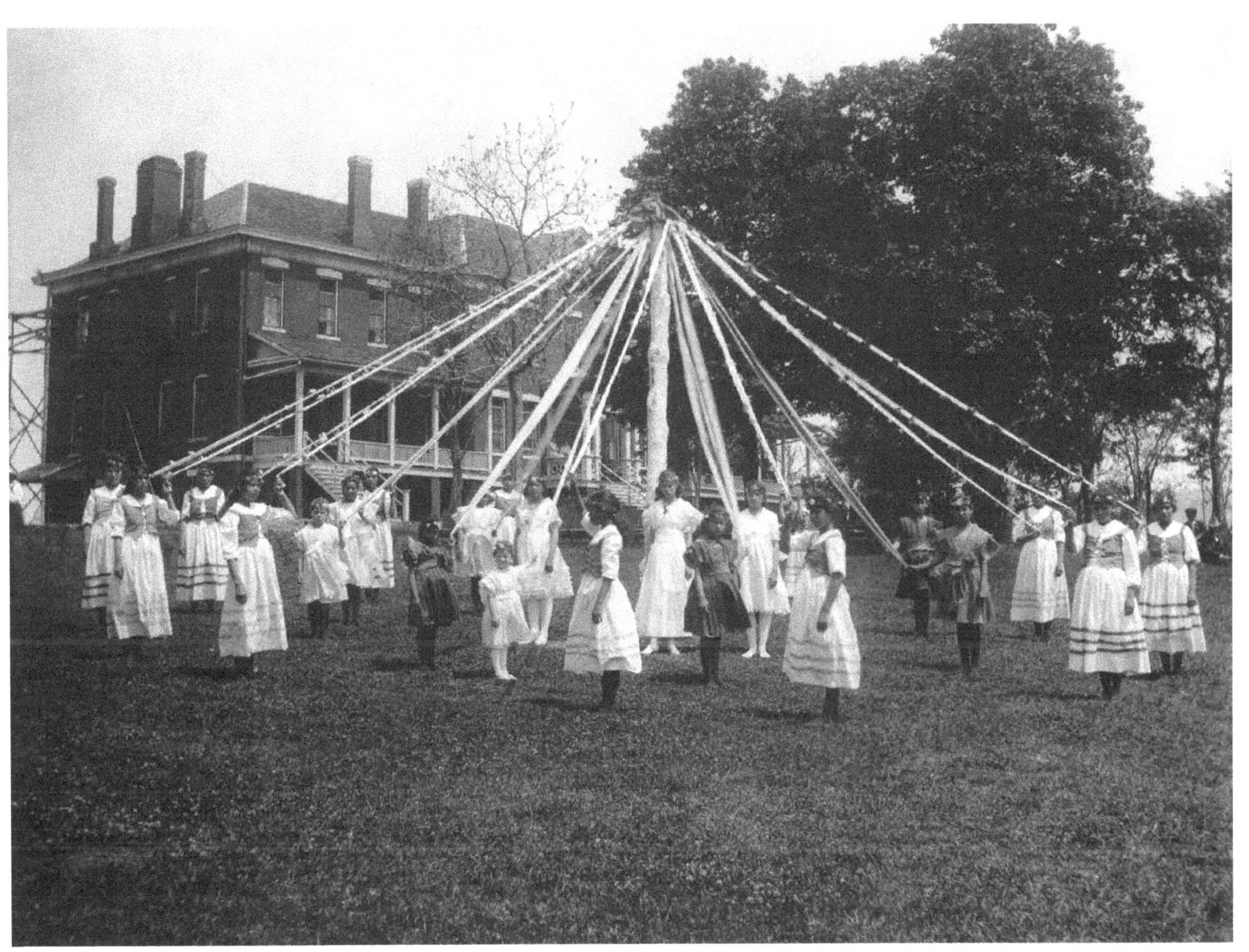

Girls of the Cherokee Orphan Asylum twirl around the maypole in 1921. The orphans' home was relocated just outside the Cherokee capital of Tahlequah after a disastrous fire destroyed the original building near Salina.

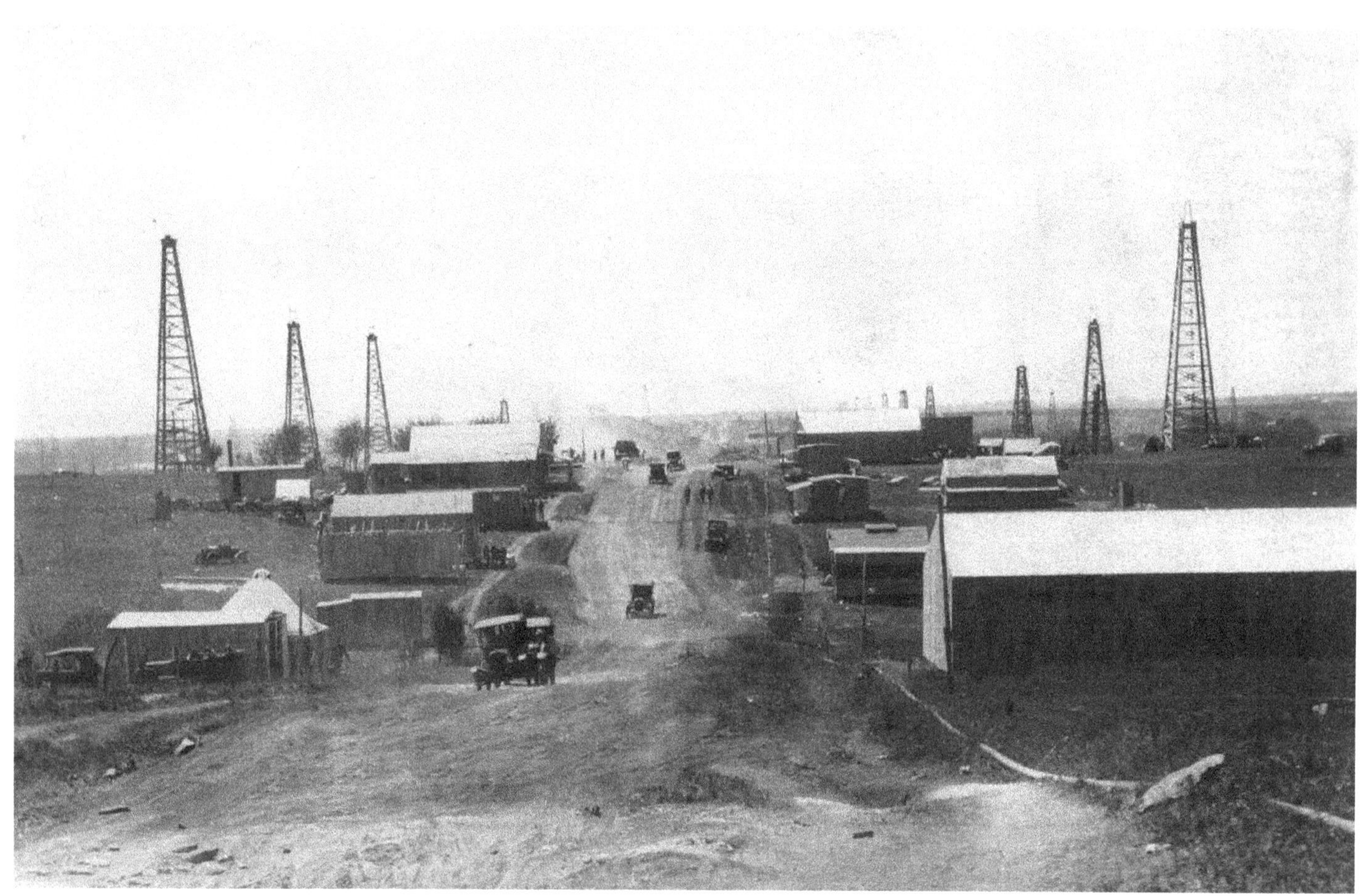

West Duncan Oil and Gas Field, 1921. Duncan had been a successful market town for over 30 years when this large field was discovered in 1918. Duncanites were able to resist the oil-boom fever and maintain steady growth for decades. Here the view is from Oil City. Gas City was just miles south.

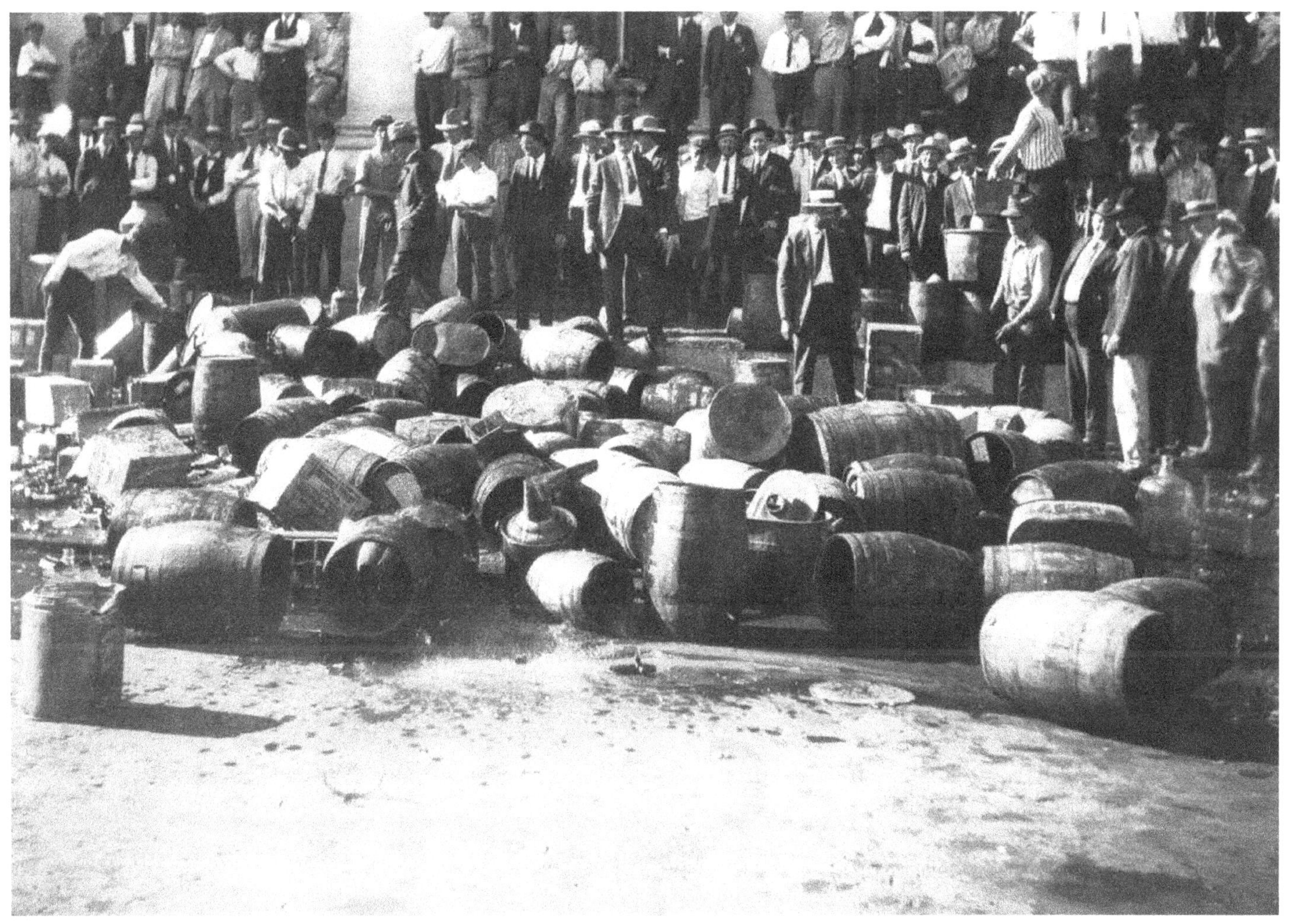

Federal agents destroy 2,000 gallons of liquor in Oklahoma City, ca. 1921. Prohibition was nothing new to Oklahoma when the Eighteenth Amendment banned liquor nationwide in 1920; what was new was the enforcement of prohibition. Federal agents had their hands full in the state: "The stills are as thick as flies here," one complained.

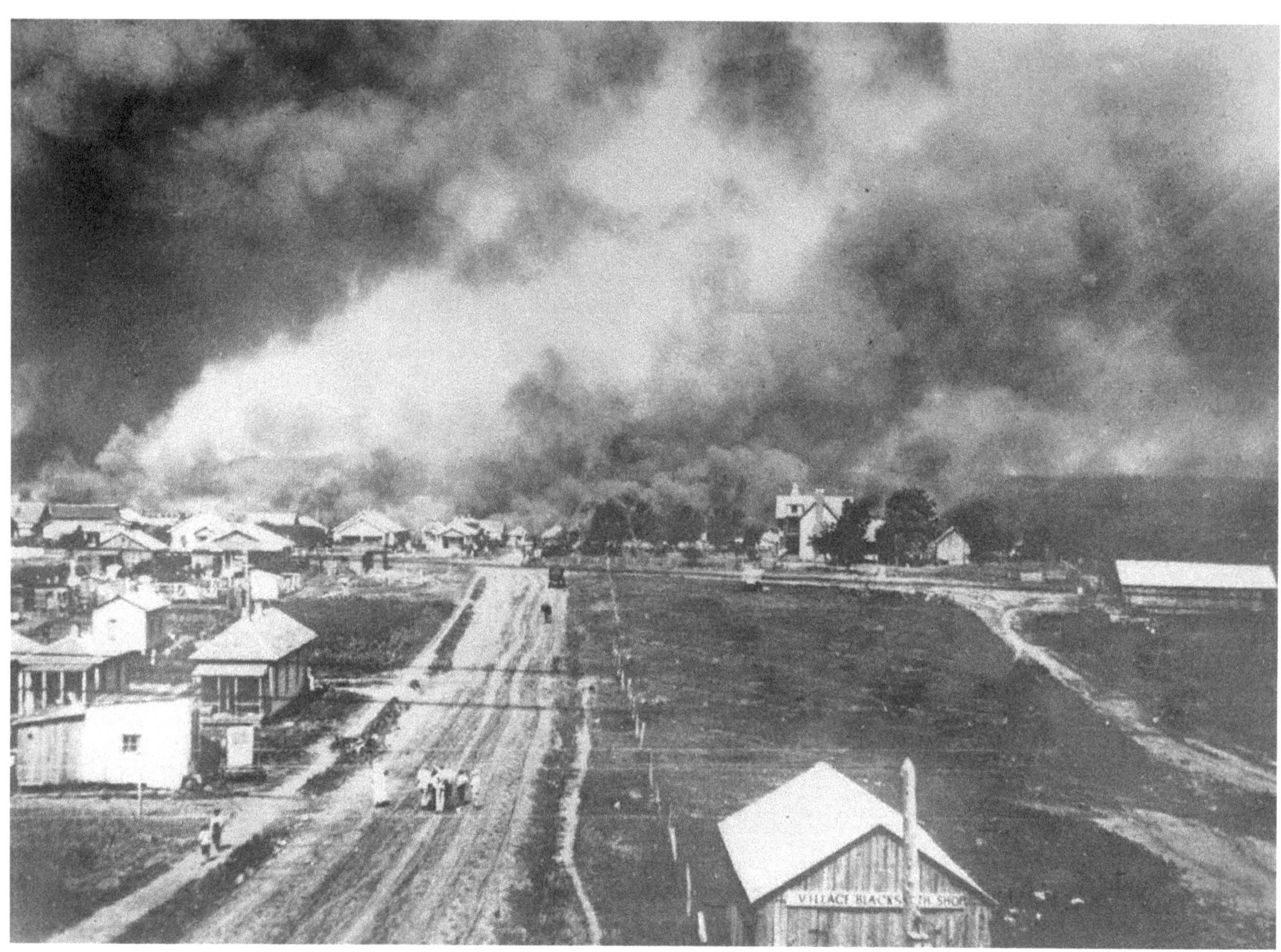

Black Wall Street burns in Tulsa, May 31–June 2, 1921. A misunderstanding fueled by hate and fanned by the city's newspaper led to a confrontation between white and black residents over the safety of a black man threatened with lynching. When the confrontation escalated, violence erupted in the prosperous African-American section known as Black Wall Street, with many homes and businesses burned. By the time the state militia had quelled the racial violence, 35 city blocks were destroyed, and many residents were dead.

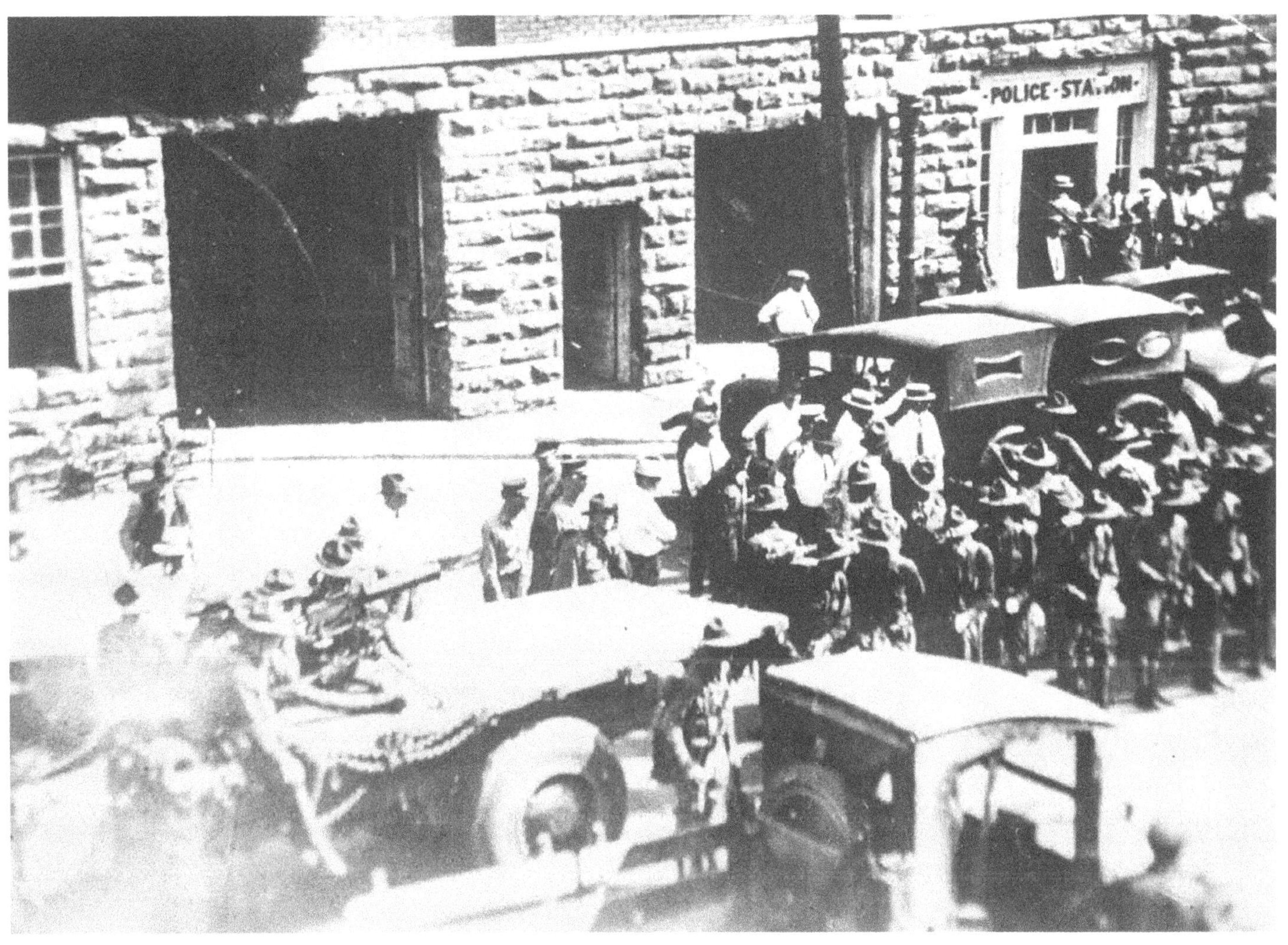

National Guardsmen near a Tulsa police station, June 1921. When violence erupted in the city's black district, the local guard units were ordered to protect the downtown area and other white neighborhoods. It was not until the arrival of units from Muskogee, Oklahoma City, and Wagoner that troops moved into the riot zone.

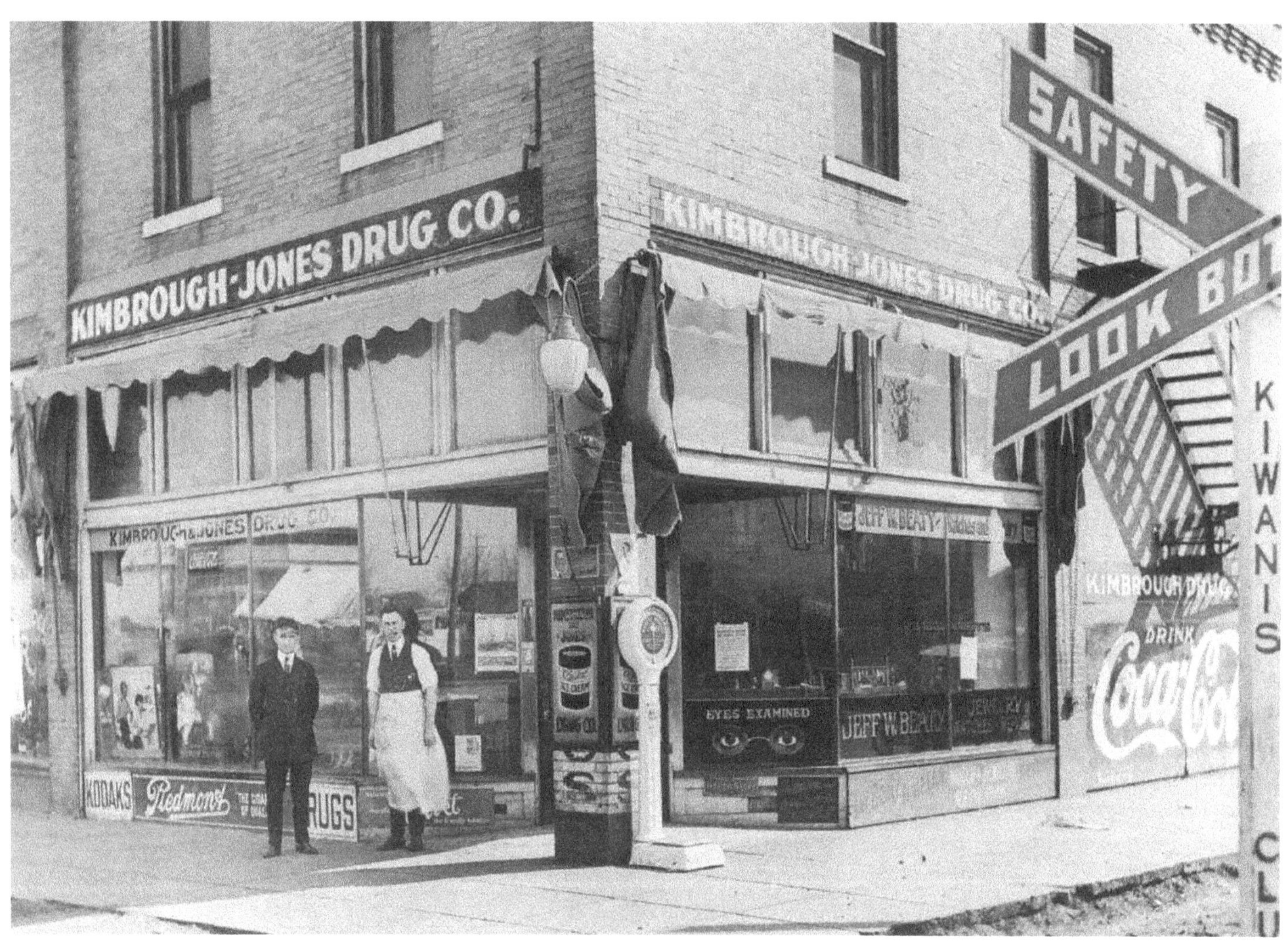

Photographed around 1921, jeweler Jeff Beaty, at left, and druggist Joe Kimbrough stand in front of the building they owned for decades at Southwest Twenty-fifth and Robinson in Oklahoma City's Capitol Hill.

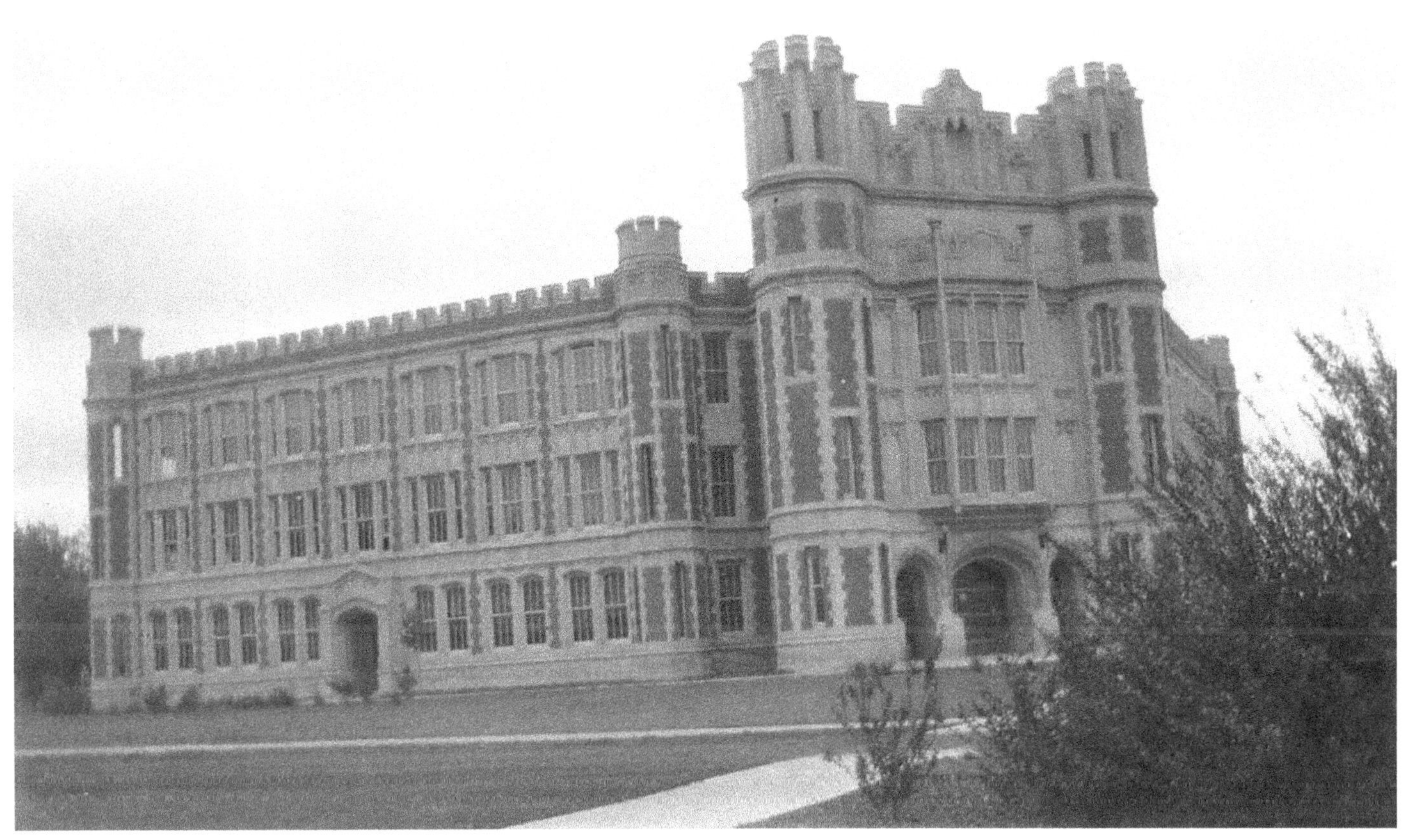

The University of Oklahoma's Holmberg Hall, Norman, 1922. Built in 1918 for the university's music program, the building features a round, European-style auditorium in the center. Famous guests have included President William H. Taft, William Butler Yeats, and composer Aaron Copland.

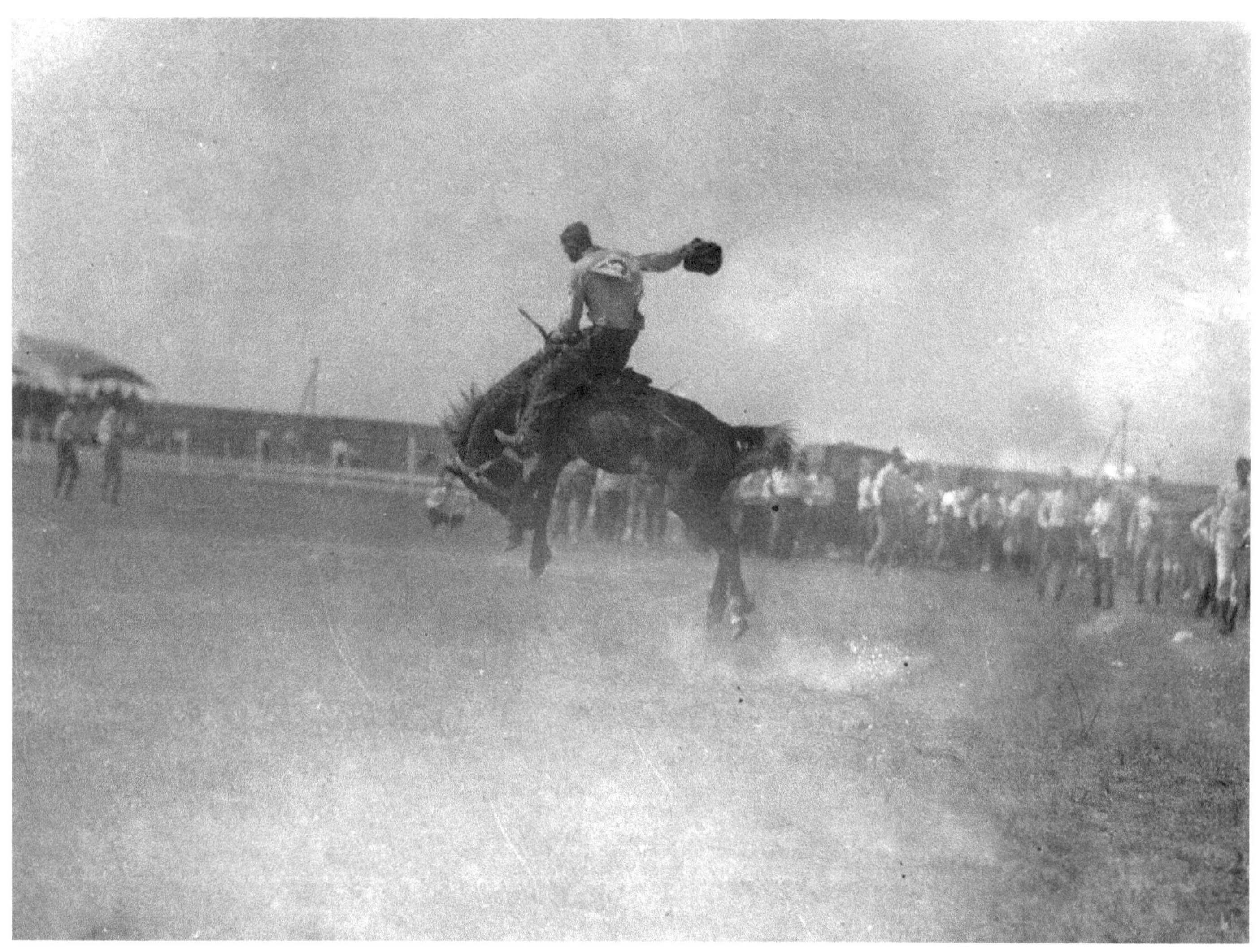

A cowboy named Nollin tames a bronc named Plow Boy at the Dewey Roundup, ca. 1922. Begun in 1909, the annual Dewey Roundup was a major event on the rodeo circuit for nearly 40 years.

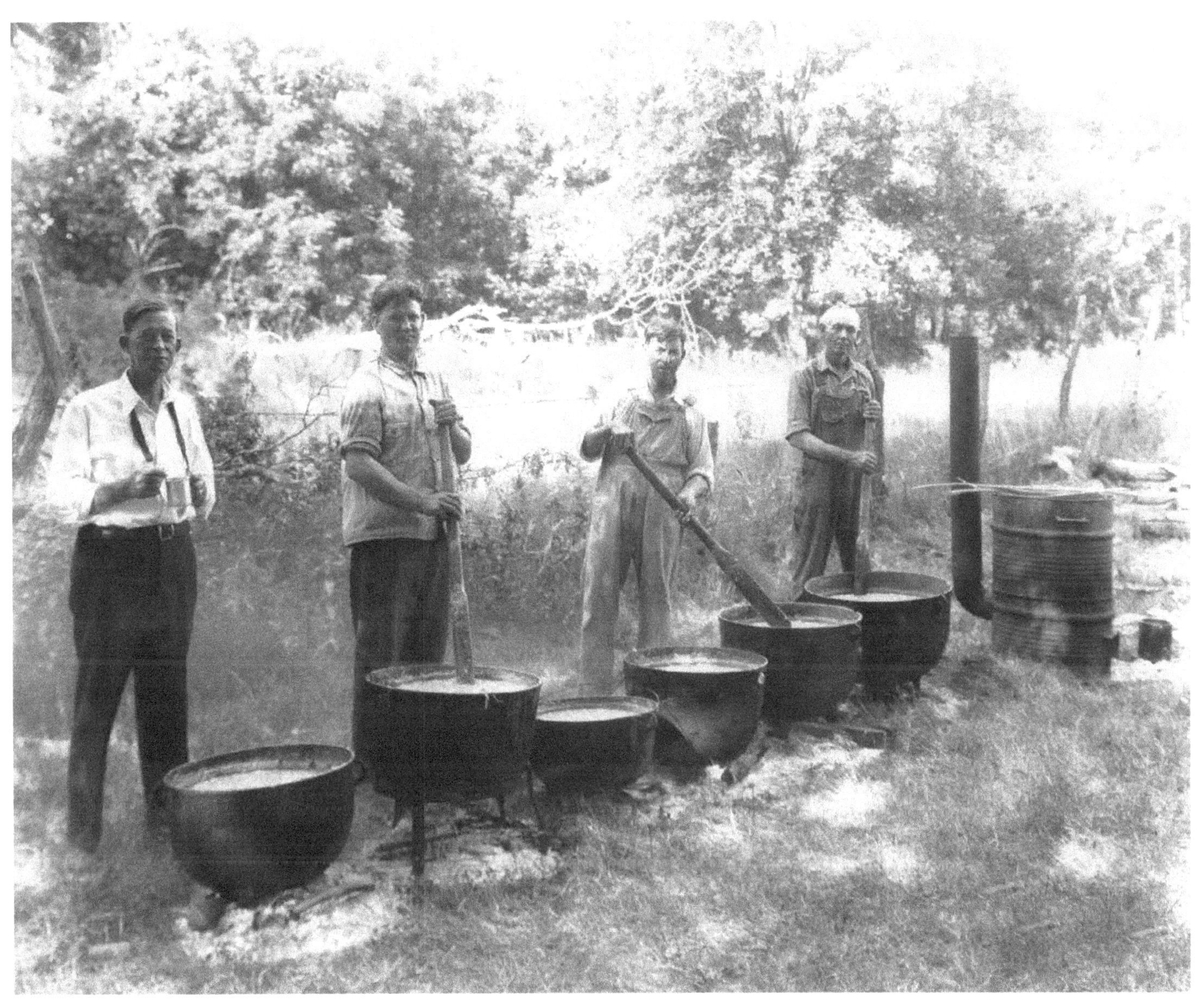

Chickasaws stir cauldrons of pashofa, a boiled mixture of cracked Indian corn and cured meat, to be served during a pashofa dance at the Chapman farm near Tishomingo, ca. 1920s. A pashofa dance is a ritual for the healing of the sick.

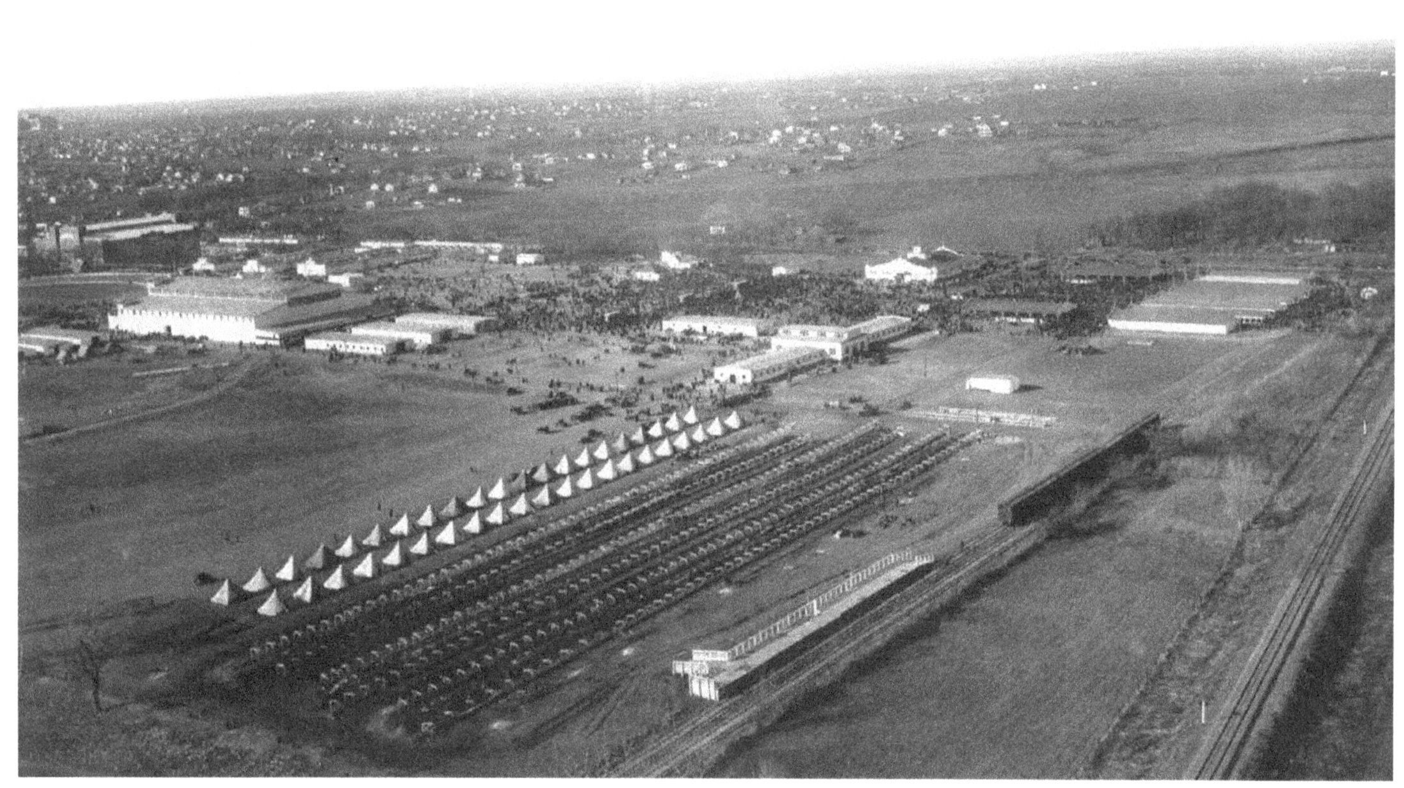

This aerial view depicts the mile-long barbecue pits used during the inauguration gala of Governor Jack Walton at the fairgrounds in Oklahoma City, January 9, 1923. Crowds estimated at about 150,000 ate their fill during an event filled with superlatives, where "boys from the forks of the creek mingled with sons of wealth."

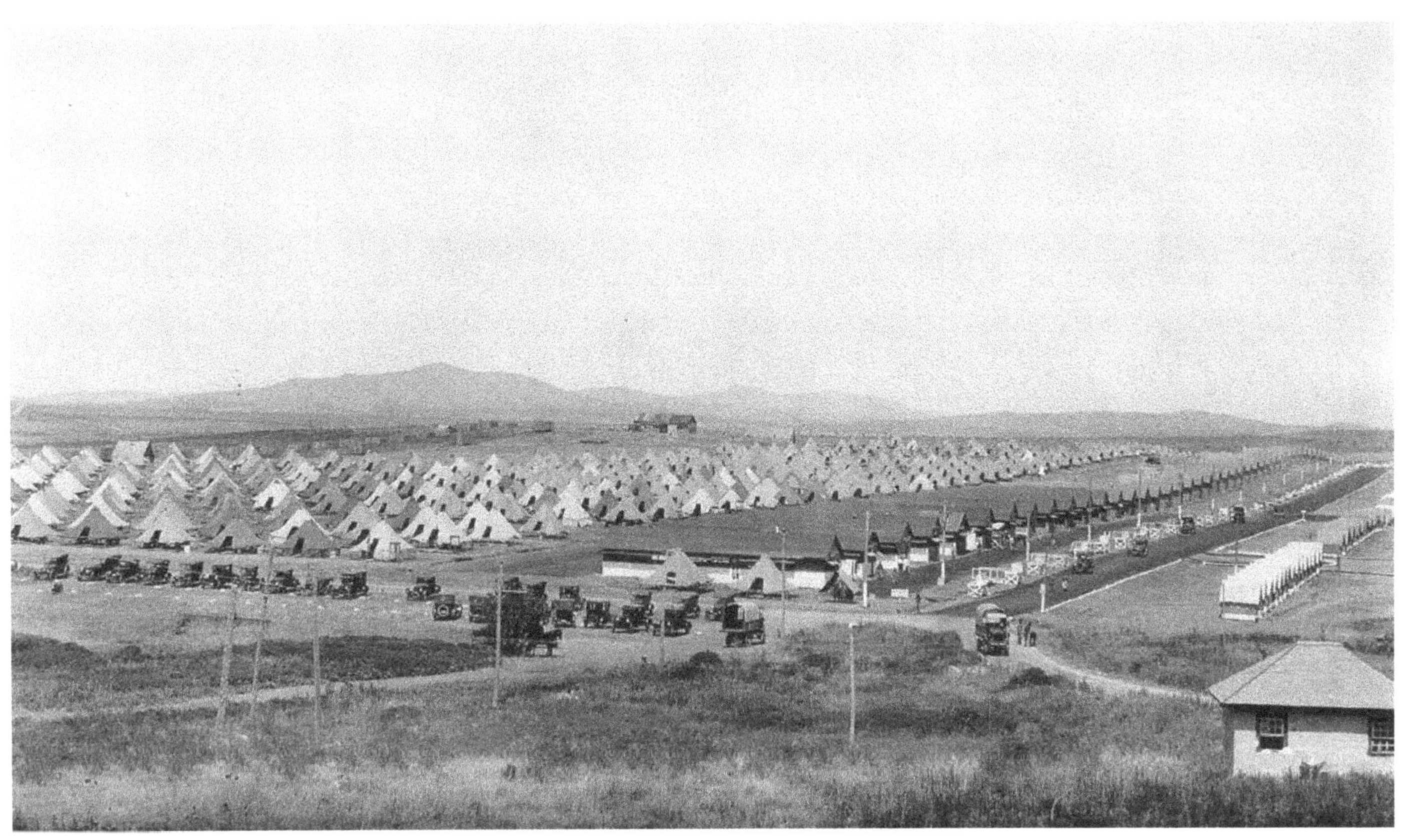

Camp Wolf, Fort Sill, 1923. This view was likely captured during the summer training exercises of National Guard units from around the country. The Guardsmen received a distinguished guest that summer in the person of General John J. Pershing.

A gusher at Okemah, February 21, 1922. Unlike towns such as Duncan, which tried to manage growth during oil booms, Okemah embraced the arrival of the wildcatters wholeheartedly and even permitted drilling on city lots. This is one of the first wells to come in near Okemah.

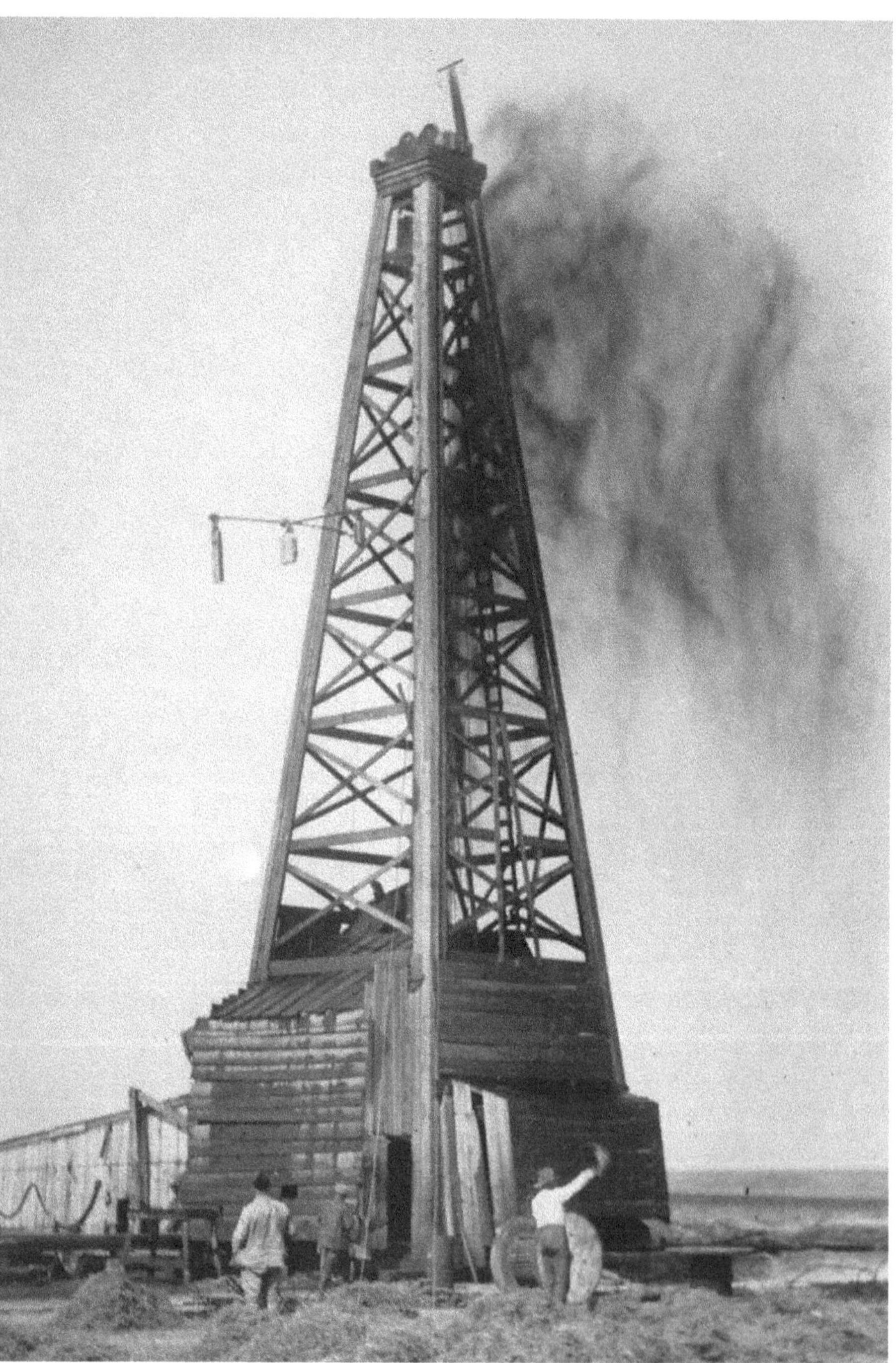

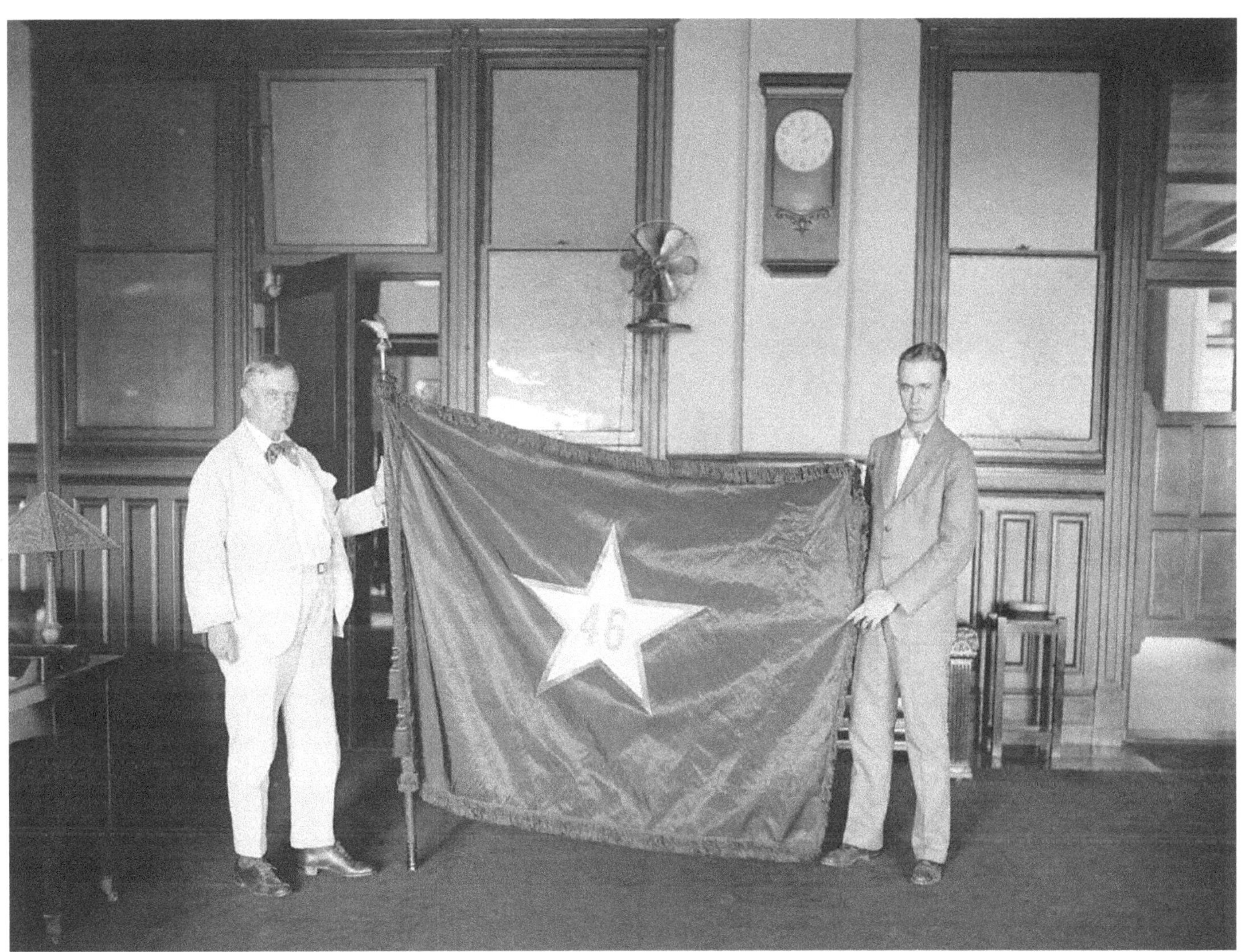

An enduring casualty of the red scare of the 1920s is the first Oklahoma state flag, seen here in August 1924. First commissioned in 1911, the bold red flag with white star and blue "46" was outlawed in 1925 because reactionary officials feared it suggested communism. It's still illegal to display the flag in Oklahoma.

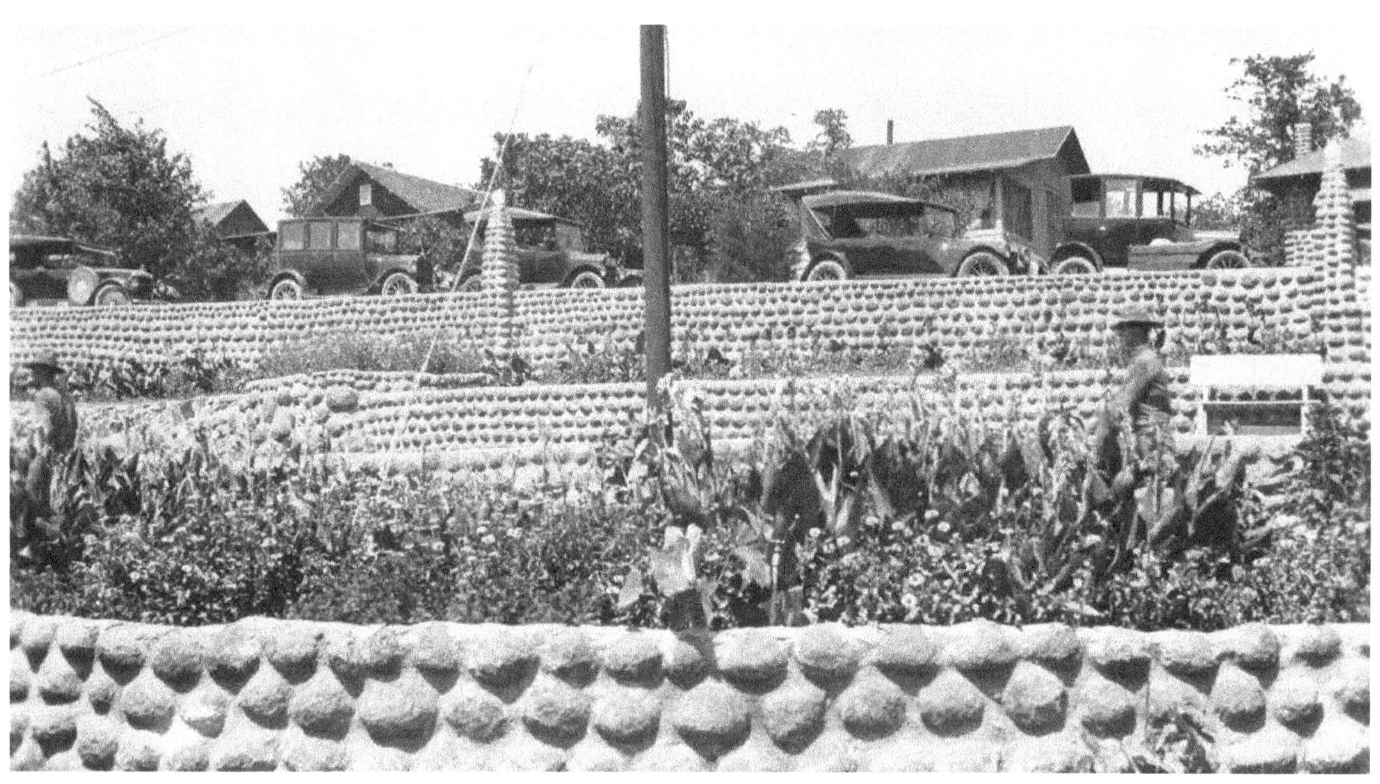

Medicine Park was a planned tourist and resort area near Lawton. Developers built the resort around the healing qualities of nearby Medicine Creek, but it was the naturally round, granite cobblestones found only in the Wichita Mountains that gave the town its unique character, as seen here in the 1920s.

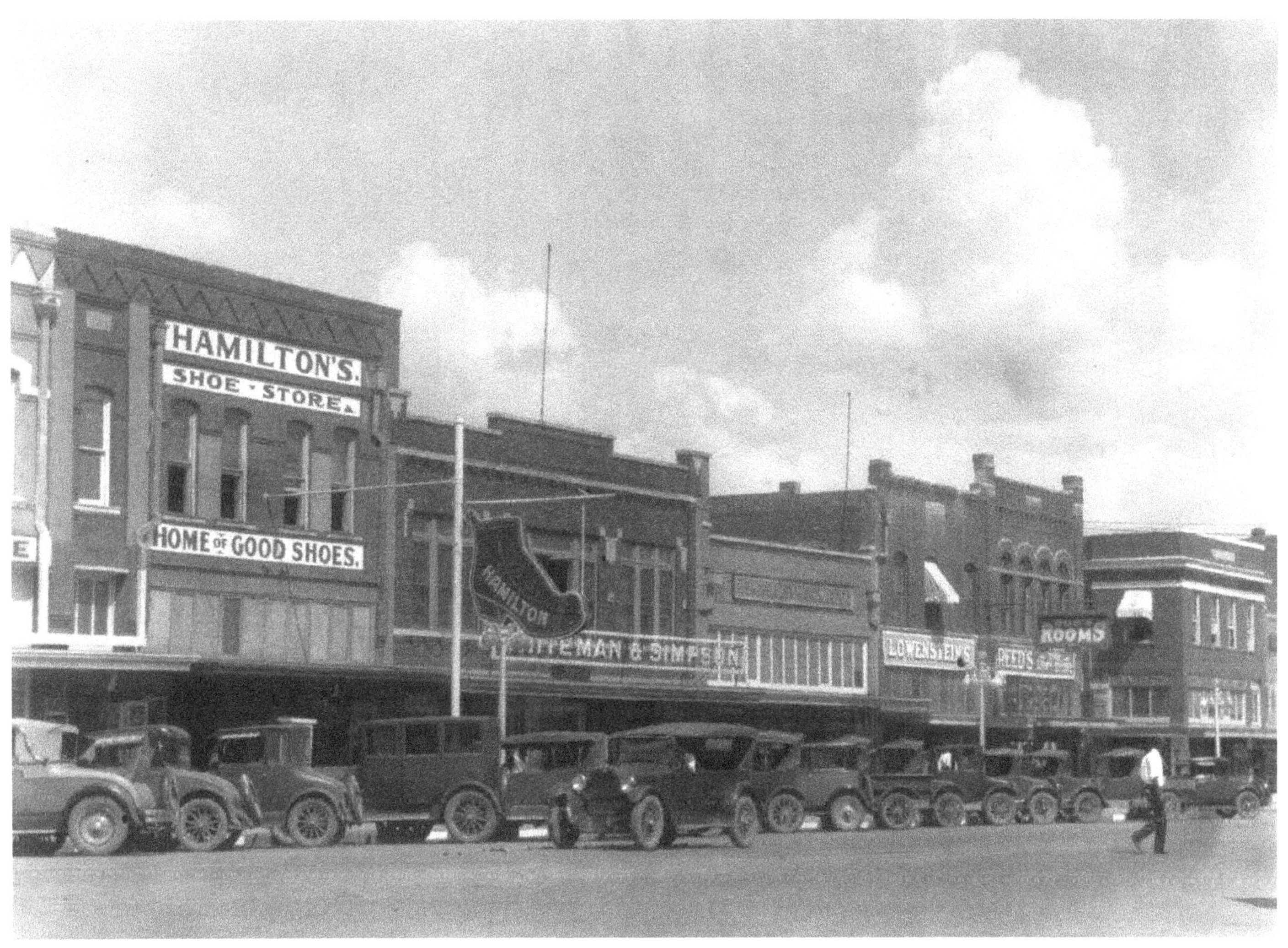

Downtown Ardmore, 1925. A diversified economy helped Ardmore recover from devastation twice. In 1895 a fire swept through the wooden buildings downtown; and in 1915 a tank car full of gasoline exploded, leveling dozens of downtown buildings and sending a river of flaming liquid through the streets, torching everything in its path.

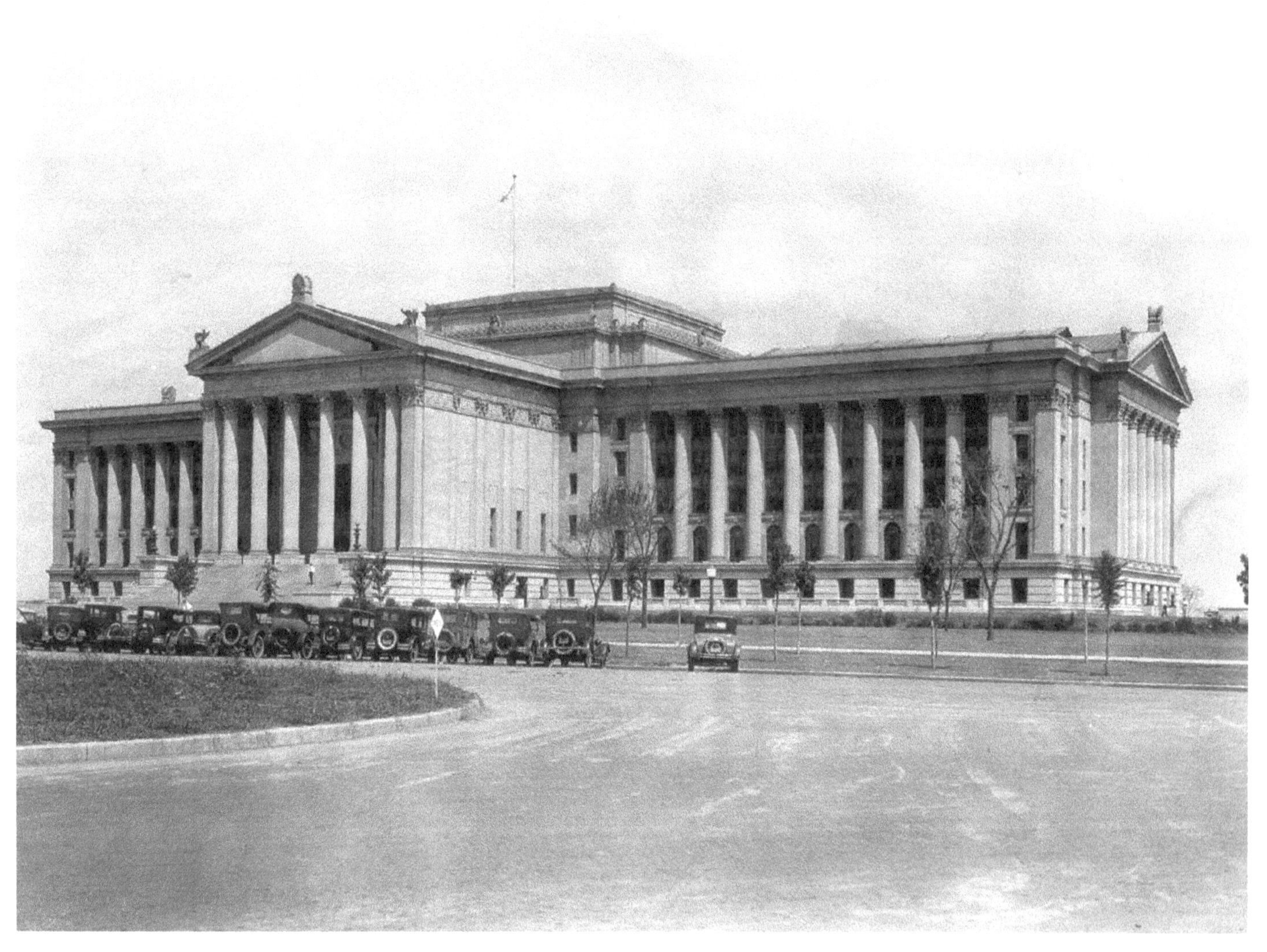

Designed by Solomon Layton, the Oklahoma State Capitol opened in 1917, but wartime penuriousness prevented the completion of the dome. The scene here is in 1926, just a few years before oil wells began sprouting on the lawns.

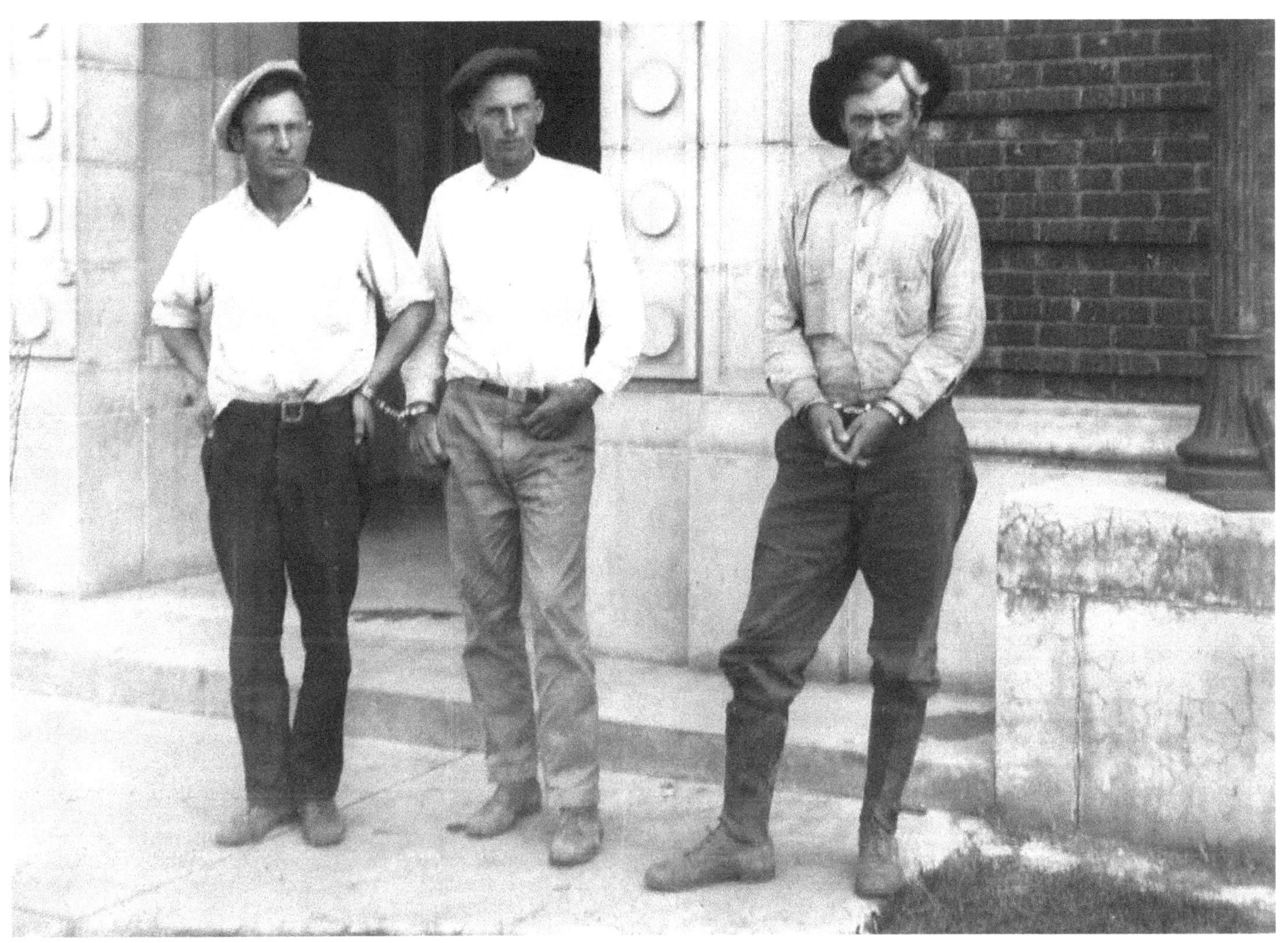

These three desperadoes were apprehended after state police received a tip that they planned to rob the bank in Wright City in June 1926. State officers followed two of them as they entered the bank, while the McCurtain County sheriff nabbed the driver of the getaway car.

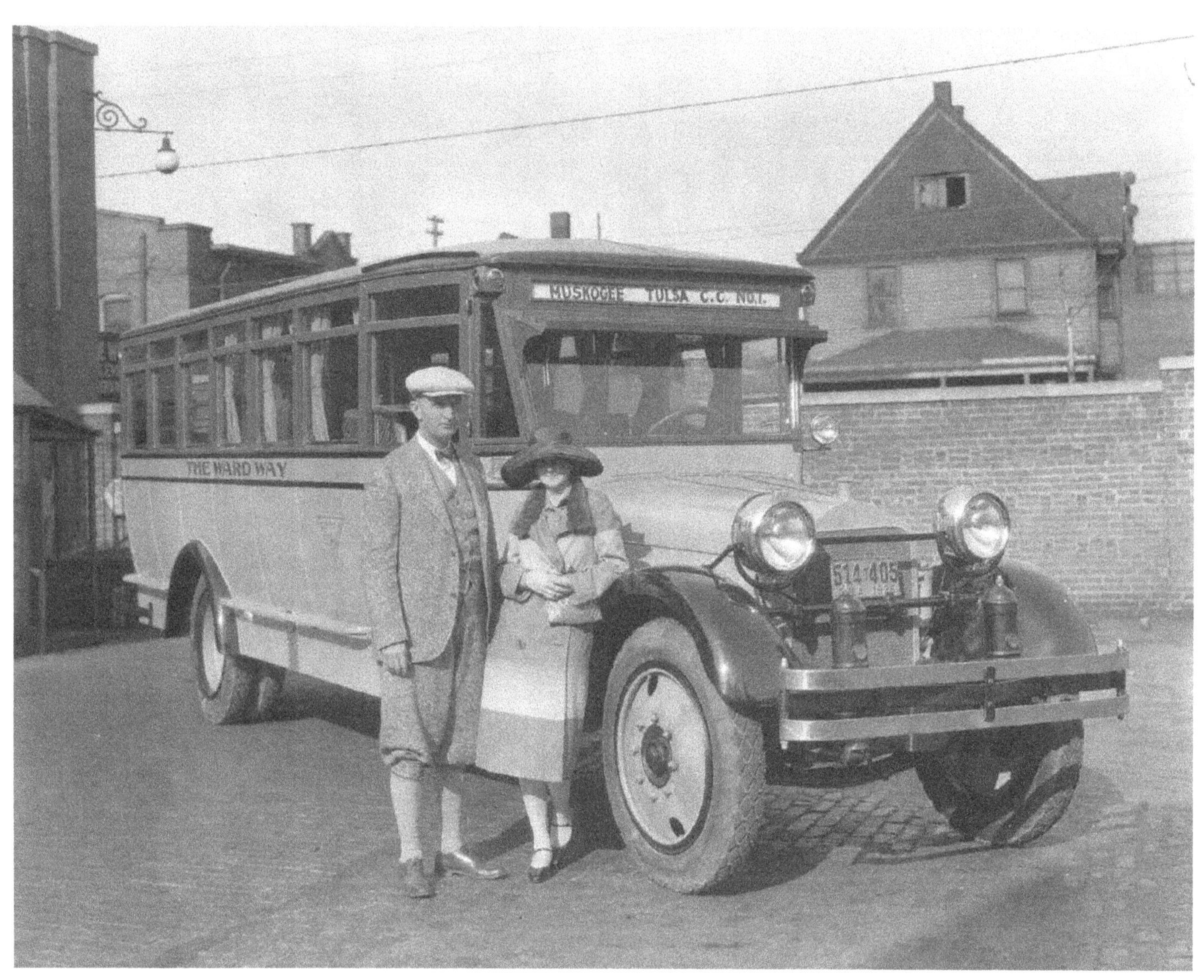

Passengers in Muskogee wait to board a Ward Way Lines bus bound for Tulsa, 1926. Muskogee was the de facto capital of Indian Territory and, until eclipsed by Tulsa in the 1920s, was the second-largest city in the state.

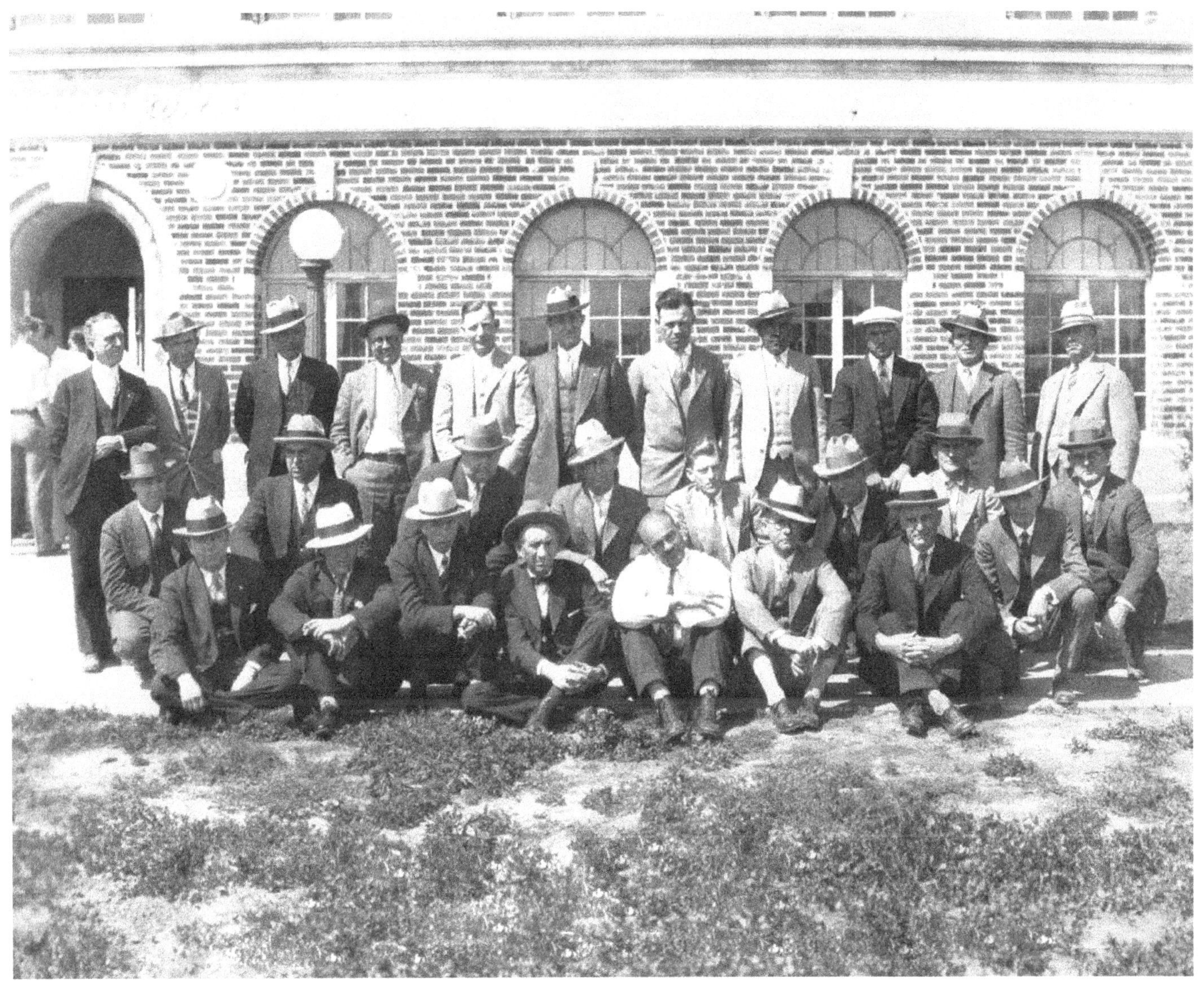

These men availed themselves of the "Southwestern Lumbermen's Association Short Course for Builders" offered at Oklahoma A&M College in Stillwater in 1928.

Following Spread: The pageantry of the Real Wild West Show at the Miller Brothers' 101 Ranch, 1927. The Miller Brothers balked at the term rodeo and always billed their popular shows as roundups because of the diversity of entertainment they offered. But rising costs, bad weather, and competition with movies made the 1927 season one of failure for the 101 Ranch, and by 1931 the Miller Brothers' empire had collapsed.

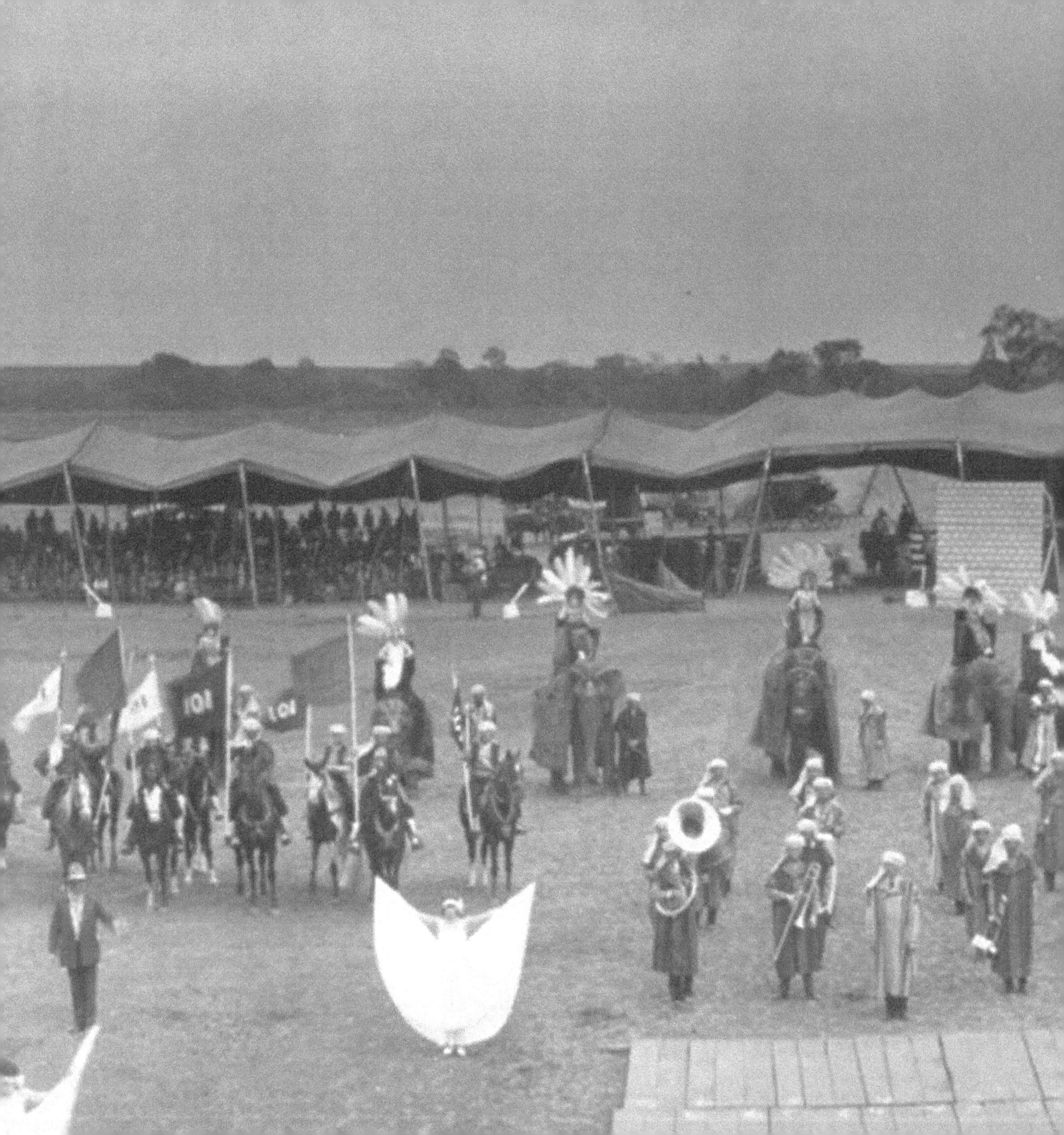
101
101

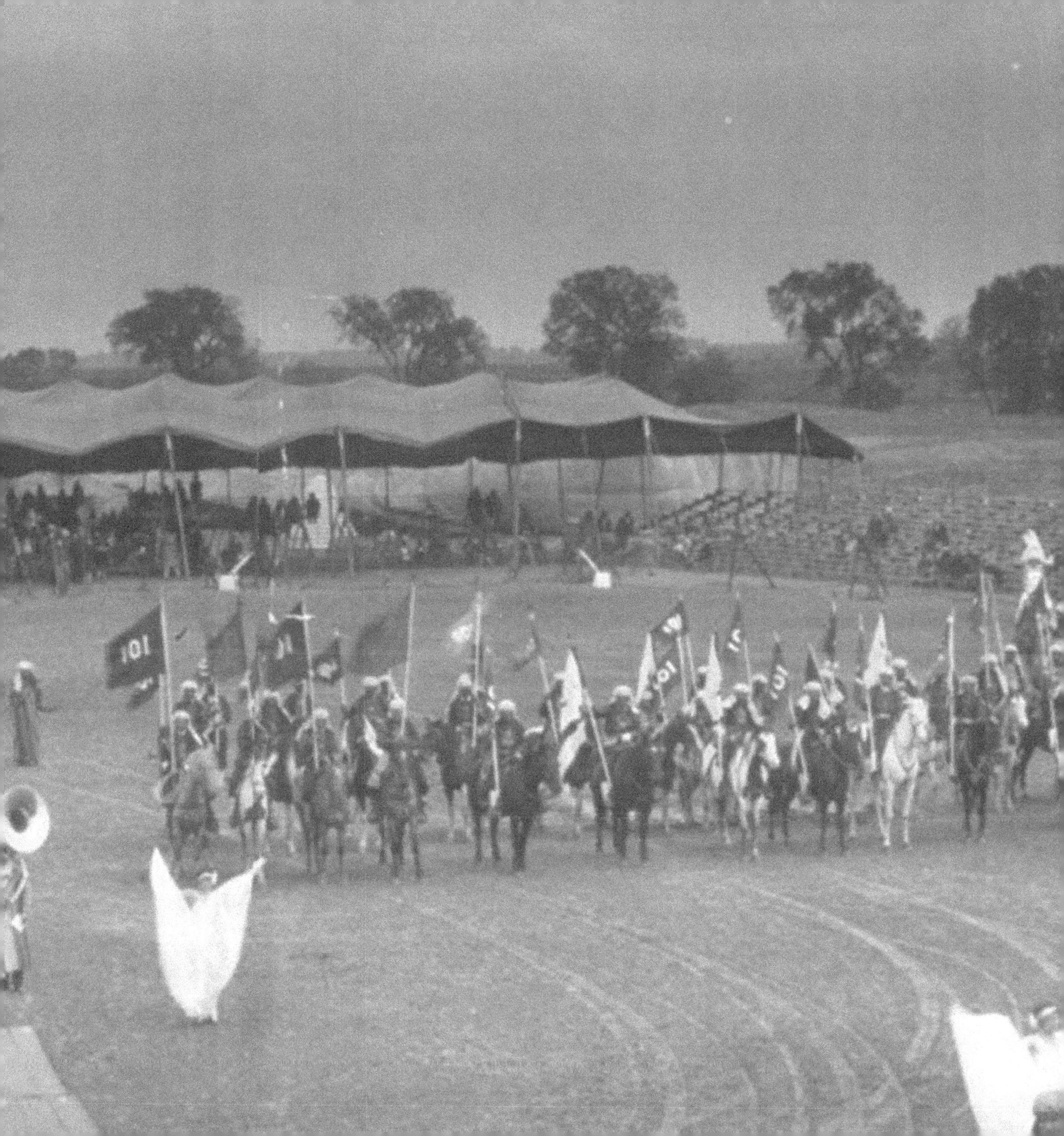

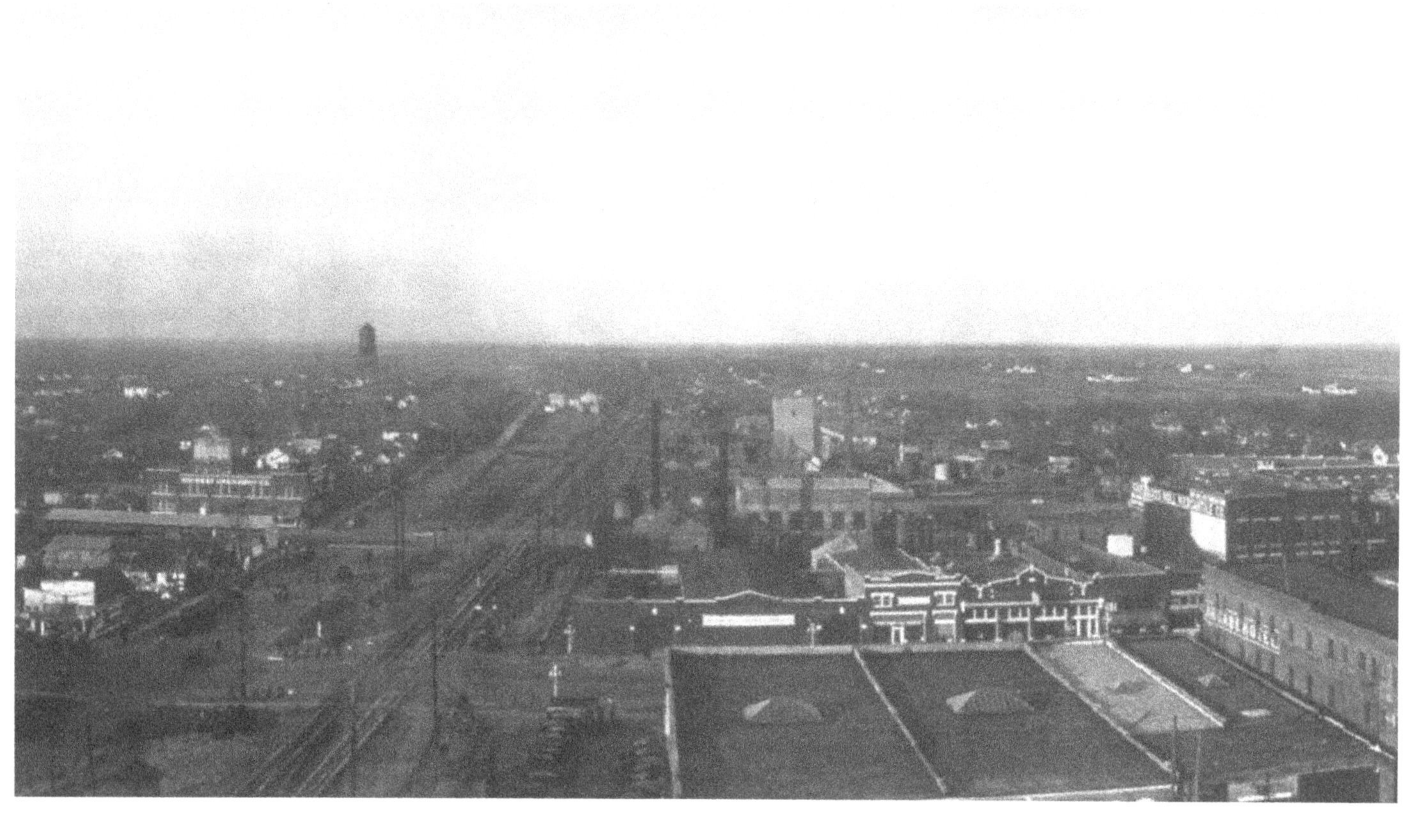

Ponca City, 1928. This view taken from the grain elevator on Central Avenue depicts Ponca City at the height of its golden era. The year was one of change for the oil center, as E. W. Marland lost control of his oil company to New York financiers and the firm was renamed Continental Oil Company, or CONOCO.

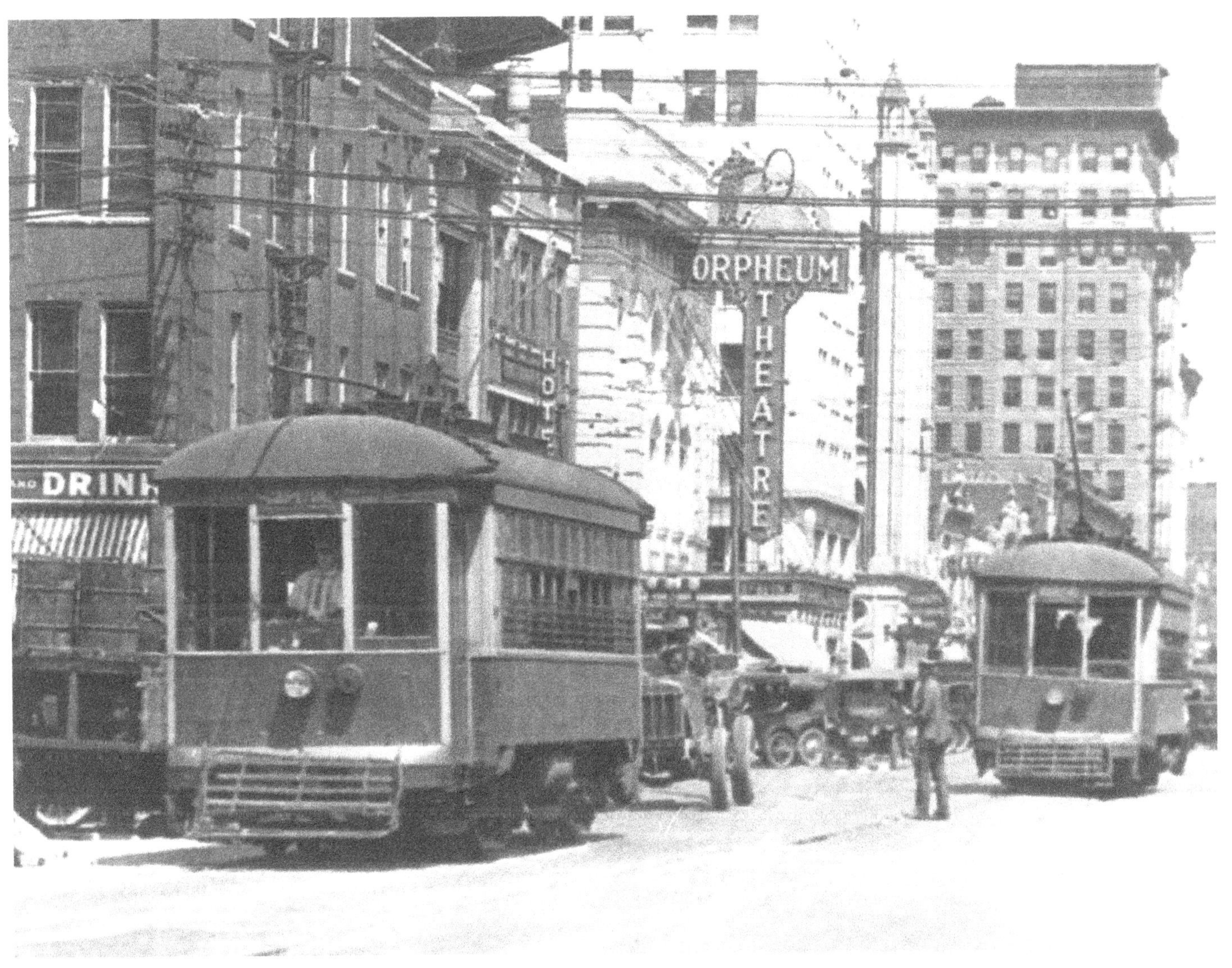

Beginning in the early twentieth century, the Greek-immigrant Sinopoulo family entertained Oklahoma City for decades, first with Delmar Garden, then the Overholser Theatre, and later the Midwest Theatre. The Overholser was revamped as the first-class Orpheum Theatre, seen here at 213 West Grand, ca. 1925, with streetcars rumbling past.

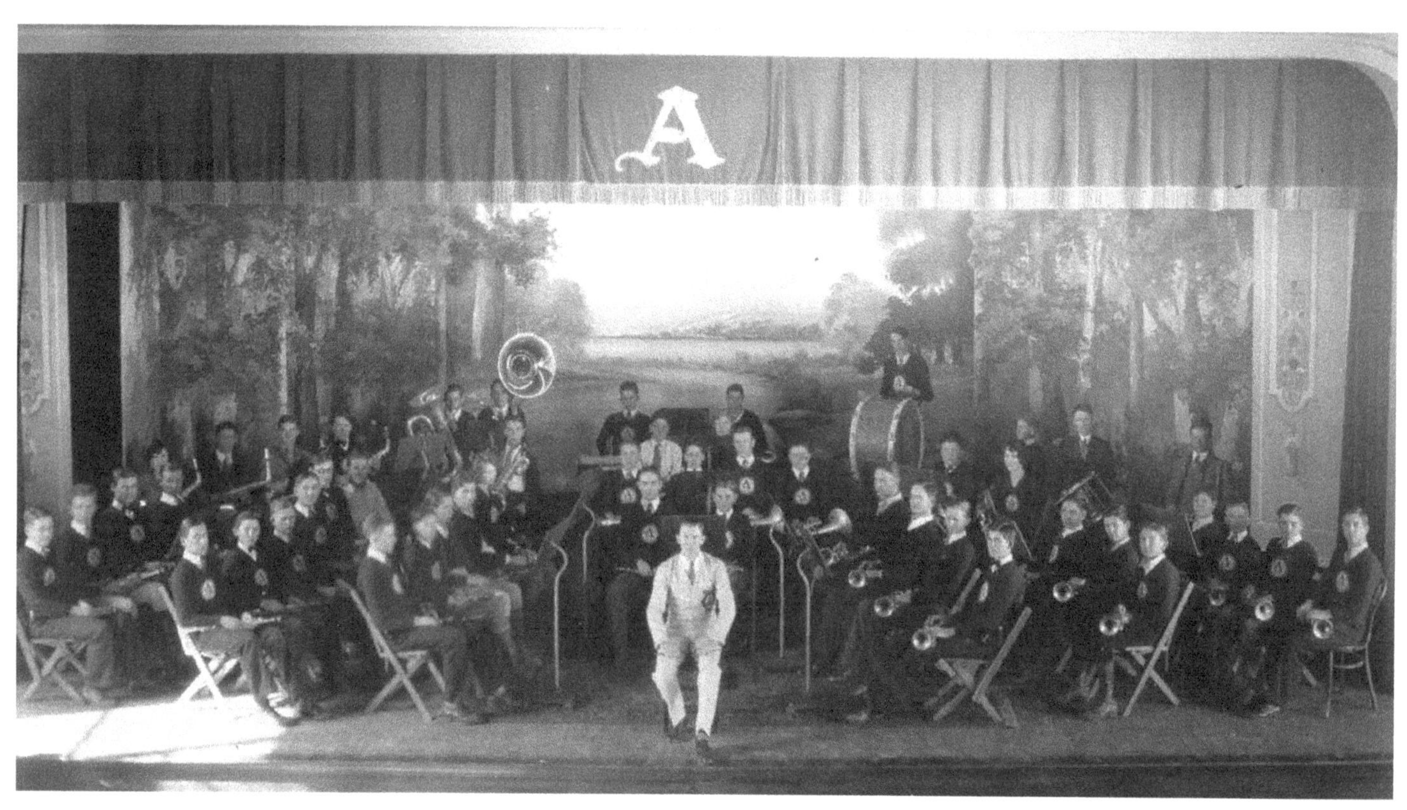

The 1929–1930 Ada High School Band poses on stage.

A Curtain of Black Rolled Down

(1930–1945)

During the first few years of the Great Depression, Oklahoma City paced the nation in new building construction, and it appeared as though Oklahoma would buck national trends and actually prosper during the economic downturn. However, while the wildcatters and roughnecks frolicked about the state, several unseen trends began to converge which would redefine the upstart state's image.

Soil erosion, agricultural mechanization, high tenancy rates, and low crop prices had already made farming in Oklahoma tenuous during the 1920s, but the drought conditions which developed in the 1930s worsened into a crisis. Finally, the massive "black blizzard" dust storms, which swallowed towns whole in the panhandle, brought cataclysmic disaster to farmers. Meanwhile, demand drops and the opening of the immense East Texas oil field produced an oil glut, and crude prices plummeted below a dollar.

Amid all these pressures, many Oklahomans looked west—to California—for relief. Some Oklahomans had family already there who beckoned them to greener pastures, while many former tenant farmers moved on in hopes of finding jobs doing the only kind of work they knew. In a musical message to them, Woody Guthrie warned, "California is a Garden of Eden . . . but you won't find it so hot if you ain't got the do-re-mi."

Still, many Oklahomans clung tenaciously to what was not taken away or blown away. Some found solace in religion, others in hard work; most of all they worked together and forged strong communities as they held out for better times. Unfortunately, the image of the poor, ragged "Okie" refugee family in a broken-down jalopy was misapplied to those that stayed behind and thus saddled the state with a negative image for decades to come.

As it did nationally, World War II jump-started the state's economy, since food and crude-oil production were vital to the American war effort. Capitalizing on its central location, the state offered incentives to bring several military bases to Oklahoma, while Rosie the Riveter worked in aircraft production facilities in Tulsa and Oklahoma City.

Victory gave many across the nation new hope, and nowhere was this more needed than Oklahoma, which faced an uphill climb to mend the ravages of Mother Nature and the Depression.

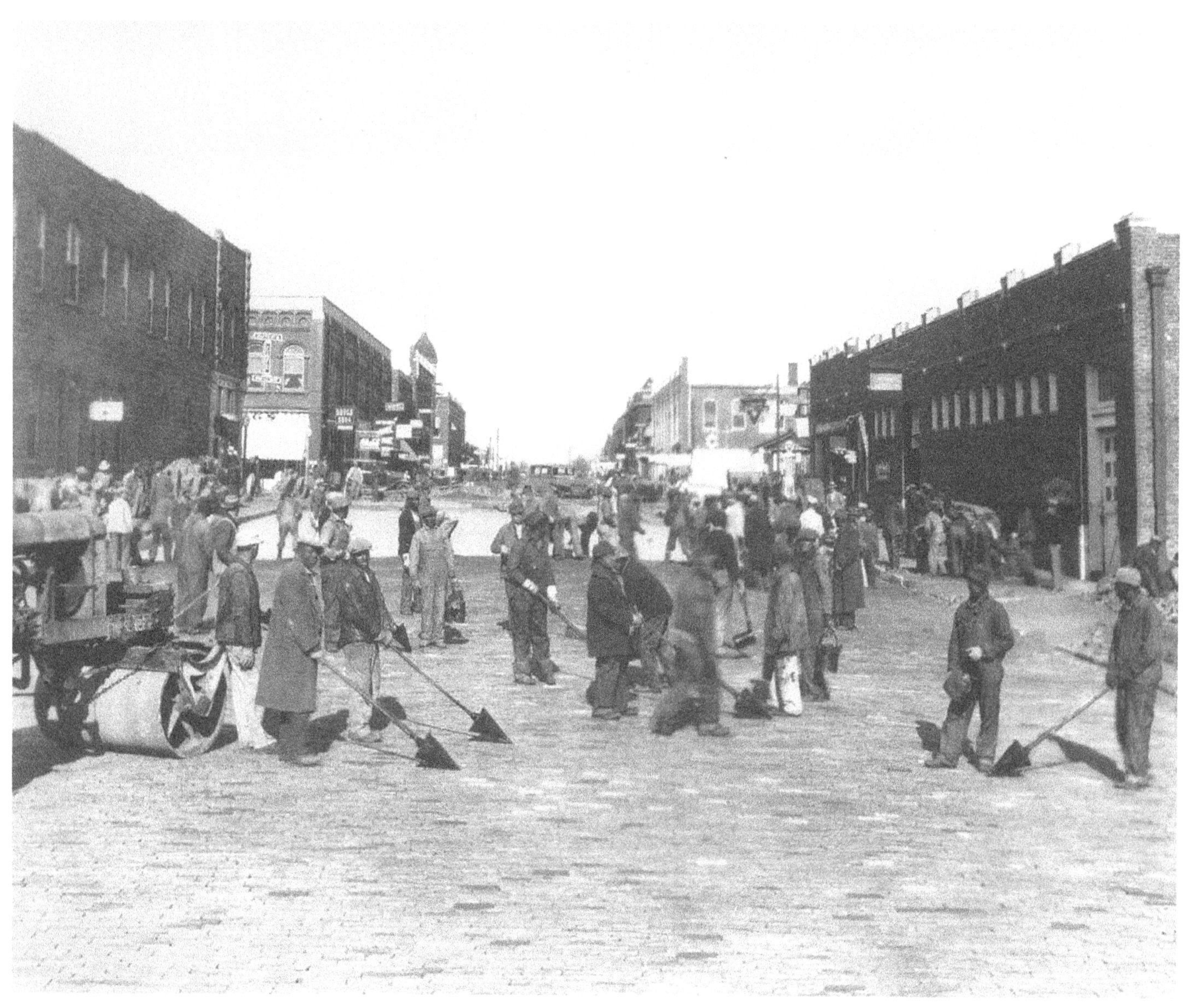

Laborers for the federal Civil Works Administration finish off a repaved section of a Guthrie street, 1933. The CWA was a temporary program established to get millions of unemployed men through the winter. The repaving work was quite difficult: laborers had to remove the bricks, clean them, roll the dirt path flat, then relay the brick.

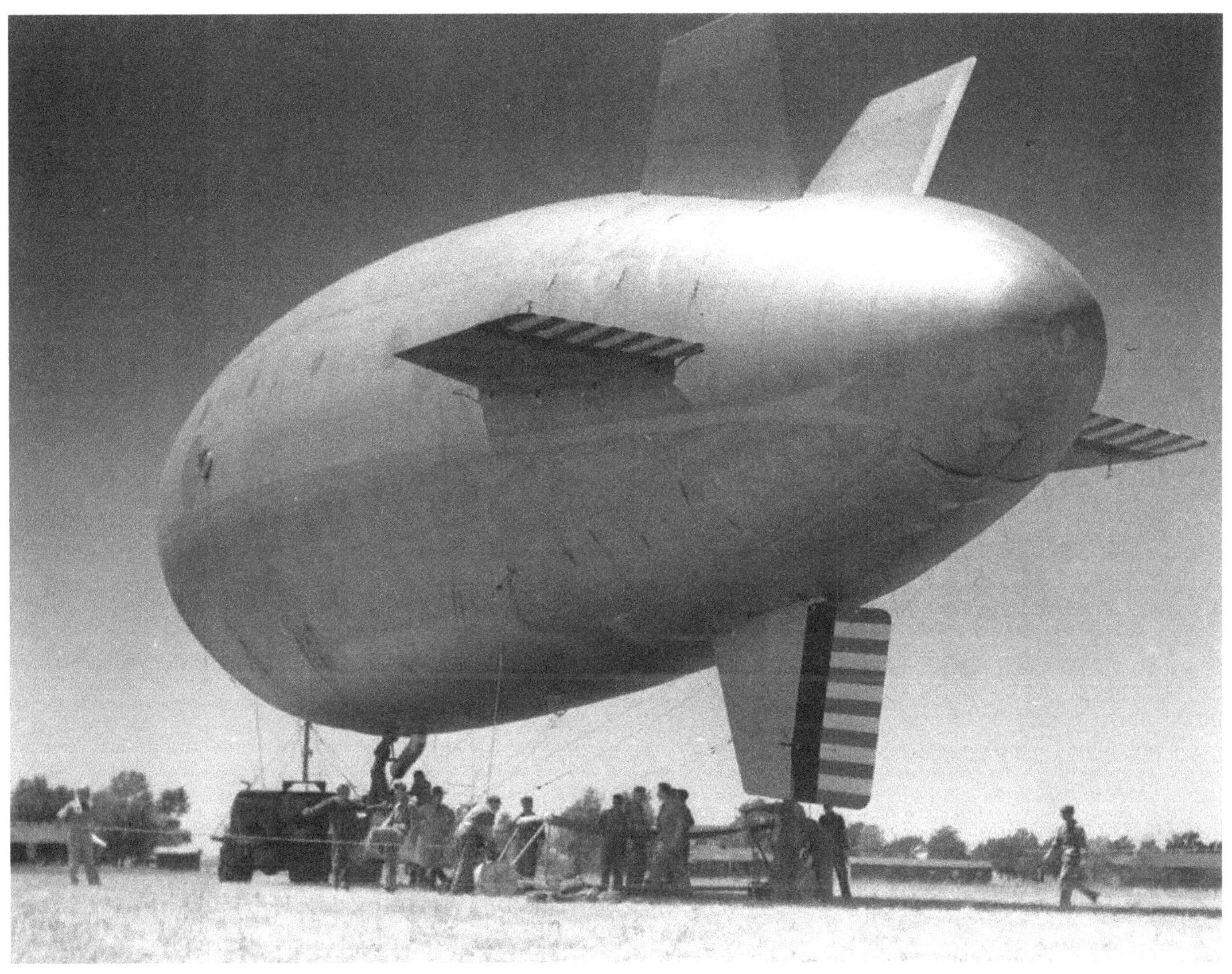

This 1930s photo of an Army blimp being inflated at Sapulpa may have been taken upon the return of Sapulpa native Captain Frank Trotter to his hometown. Trotter was an ace blimp pilot, winner of several blimp races and somewhat of a daredevil, having once delivered a stack of newspapers to the top of the Empire State Building.

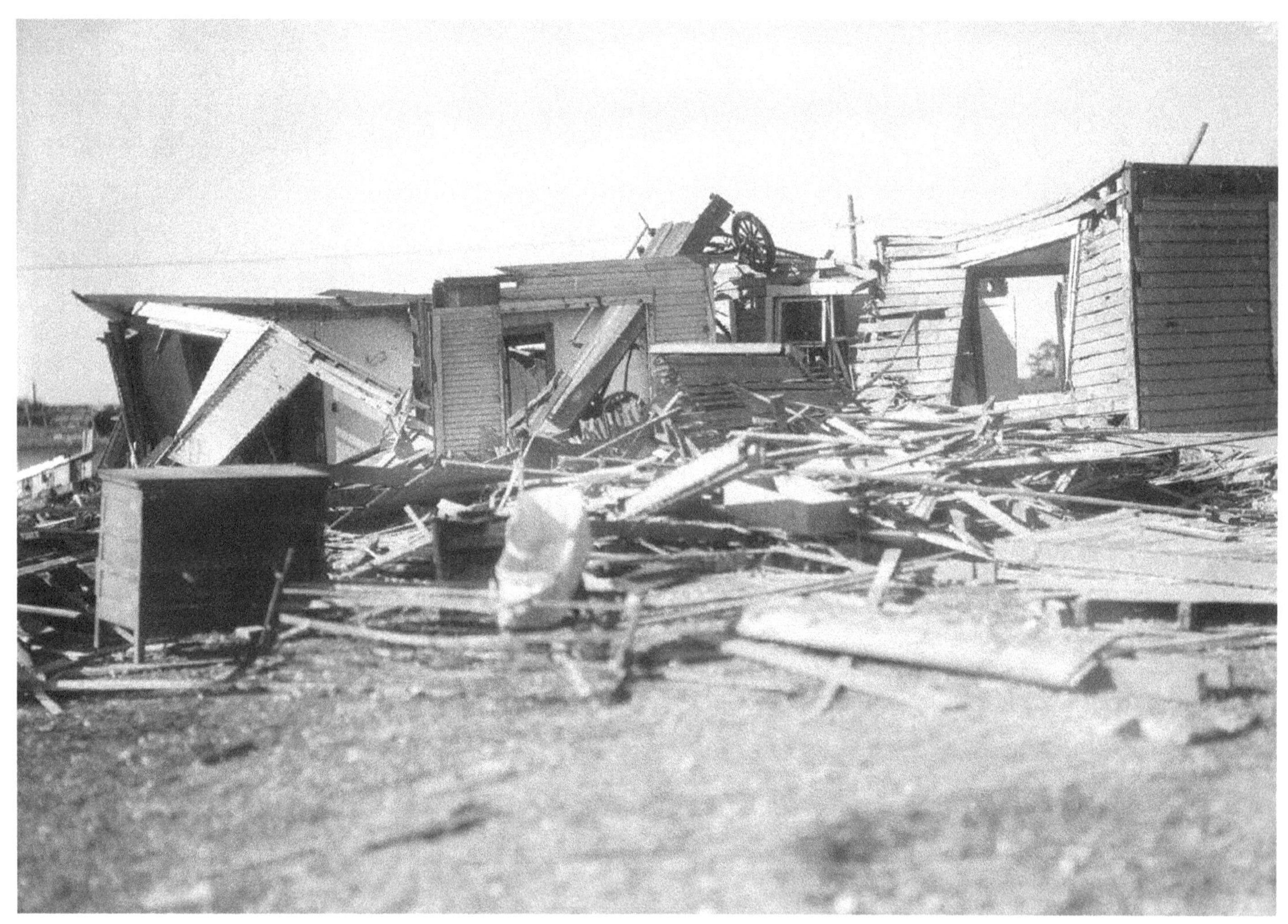

Seen here is the aftermath of a devastating tornado that struck Bethany on the afternoon of November 19, 1930. Bethany was a bustling, thriving community when the funnel touched down and wiped away most of the city in only five minutes. By nightfall, 18 were dead and 58 injured.

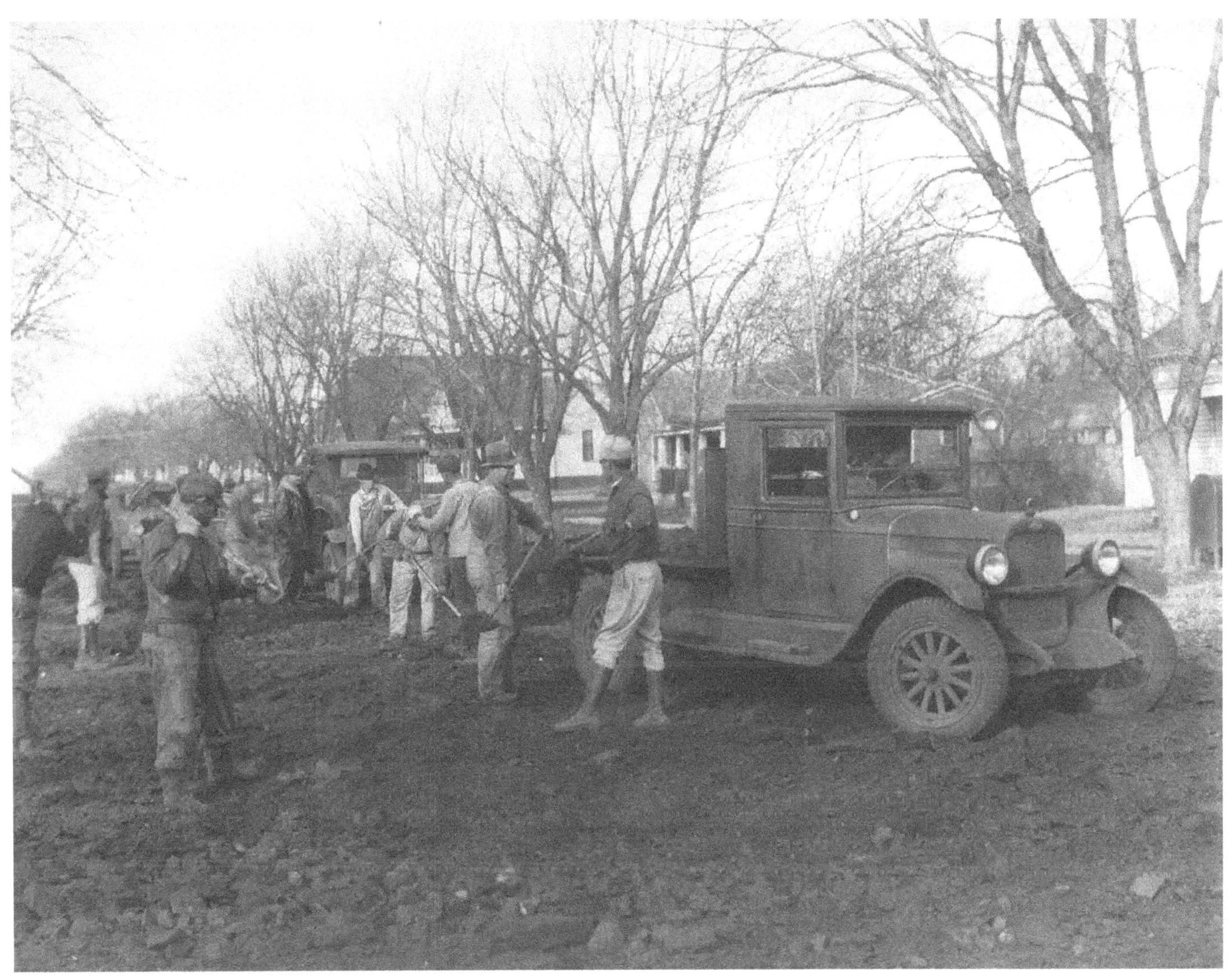

Men of the Civil Works Administration repair a city street in Yukon, 1933. The CWA was one of the earliest and costliest of the New Deal programs and ran from November 1933 through March 1934.

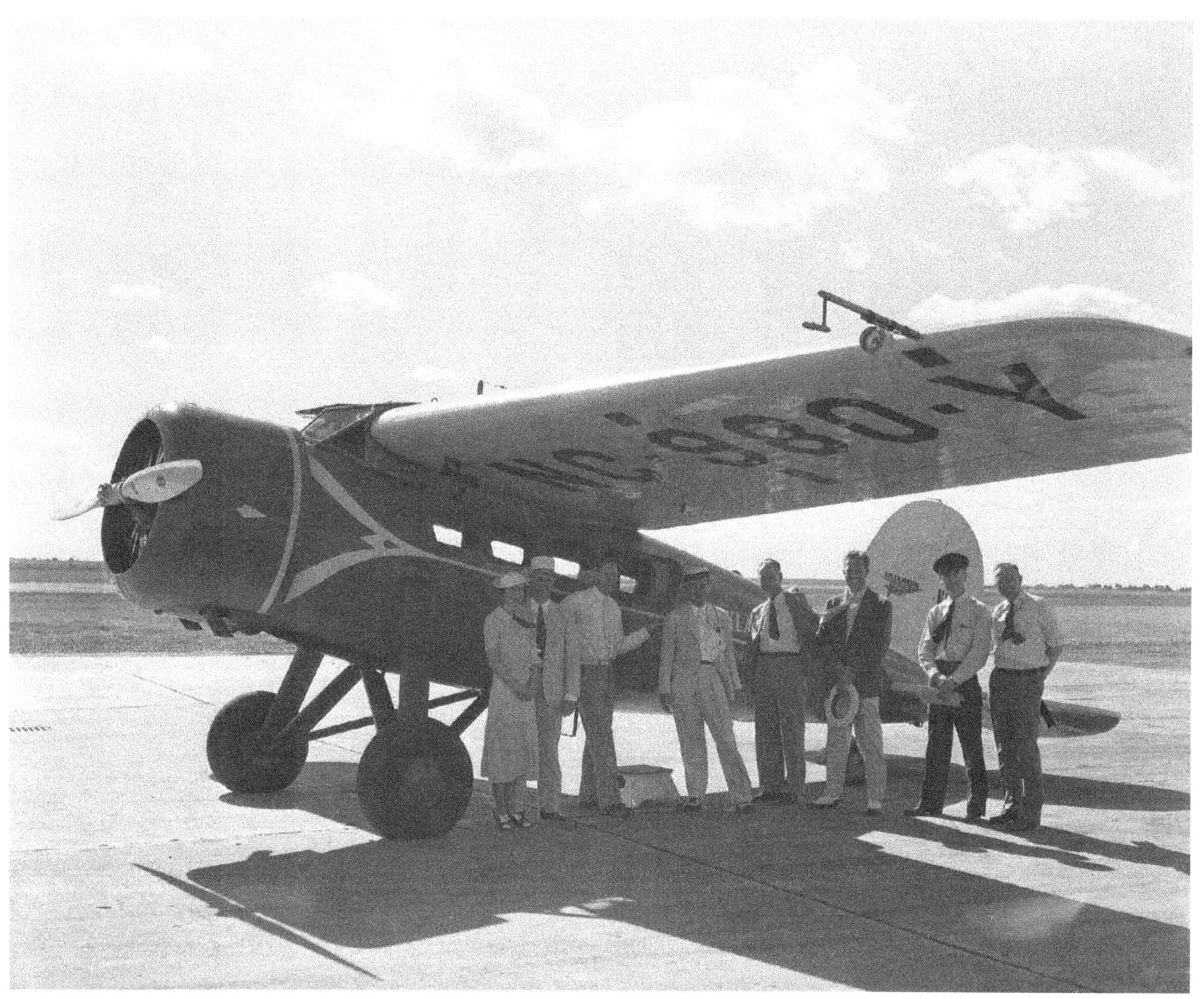

Local aviator Joel Pitts launched his Oklahoma Airlines shuttle service between Oklahoma City and Tulsa in the summer of 1935 with much fanfare. Unfortunately, the service folded around Christmas that same year. Pitts went on to have a full career as a pilot for Braniff.

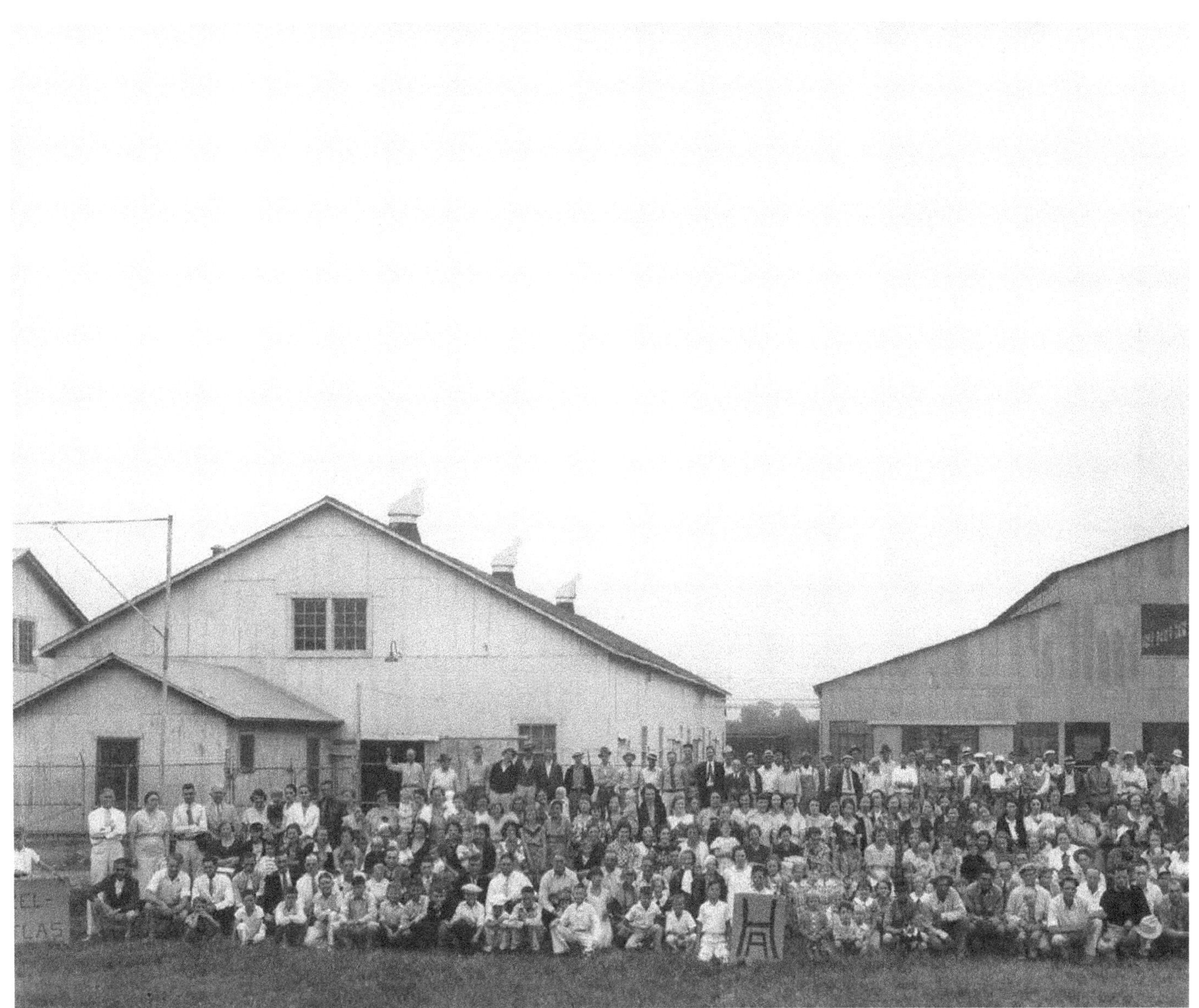

The Hazel-Atlas Glass Company was one of the nation's most prolific producers of Depression glass. Here, in 1935, the company's Ada factory celebrates its first annual Labor Day picnic.

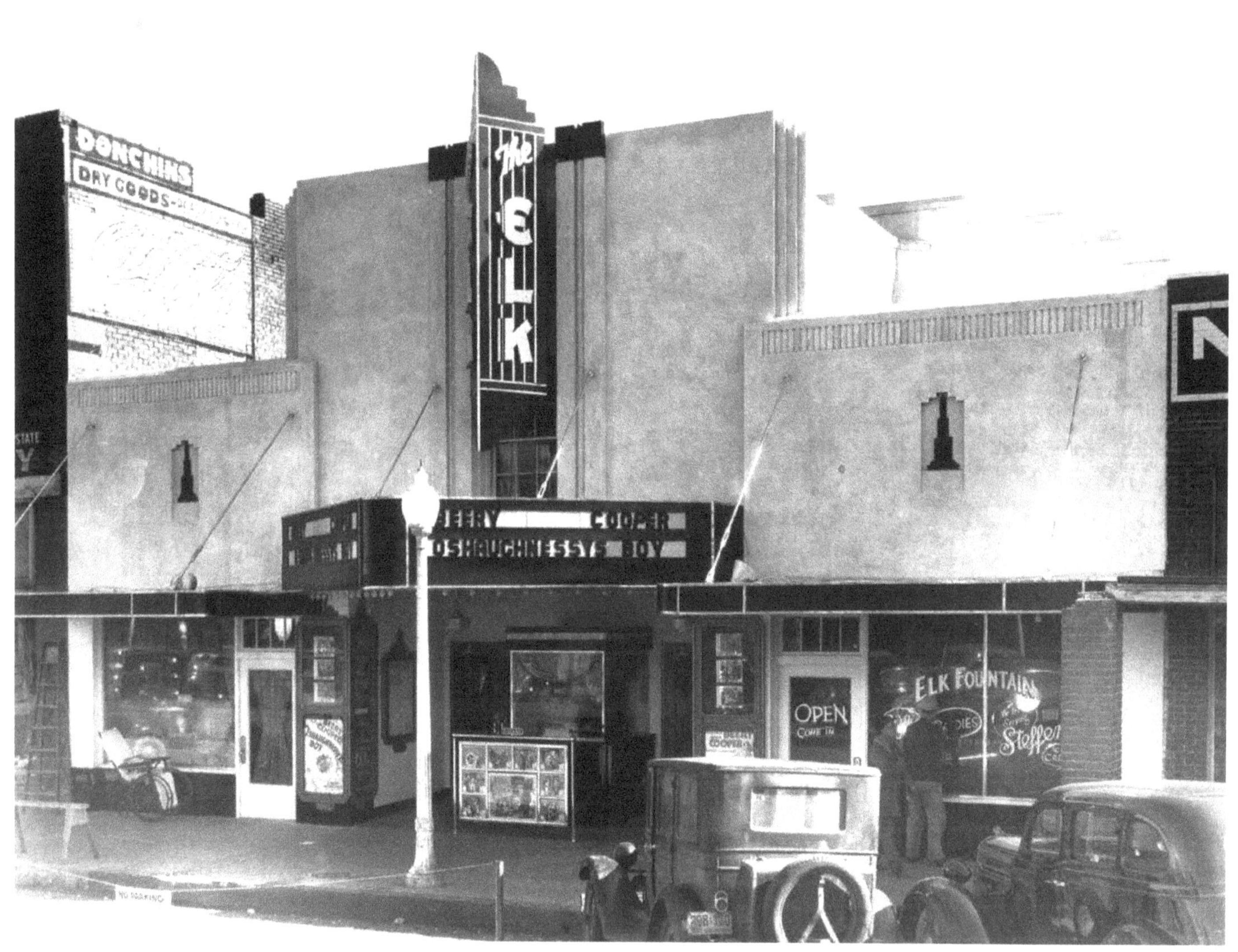

This sleek, art-deco movie palace, designed by noted Southwest architect W. Scott Dunne, has graced Elk City's stretch of Route 66 since 1935. Here the Elk is featuring the 1935 movie *O'shaughnessy's Boy,* starring Wallace Beery and Jackie Cooper.

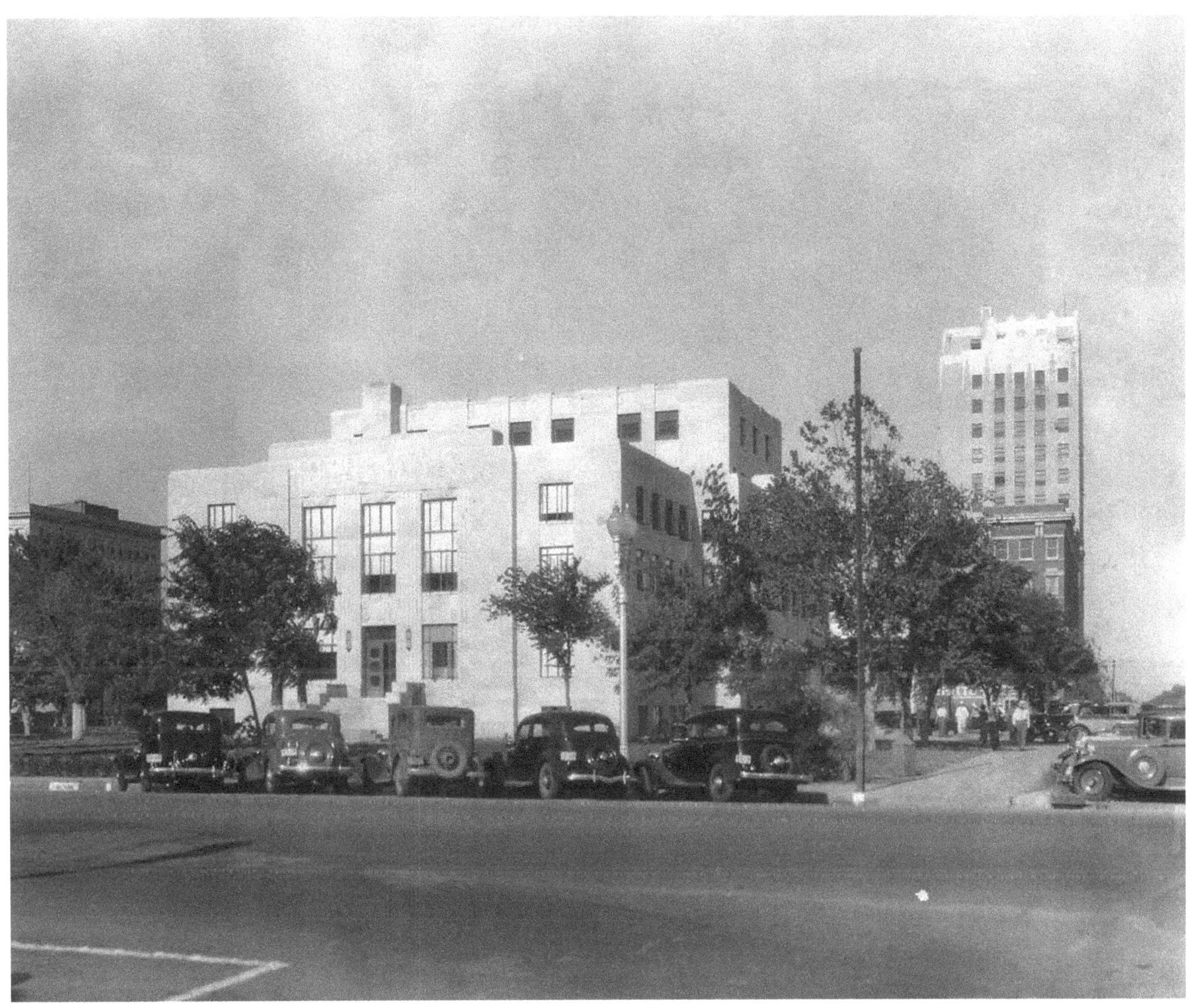

Garfield County's new courthouse is seen here on the square in Enid, ca. 1936. Formed in 1893, Enid proved to be quite adept at luring railroads and grain elevators, and quickly became the undisputed capital of northwestern Oklahoma and the state's fourth-largest city.

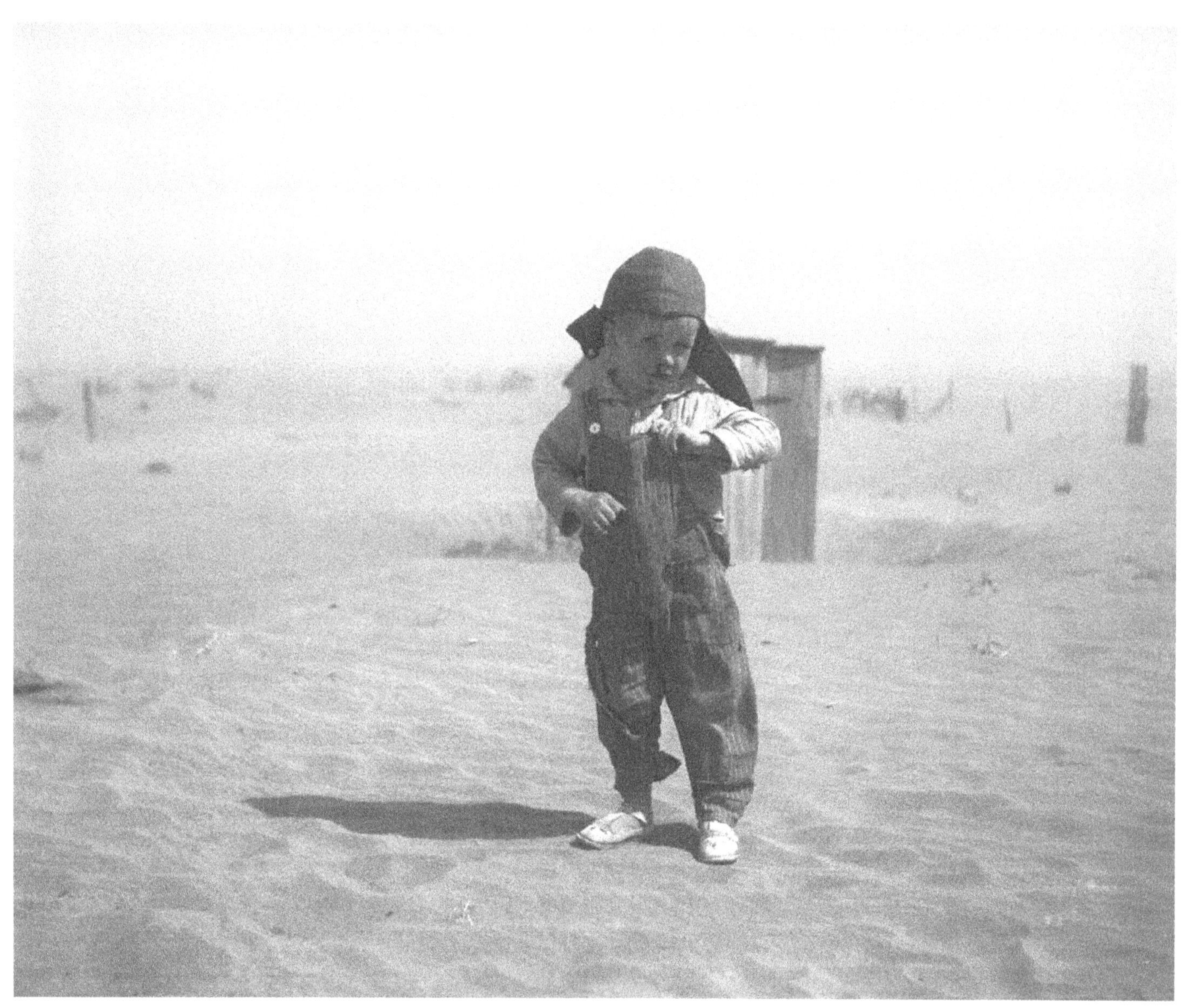

The subject of this Arthur Rothstein photo of a young boy in Cimarron County in 1936 is probably three-year-old Darrel Coble, who lived in the area his whole life and later said, "I don't really know why I like living here. I guess just 'cause this country's home."

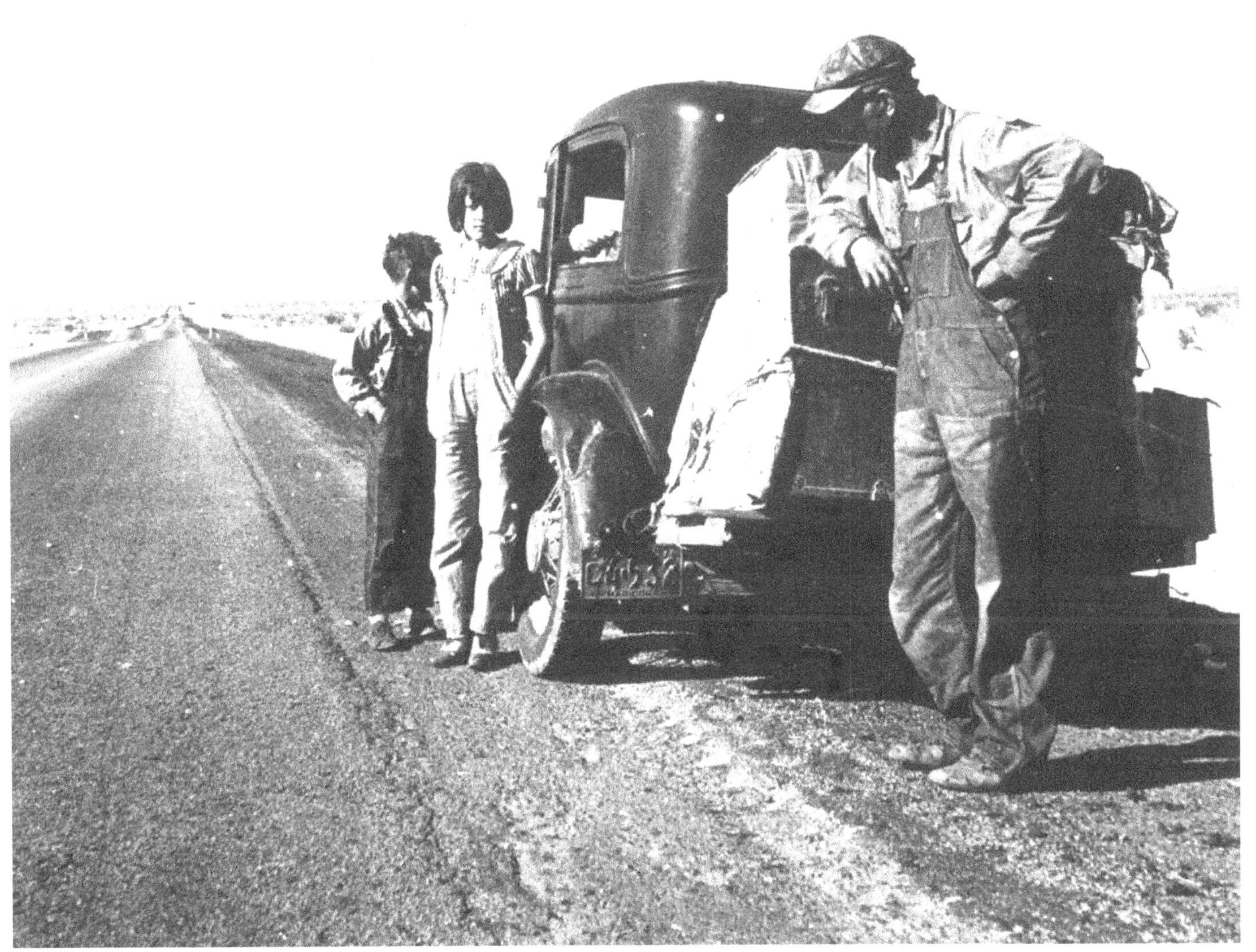

A migrant Okie family on the road, presumably headed west. Oklahoma suffered a net loss of nearly a half million people through the 1930s. Most of those who took to the road were victims of economic and agricultural transitions, but the most famous were the few who were victims of the Dust Bowl.

This was the view north up Broadway from Grand during a dust storm in Oklahoma City in the mid-1930s. On one January day in 1935, a 9,000-foot-high dry wind raised the temperature from 40 to 75 degrees and coated the city in reddish-yellow dust, with visibility reduced to a half-mile.

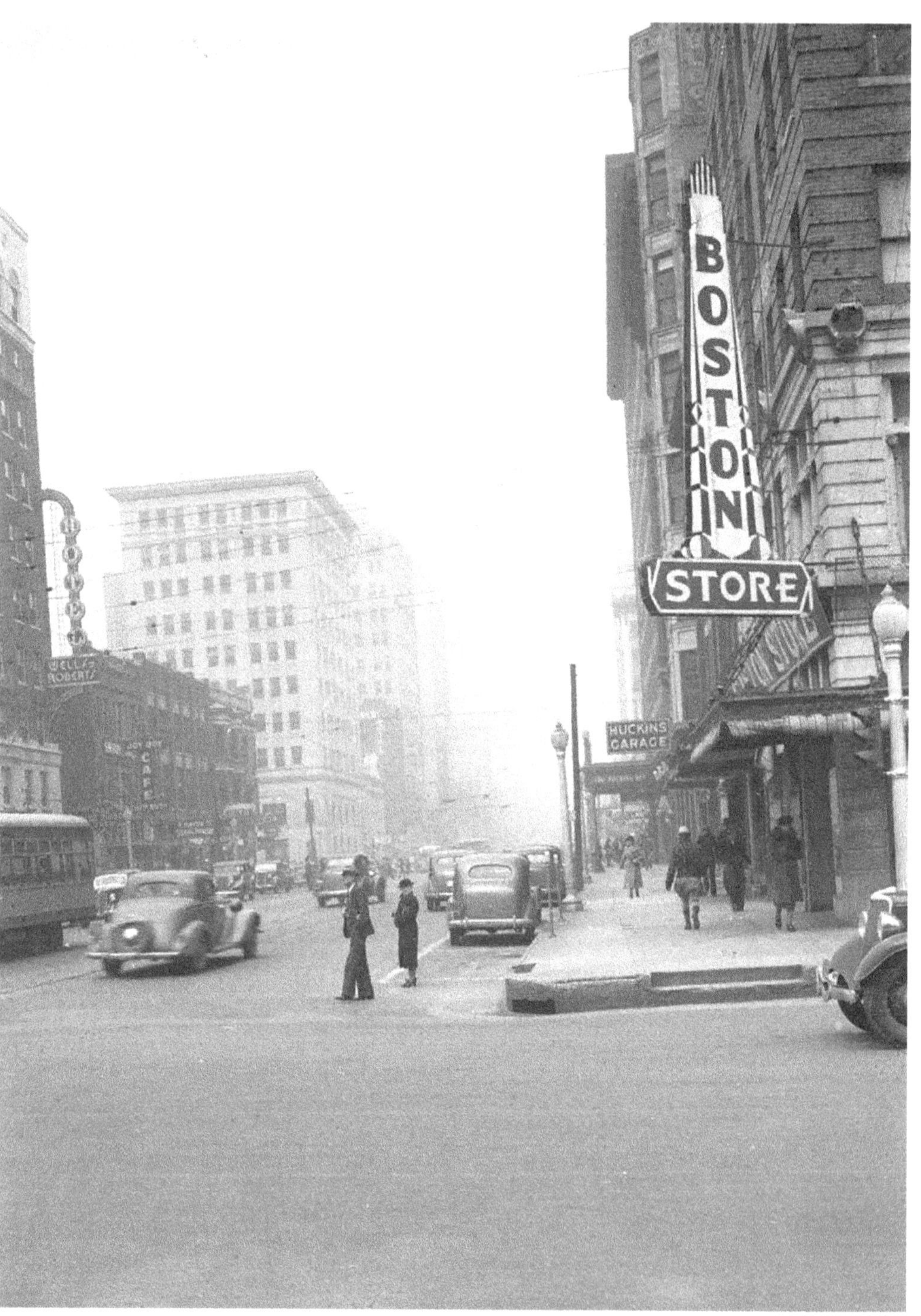

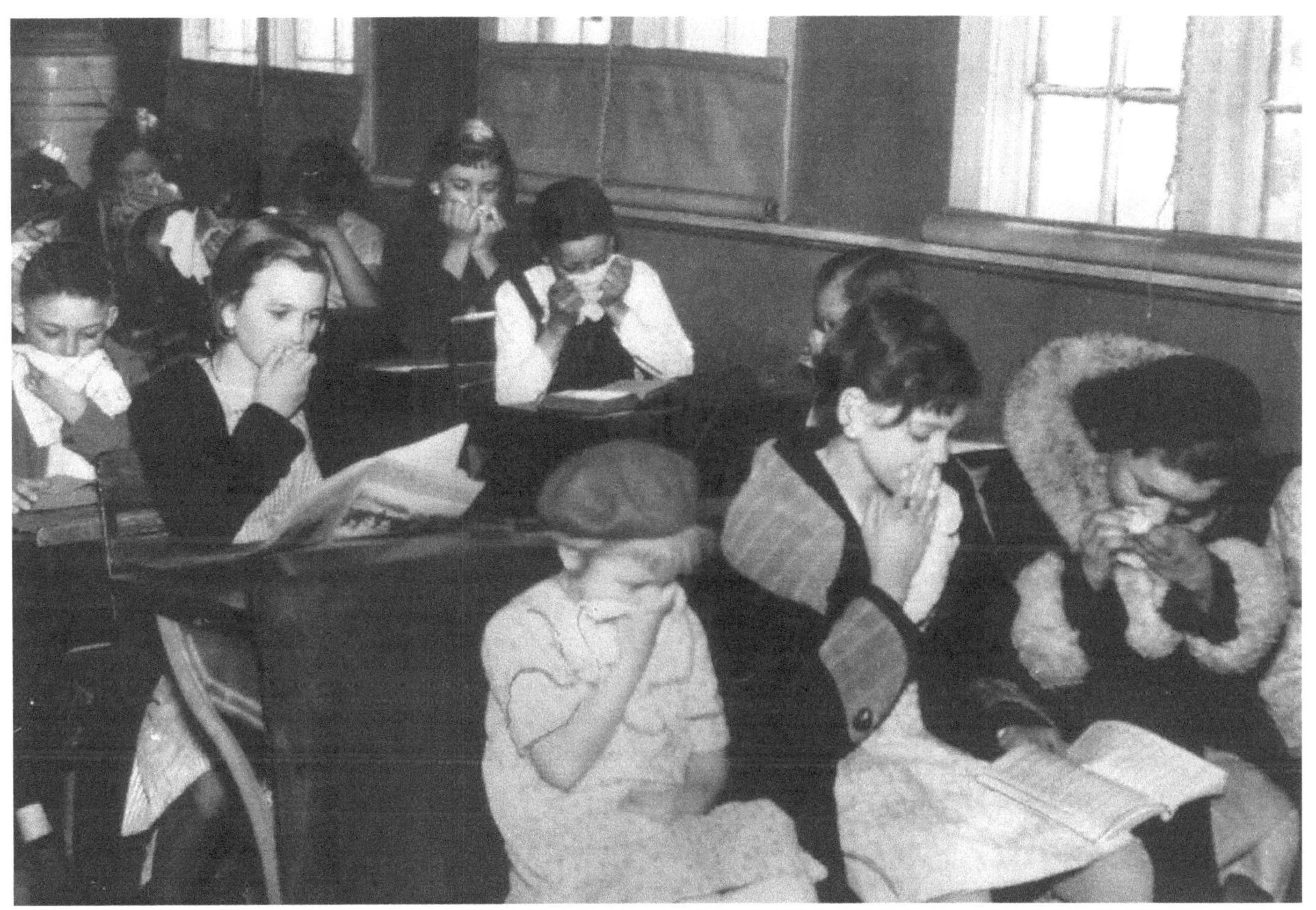

The spring of 1935 brought some of the era's fiercest dust storms to the northwestern and panhandle sections of the state. Even hiding indoors was no sure protection from "dust pneumonia," and a wet cloth for the mouth and nose were standard issue, as seen in this classroom.

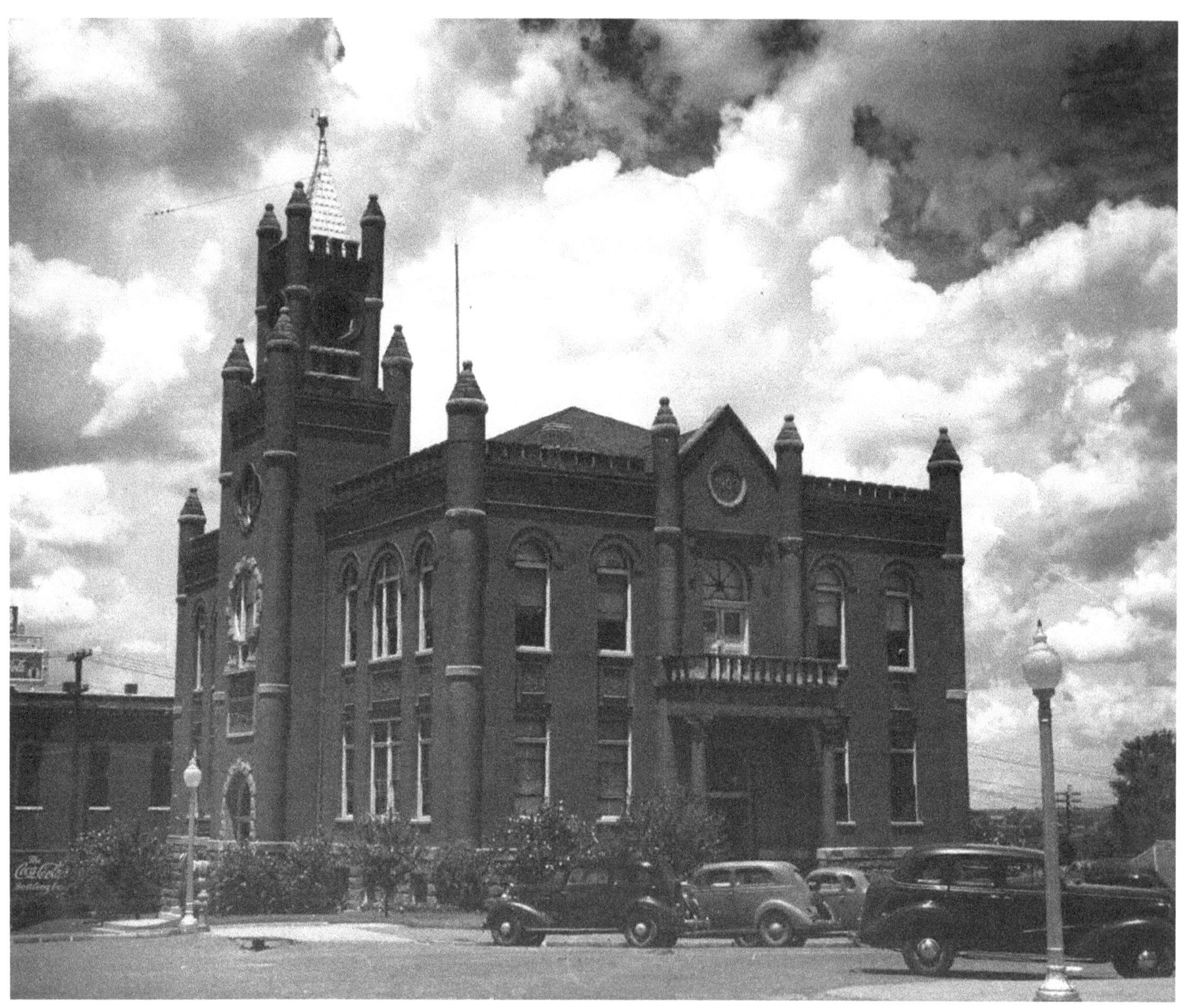

Guthrie's City Hall was designed by Joseph Foucart and erected in 1902 with an eye toward becoming the state capitol. It served as the meeting site of the state constitutional convention in 1906-7. Seen here in the mid-1930s, the ornate structure fell to the wrecking ball in 1955 after years of neglect.

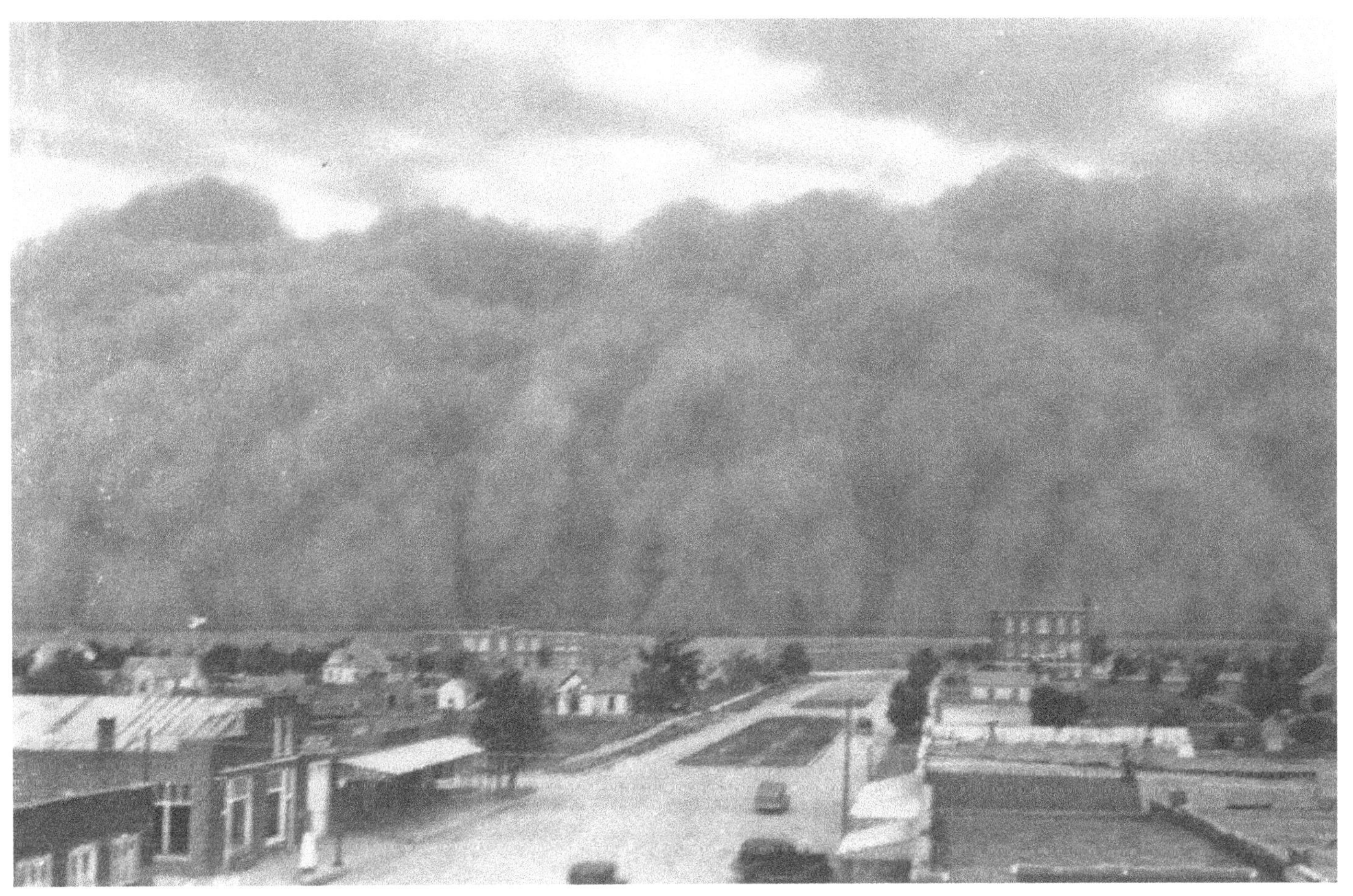

This dramatic scene shows the peaceful town of Hooker just moments before an 18,000-foot-high dust storm envelops it in tons of top soil on June 4, 1937.

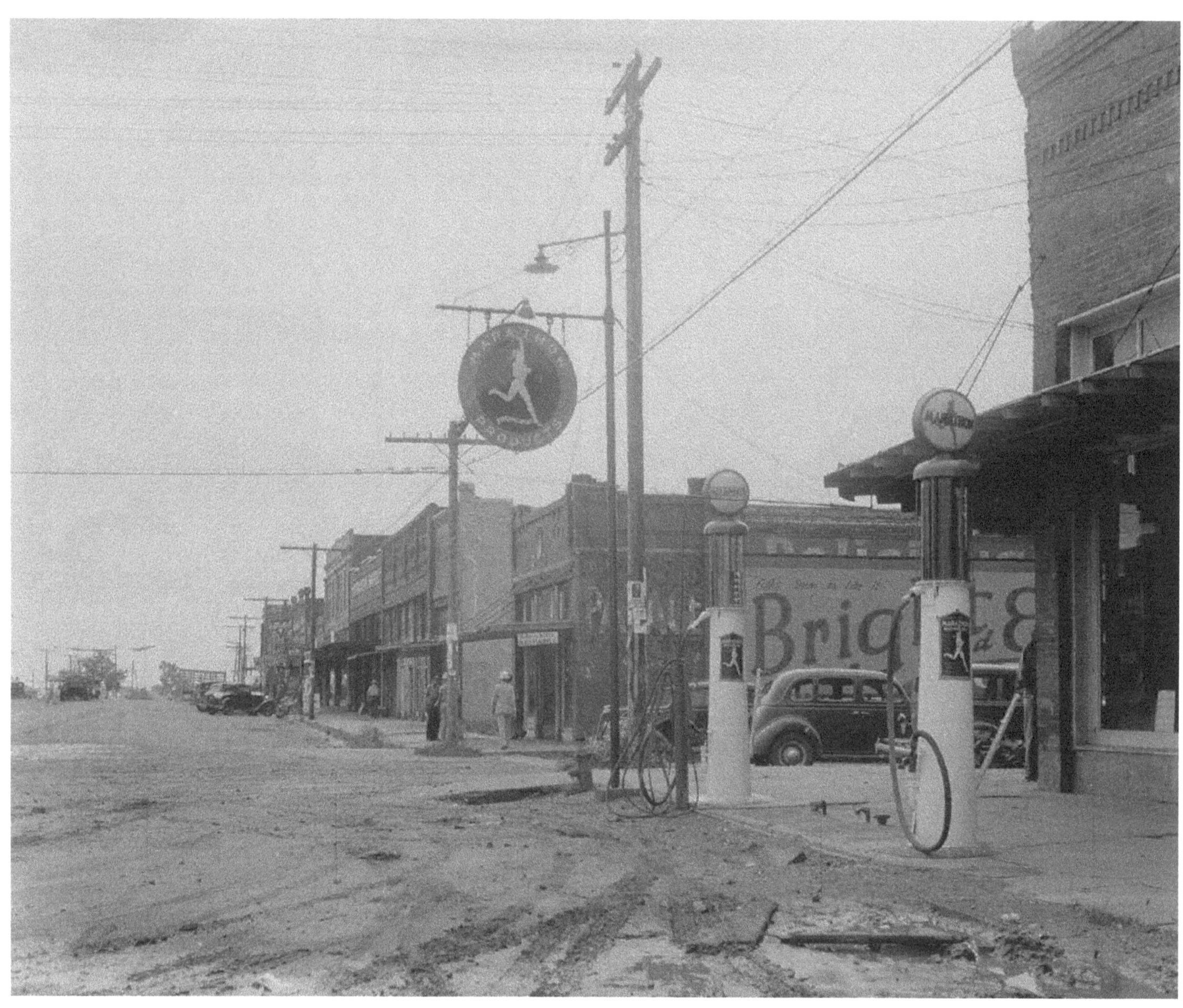

Dorothea Lange snapped this photo of downtown Caddo in 1938 to illustrate the decimation of small towns during the Okie migrations. Caddo grew up around a depot on the Katy Railroad in 1872. The Katy was the only road authorized to cross Indian Territory, and Caddo grew quickly as a market center—but only for a short while.

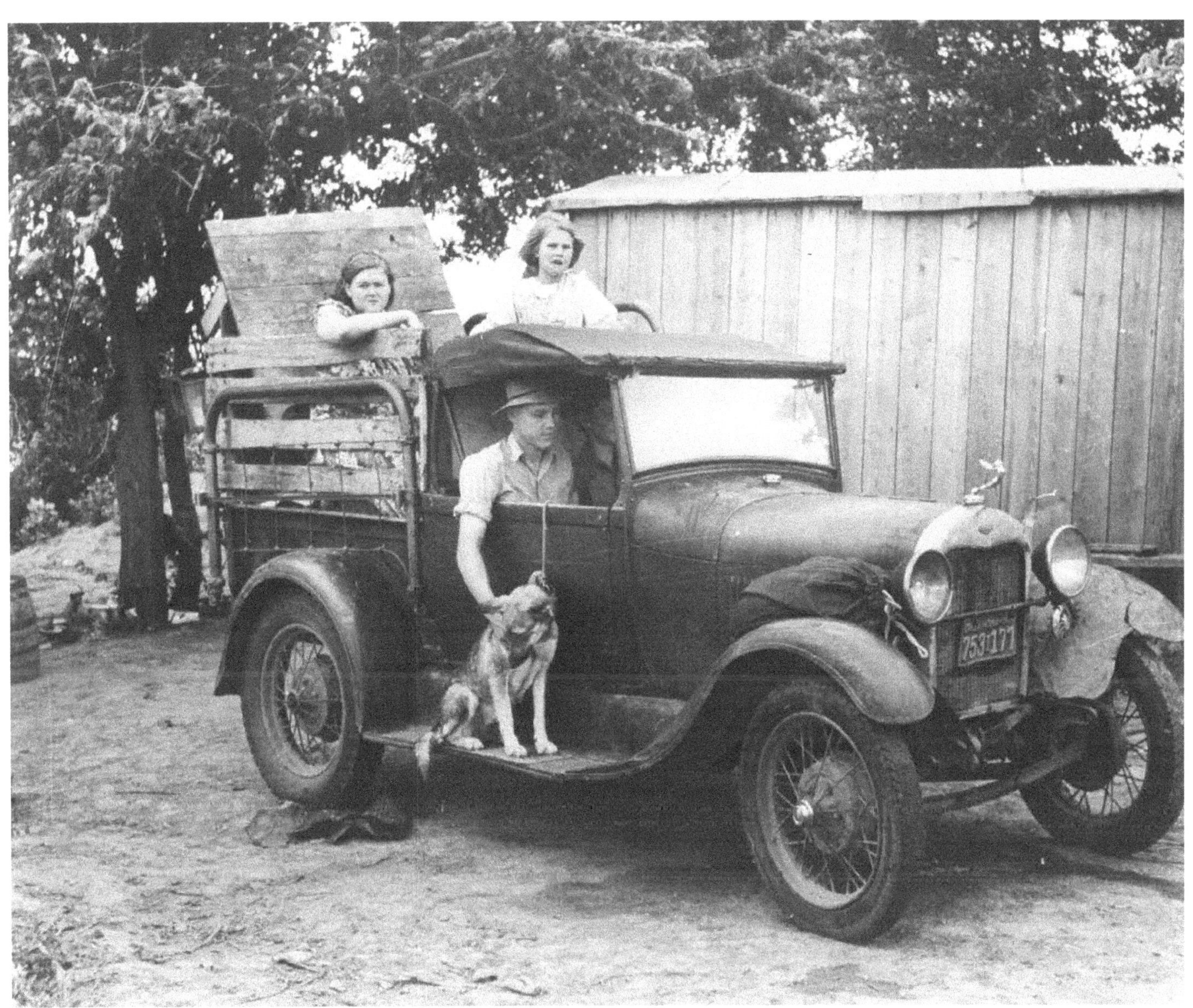

A family near Muskogee, packed up and ready to go to California, July 1939. Oklahomans had been migrating to California in the decades before the Okie migrations, and many of those who left in the 1930s were answering calls by their families to join them in better conditions out west.

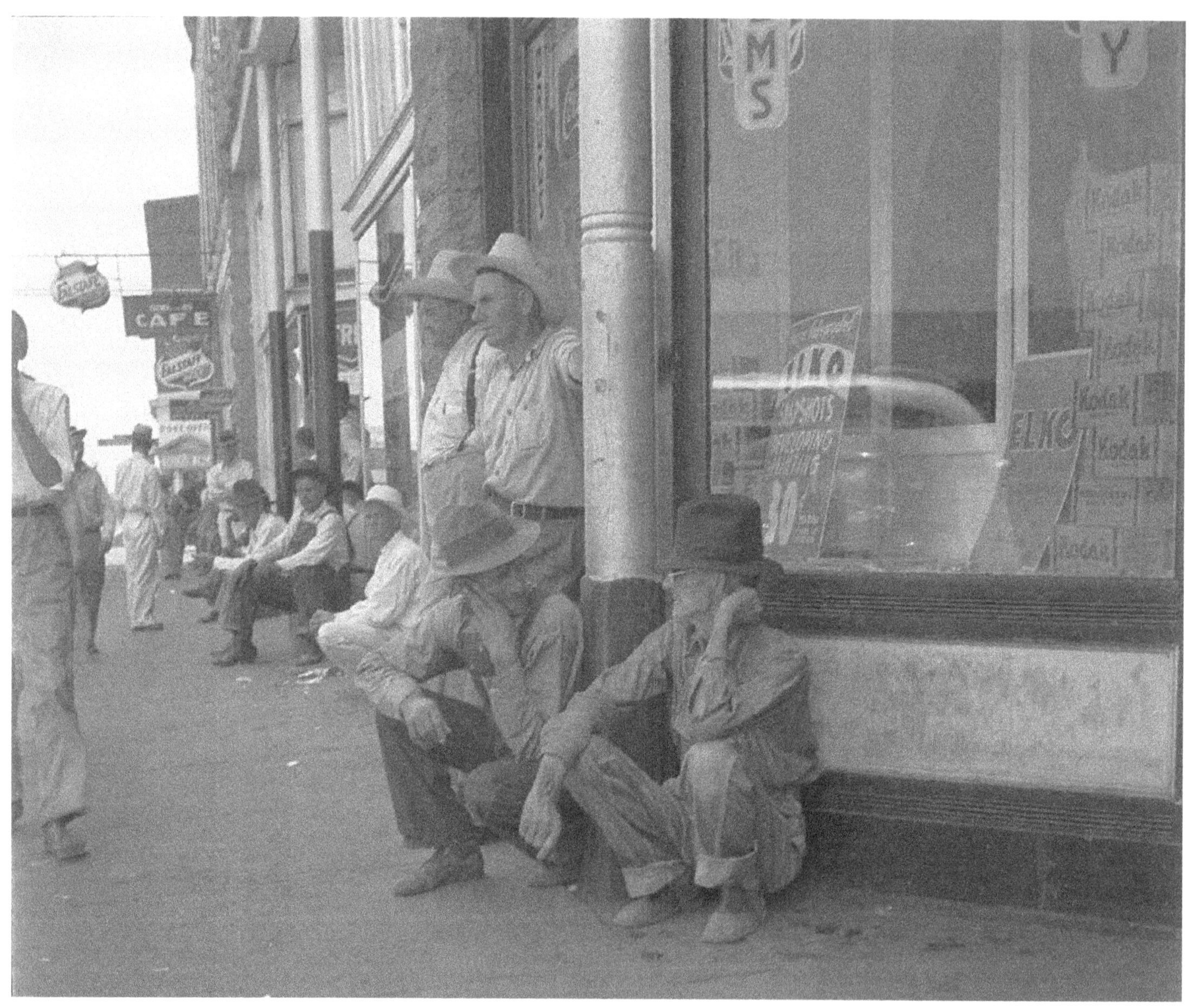

Idle farmers loiter on a street corner in Sallisaw, the home of John Steinbeck's Joad family, in this 1936 photo by Dorothea Lange. While farmers in northwest Oklahoma were beset by dust storms, farmers in the east were troubled by drought, low prices, foreclosures, and mechanization. Many left for what they thought were greener pastures out west.

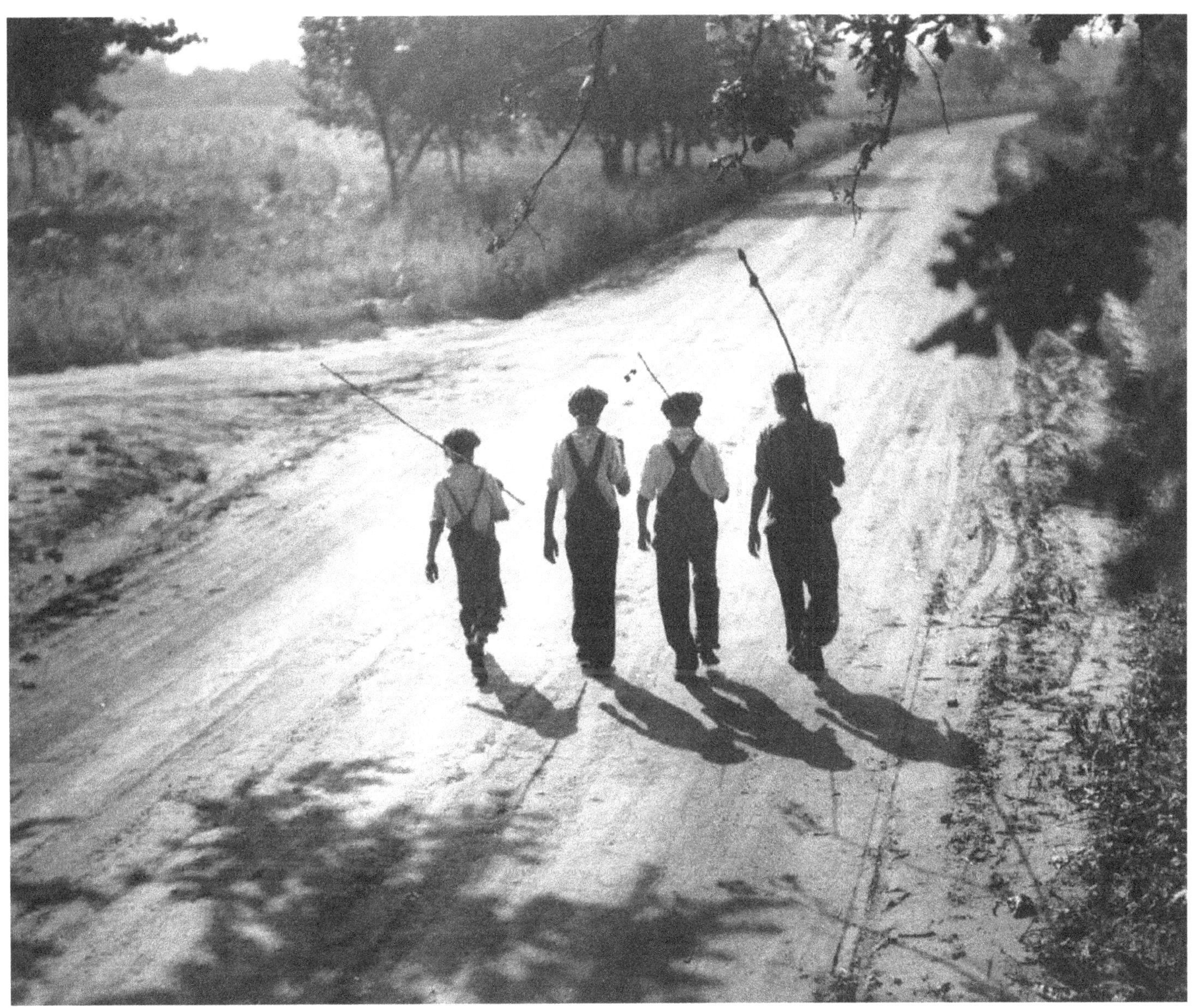

An end to innocence: boys headed for a fishing hole near Muskogee, 1937. Boys like these would experience great change in Oklahoma and the nation as they endured a childhood in the Depression and attained young manhood serving in World War II.

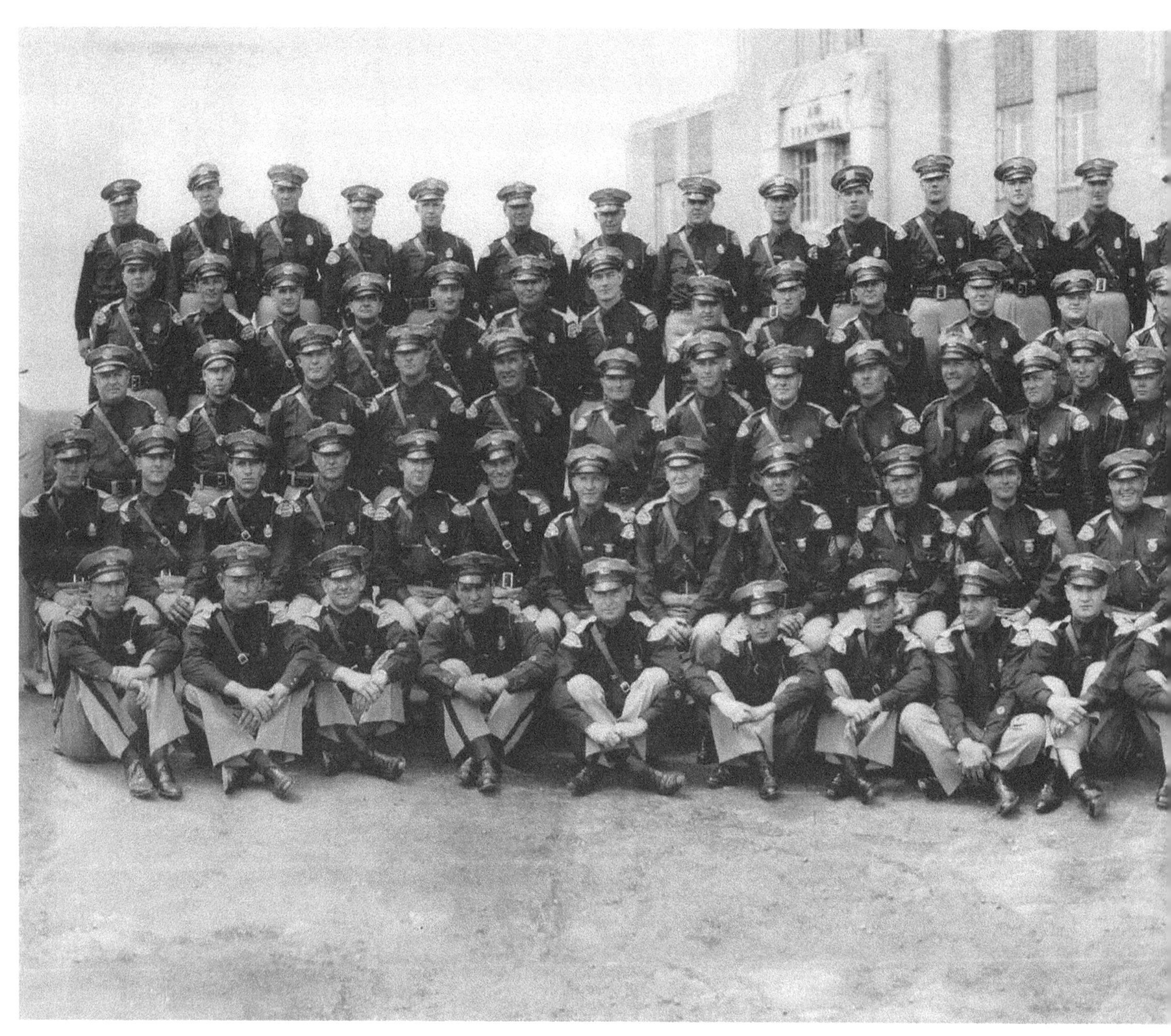

Concerned about the state's deadly roads, Governor Marland formed the Oklahoma State Highway Patrol to enforce a slew of new traffic laws in 1937. Oklahoma drivers had never had licenses or rules, so these first patrolmen, seen in 1938, were specially trained to be courteous and respectful. The tradition continues today.

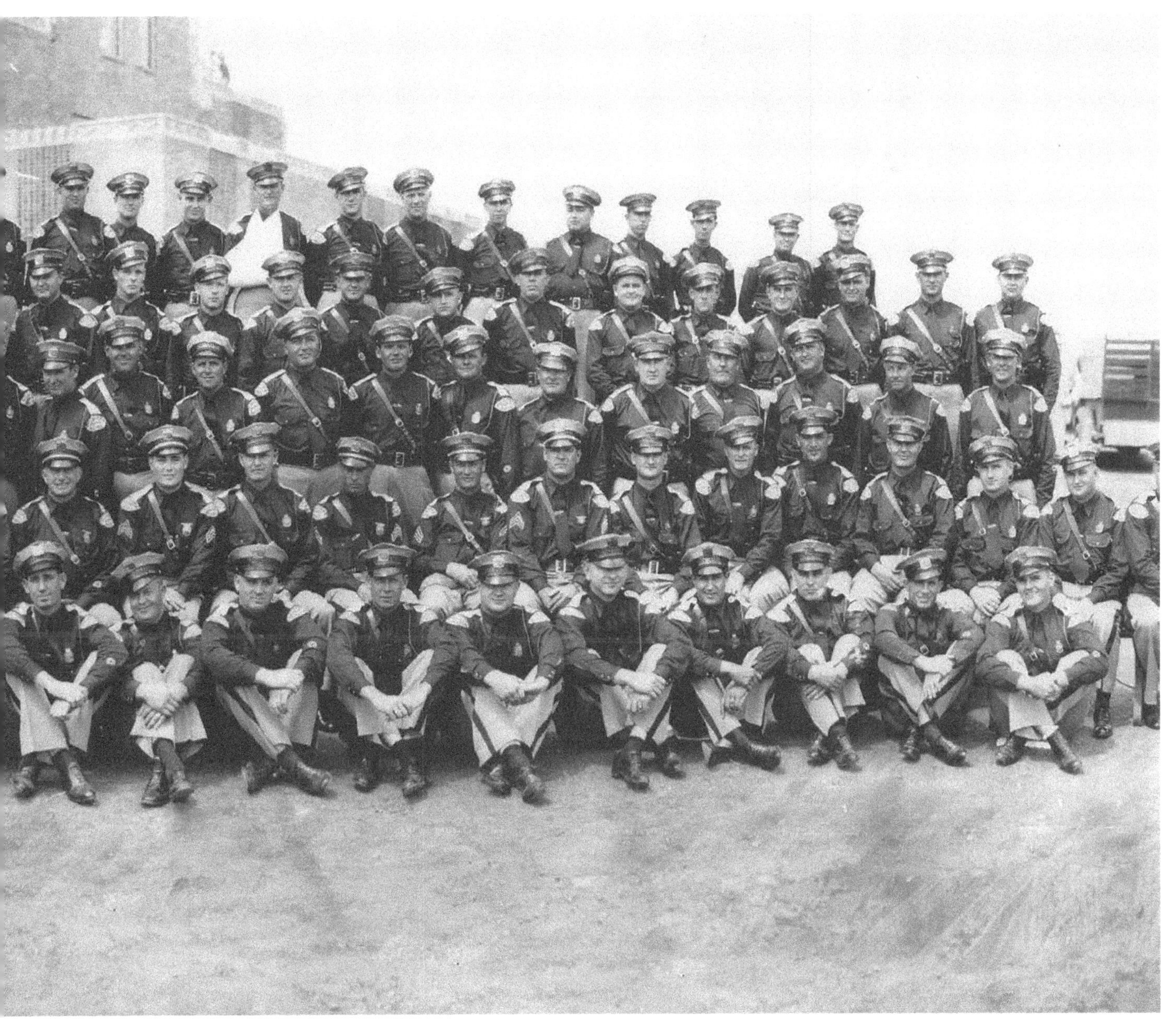

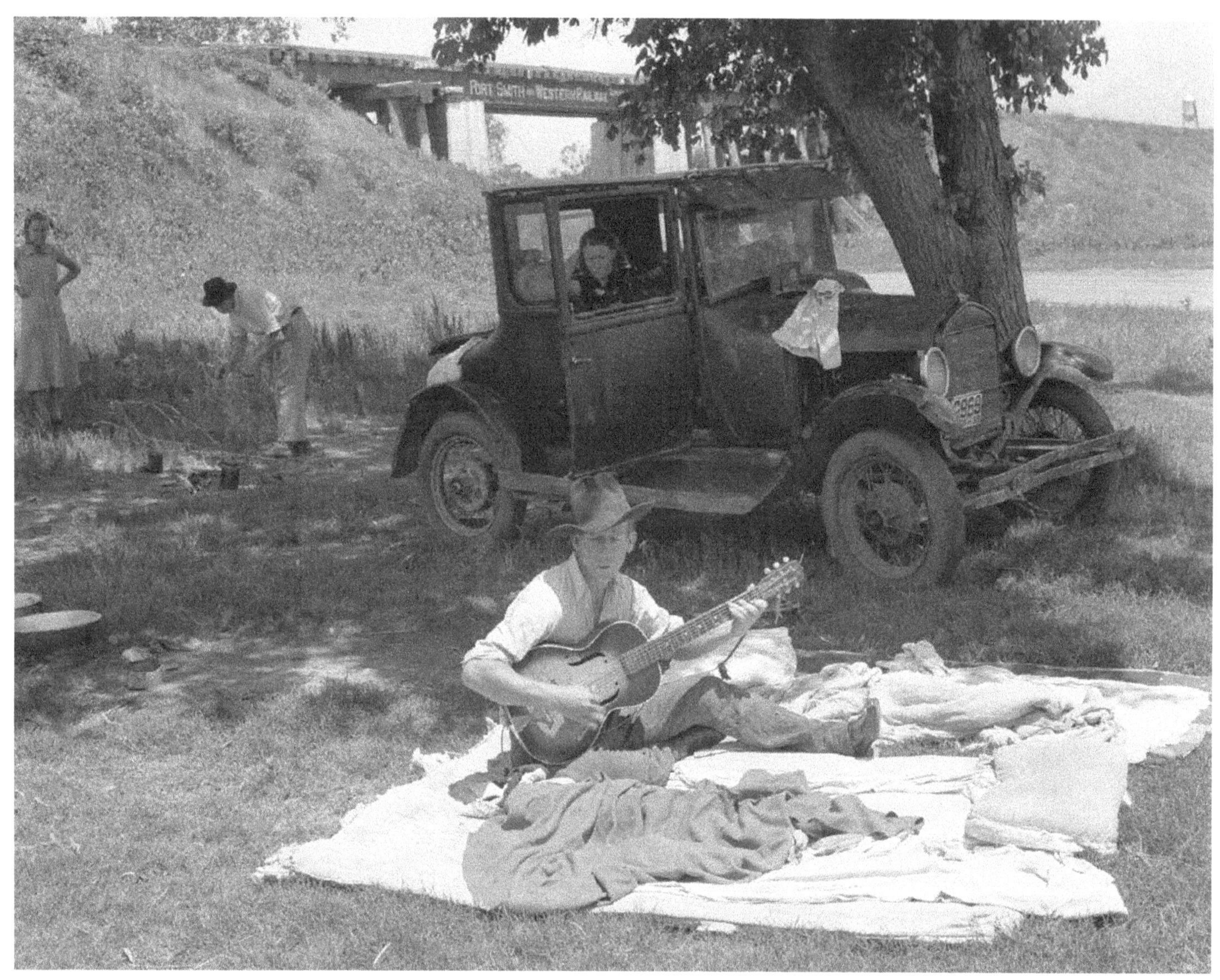

Migrant workers camped near Prague, 1939. Not all migrants went west to work in California's fields; many roamed the Southwest picking up government jobs or performing odd jobs to carry them to their next meal. Photographed by Russell Lee, this fellow evokes the image of another Oklahoman, Woody Guthrie.

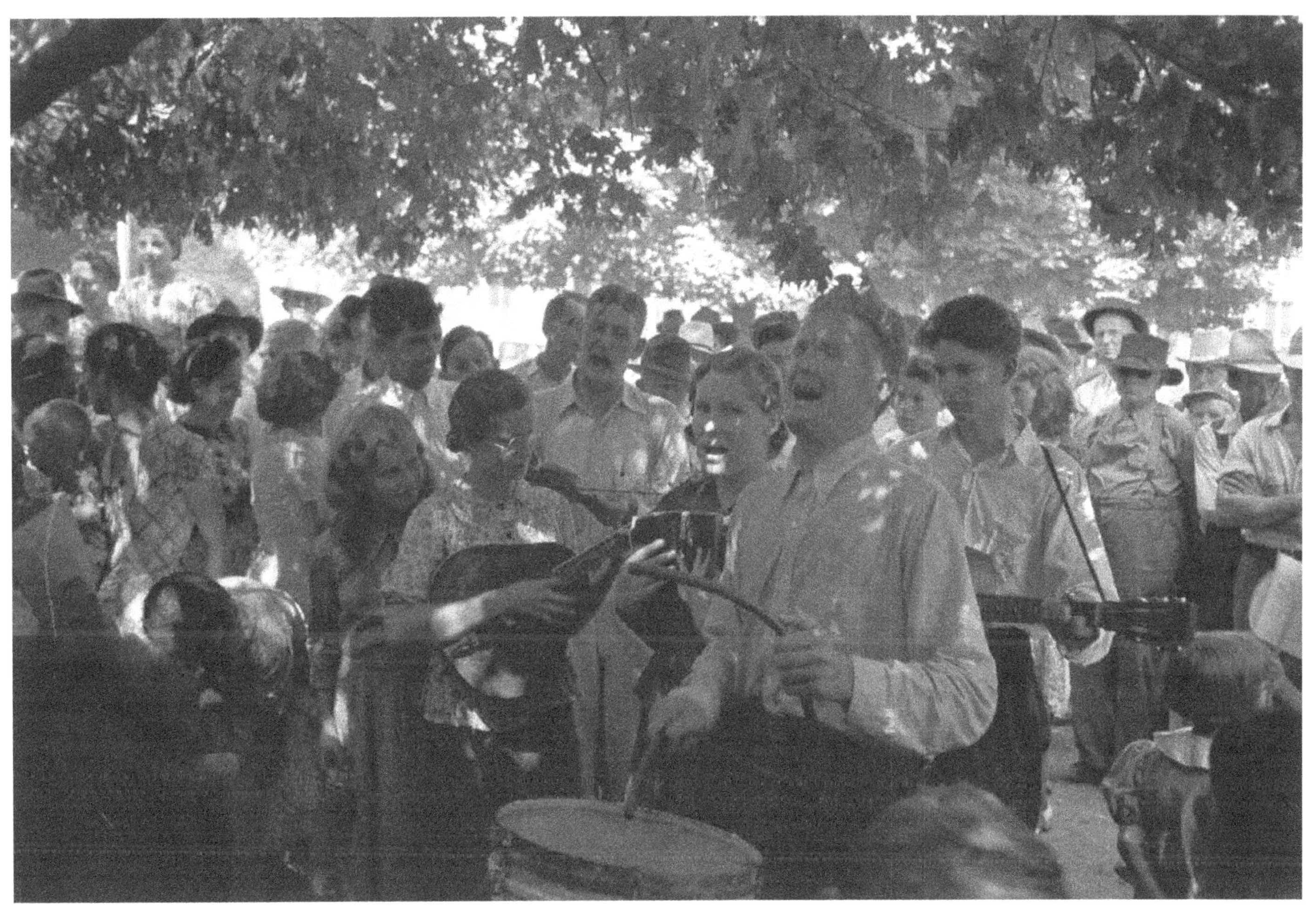

Oklahoma was settled largely by adherents to evangelical movements in mainstream Protestant denominations, and a number of newly formed ones as well. Revivals, like this one in Tahlequah in 1939, were a common sight throughout the state, but especially so during the challenging times of the Depression.

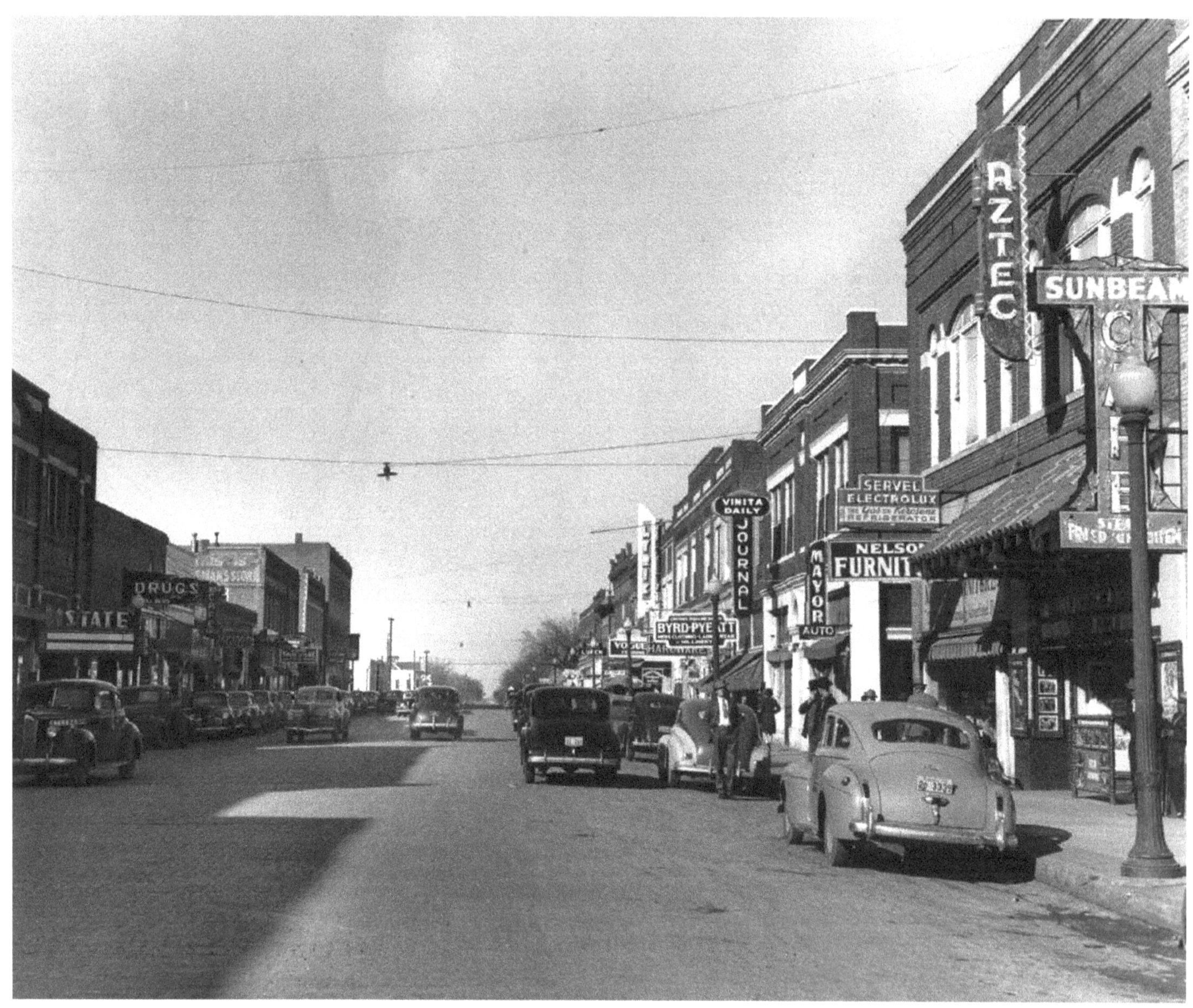

Route 66 as it passes along Vinita's Wilson Street in 1939. Established along the Katy Railroad in 1872, Vinita was one of the first towns in the state to incorporate.

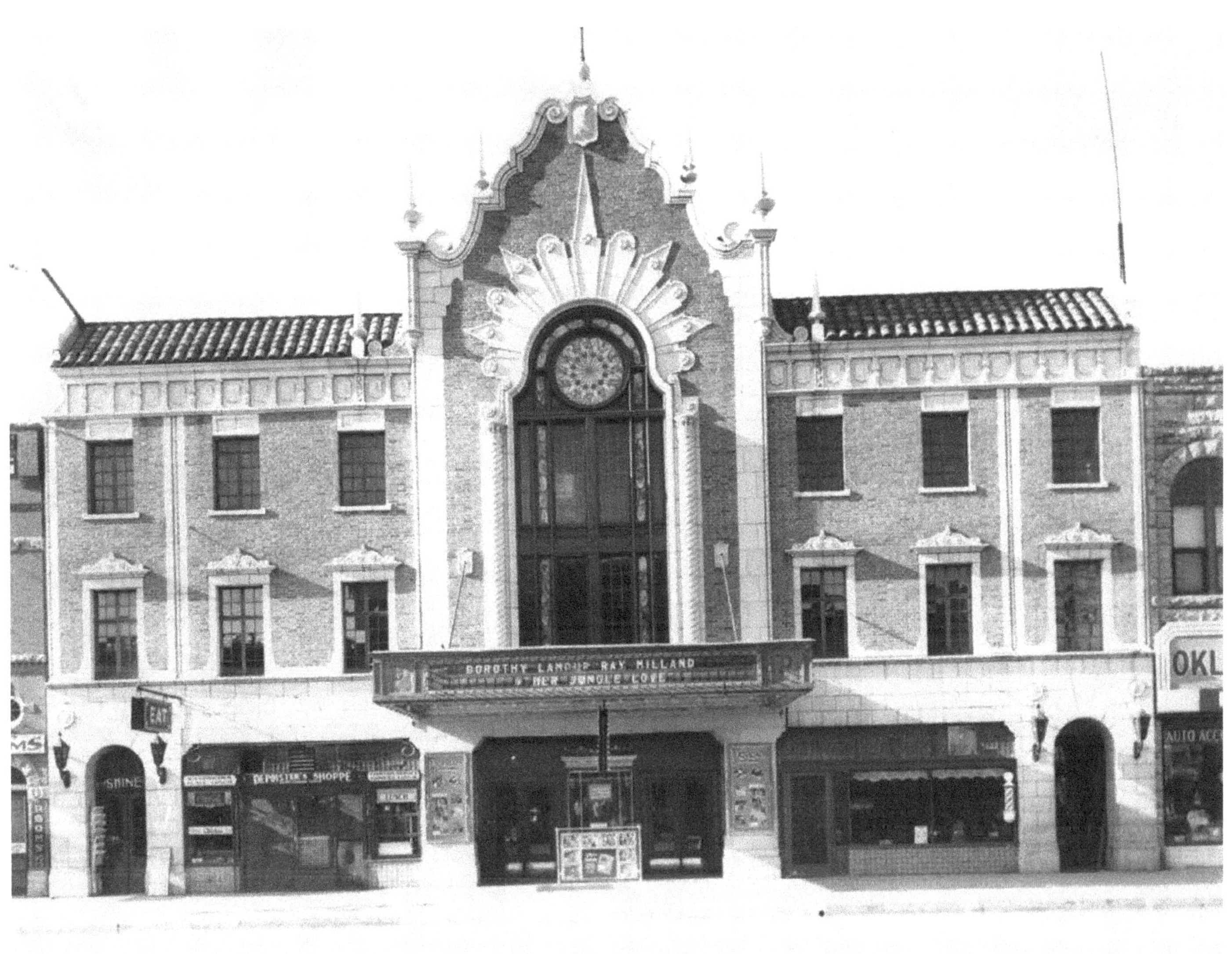

The Poncan Theatre, seen here around 1938, is a fine example of the Spanish Revival style found throughout the architecture of Ponca City's golden era. The theater was built to accommodate silent movies, but talkies debuted the same week it opened in 1927. The Poncan is still an active theater for plays and films.

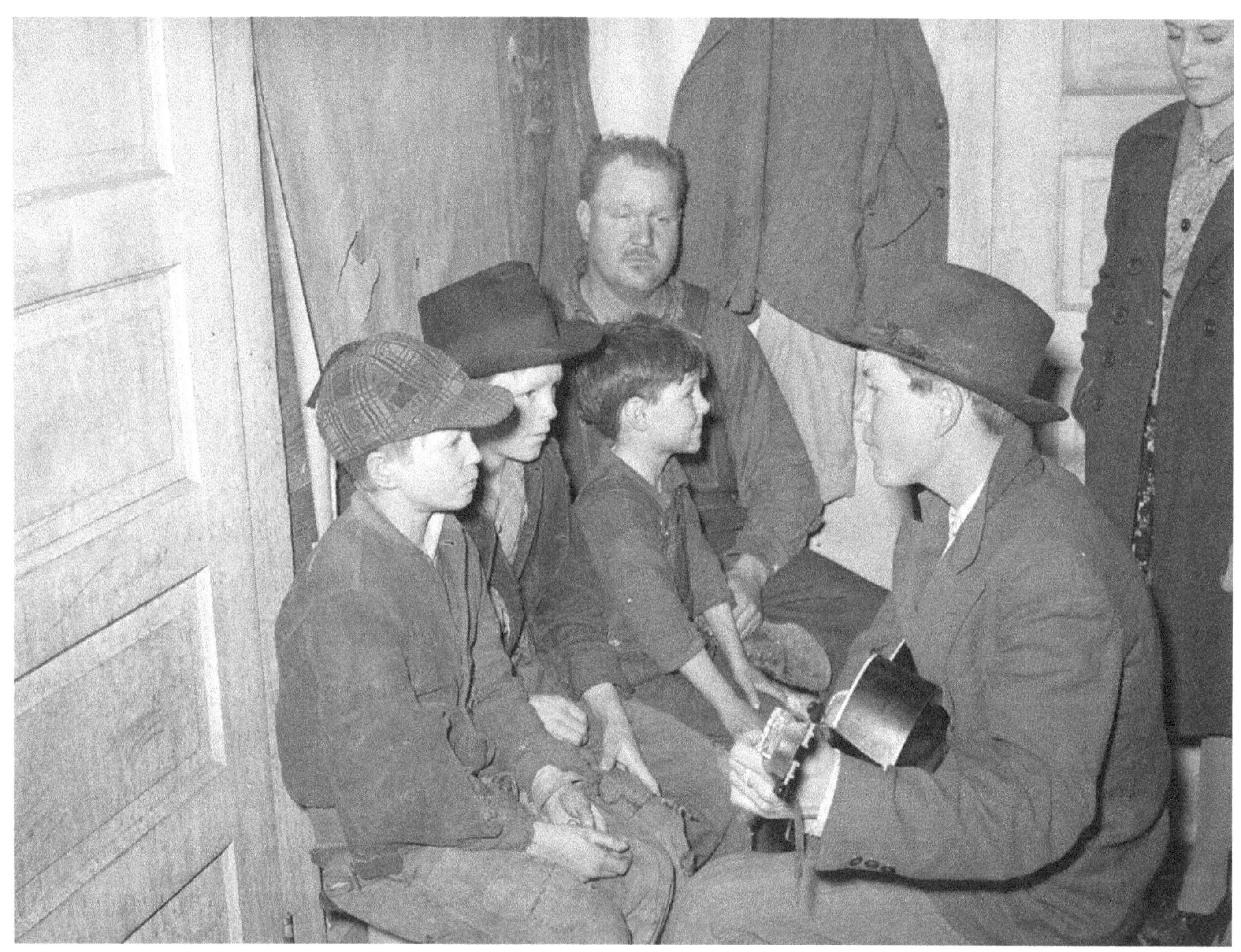

Farm Security Administration lensman Russell Lee captured this scene during a community gathering in McIntosh County, 1939. The barn dance and the play party were folk traditions carried to Oklahoma by its earliest settlers, and many such entertainments continued into the 1950s before urbanization began to diminish them.

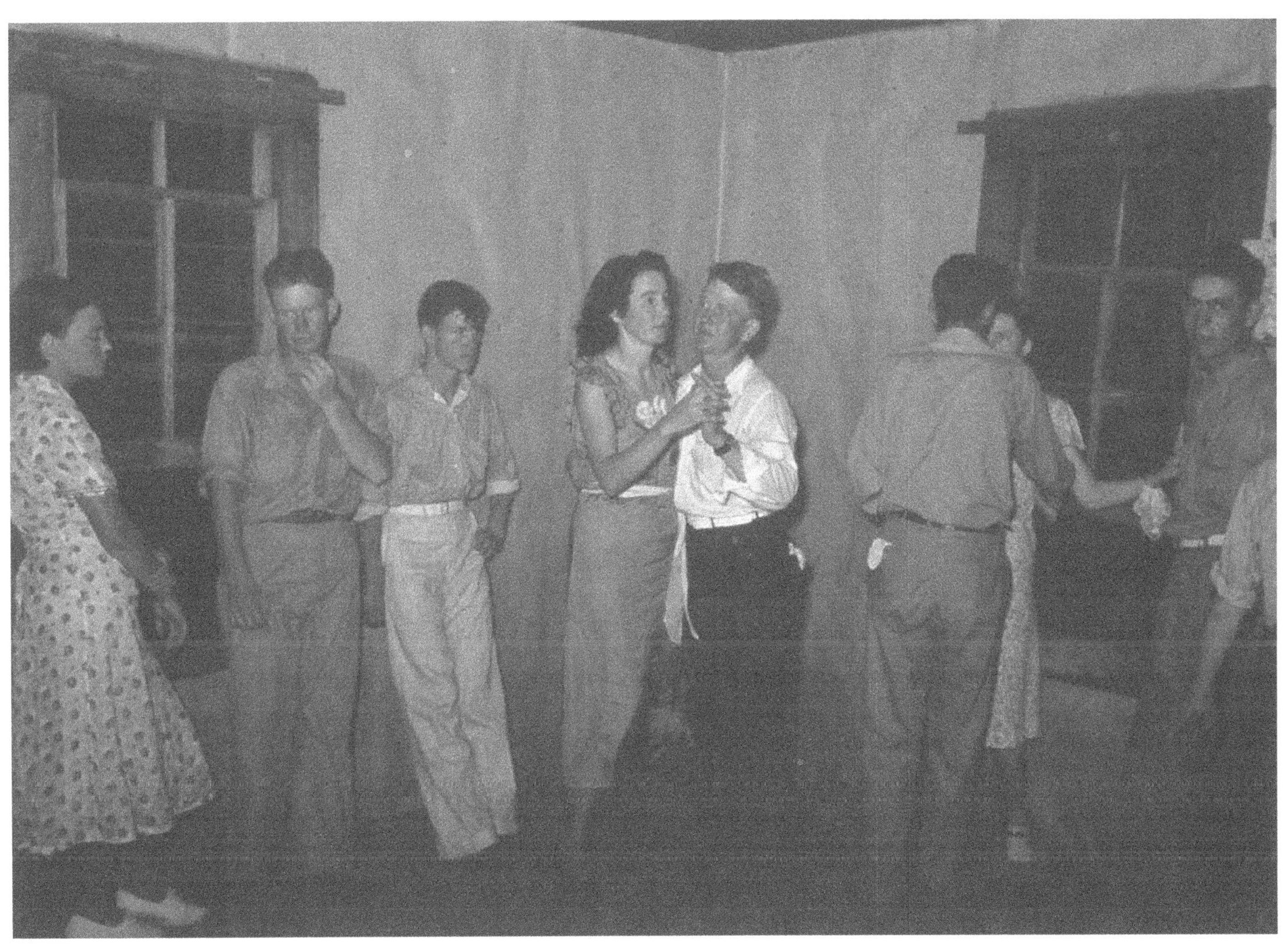

Another image from Russell Lee's series on life in McIntosh County shows a typical dance scene of the era. Gatherings were usually held in farmhouses or barns and involved dances, party games, and potluck meals.

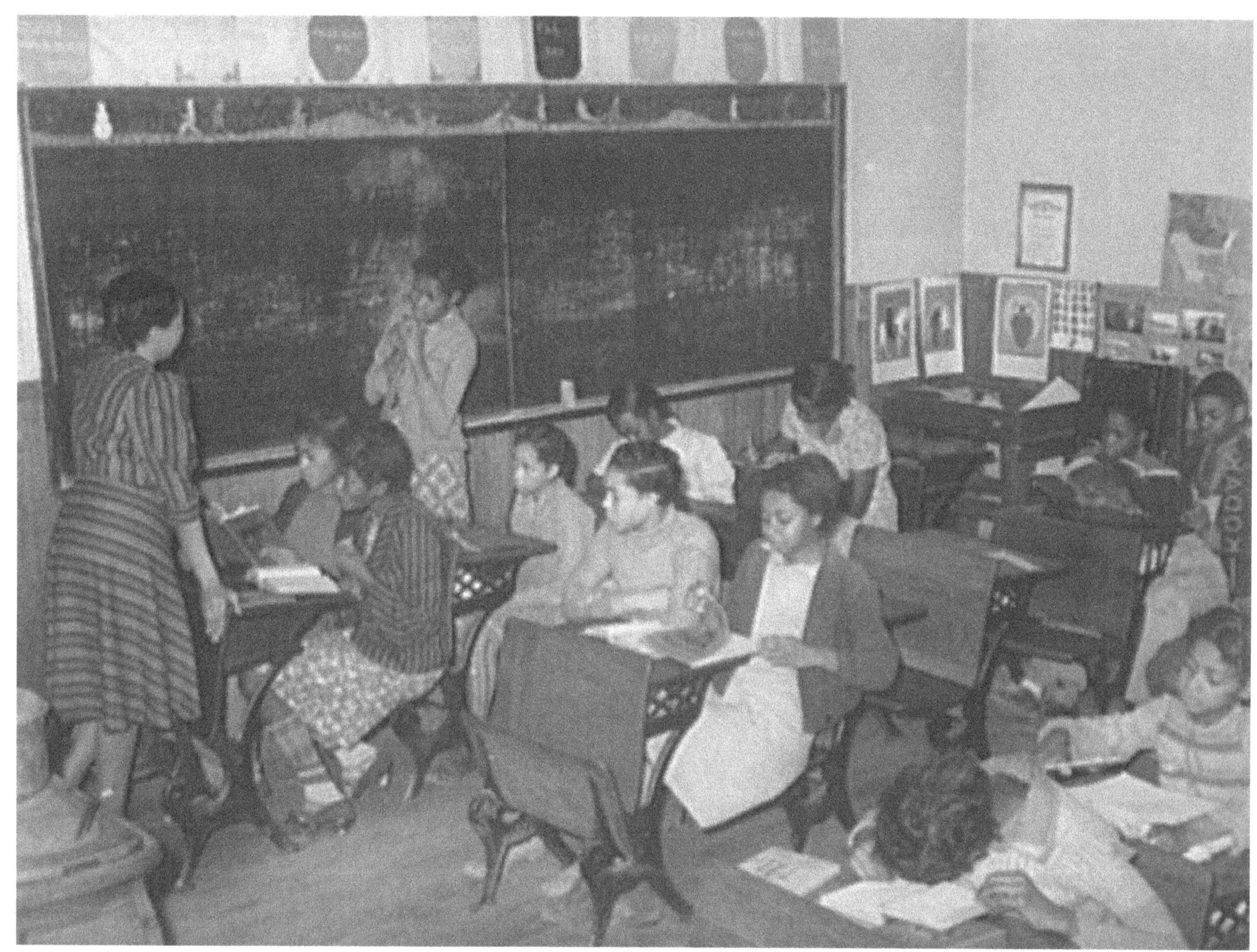

This scene of African-American students in a rural separate school near Tabor in 1940 would change dramatically in the 1950s when Governor Raymond Gary consolidated and integrated thousands of schools across the state.

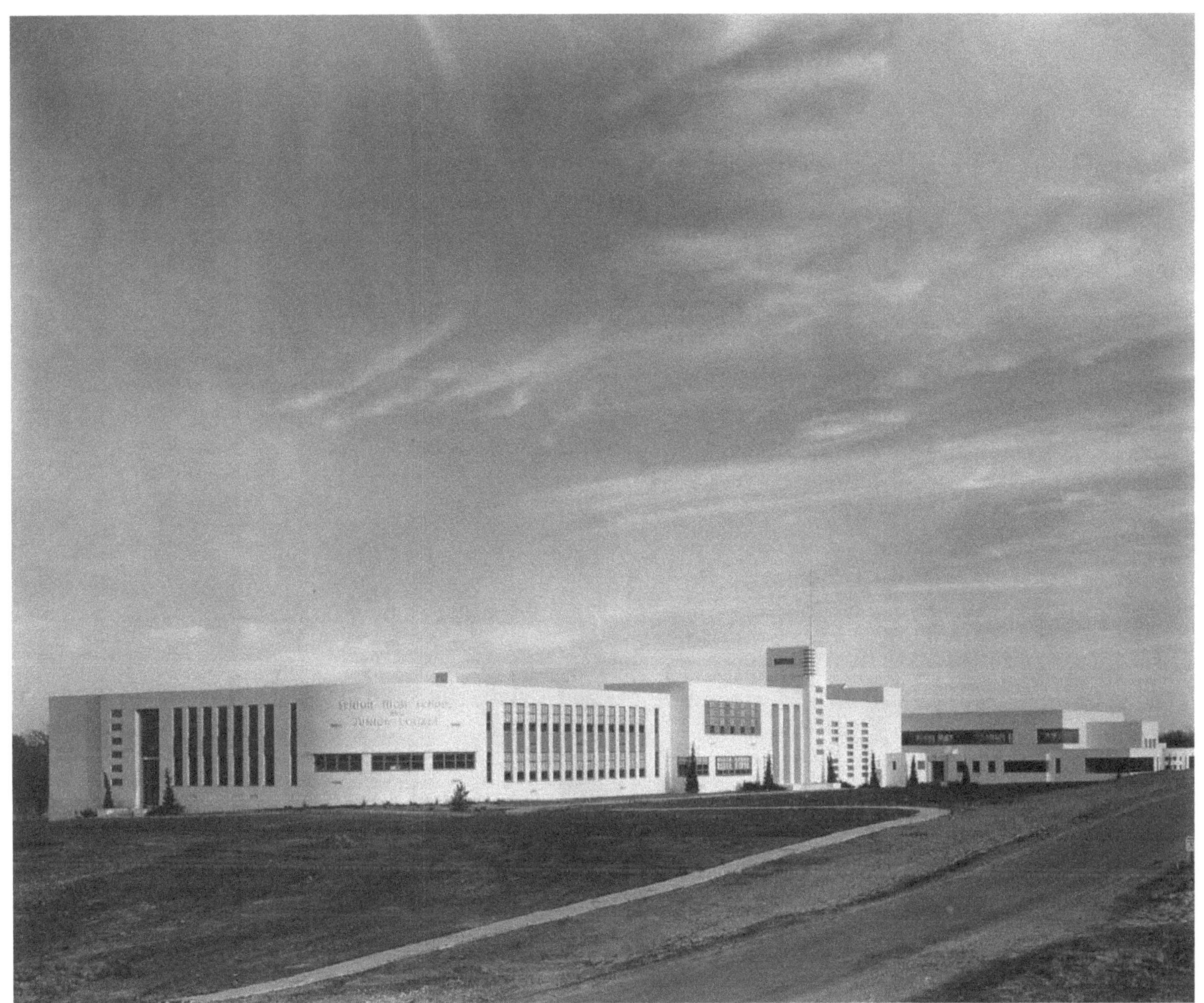

Bartlesville's College High was so named because it included a high school and junior college when it was built by the Public Works Administration. The streamline-moderne school building, seen here in 1940, is still in use as a high school but no longer includes the junior college.

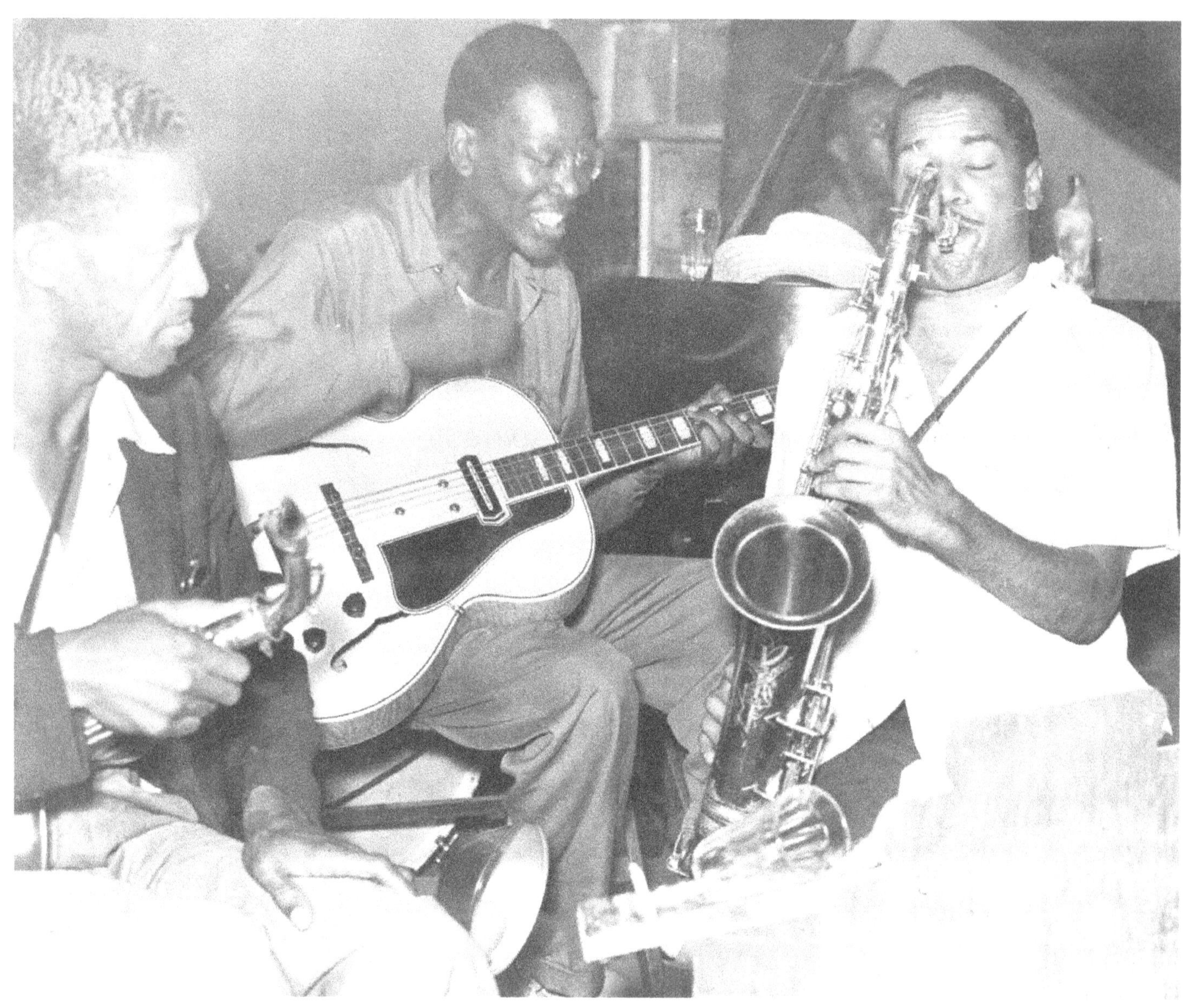

Jazz guitar legend Charlie Christian, who grew up in Oklahoma City, reunites with old friends at Ruby's Grill in the city's Deep Deuce following a tour with Benny Goodman, 1940.

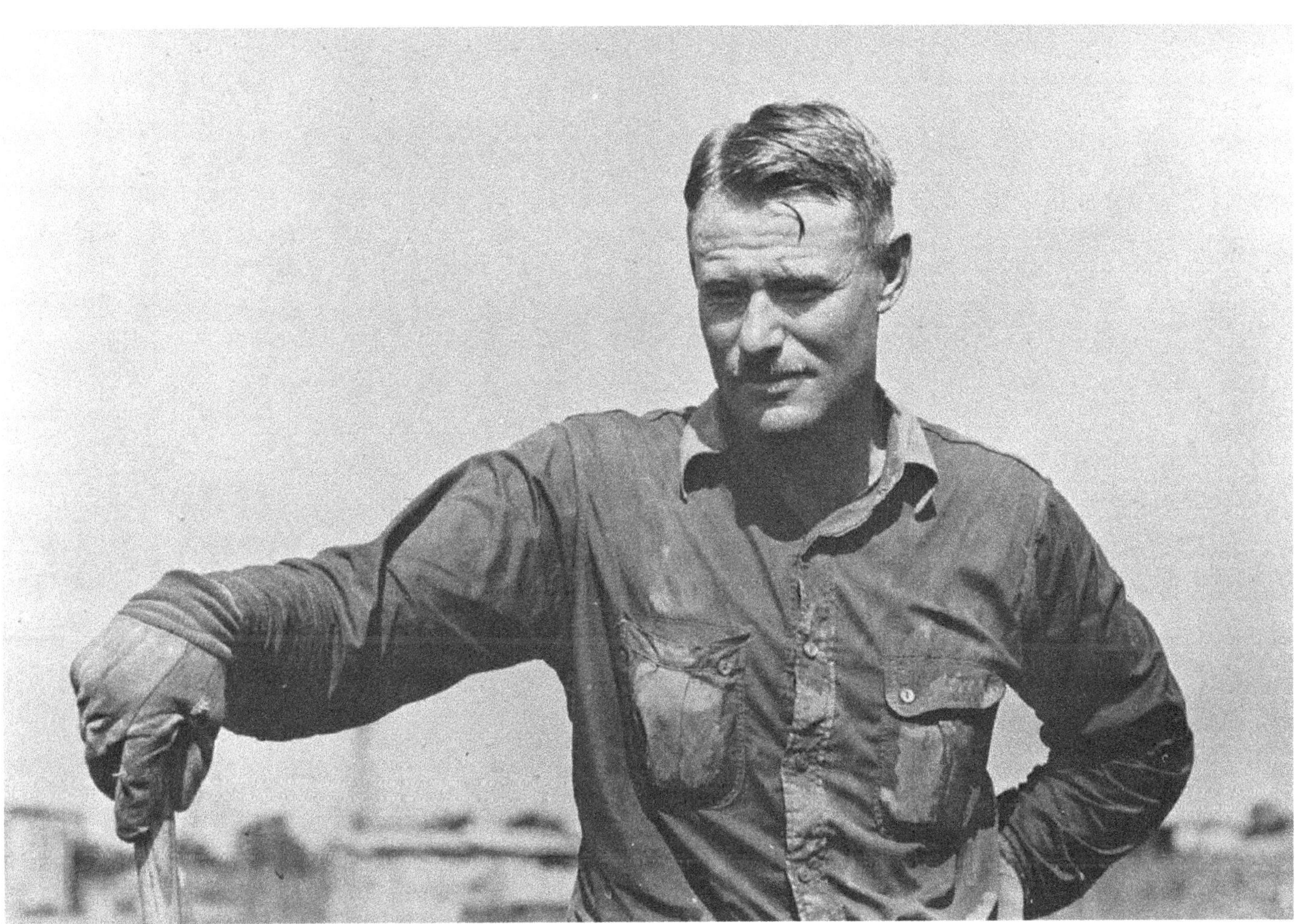

The oil industry buffered the state's economy from some of the worst effects of the Depression by offering employment to thousands of workers. As this roustabout in the Seminole Field would attest, most of the work was difficult, dirty, and dangerous, and living conditions were often squalid.

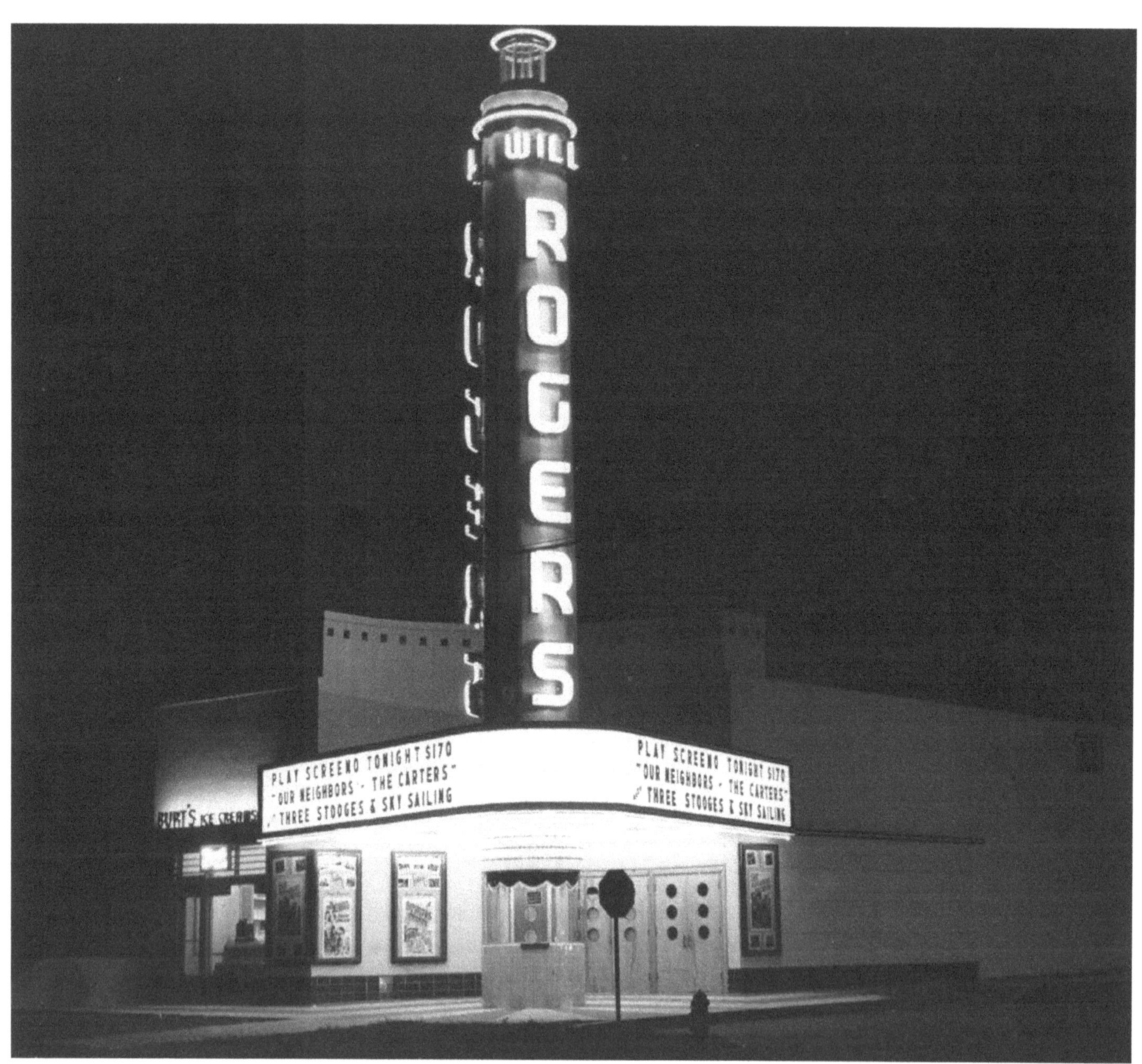

Tulsa's Will Rogers Theatre was a fixture on Eleventh Street from 1941 to 1976. Its sister theater, also designed by Southwest architect Jack Corgan, still stands in Oklahoma City on Western Avenue.

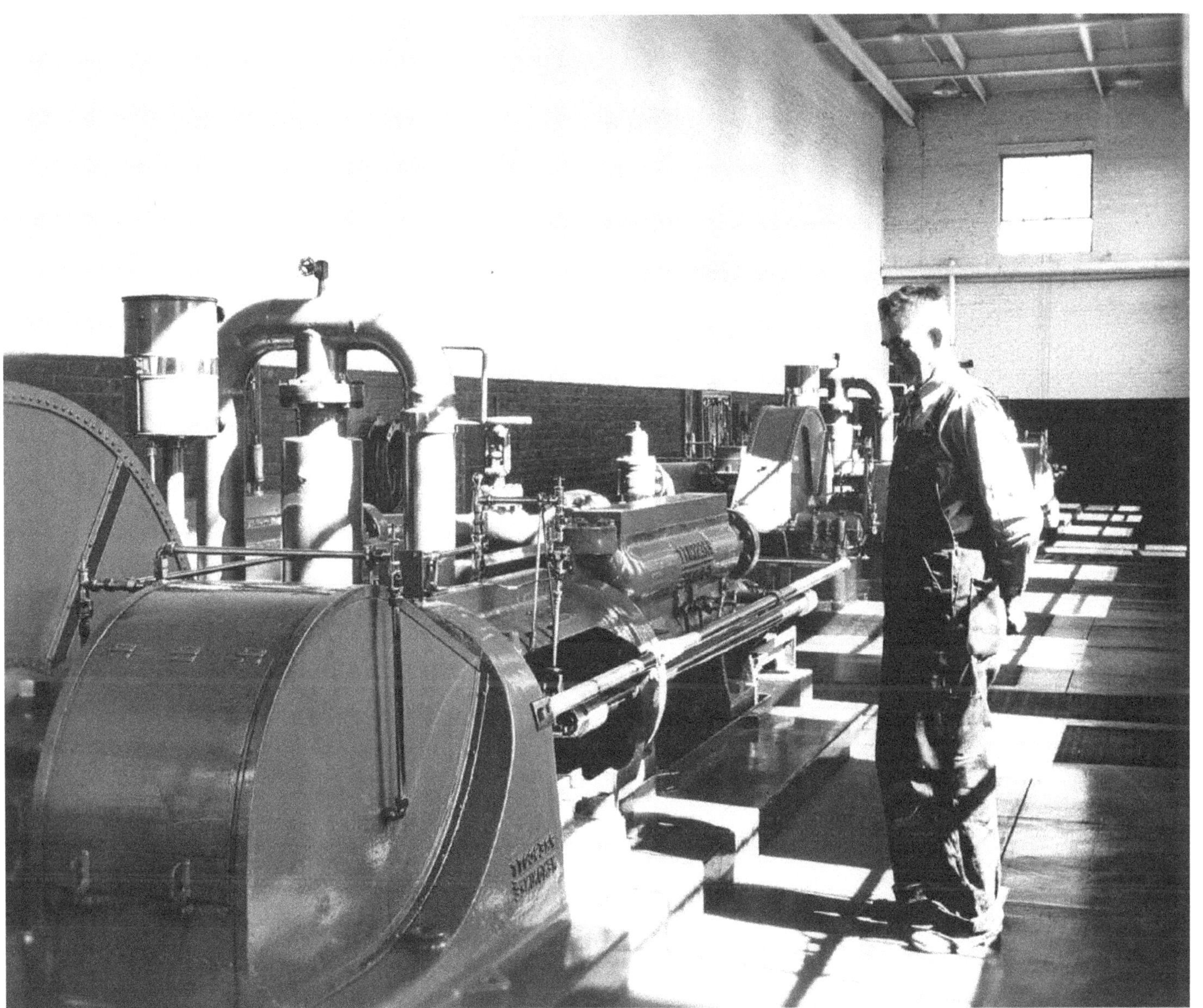

A mechanic tends his machinery at the Great Lakes Pipeline pumping station in Tulsa, November 1942. The station was one of five in the state that pumped gasoline to Ponca City and from there to Chicago and the upper Midwest. At the time, the 1,400-mile route was the longest gasoline pipeline in the world.

Tiger, a Great Dane mascot at the Enid Army Flying School, earned his sergeant's stripes by waking the men in his barracks every morning. Here, in 1942, Lieutenant Robert Davidson poses with Tiger next to a plane at what would become Vance Air Force Base in 1948.

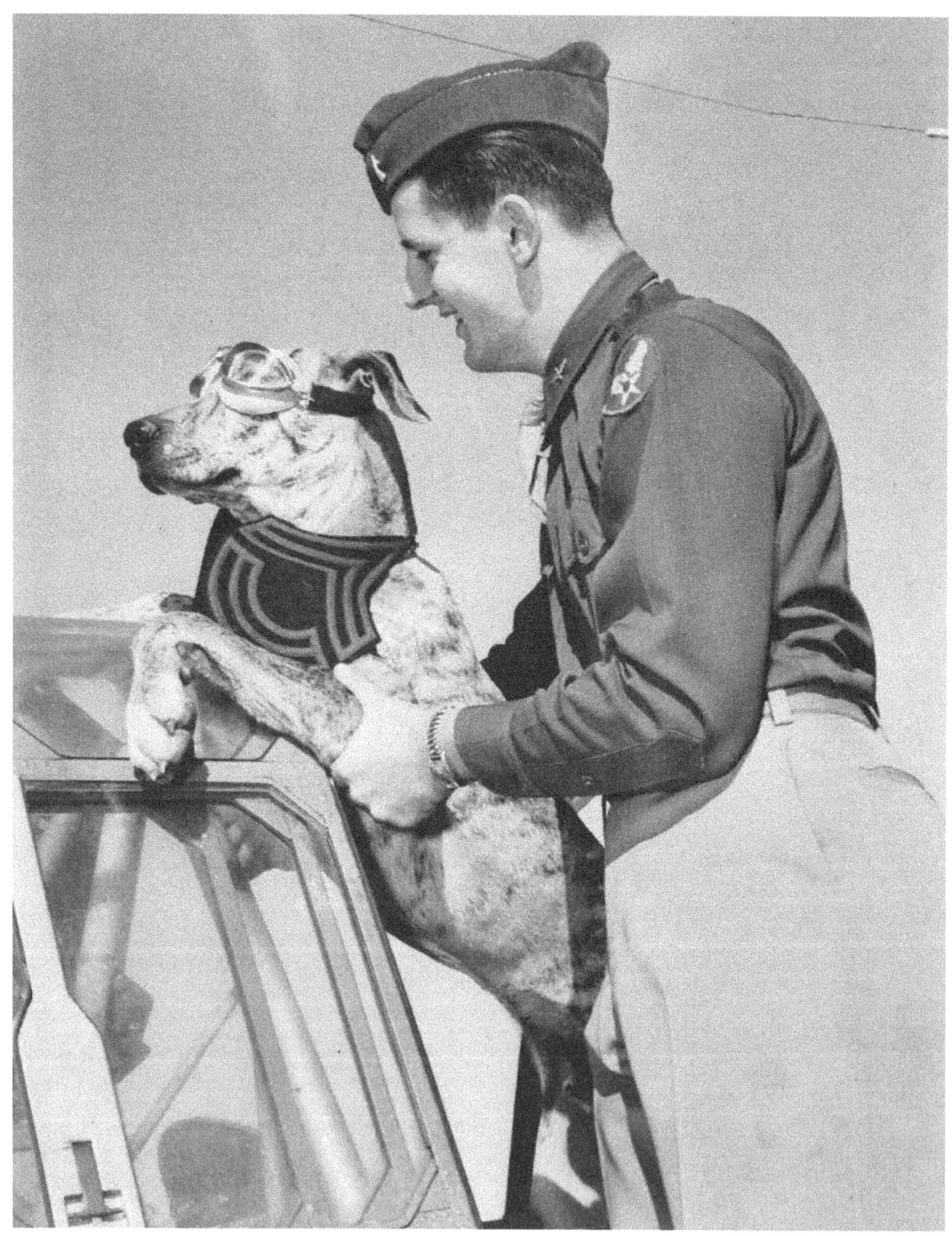

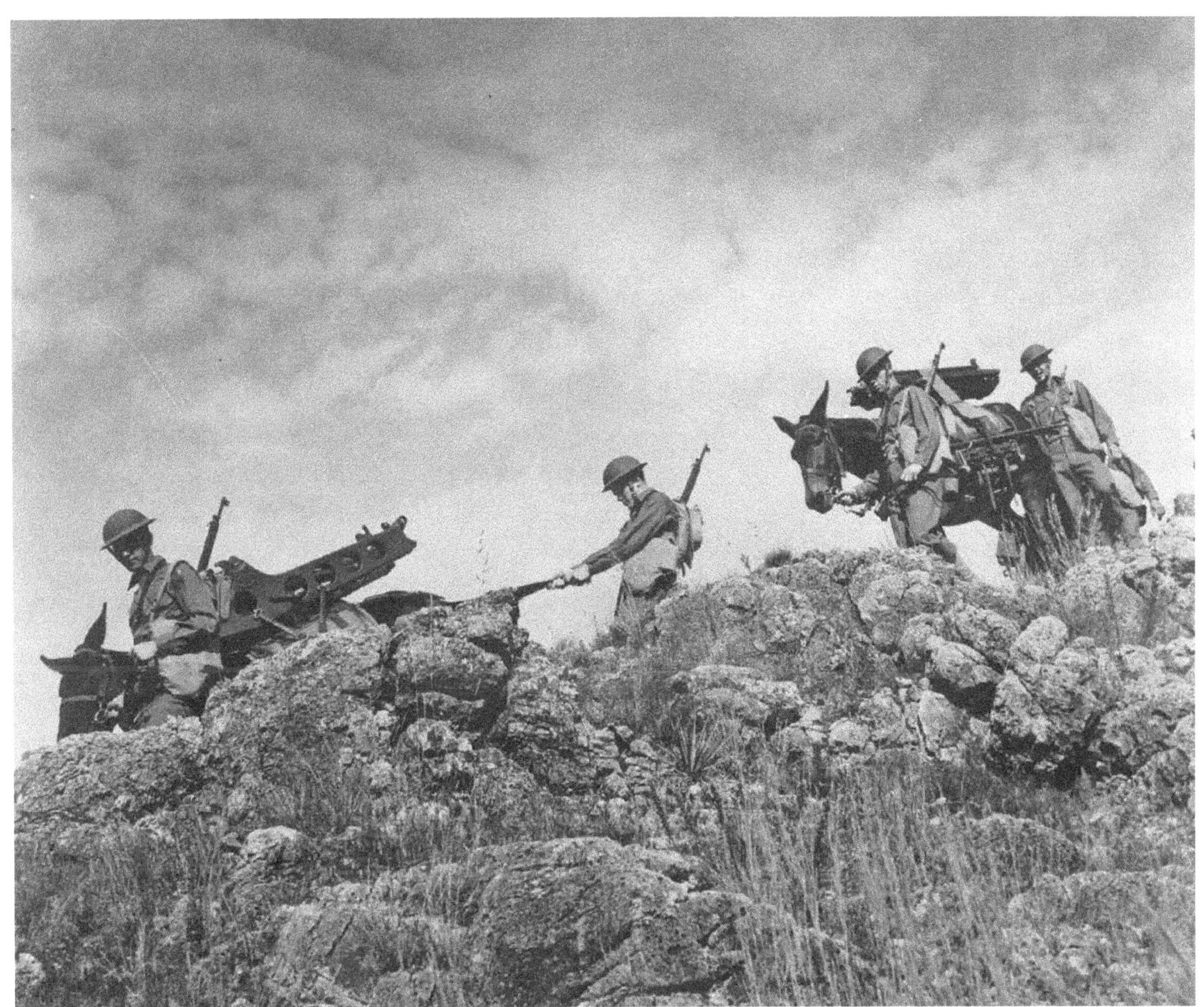

Pack mules train with artillerymen at Fort Sill in 1942. Training in the rugged Wichita Mountains proved to have been quite useful when American soldiers in World War II moved into similar terrain during the Italian campaign of 1943-44.

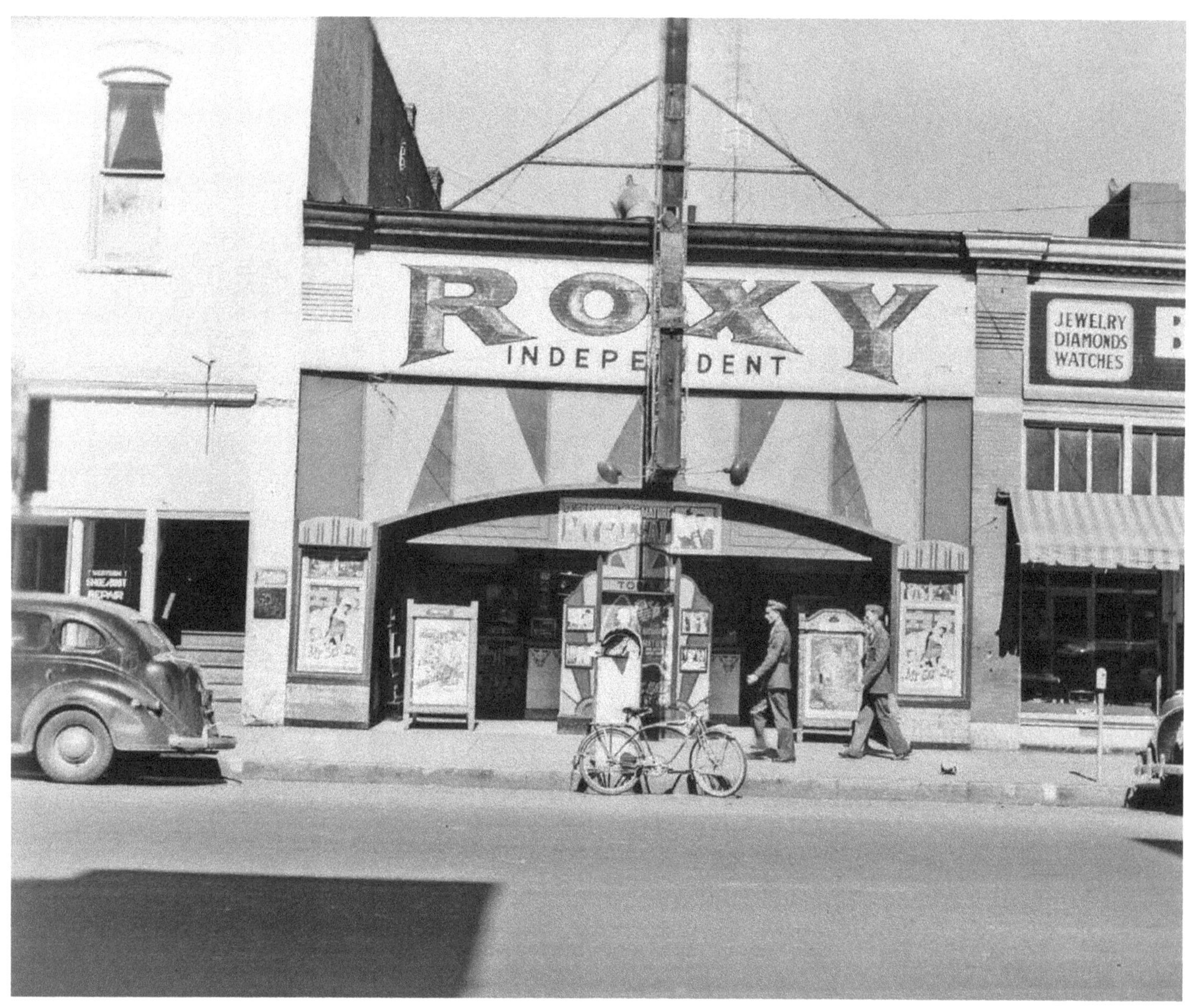

Soldiers stroll by the Roxy Theatre in Muskogee, 1942. Muskogee was the home of two military installations: the Muskogee Army Airfield, and the Army's Camp Gruber, which doubled as a prisoner-of-war camp.

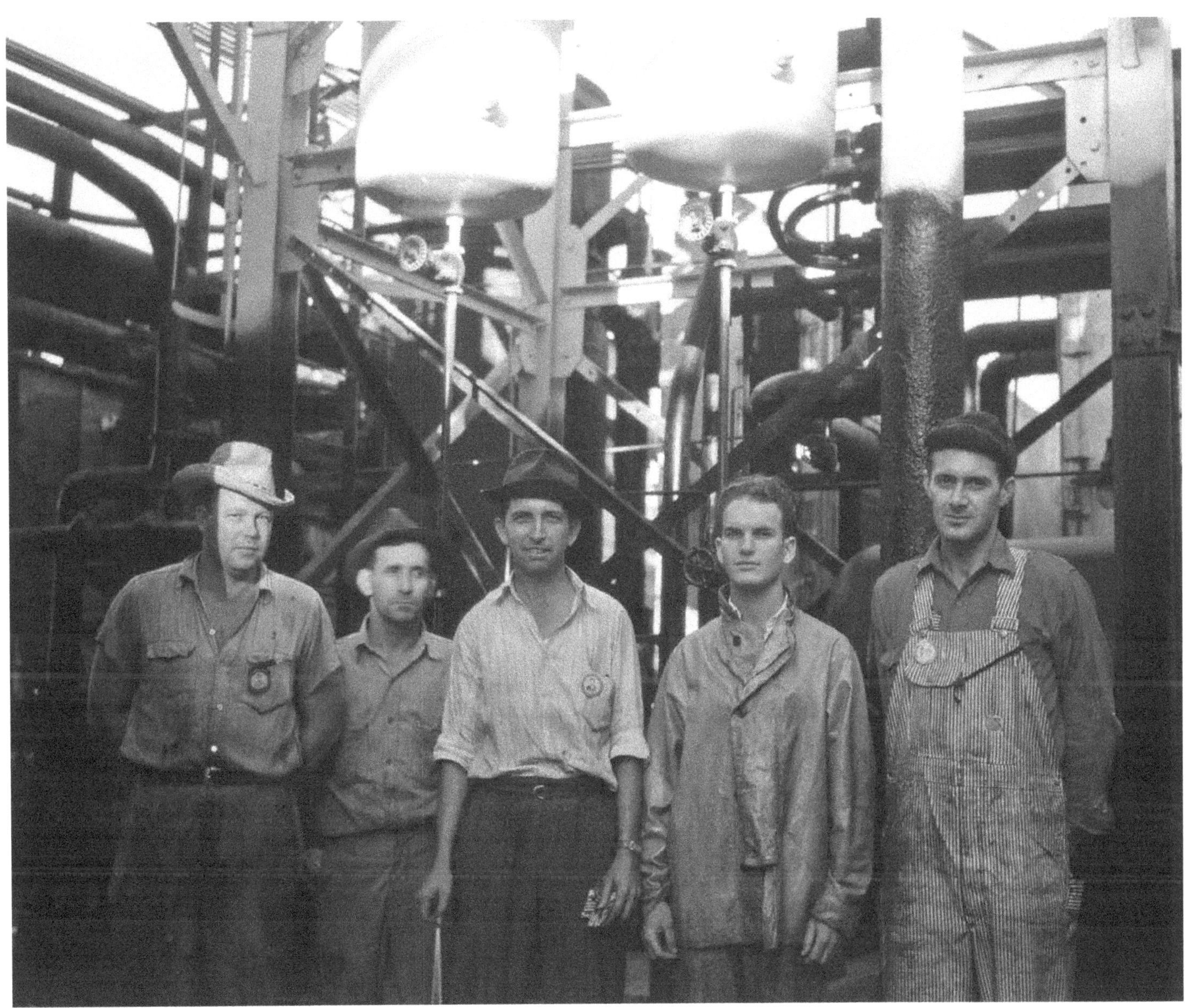

Workers at the Mid-Continent Refinery in Tulsa, 1943. The year before, employees of the refinery ended a lengthy and costly strike that inspired activist folksinger Sis Cunningham to pen a protest song with the lyrics: "All those anti-union ginks / Had better watch their step, by jinks / Or they too will hang from the derrick."

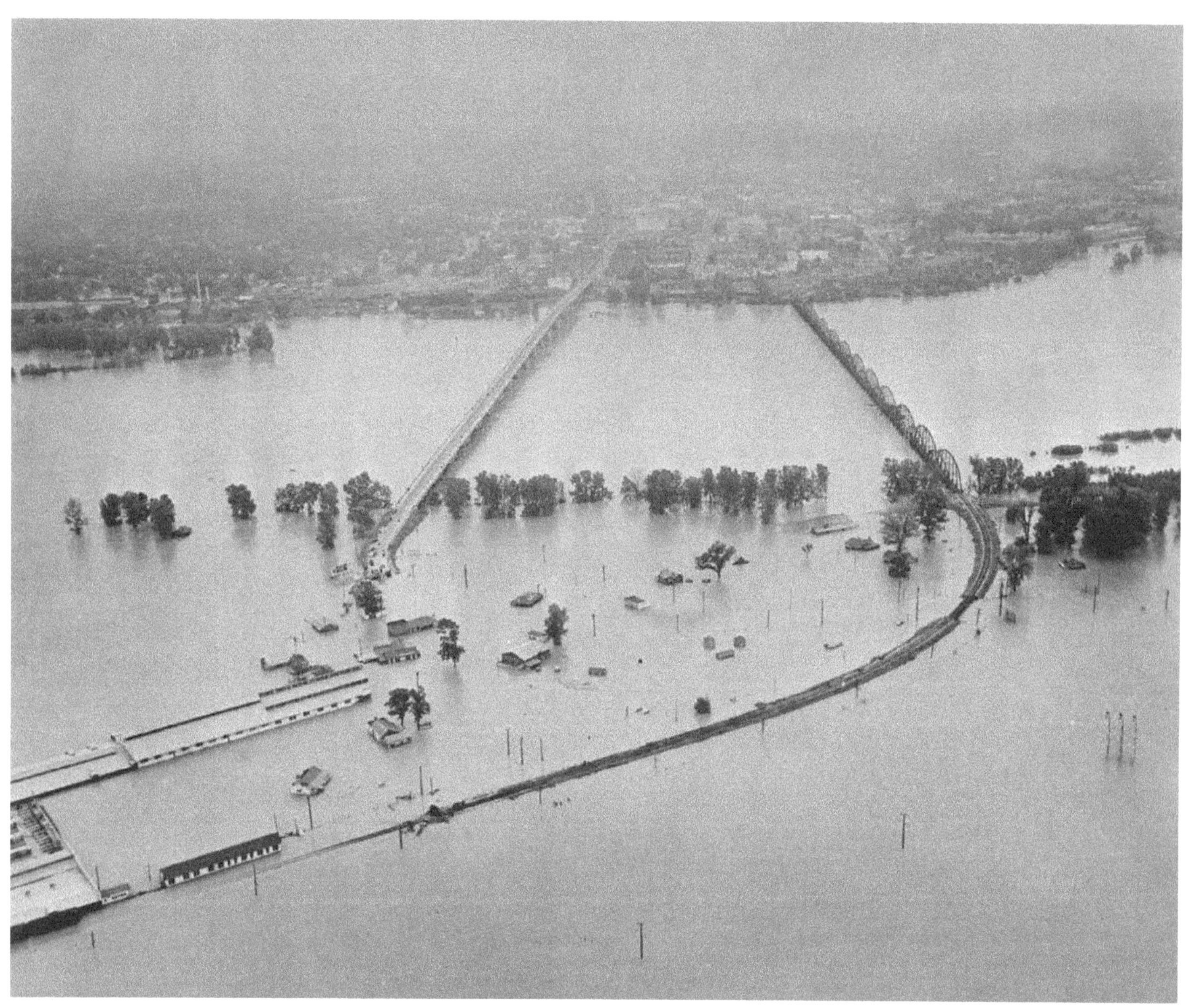

In May 1943 the Arkansas River rose to 110-year-high levels, flooding 600 city blocks of Fort Smith, Arkansas, seen at top, and obliterating nearly a third of the rich bottomlands of Oklahoma's Sequoyah County. Homes from the town of Moffett, Oklahoma, are shown floating away in the flood; those that weren't adrift were socked in with six feet of sand.

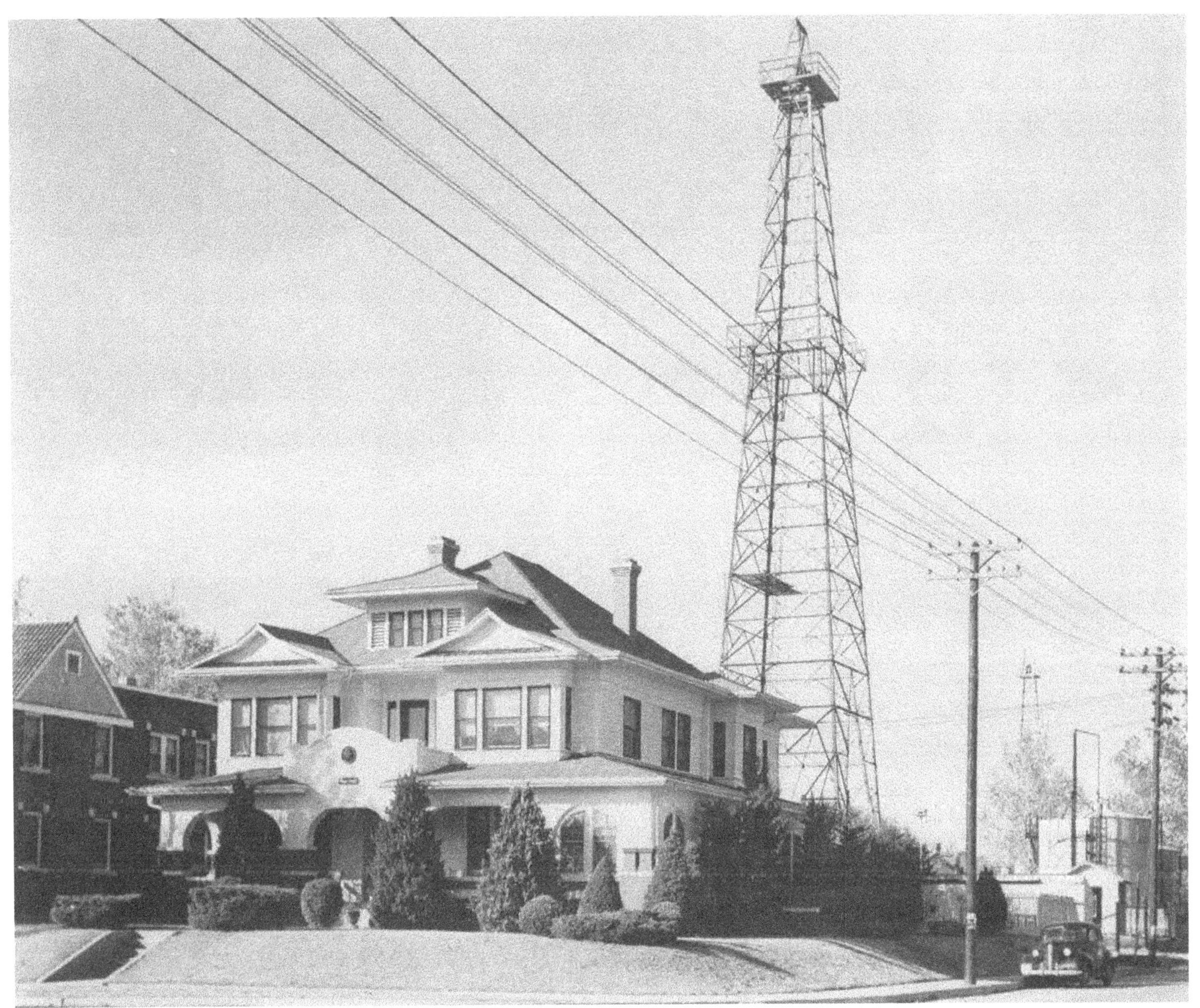

An oil derrick has sprouted in the garden of a northeast Oklahoma City home, 1944. Few yards in that quarter of the city—not even the State Capitol grounds—escaped the driller.

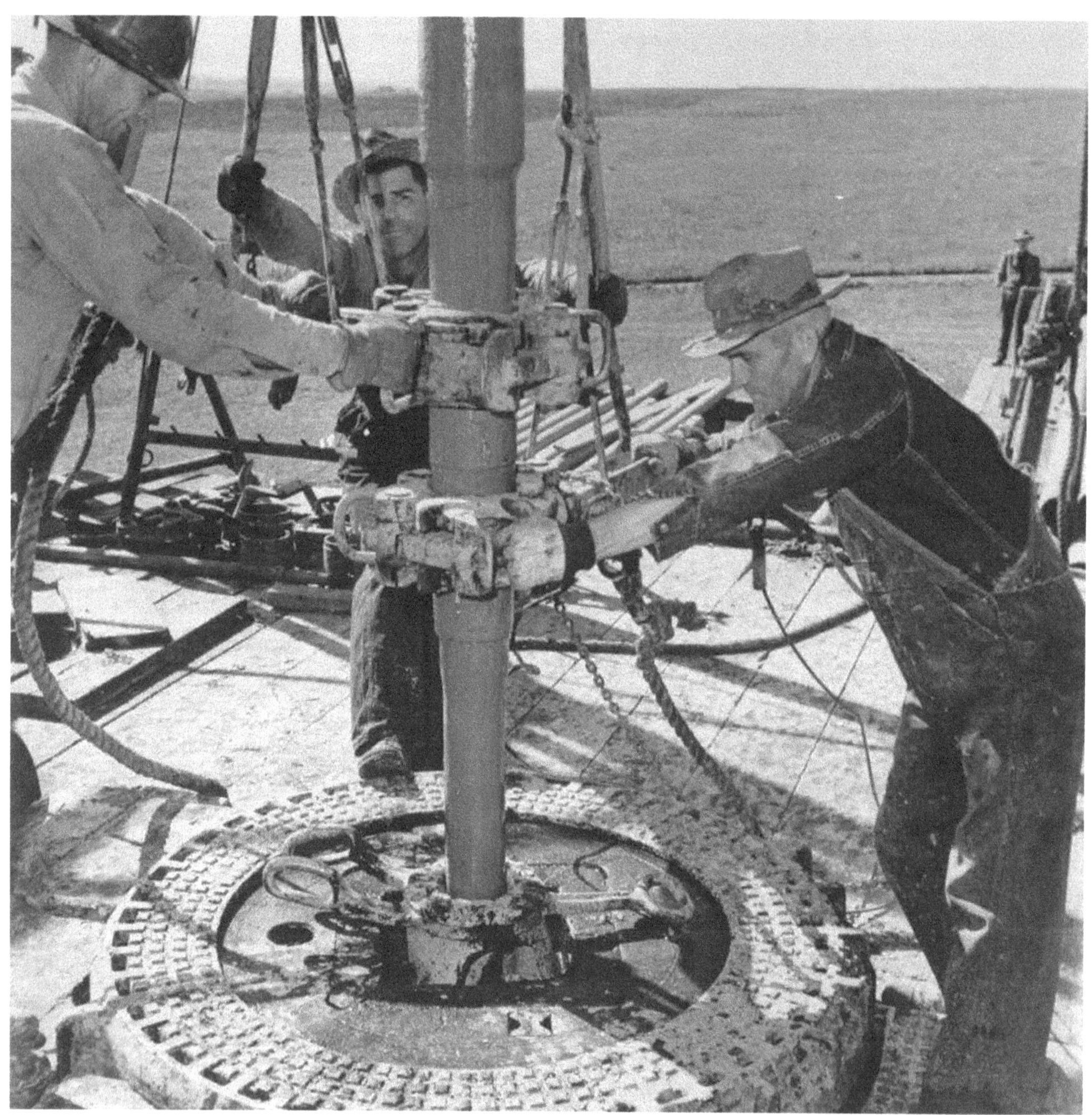

Wildcatters work to bring in a well, 1944. America's oil production was critical to fueling the thirsty war machines in the fight against fascism. Oil workers were reminded that one bombing run by a B-24 bomber used 1,800 gallons of fuel—enough to power the average American car for five years.

I'VE NEVER BEEN TO HEAVEN, BUT I'VE BEEN TO OKLAHOMA

(1946–1968)

Following World War II, Oklahoma was faced with serious challenges as it began the recovery from the Great Depression. Significant damage was done to the agricultural system from soil erosion and dust storms, and industrial development around the state was limited by a lack of infrastructure. Depopulation was also a significant problem, as the state had to cope with net losses from migration throughout the Depression and war years.

Complicating matters was the negative image Oklahoma earned from the Okie migrations and the Dust Bowl. Many in the state, especially the young, had a crisis of confidence, and the state began to see a new migration—what is today called a "brain drain"—in which some of the state's brightest young people left for greater opportunity in other states. To combat that trend and to revive the spirits of traumatized Oklahomans, much emphasis was placed on promoting a positive image; the most prominent examples were the University of Oklahoma football team and the 1957 Semi-Centennial celebration.

Fortunately, the state was blessed with strong leadership during this period, chiefly in the person of Governor (later Senator) Robert S. Kerr. Kerr transcended the contentious politics present since territorial days and provided the blueprint for recovery. Working with other strong leaders like Mike Monroney (later known for fostering Oklahoma's aviation industry), Kerr saw a chemistry of combined federal and state programs as a way to modernize the state and diversify its economy. The establishment of military bases, rural electrification, education reform, and water impounding were notable during the postwar period. The most striking of these programs was the construction of hundreds of large and small dams that together transformed a state with a reputation for droughts and dust storms into a state with nearly as many miles of shoreline as America's Atlantic, Gulf, Pacific, and Arctic coasts combined.

Oklahoma was also blessed with reform-minded governors like Raymond Gary and J. Howard Edmondson. These "good government" leaders supported many measures to modernize the state, including challenging and dismantling barriers to civil rights. Although the Five Civilized Tribes had sometimes been slave owners, and Jim Crow segregation came with statehood, Oklahoma did not have many of the lasting scars of slavery as did states in the Deep South. Consequently, Oklahoma's civil rights transition was relatively peaceful compared to other states.

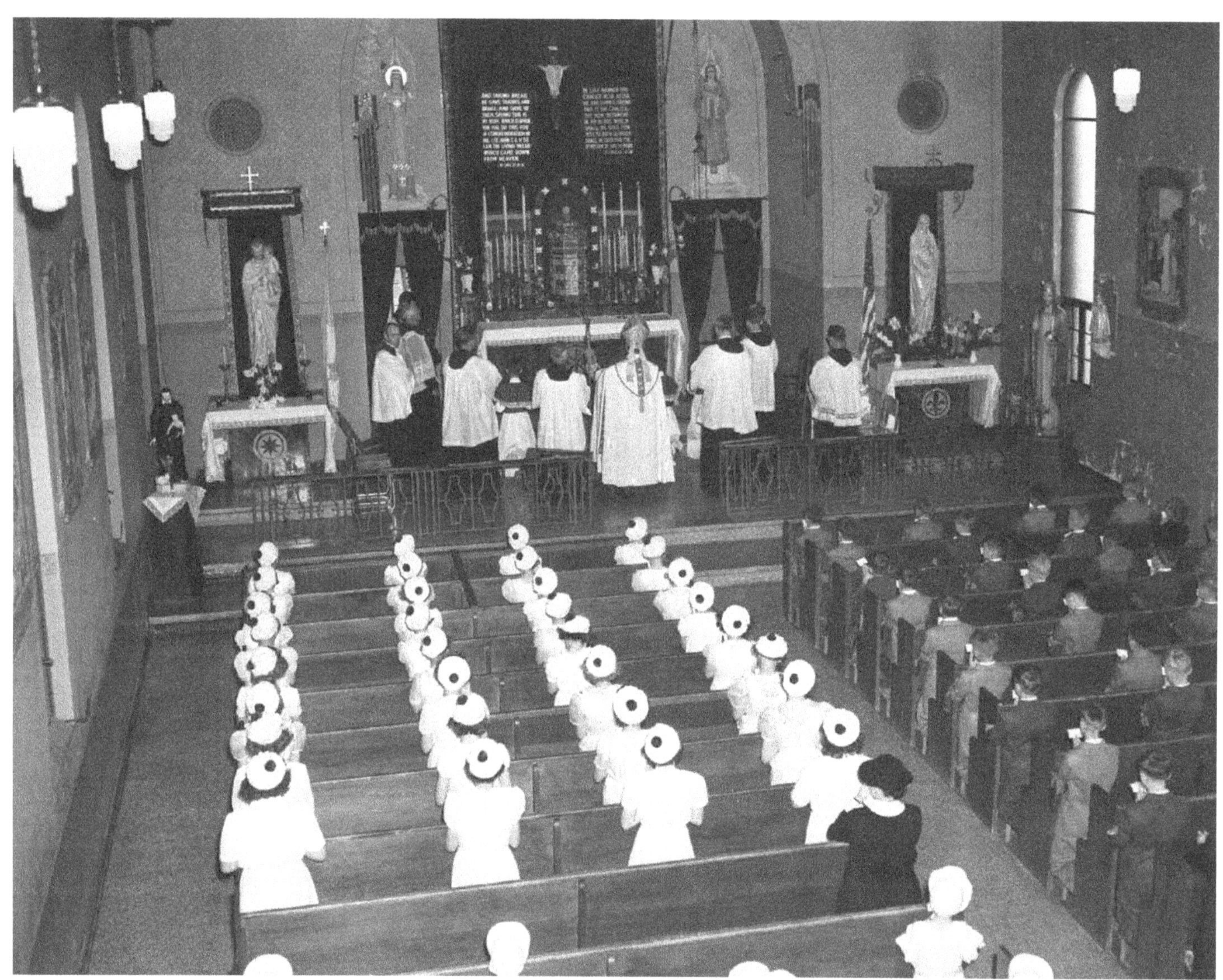

The children of St. Joseph Industrial School and Orphanage attend mass, 1946. The orphanage was established in 1911 west of the new town of Bethany and would eventually include a home for unwed mothers and a seminary.

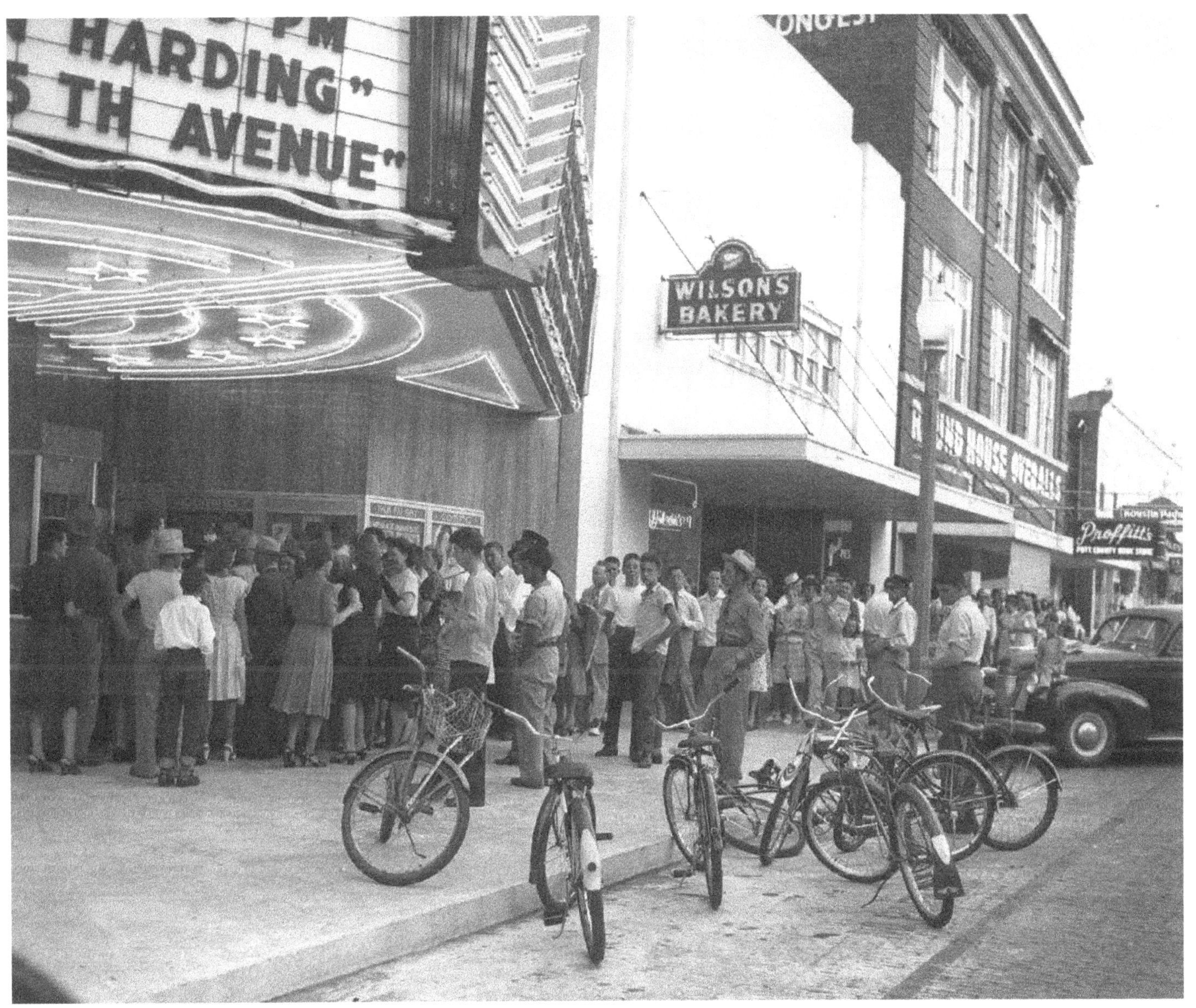

The Hornbeck Theatre in downtown Shawnee, July 1947. After Shawnee won the Pottawatomie County seat from Tecumseh in 1930, economic diversity and a central location helped it remain a viable city.

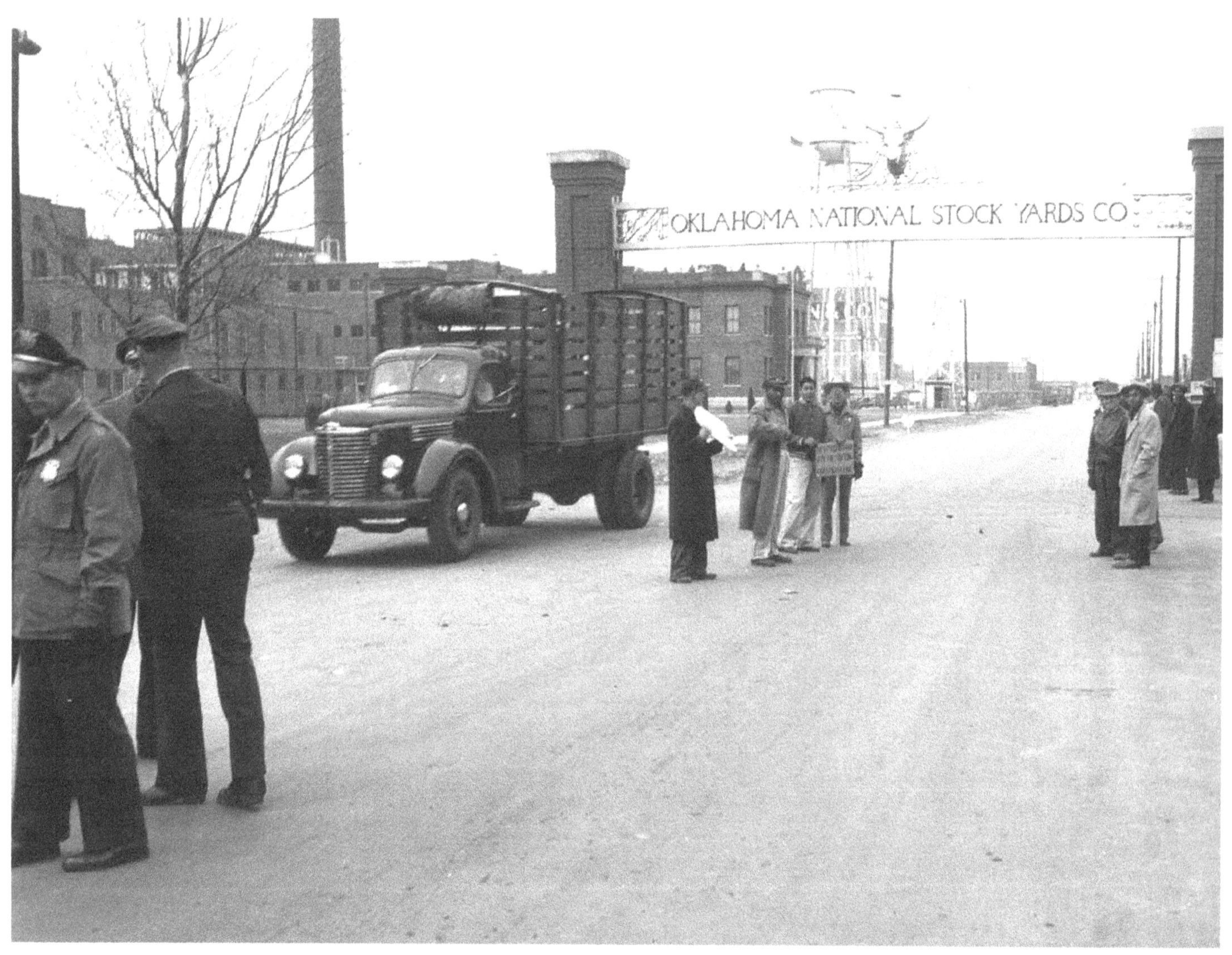

Pickets mill around near the entrance to the Oklahoma National Stock Yards in Oklahoma City, 1948. Throughout much of the spring that year, meatpackers in the city took part in a nationwide strike by the national union. Workers met violence and death in other cities, but the strike was largely peaceful in Oklahoma City.

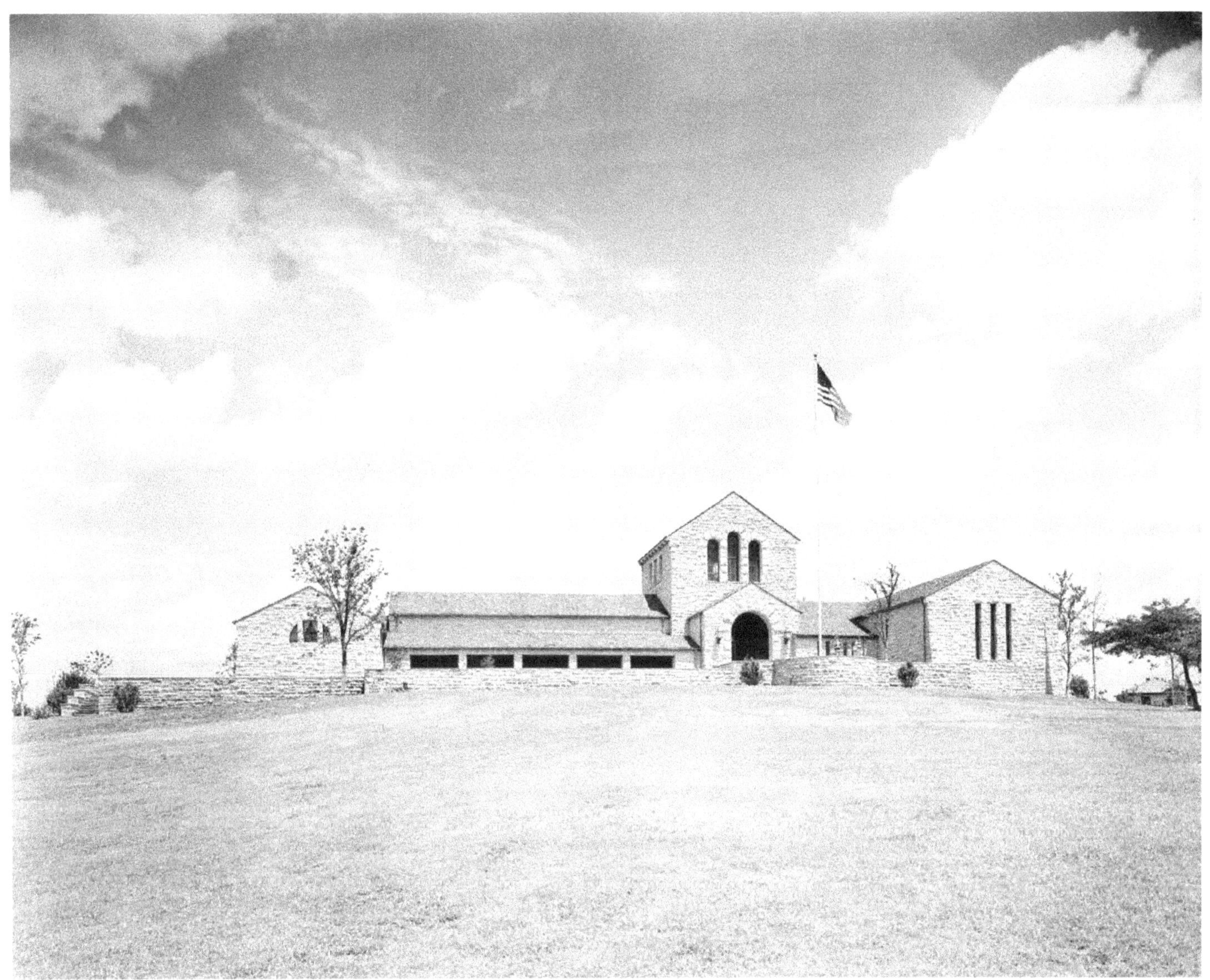

The Will Rogers Memorial in Claremore, seen here in 1948, was built a decade earlier on land donated by the Rogers family. Even though Rogers once said memorials ought to be living buildings and not monumental heaps of stone, the chairman of the memorial declared the place "simple and homespun. Will would have liked it."

President Harry S. Truman made one of his famous whistle-stop tours through Oklahoma during his 1948 reelection campaign. At Ardmore he left the train to address the crowd on the steps of the First Methodist Church. Although the population of Ardmore was only 20,000, police estimated 40,000 people were in attendance.

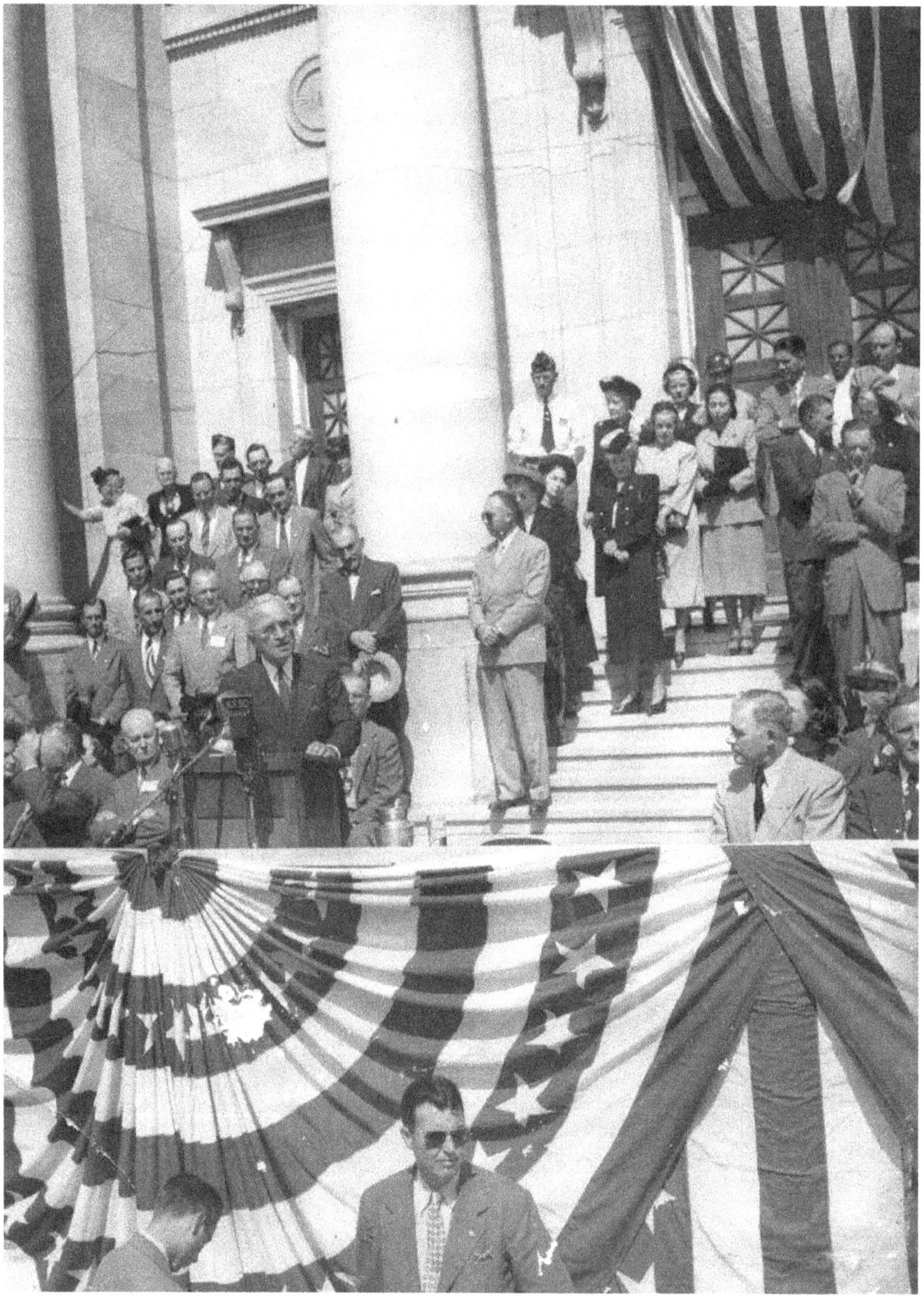

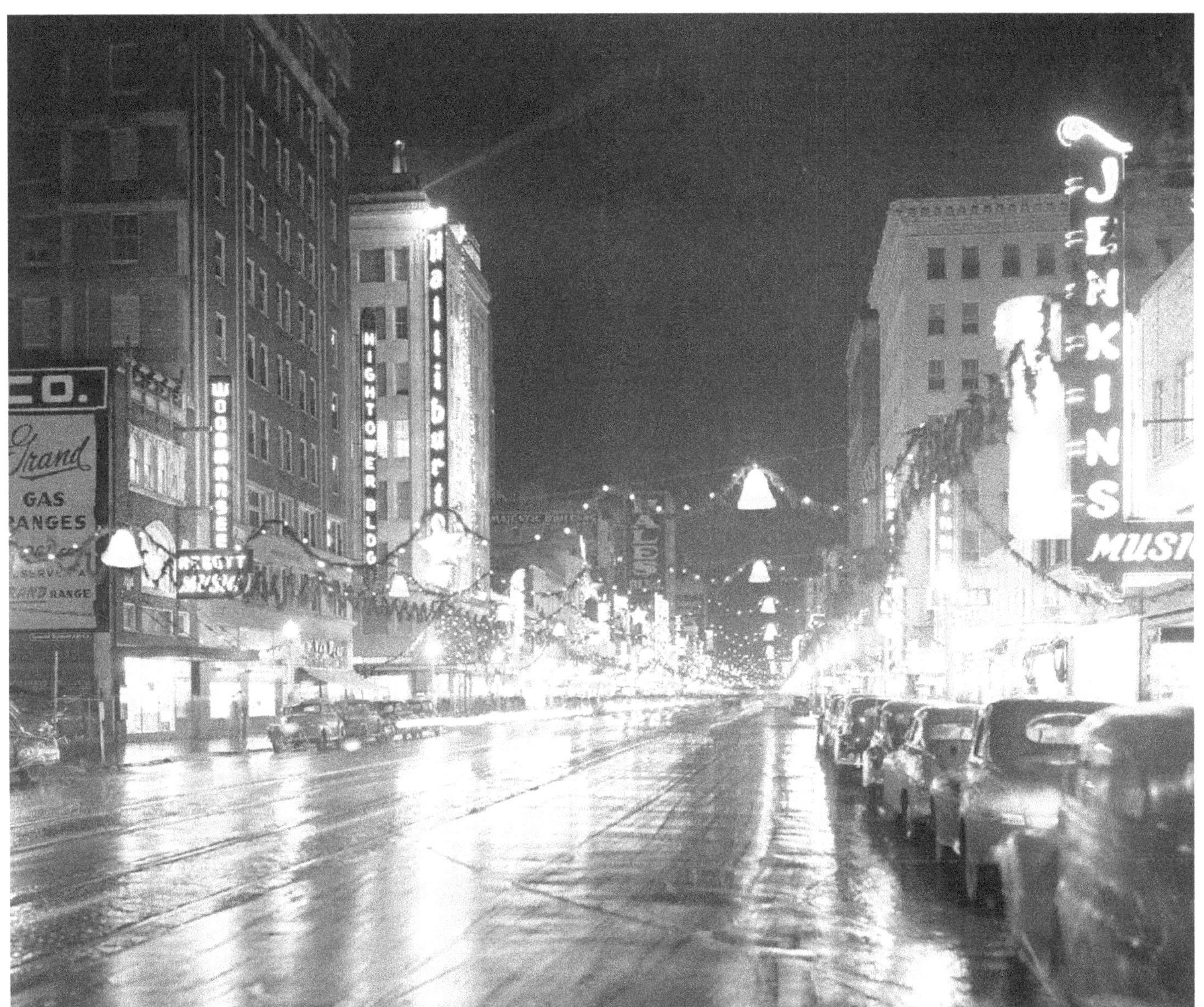

Oklahoma City's Main Street was aglow with new Christmas decorations in this view east from Walker Avenue in 1949.

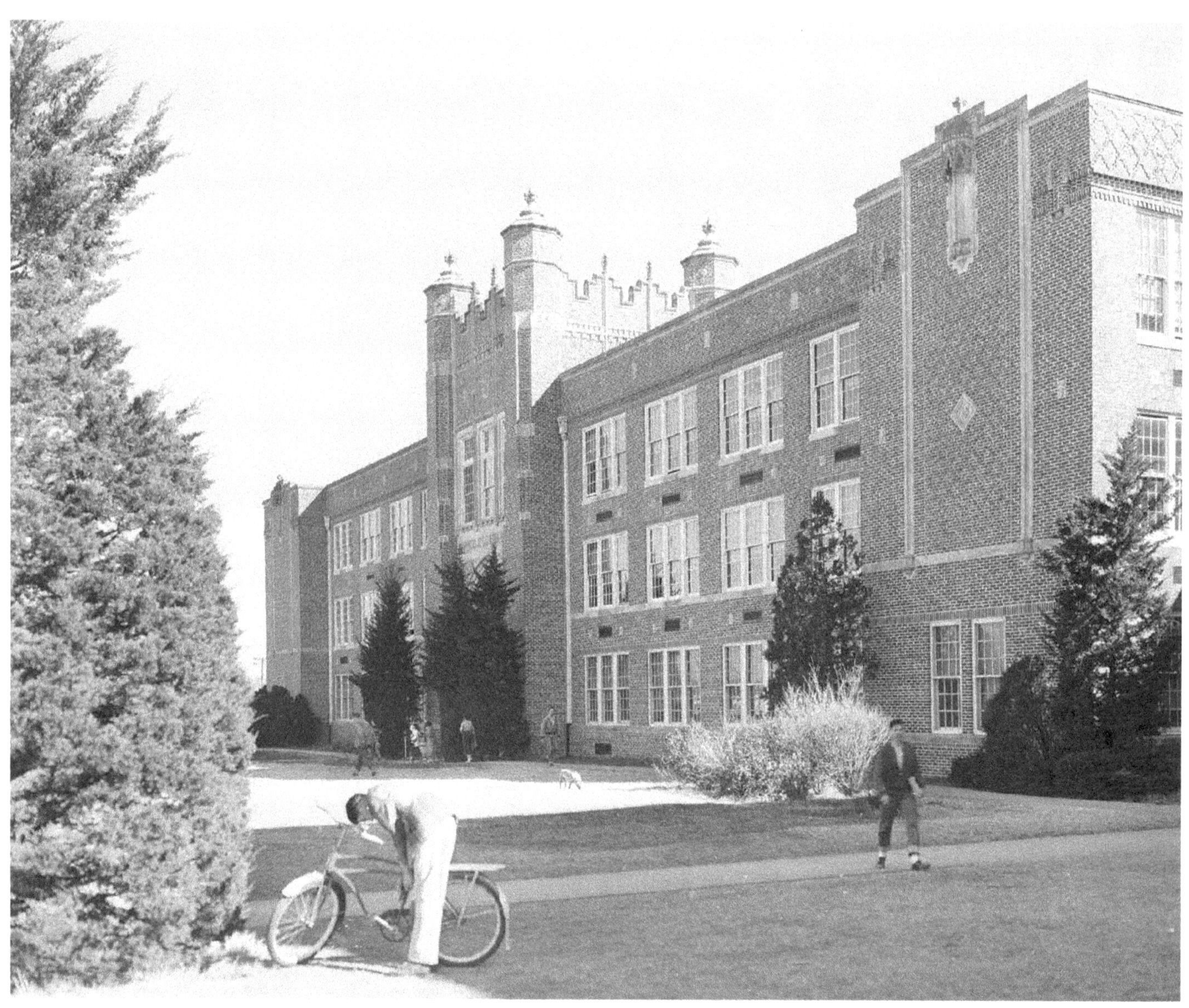

Capitol Hill High School was established in 1928 during a major building program in Oklahoma City. The school was a perennial powerhouse in football in the 1950s and was reigning state champion when this photo was snapped in the spring of 1950.

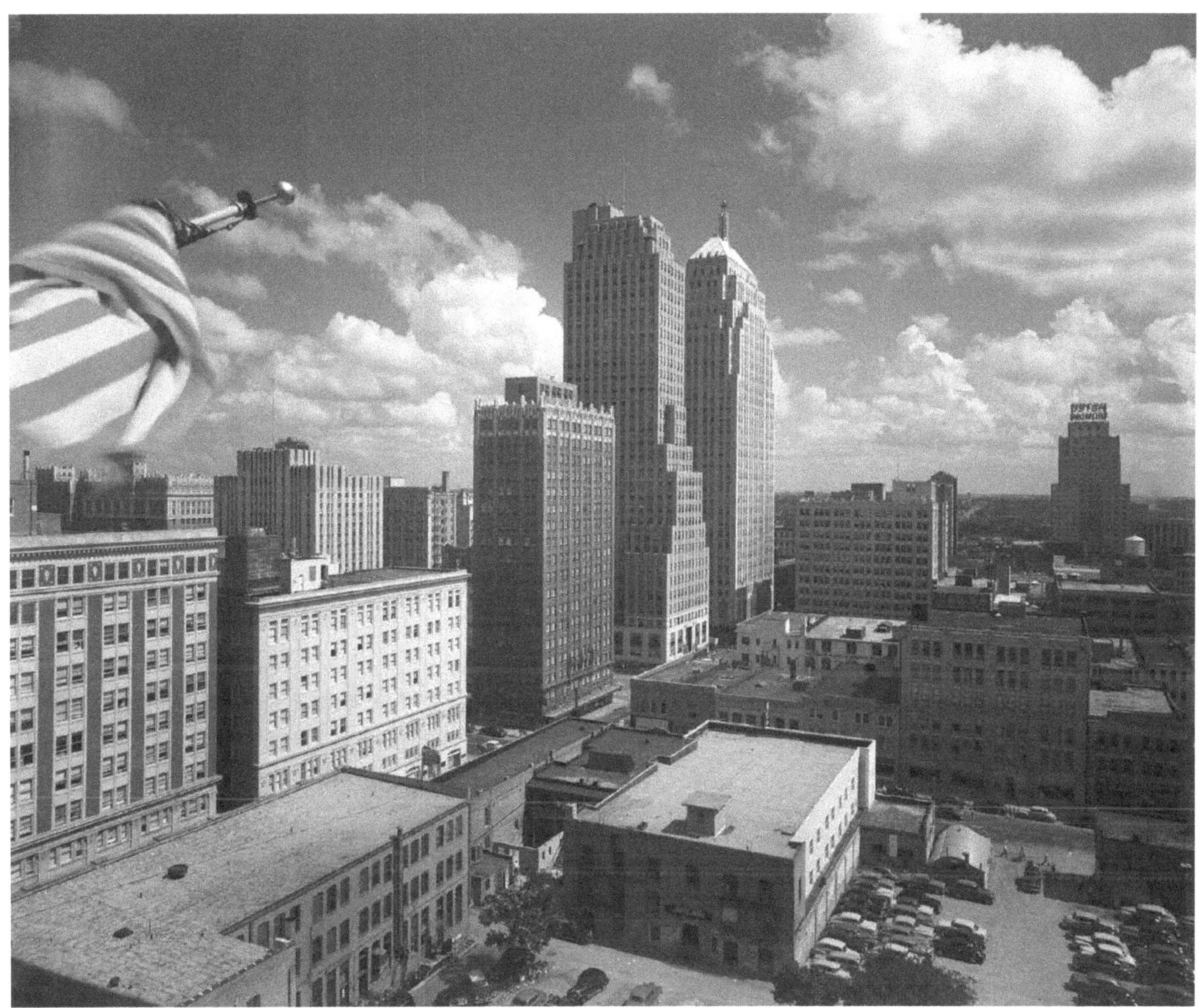

The sheer wall of the Robinson Canyon is clearly visible from this vantage point atop the Federal Building in Oklahoma City, 1950. From left to right, the tall buildings are the Braniff, Kerr-McGee, Petroleum, Ramsey Tower, and First National Bank.

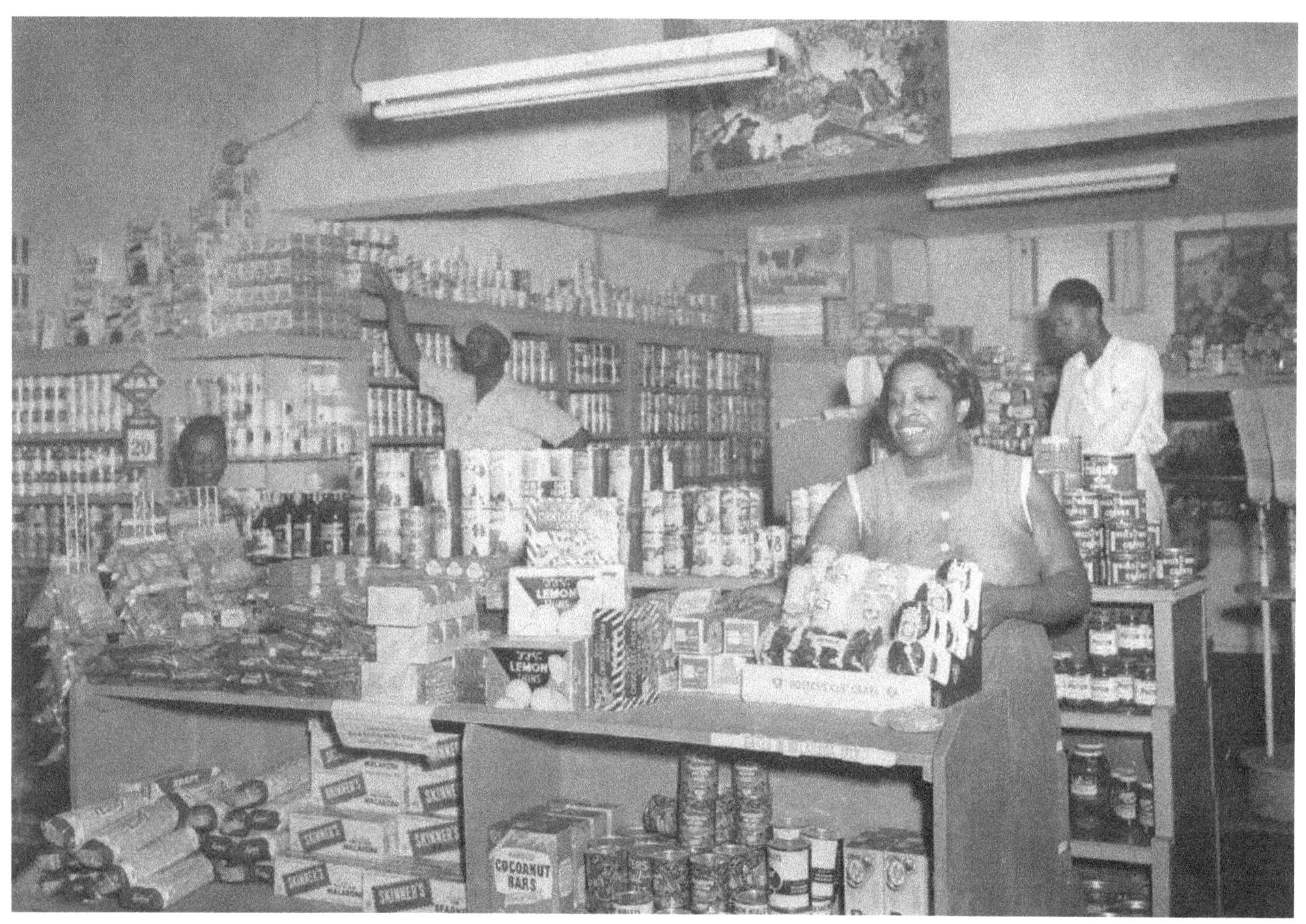

Inside Wilson's grocery store at Northeast Eighth and Kate in Oklahoma City. This neighborhood grocery had been in operation for several years when Andrew Wilson took it over around 1949. He ran it throughout the 1950s.

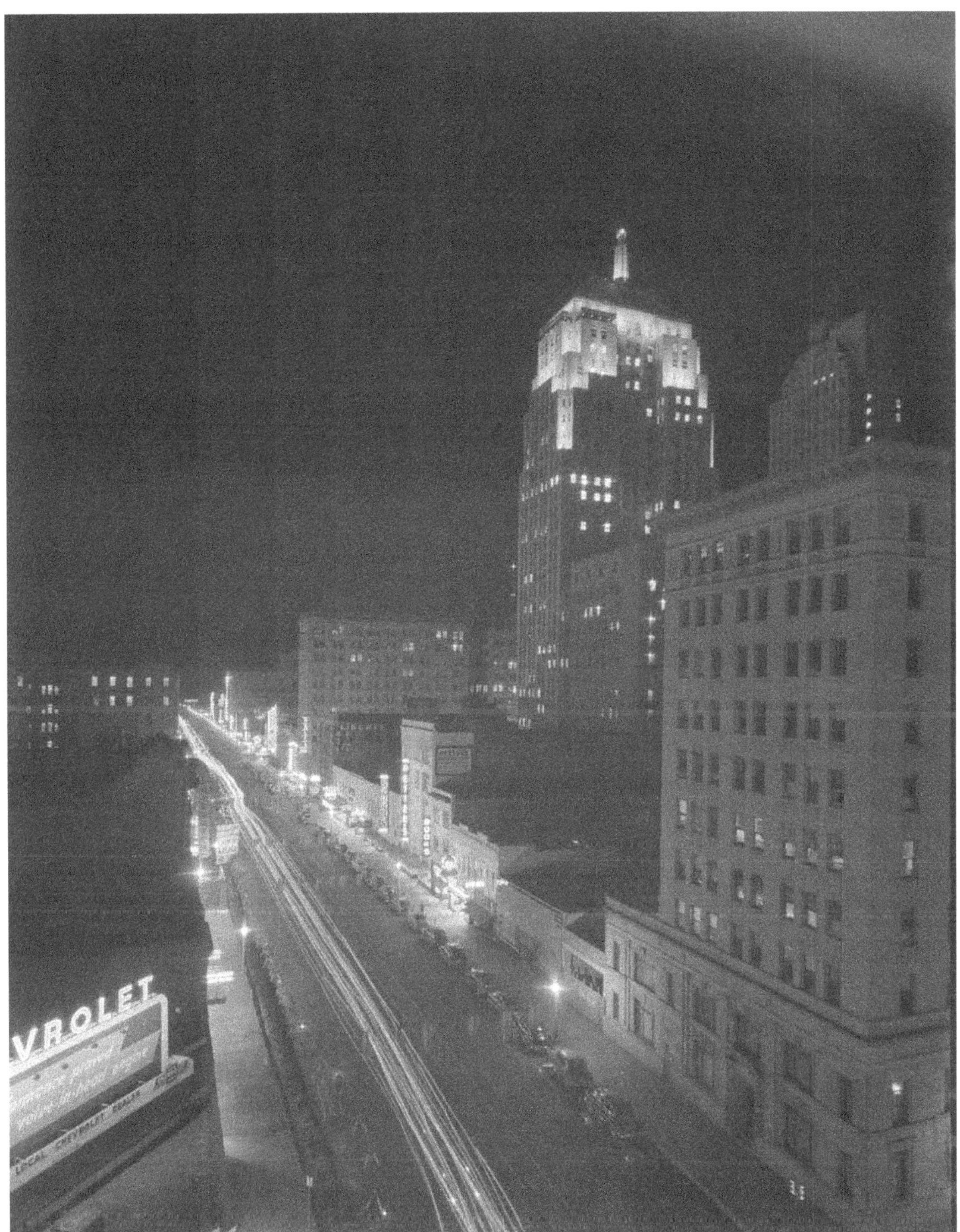

Oklahoma City's Main Street is aglow in this night view taken from the Huckins Hotel, 1951.

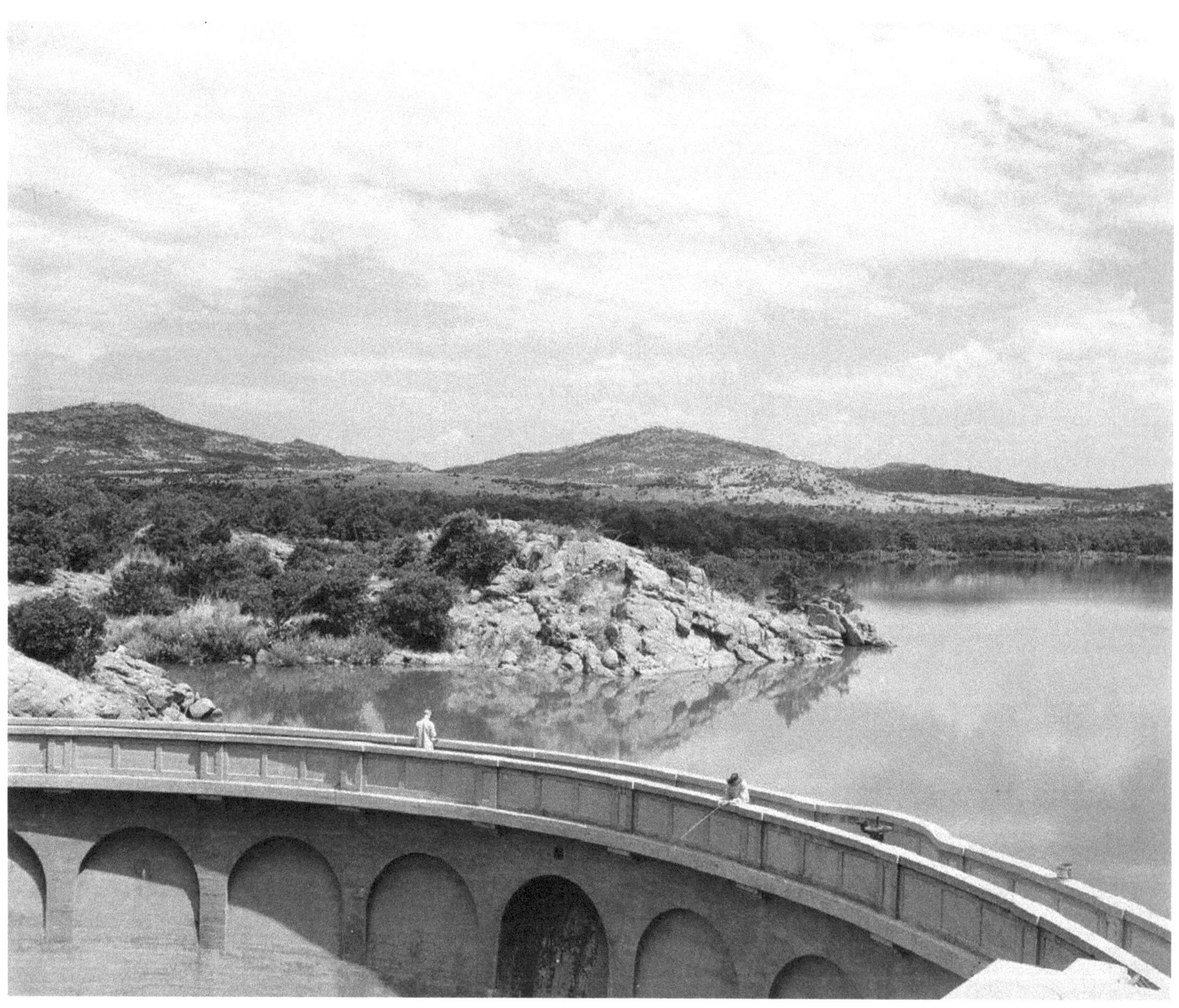

A miniature replica of the Hoover Dam, the Quanah Parker Lake Dam, seen in 1951, creates a body of water that stands in defiance of the arid Wichita Mountains all around it. Oklahoma was a willing recipient of numerous federal reclamation and soil conservation programs from the 1930s to the 1960s.

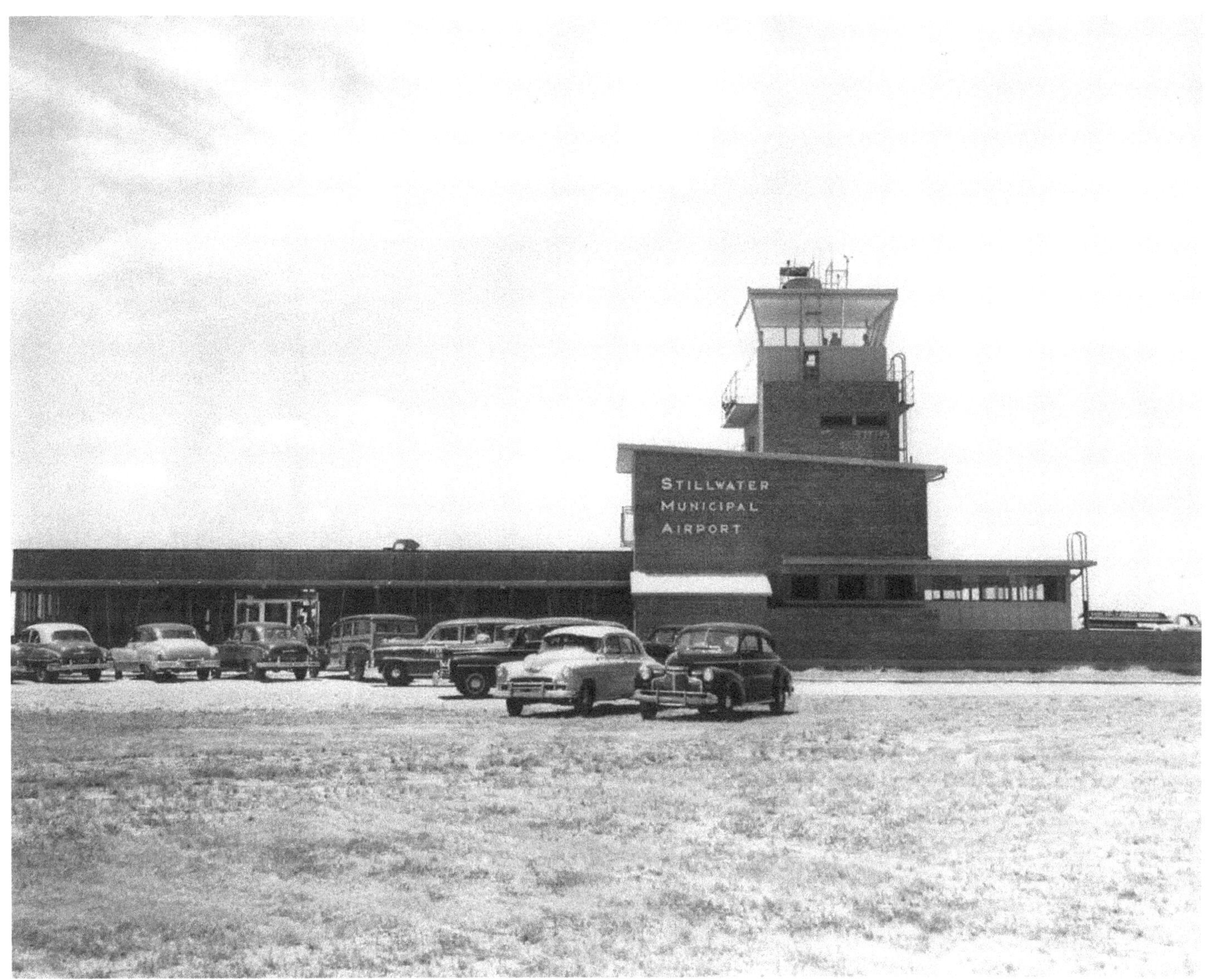

This spiffy new Stillwater airport opened in 1952 as part of a Civil Aeronautics Administration program. The new concrete runways accommodated modern commercial aircraft and earned Stillwater a regular stop on a Central Airlines route to Oklahoma City.

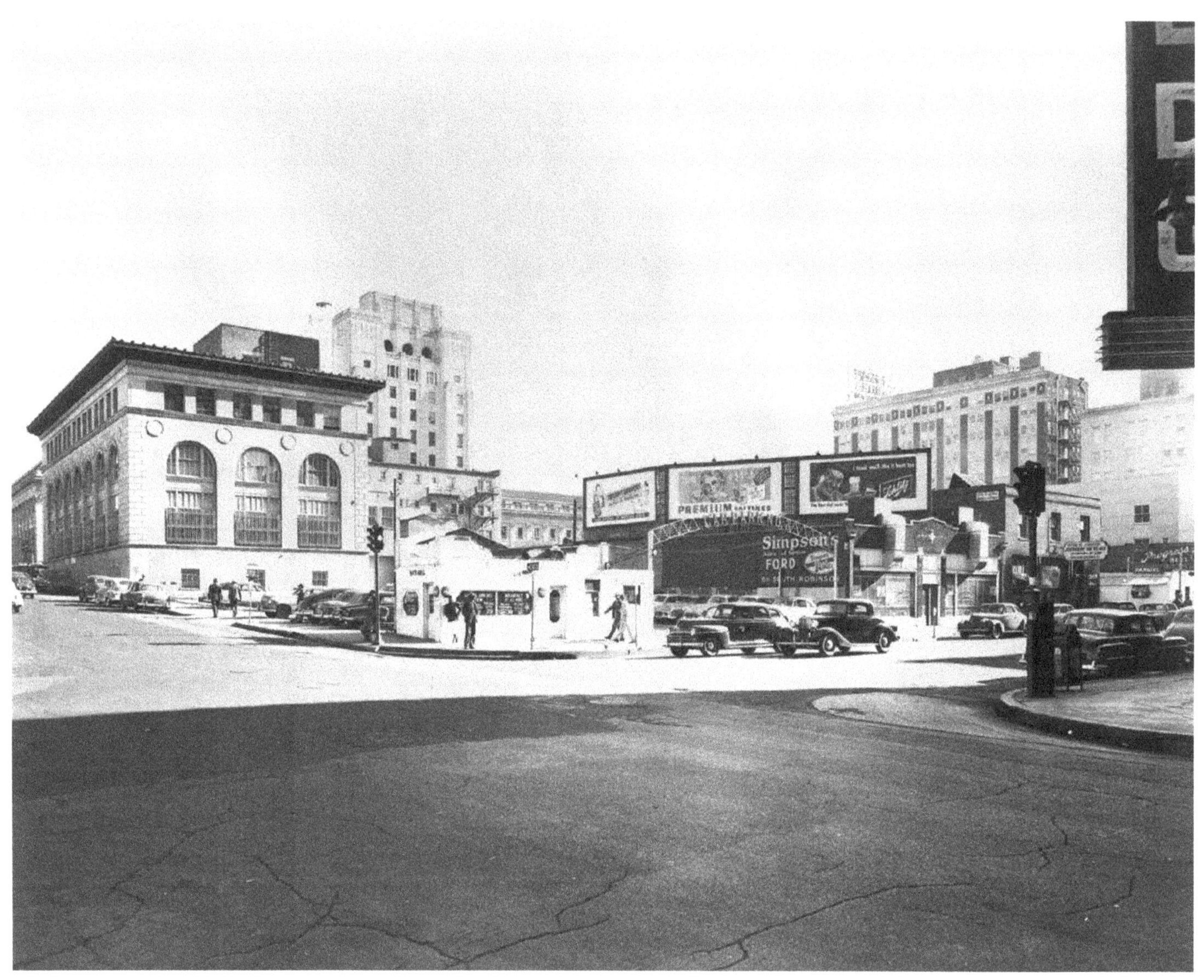

Tony's Grill, operated by Greek immigrant Tony Kiriopoulos, clings to the corner of Northwest Second and Harvey in Oklahoma City, 1952. By year's end the corner building would be razed and a five-decker parking structure erected on the site.

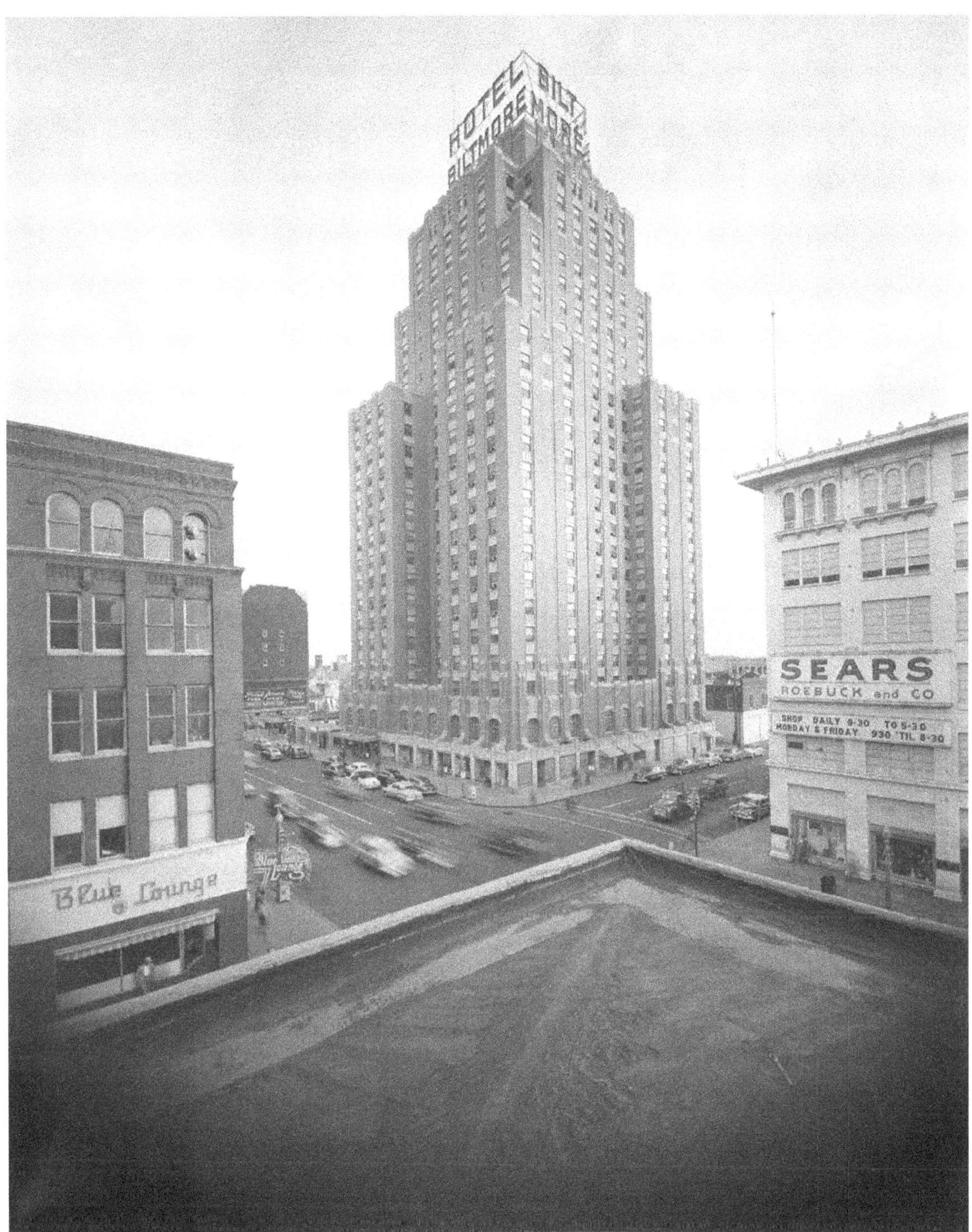

Called "a city unto itself," the Biltmore Hotel was the largest hotel in the state when it was constructed in 1932. Here the Biltmore is seen on its twentieth anniversary.

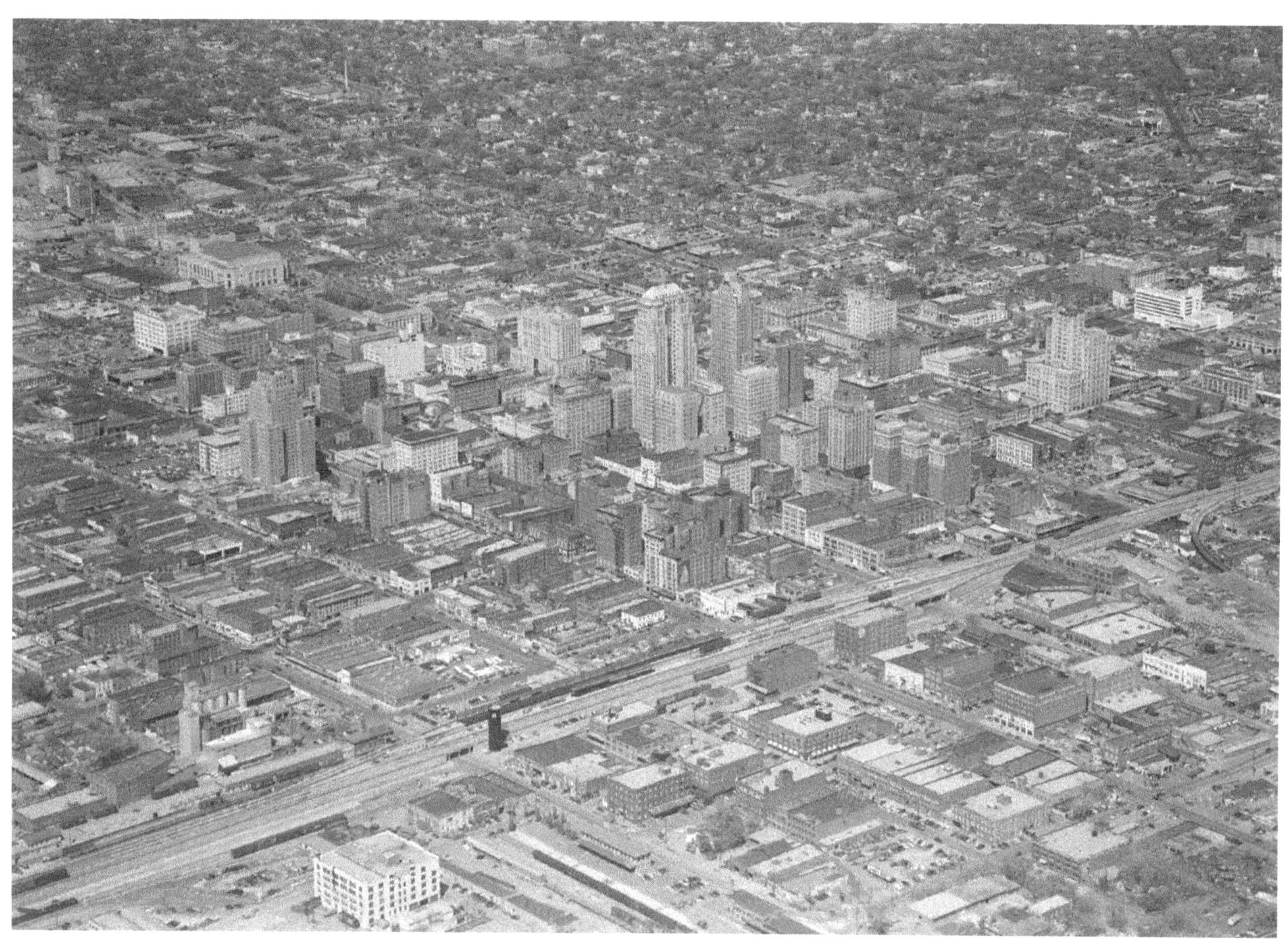

This aerial view of downtown Oklahoma City from the southeast shows it much as it was from the time of the building boom of the early 1930s to the urban renewal era of the late 1960s. Much of the area to the south of the built-up section was razed for the convention center district and Myriad Gardens.

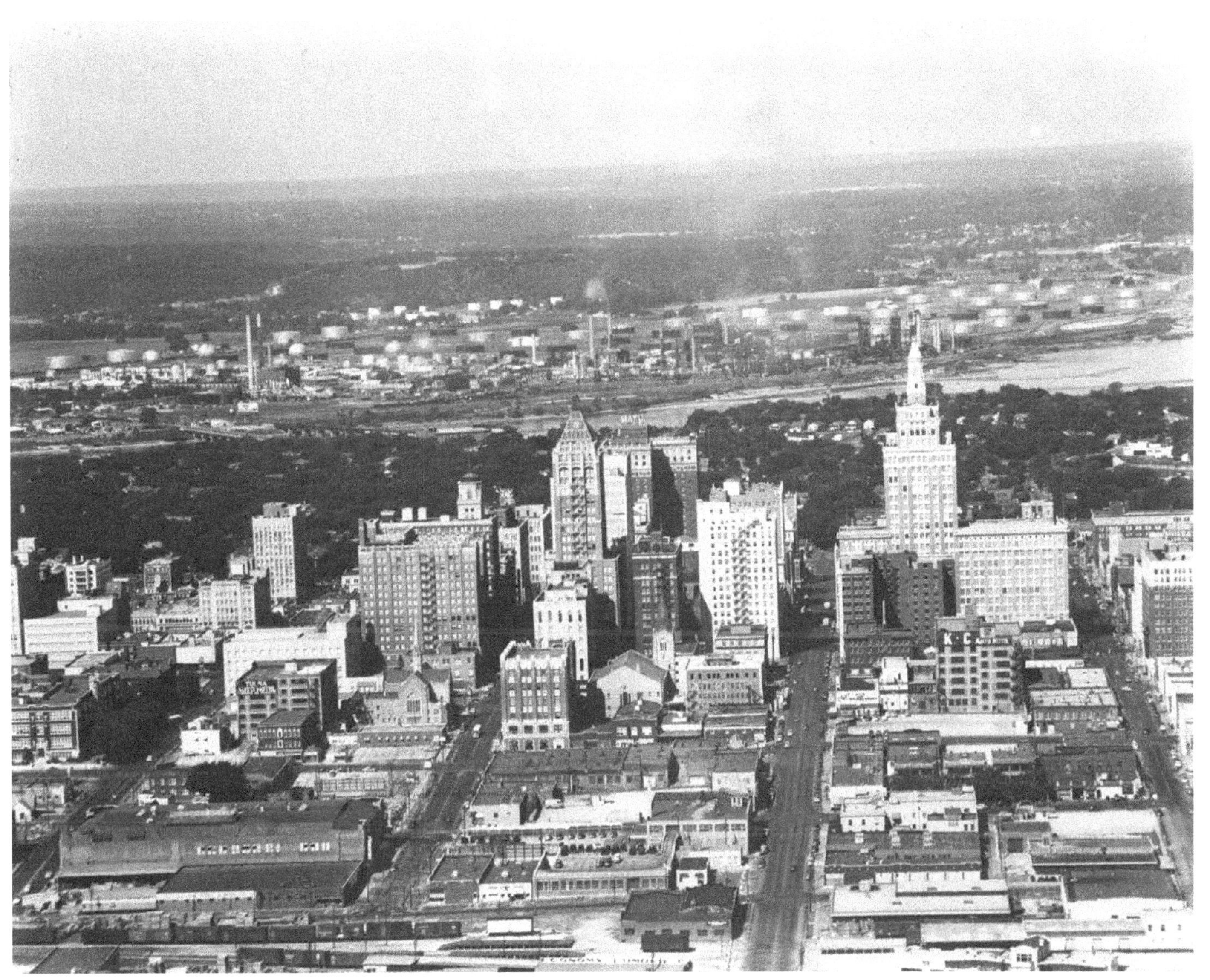

Downtown Tulsa, 1952. In the distance, across the Arkansas River, lie the massive refineries of West Tulsa.

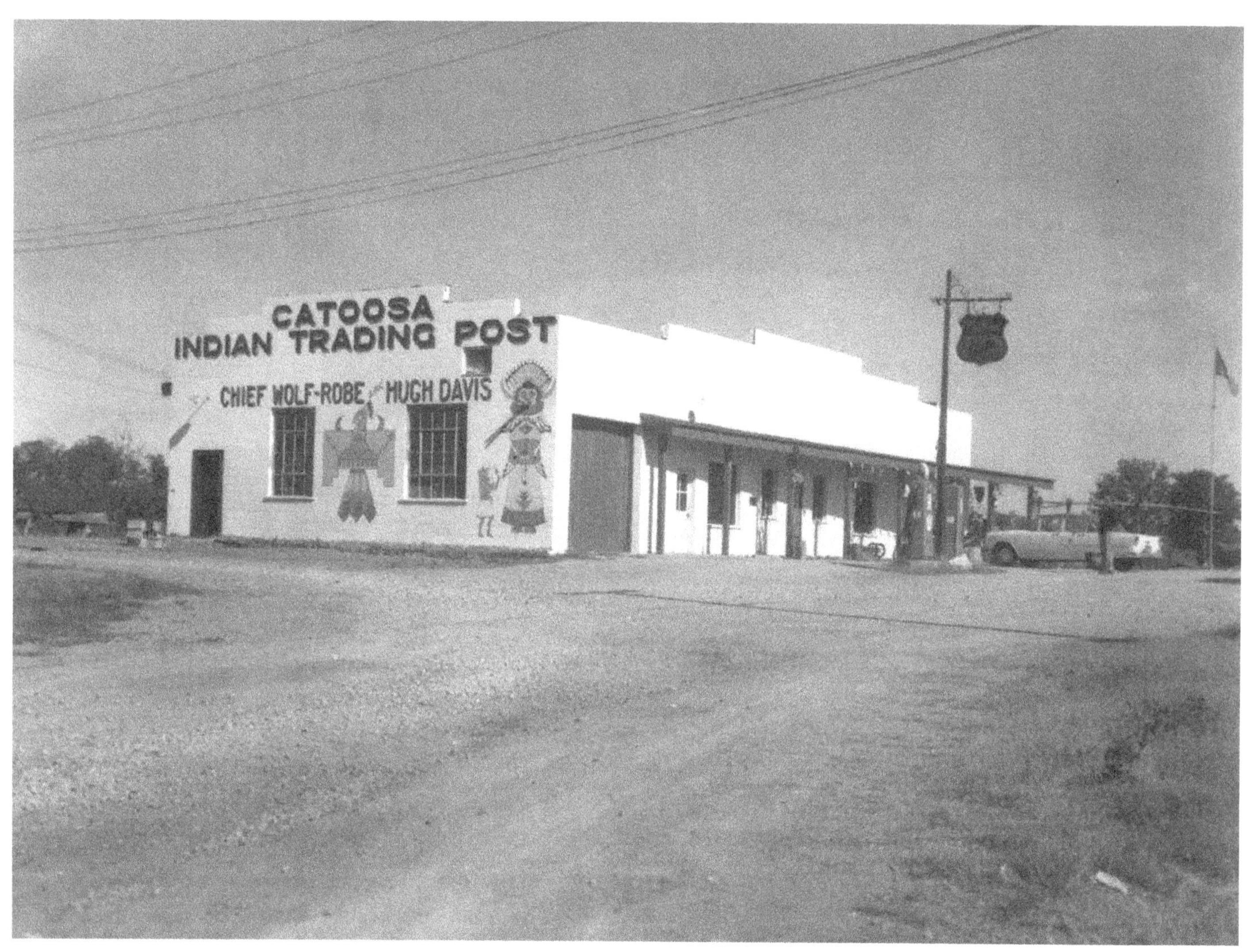

Just across the highway from its more famous sister attraction, the Blue Whale, the Catoosa Indian Trading Post was a familiar site along Route 66 in 1952. Although the trading post sold plenty of cheap souvenirs, its owner, Chief Wolf Robe, was an accomplished artist.

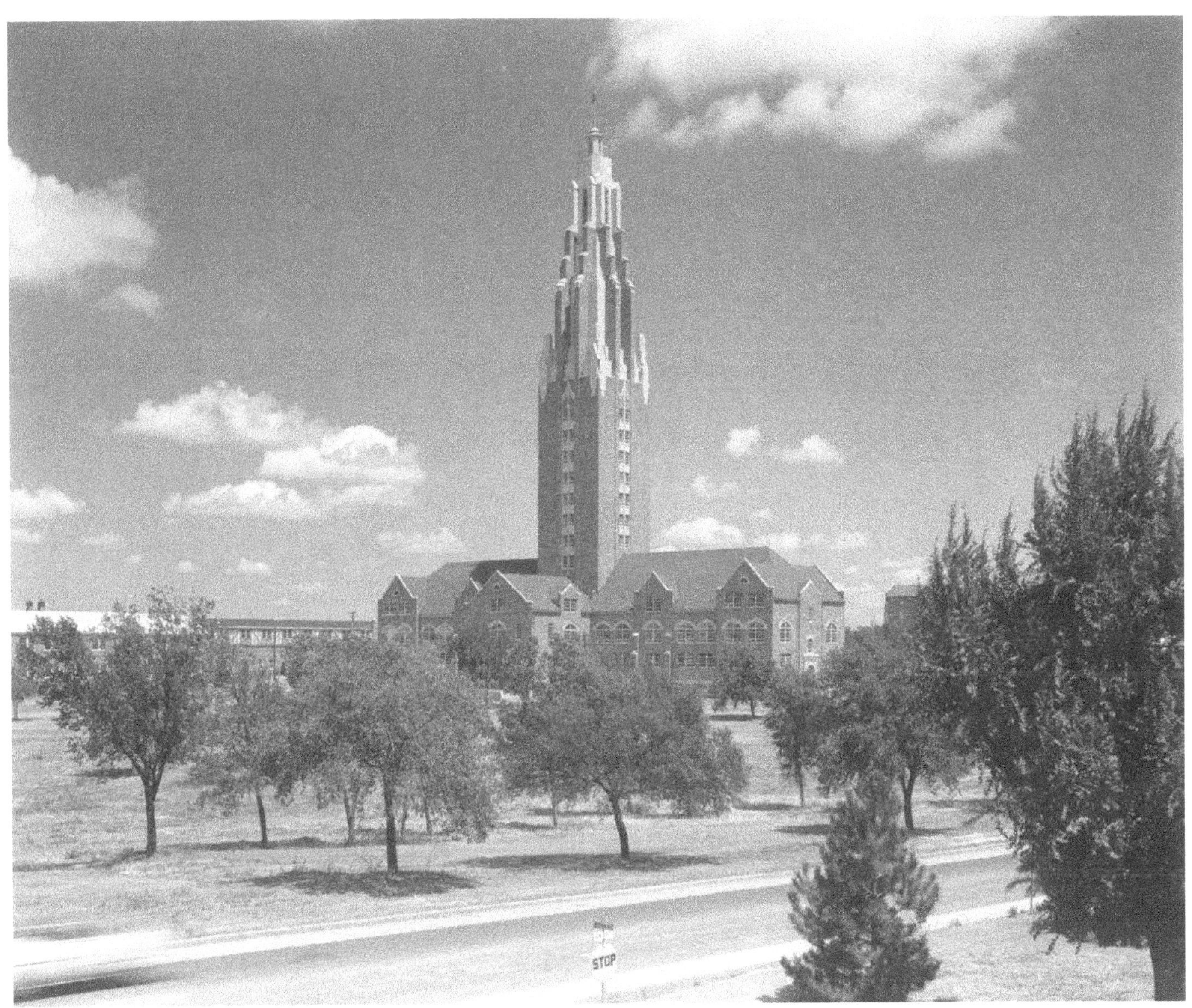

The Gold Star Memorial on the campus of Oklahoma City University was dedicated in 1953 to Methodists from the state who died during the nation's wars. The gold-plated star atop the 22-story tower has been a city landmark for decades.

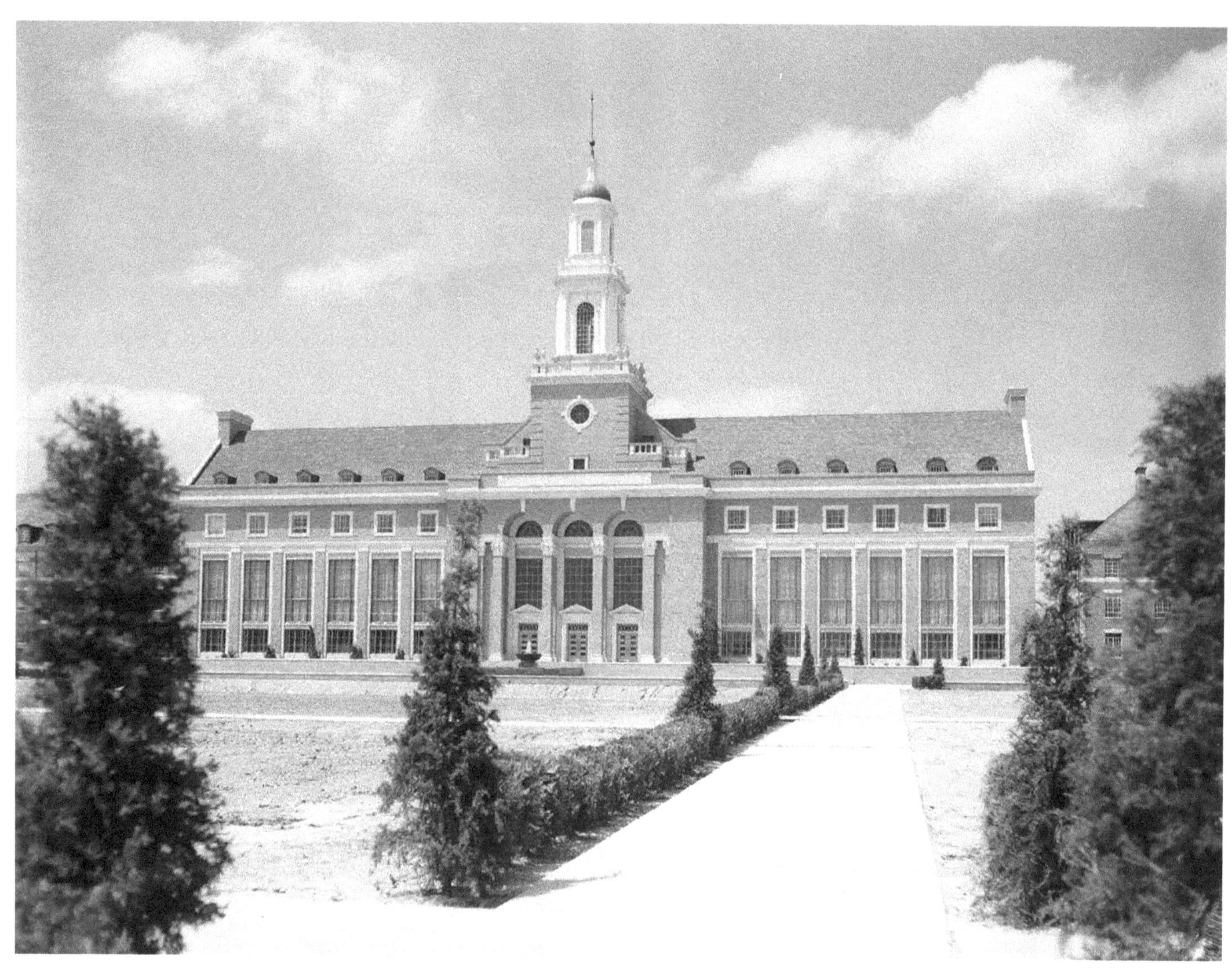

With a capacity of one million volumes, this massive library at Oklahoma A&M University was the fifth-largest in the nation when it was dedicated in 1953. Four libraries around campus were moved into the Georgian-style building.

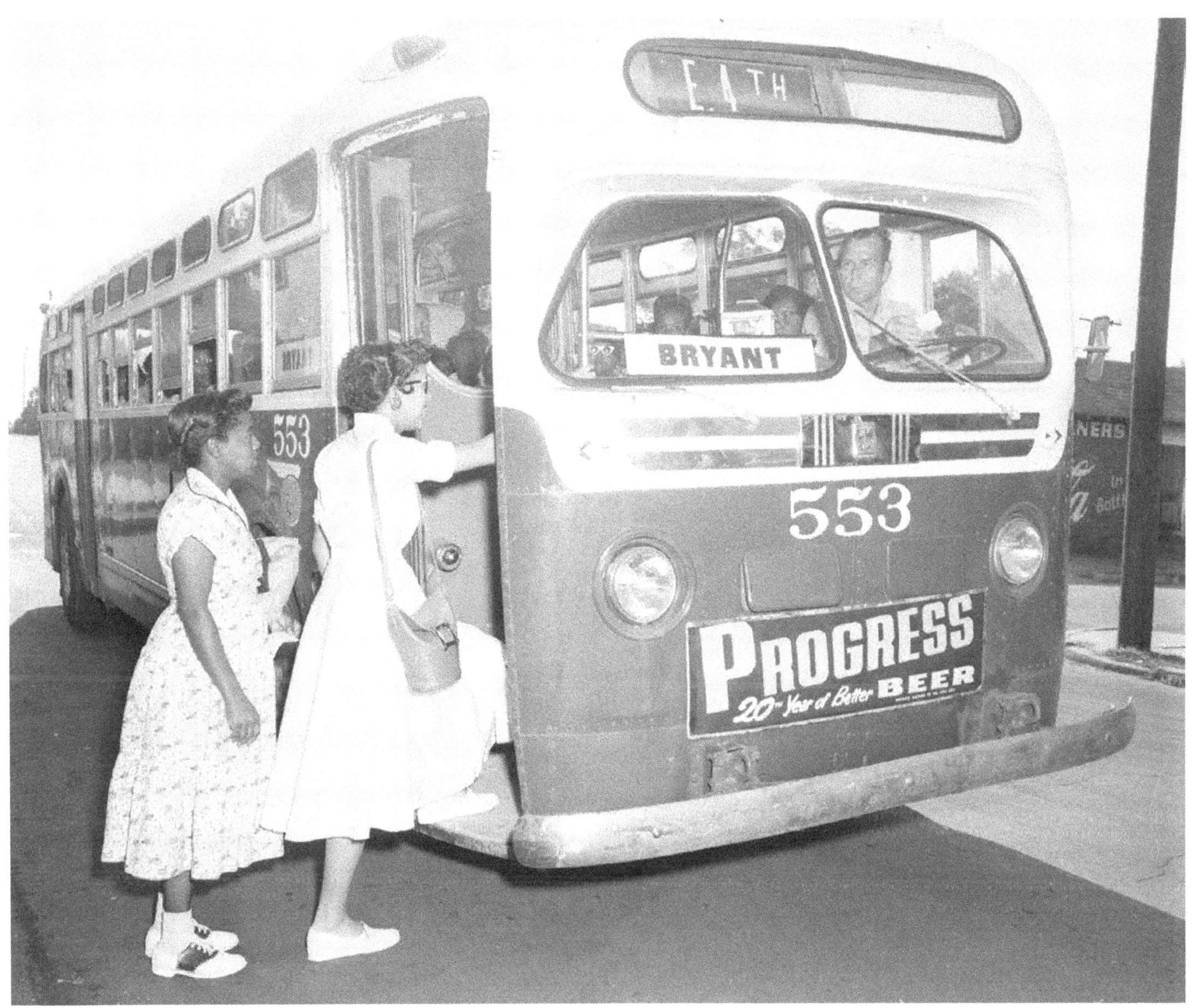

African-American riders board a bus on the Northeast Fourth route in Oklahoma City, 1953. This route was the busiest on the privately owned City Bus Company's line, largely because it was one of two routes that were essentially desegregated. African-American riders had to move to the rear seats when transferring to other routes.

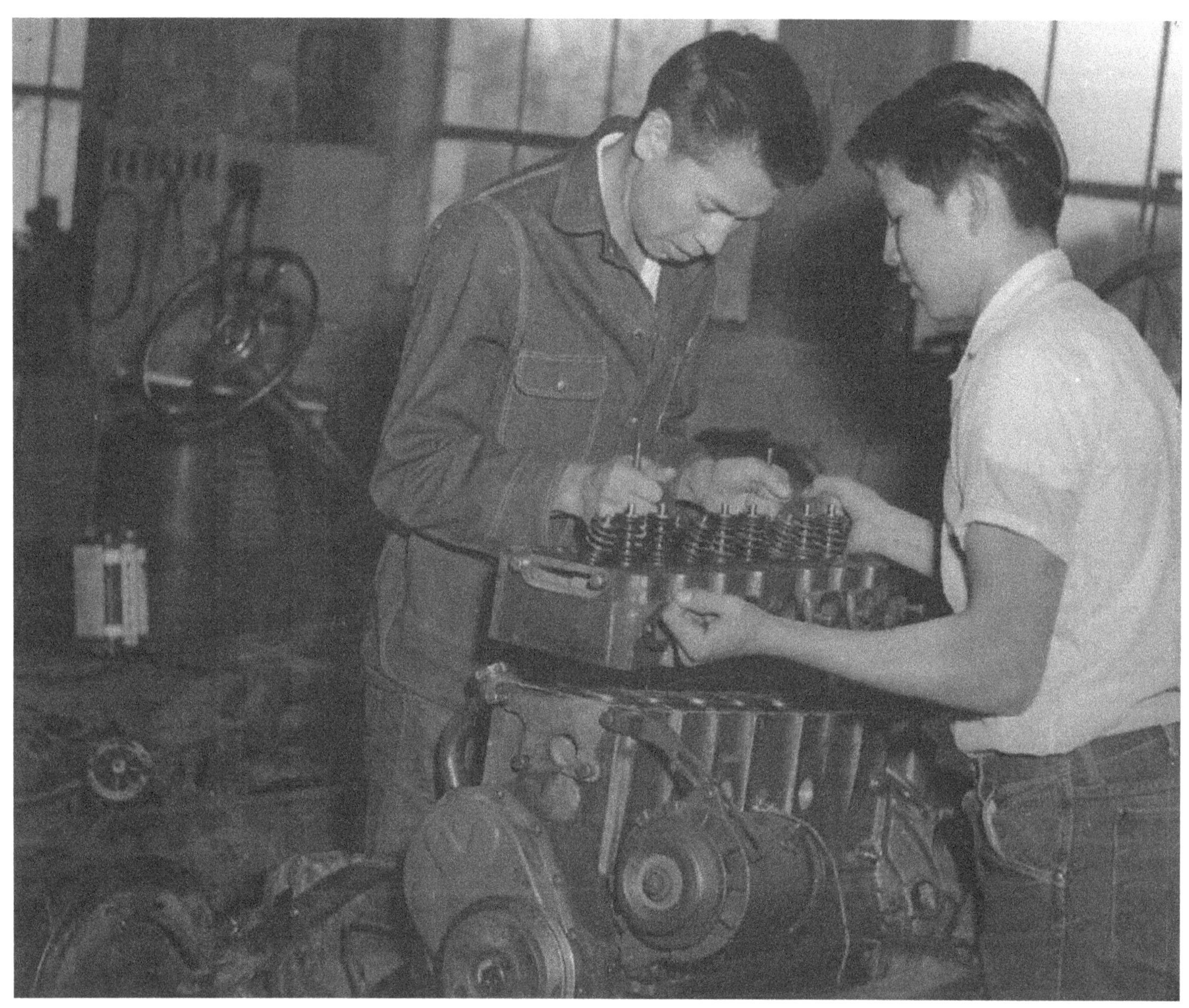

Students at the Chilocco Indian School north of Ponca City overhaul an automobile engine, 1955. Established in 1884, the federal school was initially intended to assimilate and Americanize plains Indians from southwestern Oklahoma, but later included Indian students from many tribes.

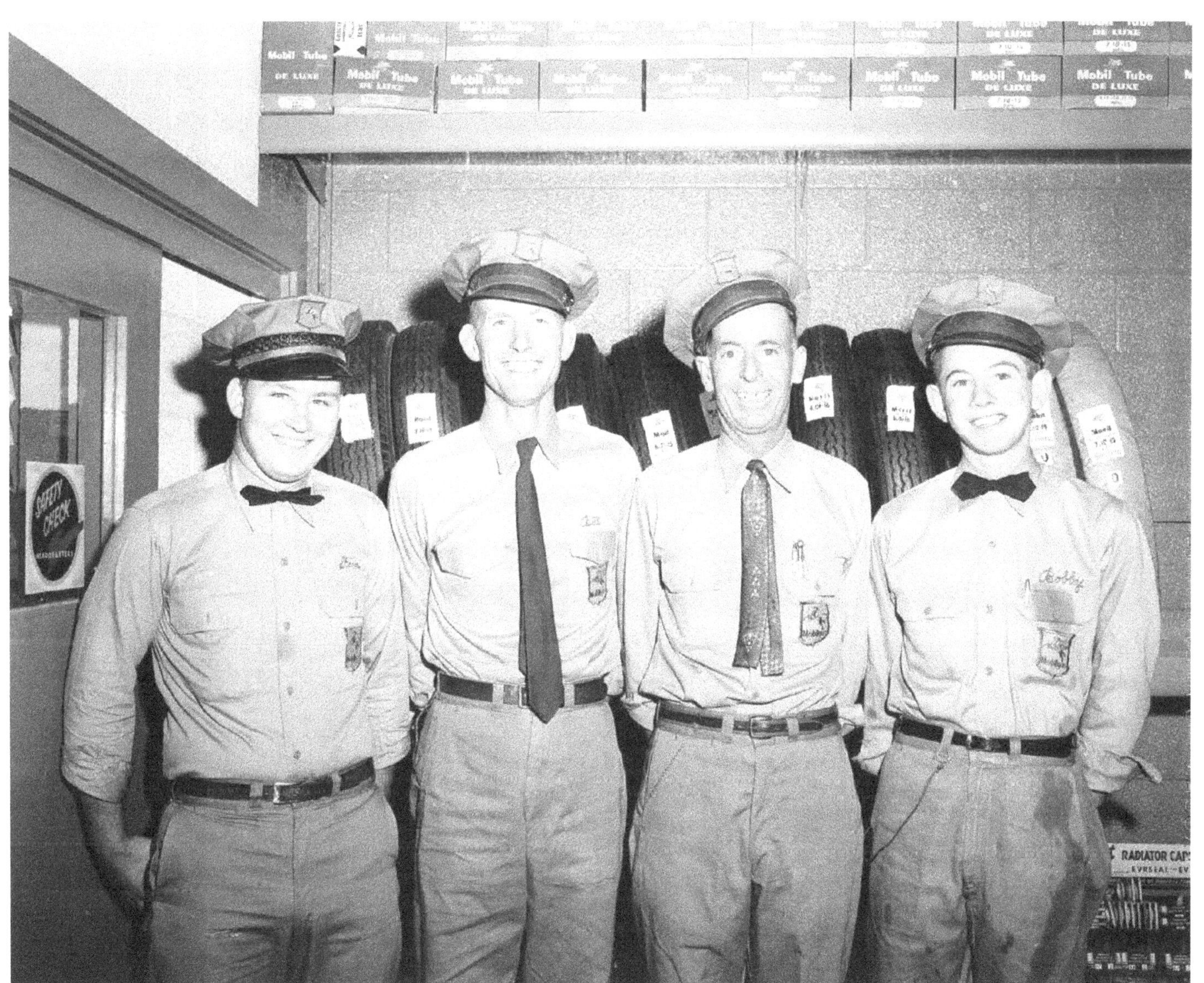

The mechanics of a Mobil gas station in Oklahoma City pose together in 1955.

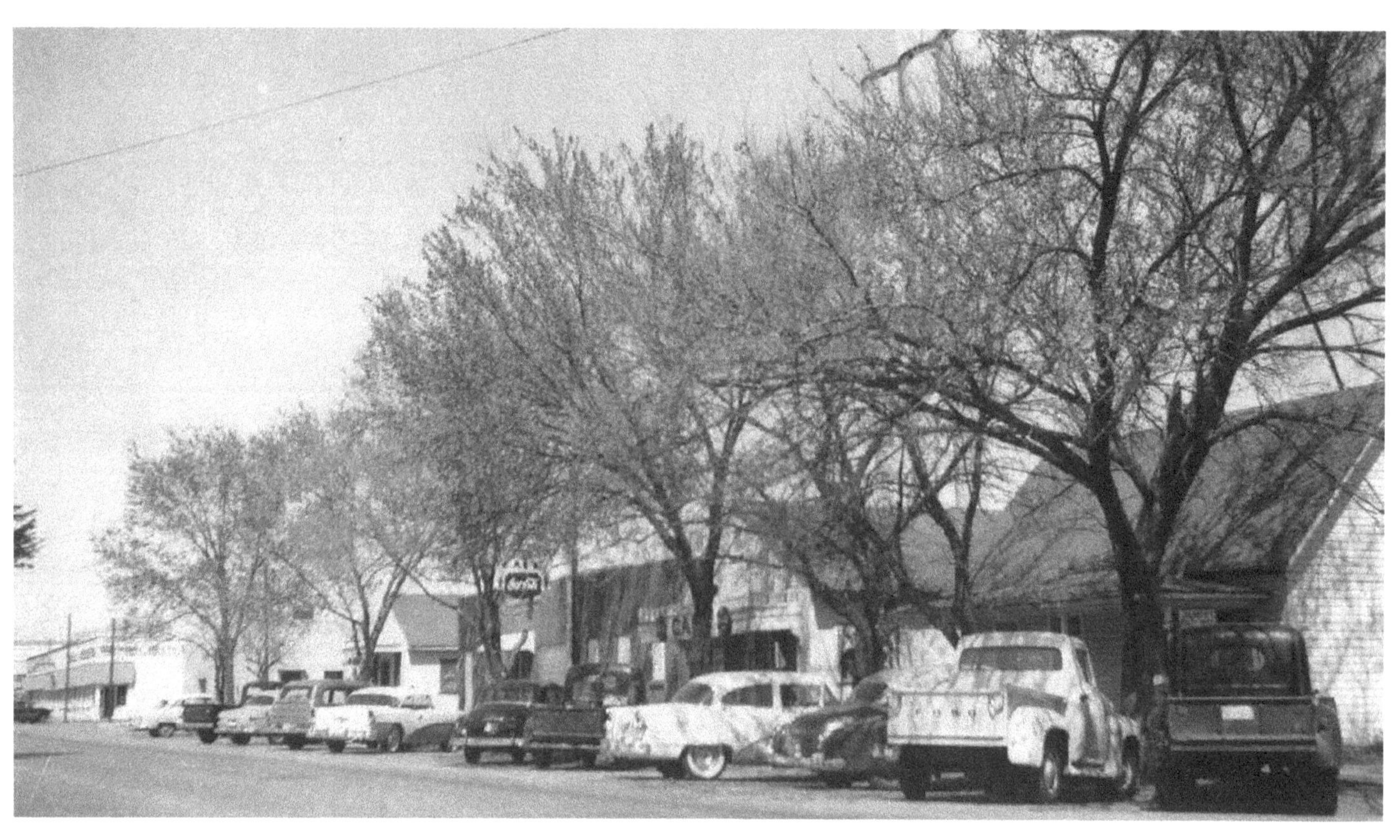

Church Avenue, Harrah, March 1956. The town took its name from its developer, early Oklahoma City real estate baron Frank Harrah. A cluster of Polish settlers in the 1890s and their parish church, St. Teresa's, gave the town a unique character it has maintained ever since.

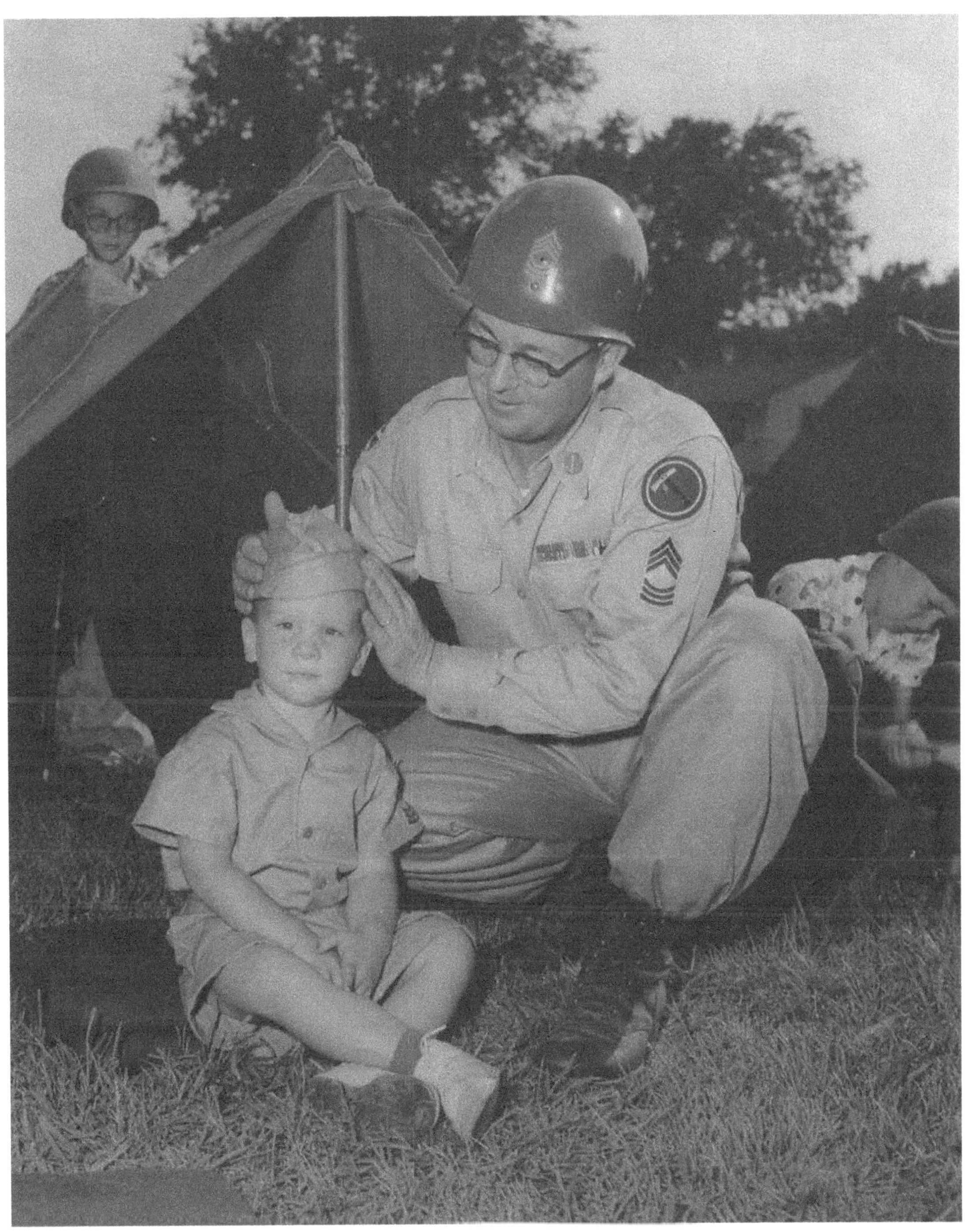

Major General Maxwell Taylor called Fort Sill's Operation Small Fry the best idea in Army public relations he'd ever seen. For two days during the annual summer camp for Army reservists, their sons and young friends could get a taste of Army life, including marching, saluting, and camping out, as seen here in 1956.

Oklahoma celebrated its Semi-Centennial in 1957 with the theme "Arrows to Atoms," which symbolized the state's rapid development from Indian Territory to modern society.

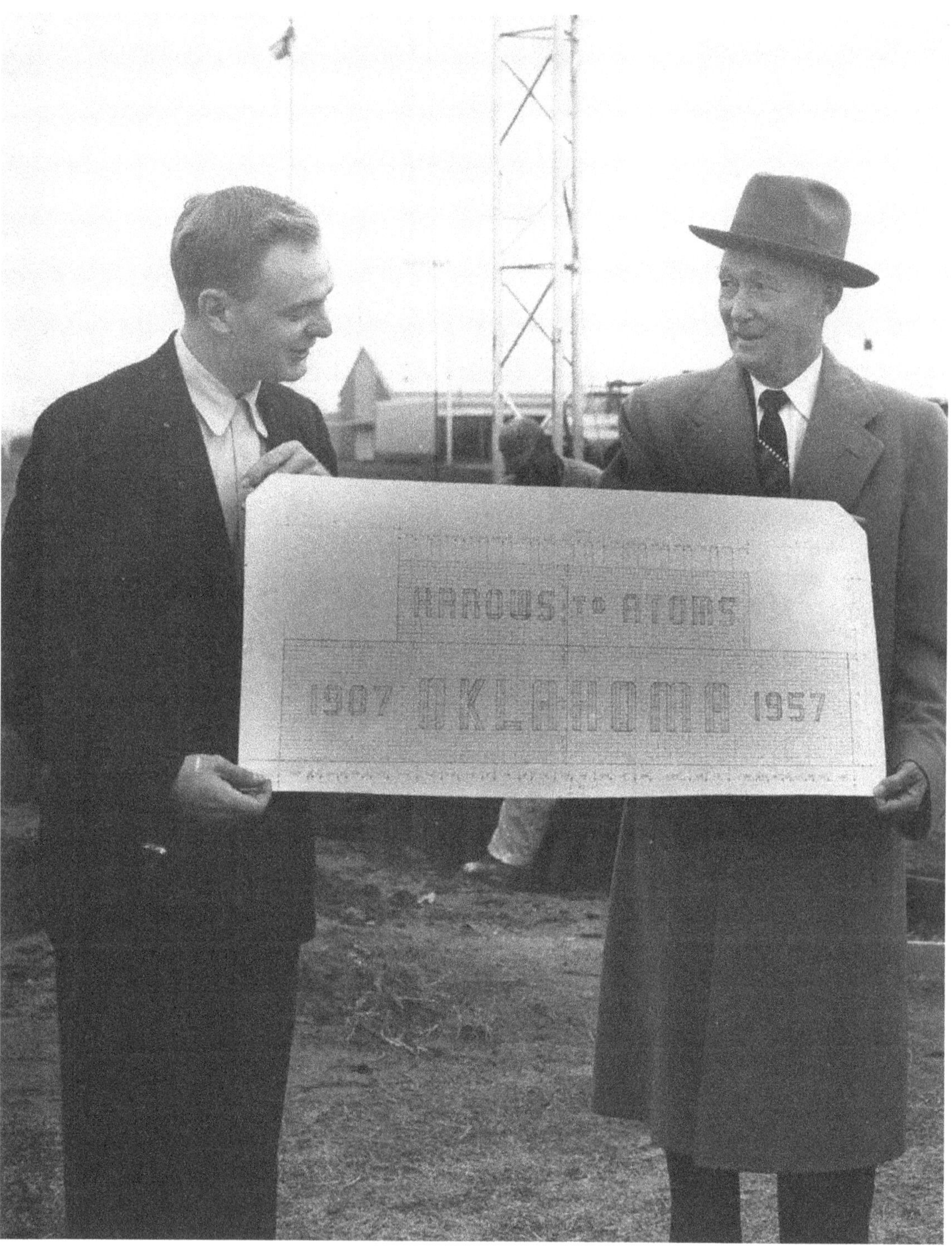

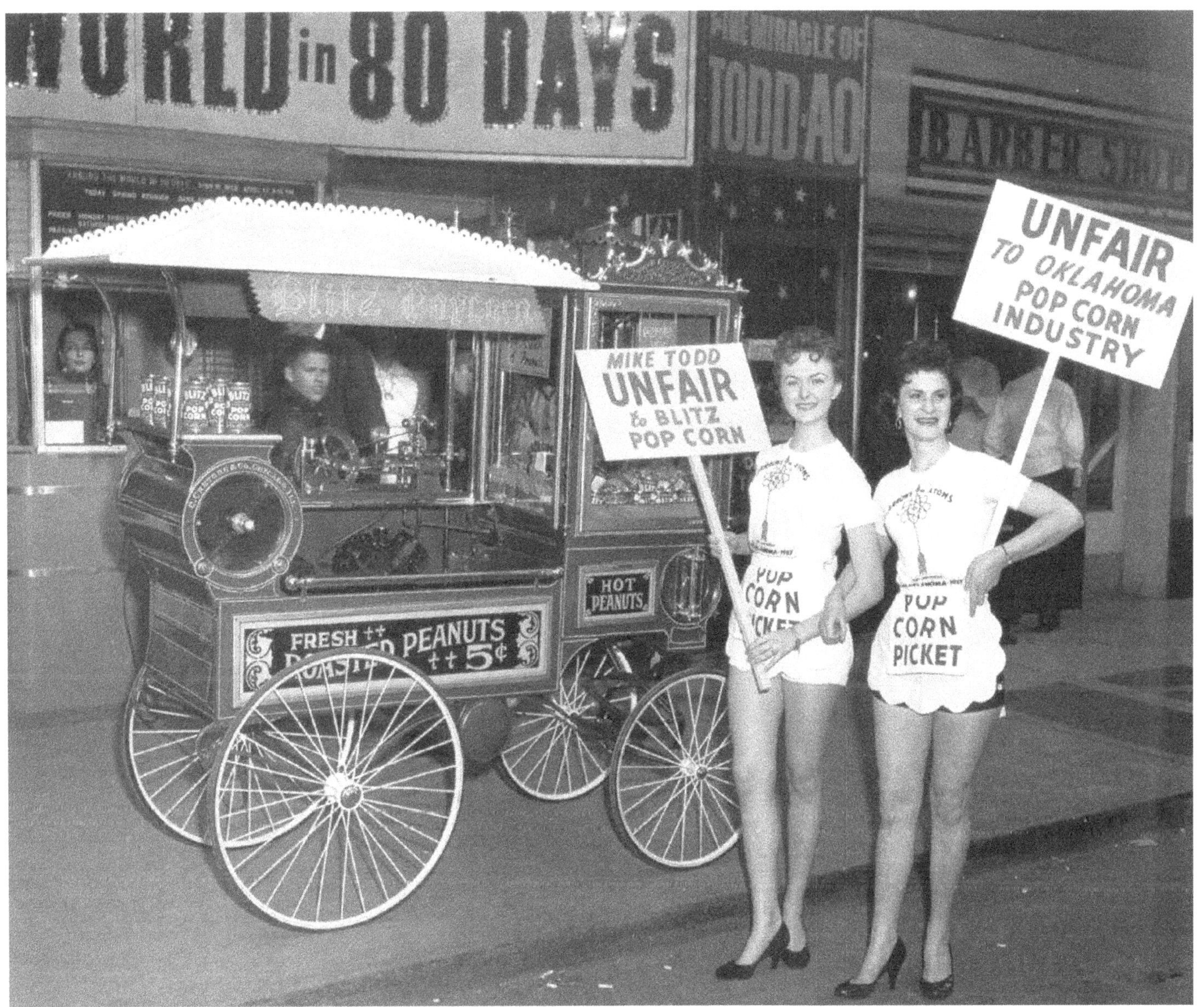

Hugo-based Blitz Popcorn made an attention-getting protest during the 1957 Semi-Centennial State Fair. The fair featured a cinema showing the Oscar-winning *Around the World in 80 Days,* and producer Mike Todd banned the sale of popcorn so viewers could marvel without distraction at the epic film.

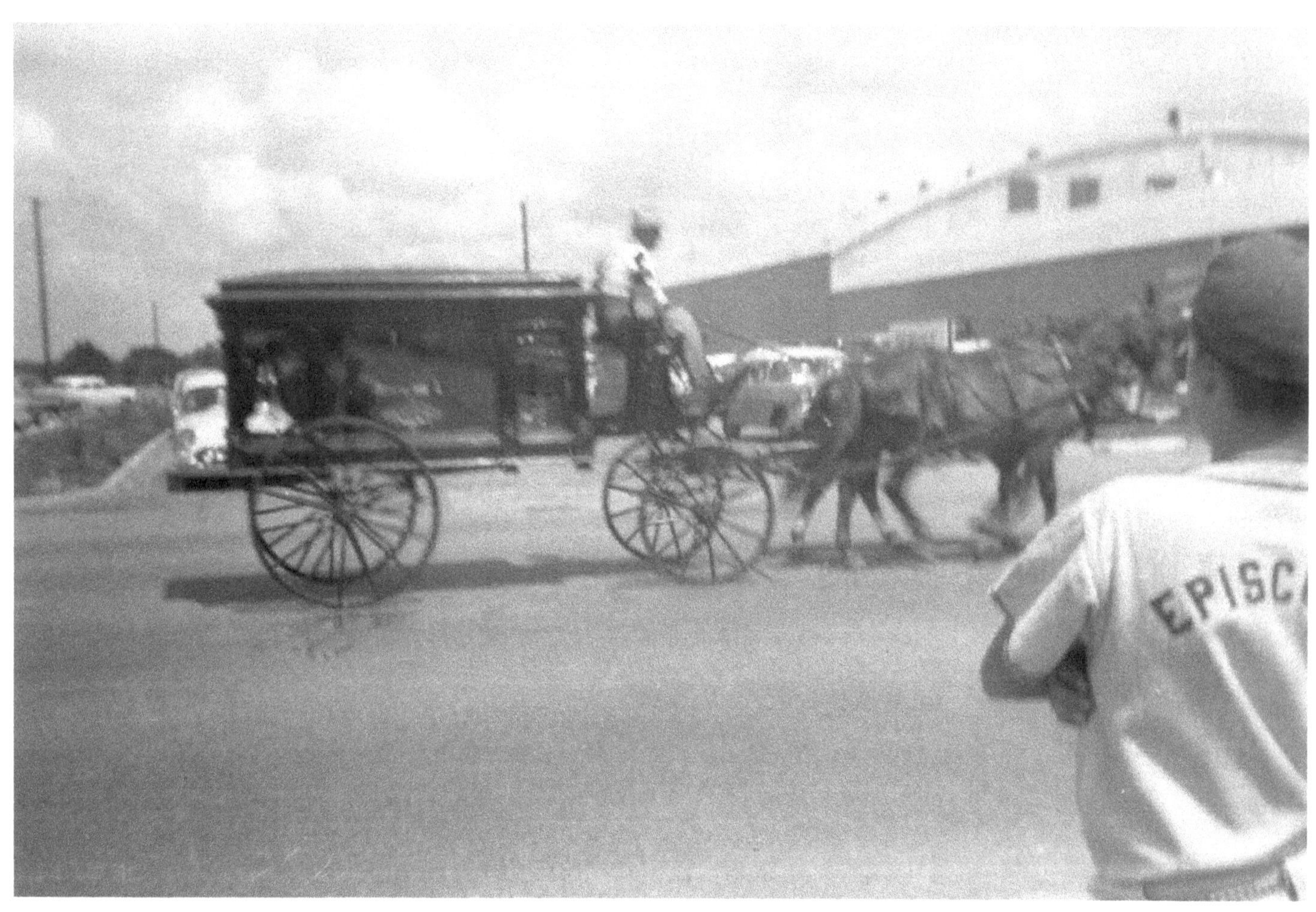

Celebrations were held throughout the year during the state's Semi-Centennial in 1957. Miami's parade in July featured a timeline of transportation from horse-drawn hearses to modern limousines.

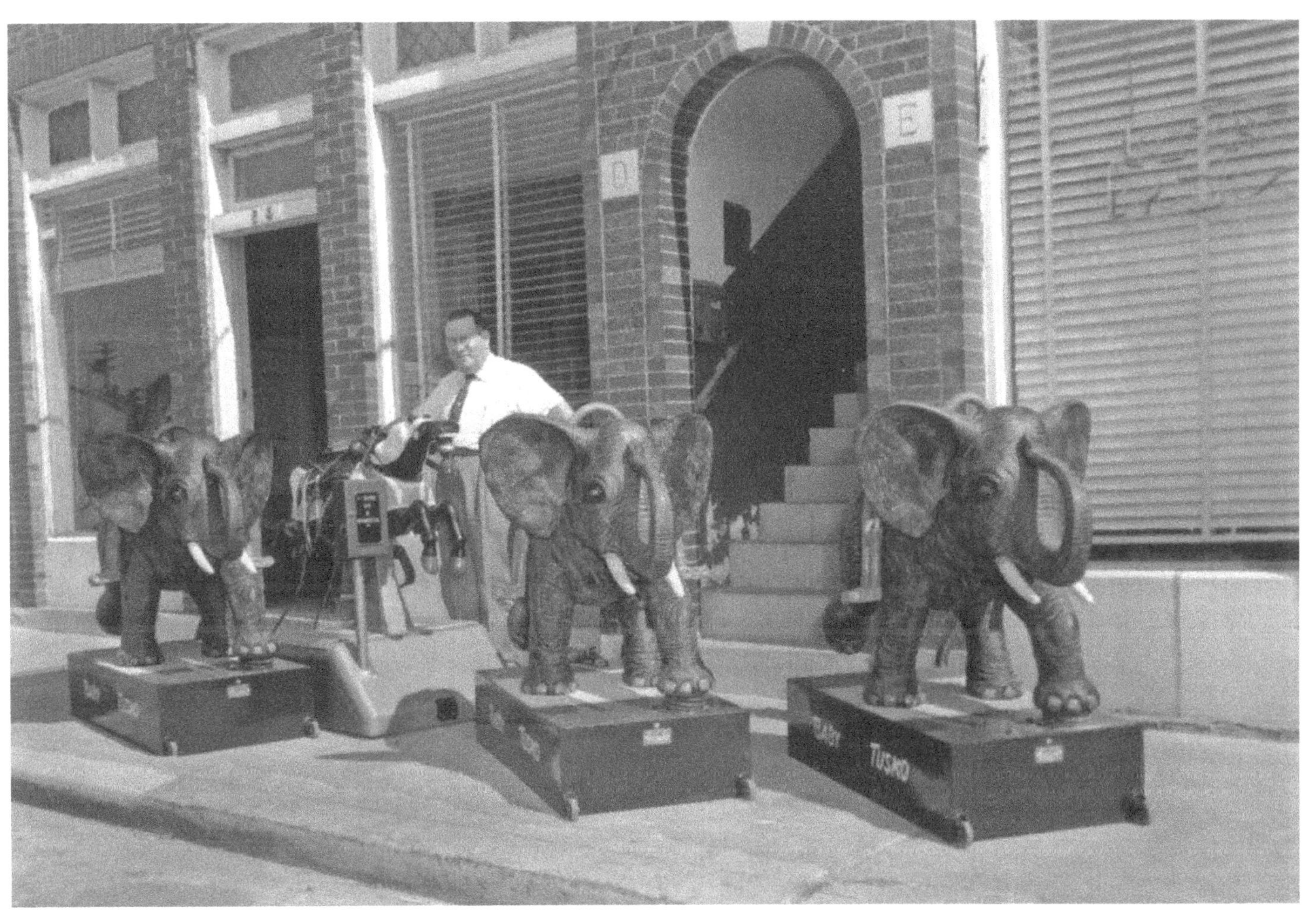

Outside Atkins Music Company in 1958, a galloping steed and three Baby Tusko rides await distribution to Oklahoma City area venues. Coin-operated animal rides were a staple feature of grocery stores and other places frequented by busy parents in the 1950s and 1960s.

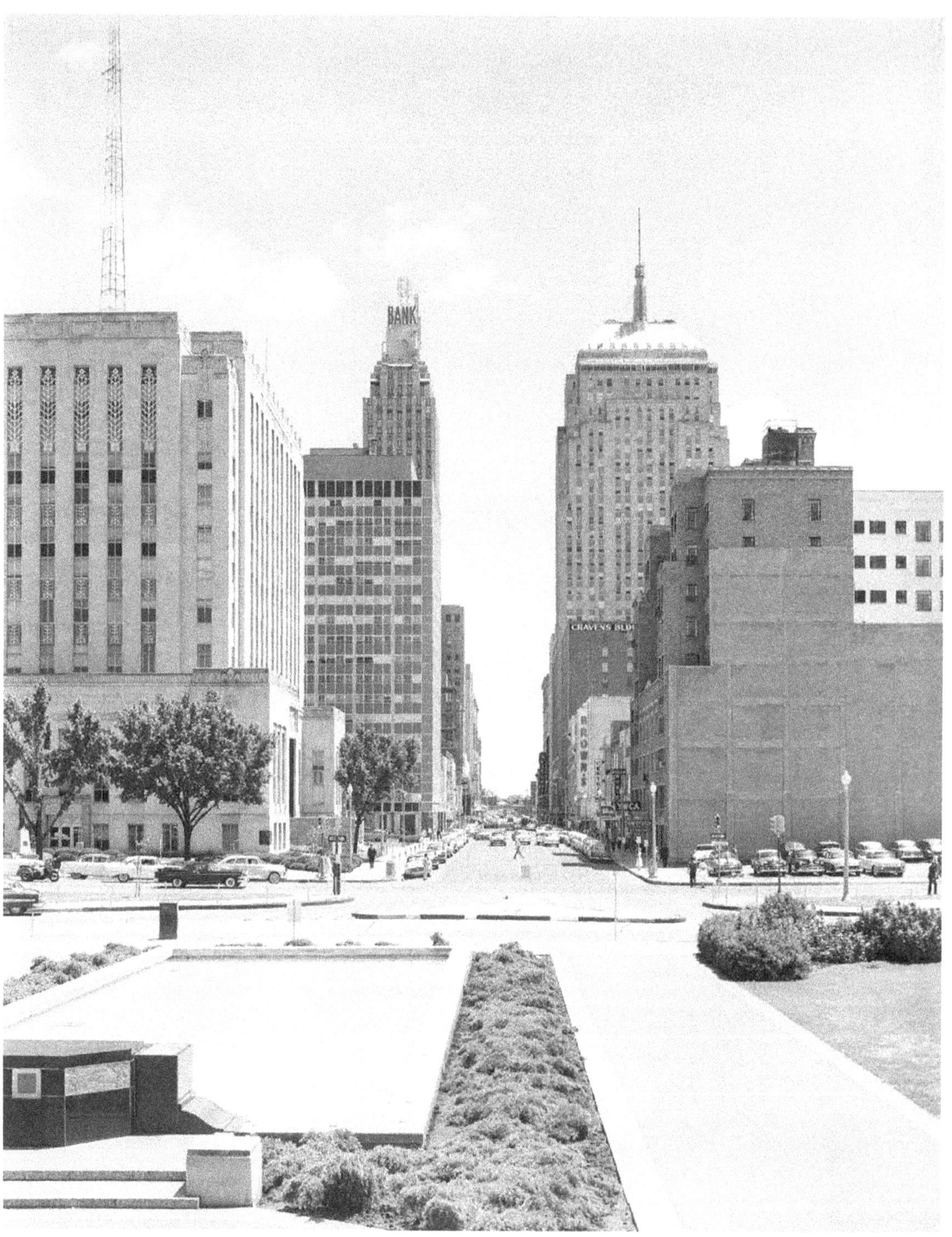

Oklahoma City's busy Park Avenue as viewed looking west from the steps of City Hall, 1958. This section of town was developed in the 1930s on a former railroad right-of-way that divided the city and caused major traffic snarls.

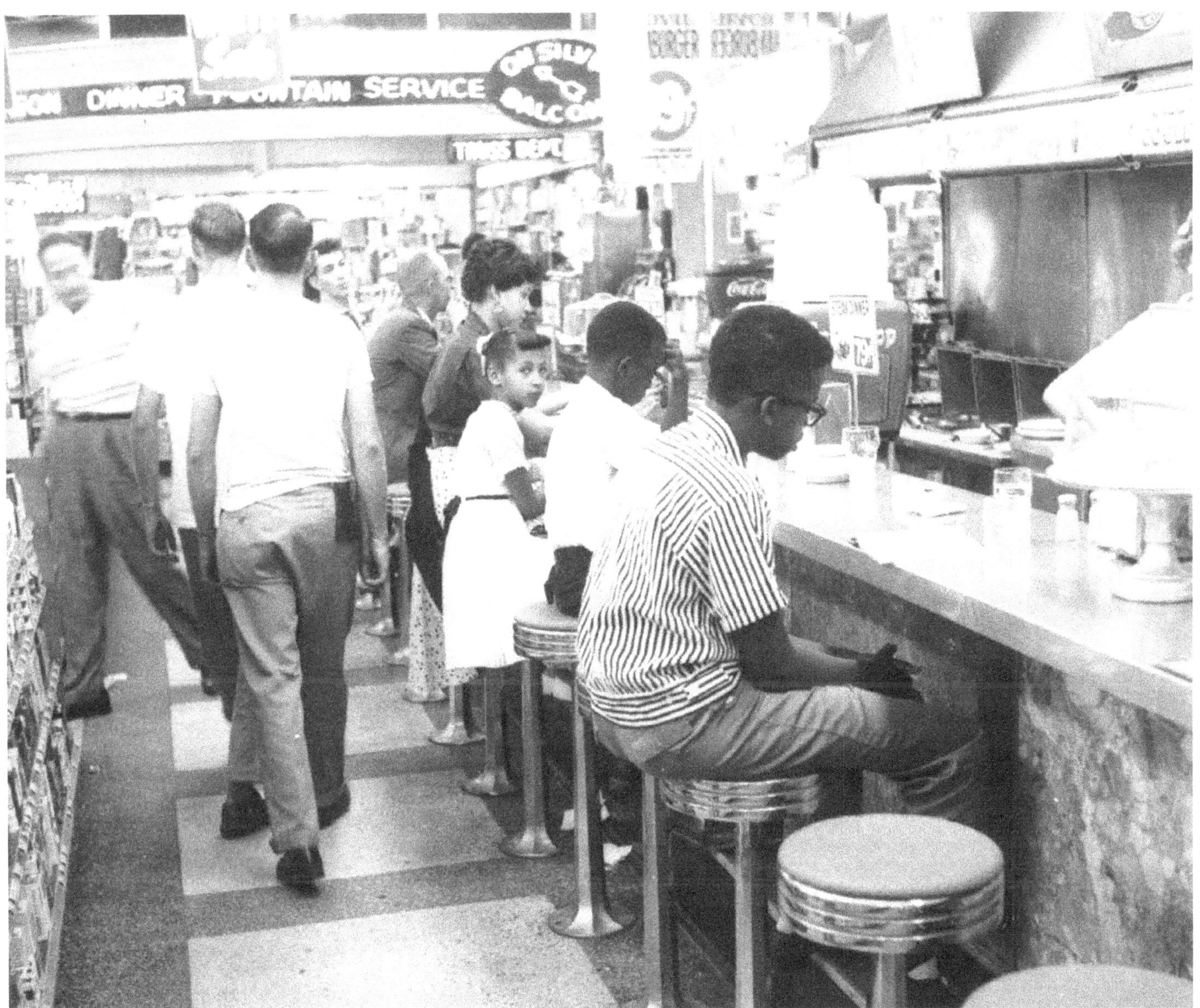

Among the nation's earliest sit-ins during the civil rights movement was the August 1958 demonstration at Katz Drug Store in Oklahoma City. Members of the NAACP Youth Council, led by Clara Luper, sat at the drugstore's fountain until management agreed to serve them. Three days later, their first battle had been won.

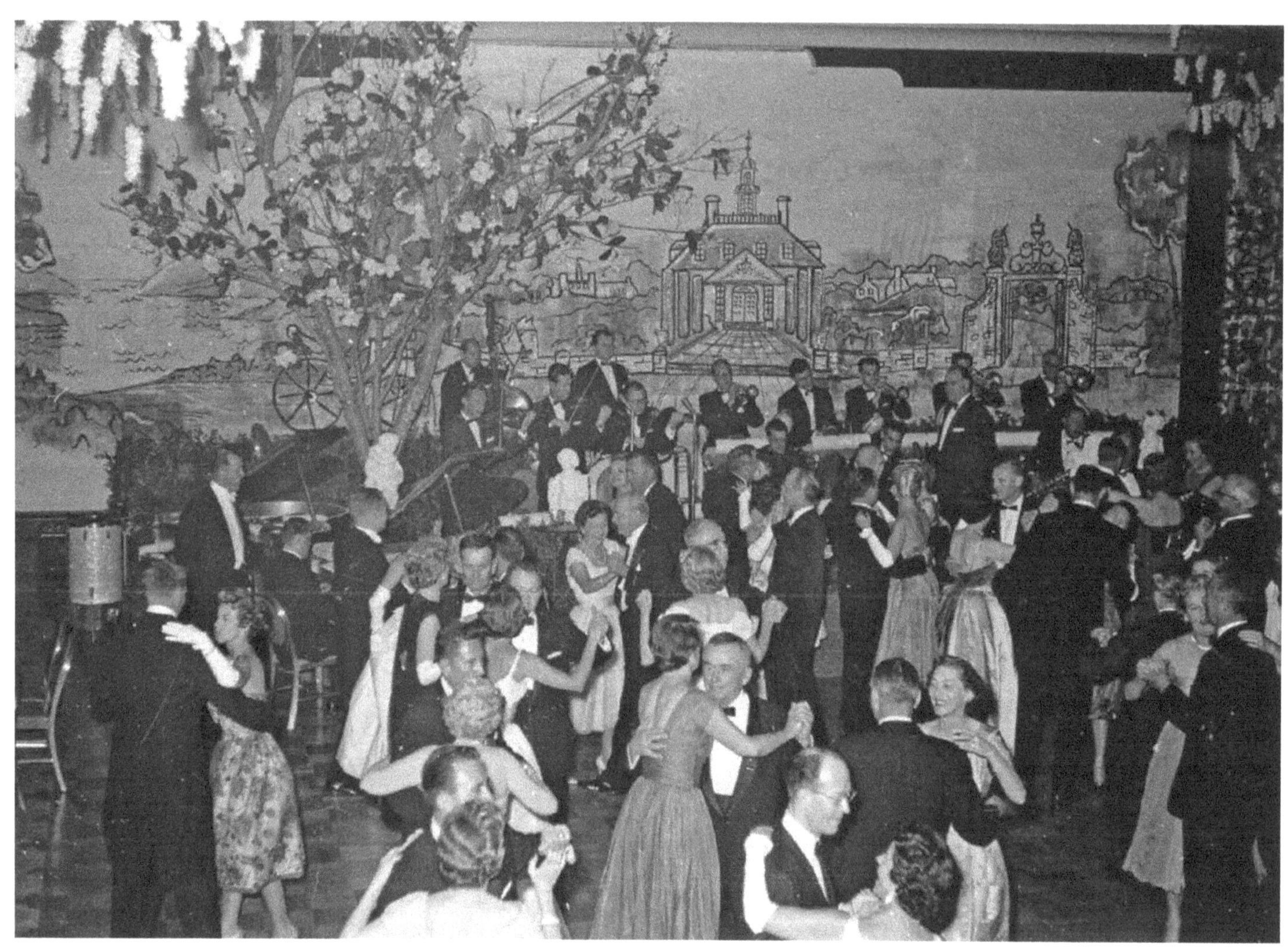

Oklahoma City's elite twirl about the Persian Room of the Skirvin Tower during the Spring Ball of 1959. The Williamsburg-themed event, which featured waiters costumed as powdered-wigged footmen, was for the benefit of the Oklahoma City Symphony.

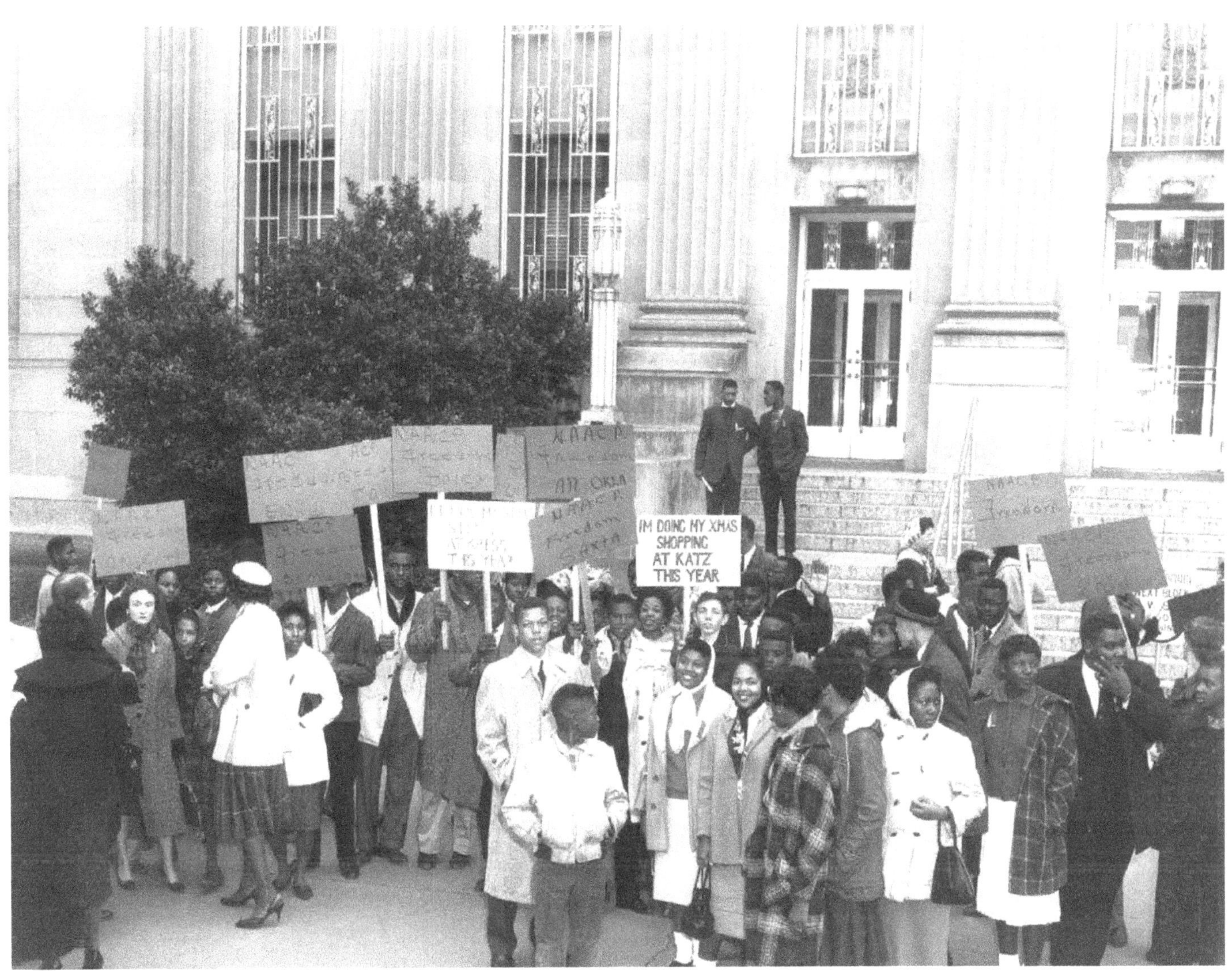

These students made several unsuccessful sit-in attempts in downtown Oklahoma City establishments in December 1960 before assembling on the steps of City Hall to sing Christmas carols and shout pep yells. Despite their earlier successes, the local "sit-inners" still had a long struggle ahead.

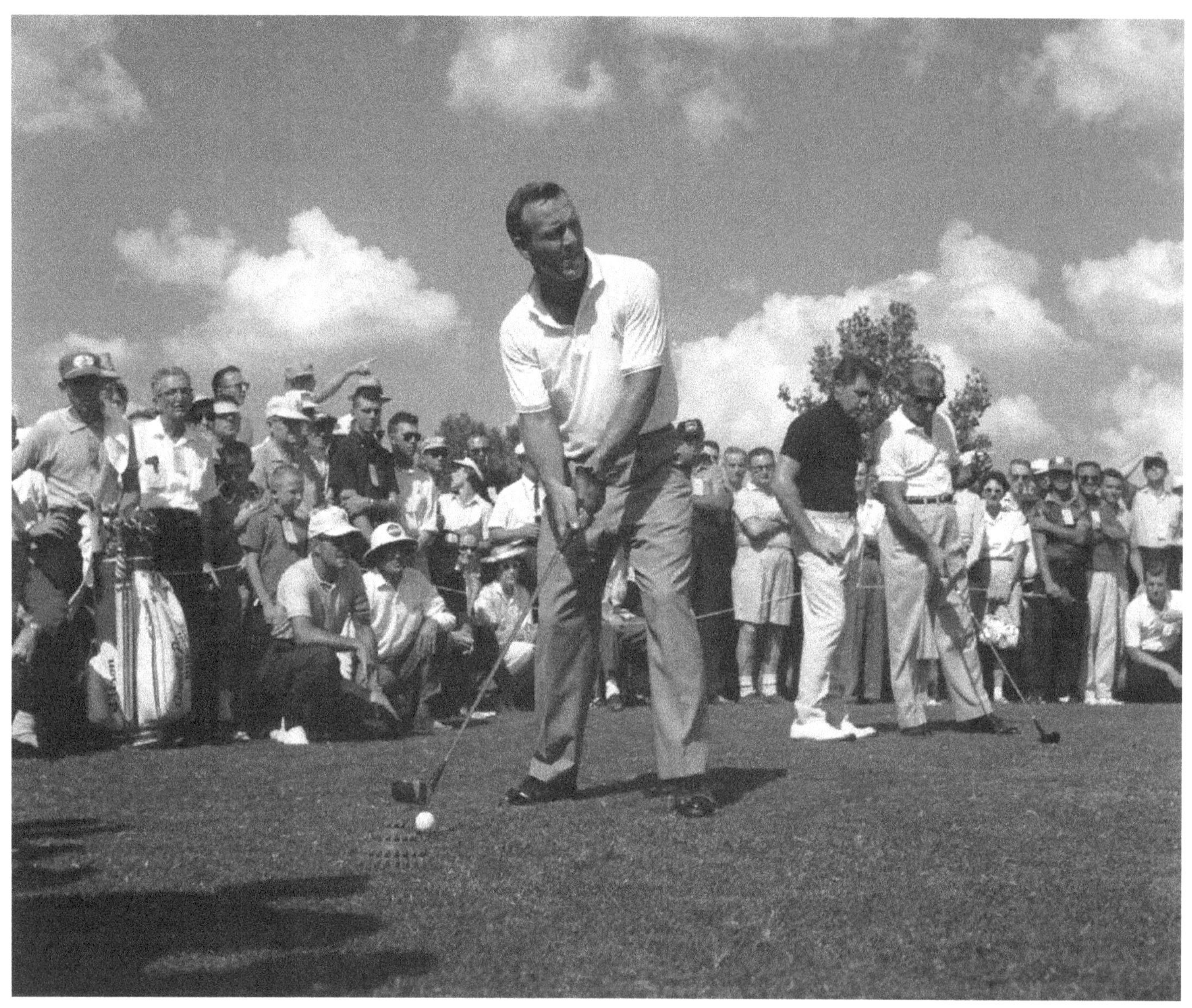

Golfing legend Arnold Palmer visited Oklahoma City's Lincoln Park course in September 1961 to square off against Gary Player as part of a 25-match series played across five nations. Palmer won the Lincoln Park match 68–75.

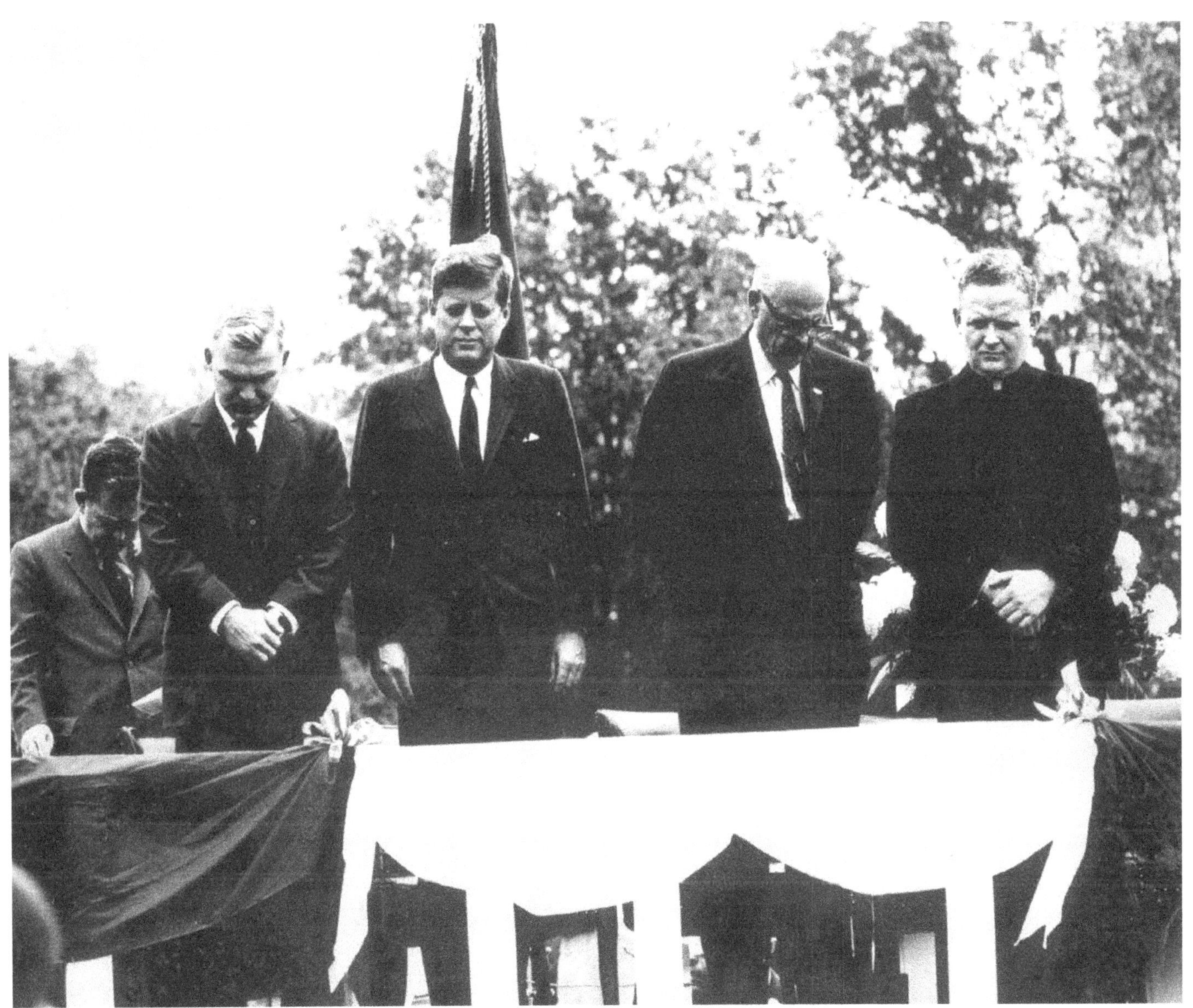

In October 1961, President John F. Kennedy arrived at the tiny crossroads village of Big Cedar to formally open the scenic highway between Poteau and Broken Bow. Here Kennedy is seen on the dais flanked by Governor J. Howard Edmondson, at left, and Senator Robert S. Kerr, at right.

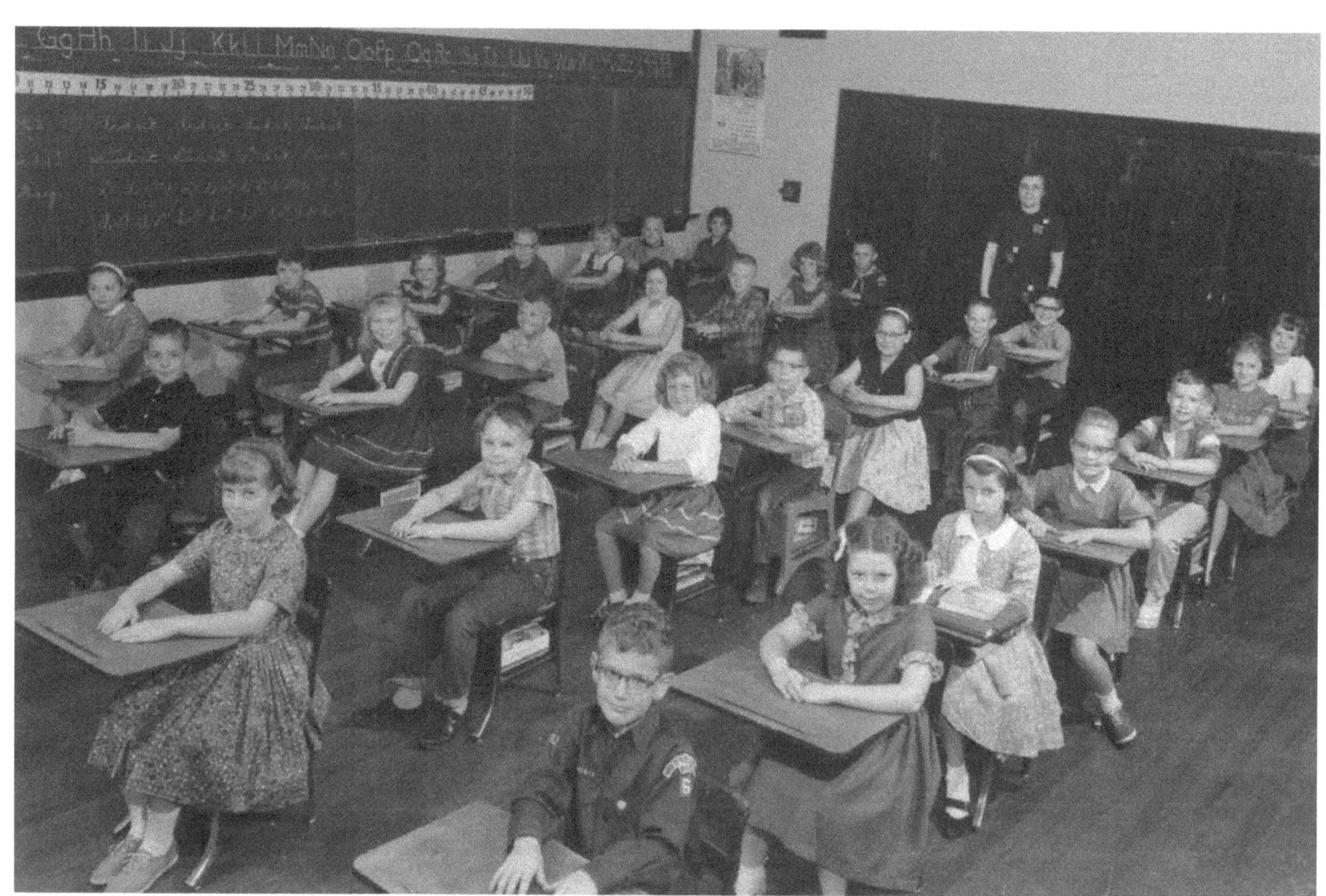

Children at attention, Guthrie Central Elementary School, 1962.

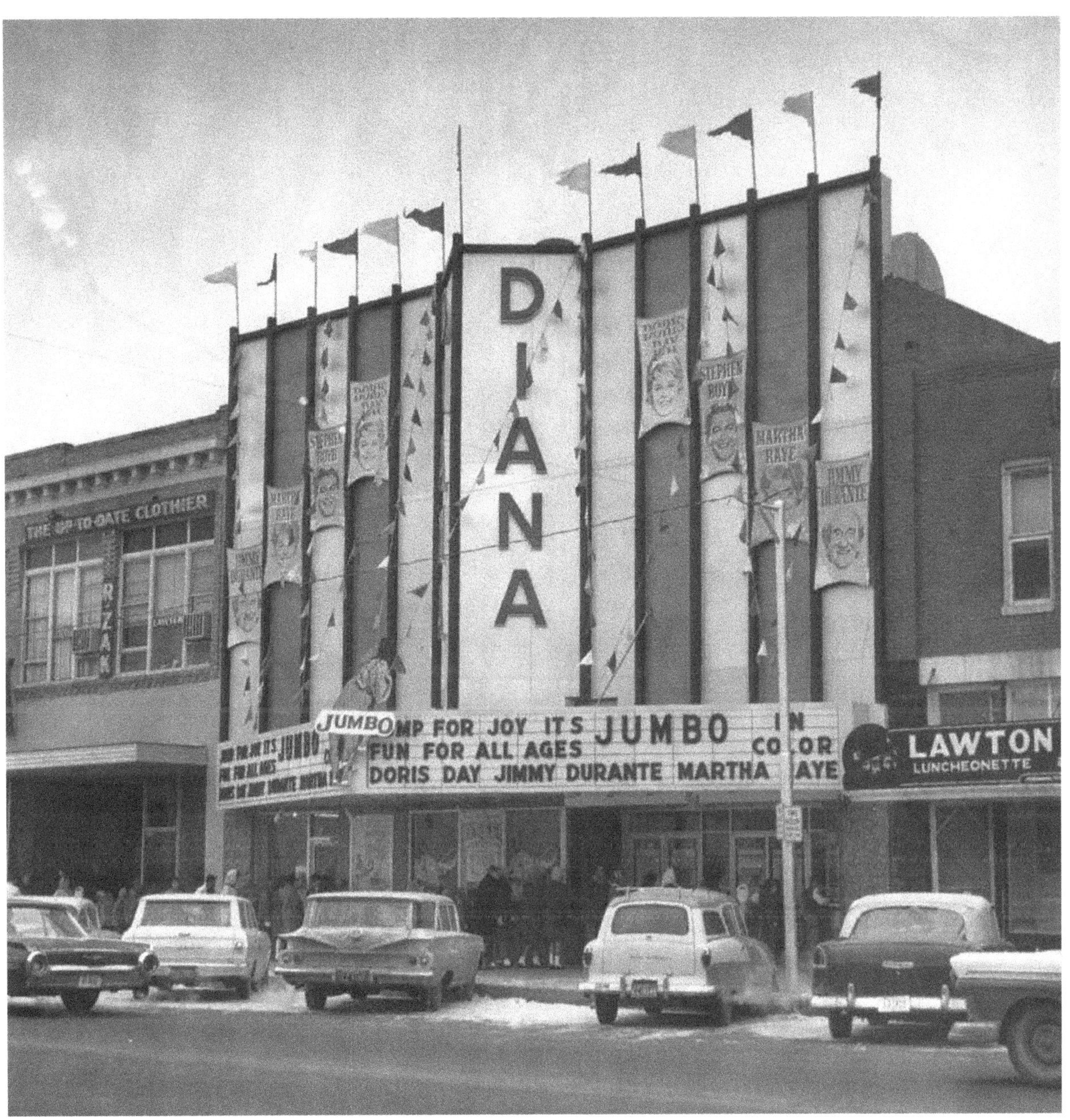

The Diana Theatre at Third and D, seen here ca. 1963, was once part of Lawton's bustling downtown. In the 1970s, Lawton officials used urban renewal funds to raze about a dozen city blocks and build a large shopping mall in place of the downtown district.

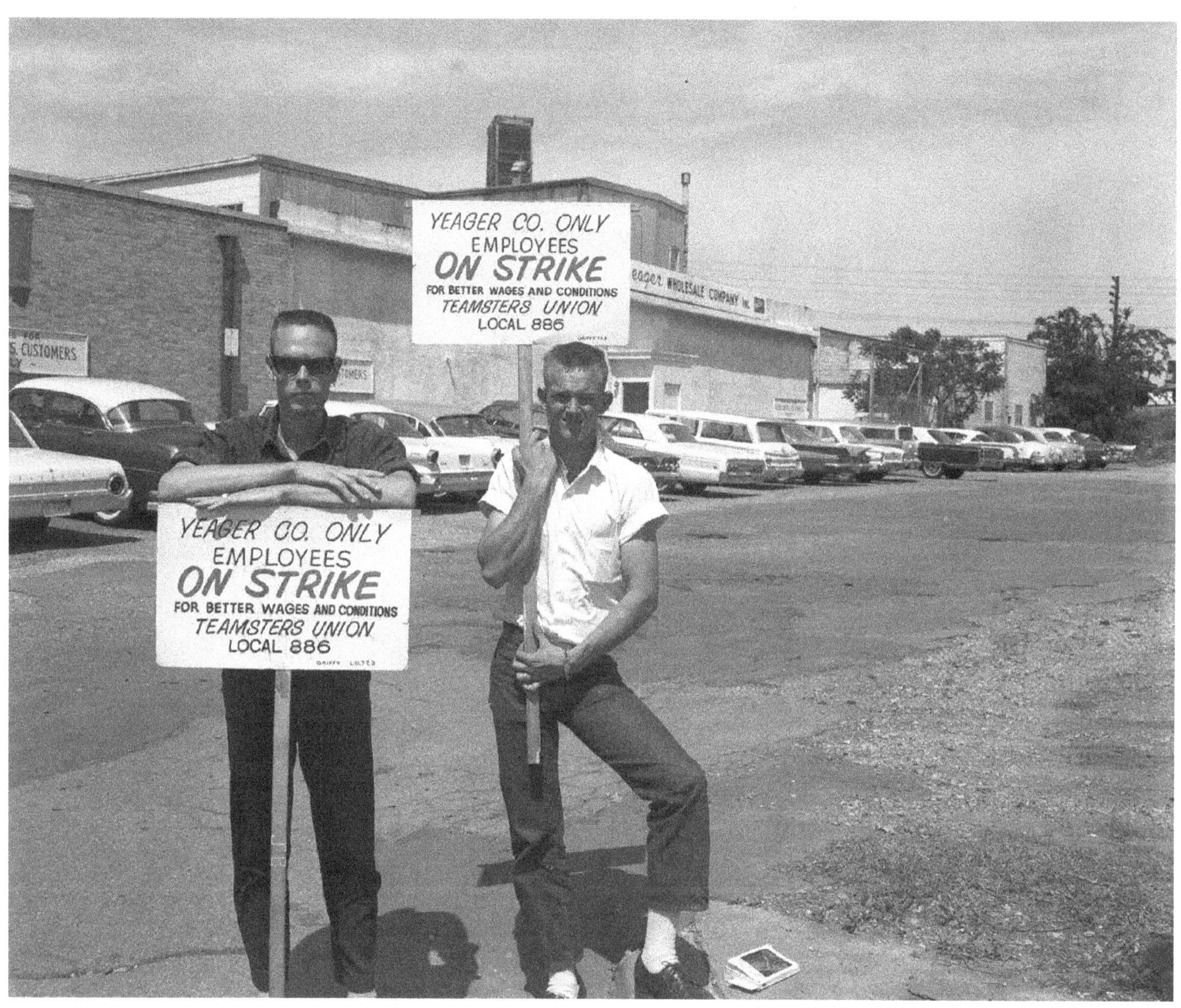

Members of the Teamsters Union strike for better pay and working conditions at the Yeager Wholesale Company's warehouse at Northwest Twenty-fifth and Broadway in Oklahoma City, May 1964.

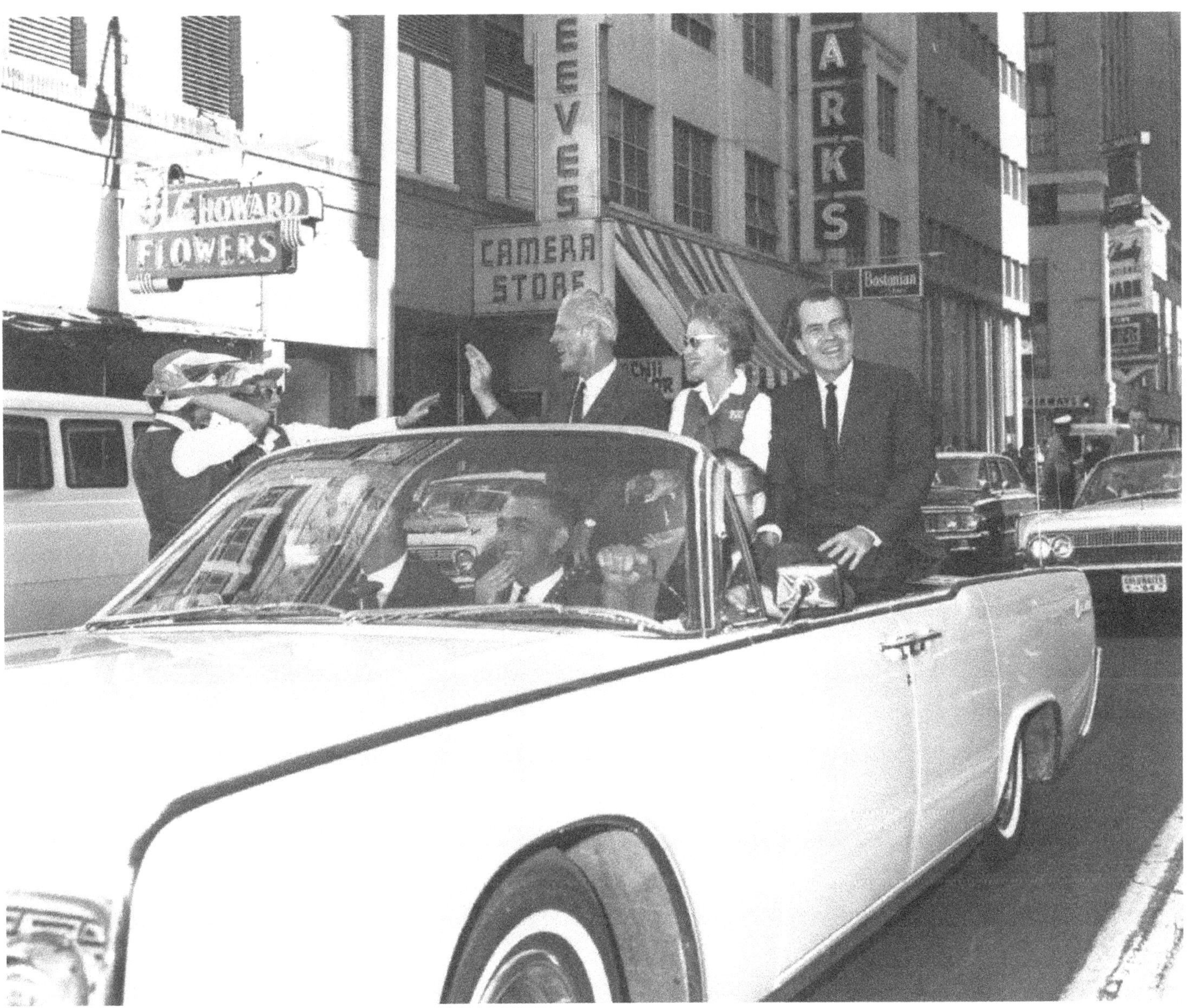

On the eve of the 1964 election, Richard Nixon visited Oklahoma City in support of his friend Bud Wilkinson, the legendary Oklahoma football coach running for the U.S. Senate. Nixon was between jobs that election cycle, but he campaigned for Republicans around the nation. Wilkinson lost his bid for office but later was a Nixon advisor.

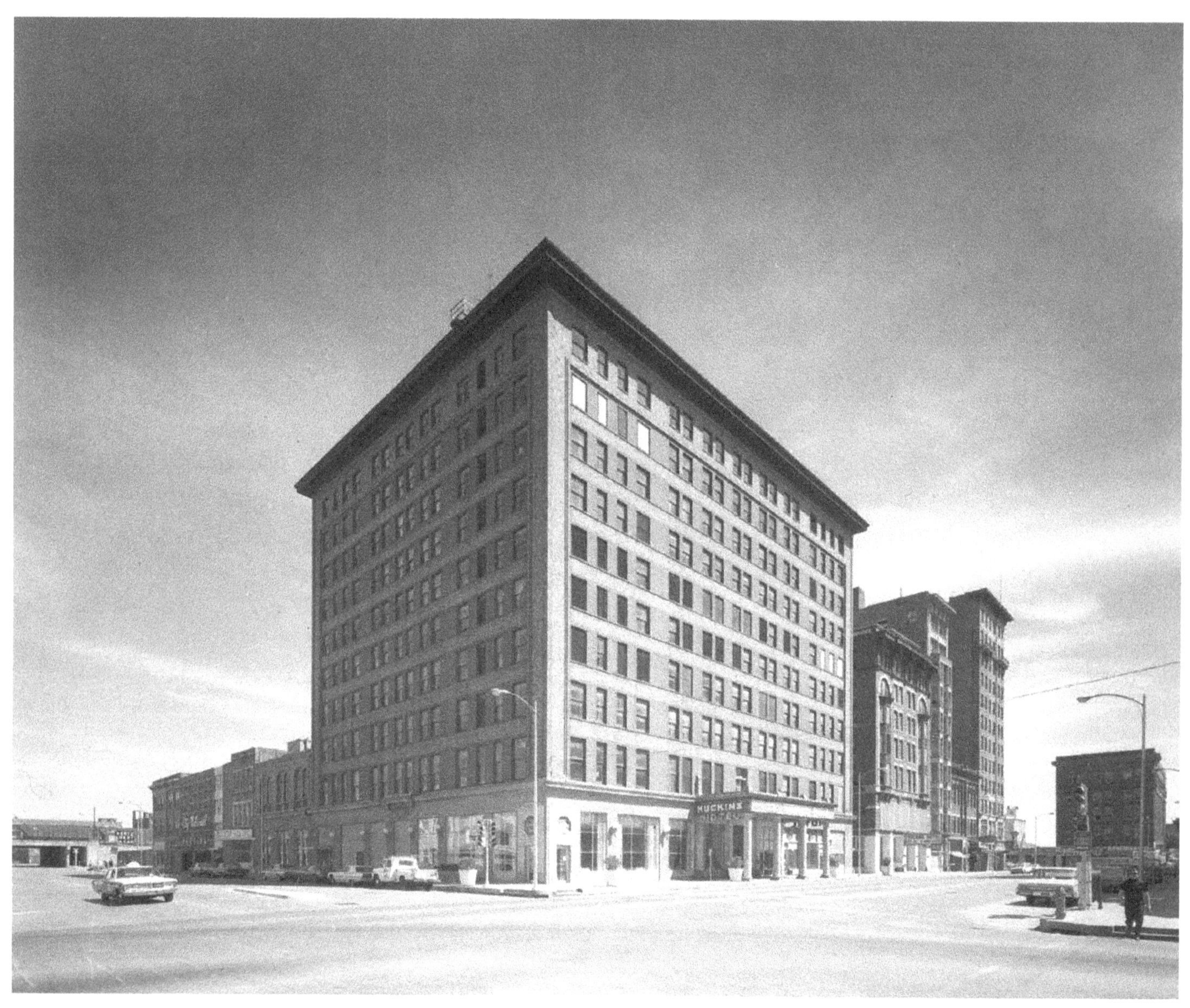

Seen in 1968, this view of Oklahoma City's Huckins Hotel shows it at the time of its auction, just prior to its demise for urban renewal. For over 50 years the Huckins had been the proverbial "smoke-filled room" of politics in the capital city.

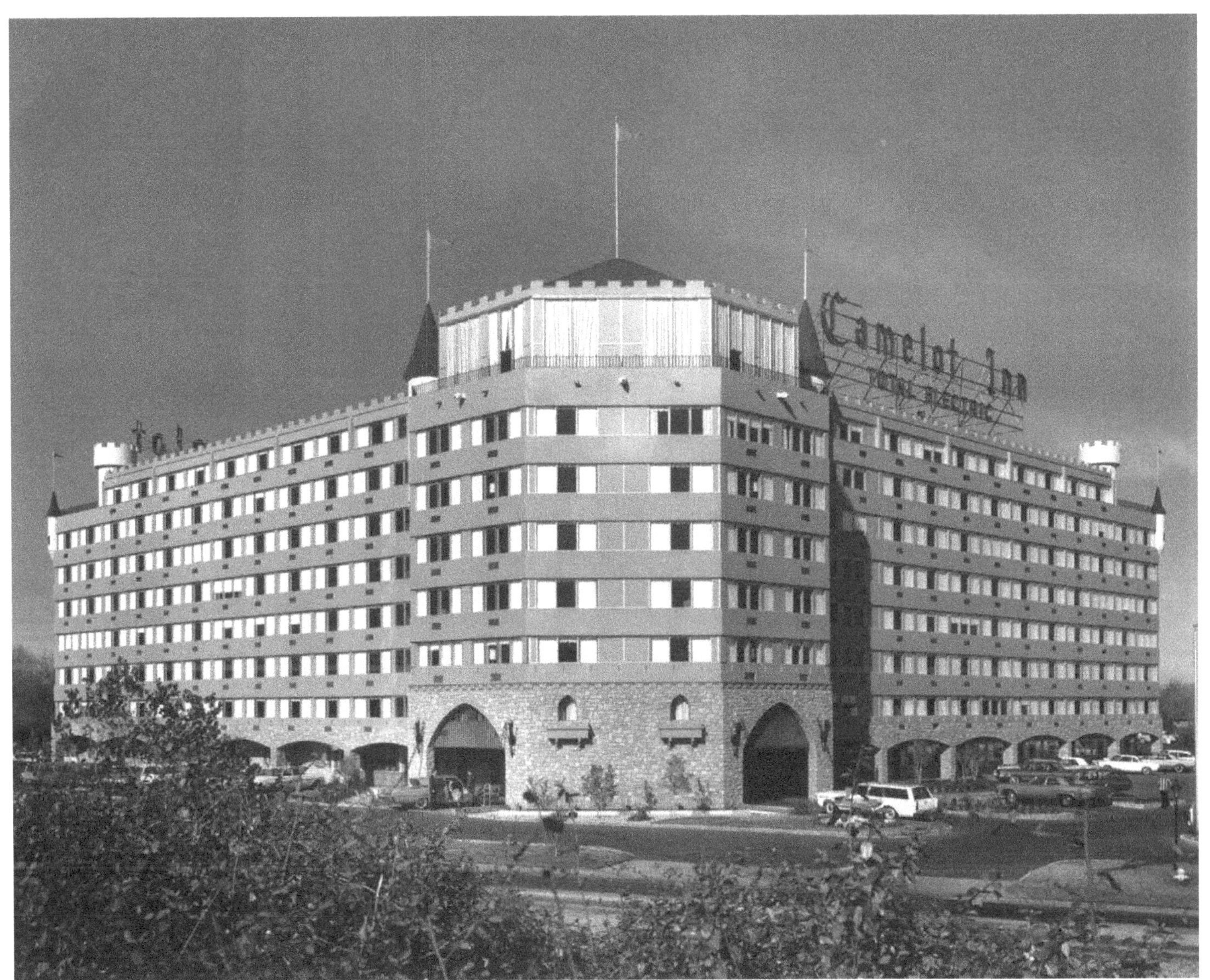

Tulsa's Camelot Hotel was brand new when this photo was made in 1966. Over its 41-year life, the moat-ringed inn played host to Tulsa's most notable guests, including Elvis Presley and Presidents Nixon, Ford, and Reagan. The Camelot's walls were breached in a final siege by wrecking crews in 2007.

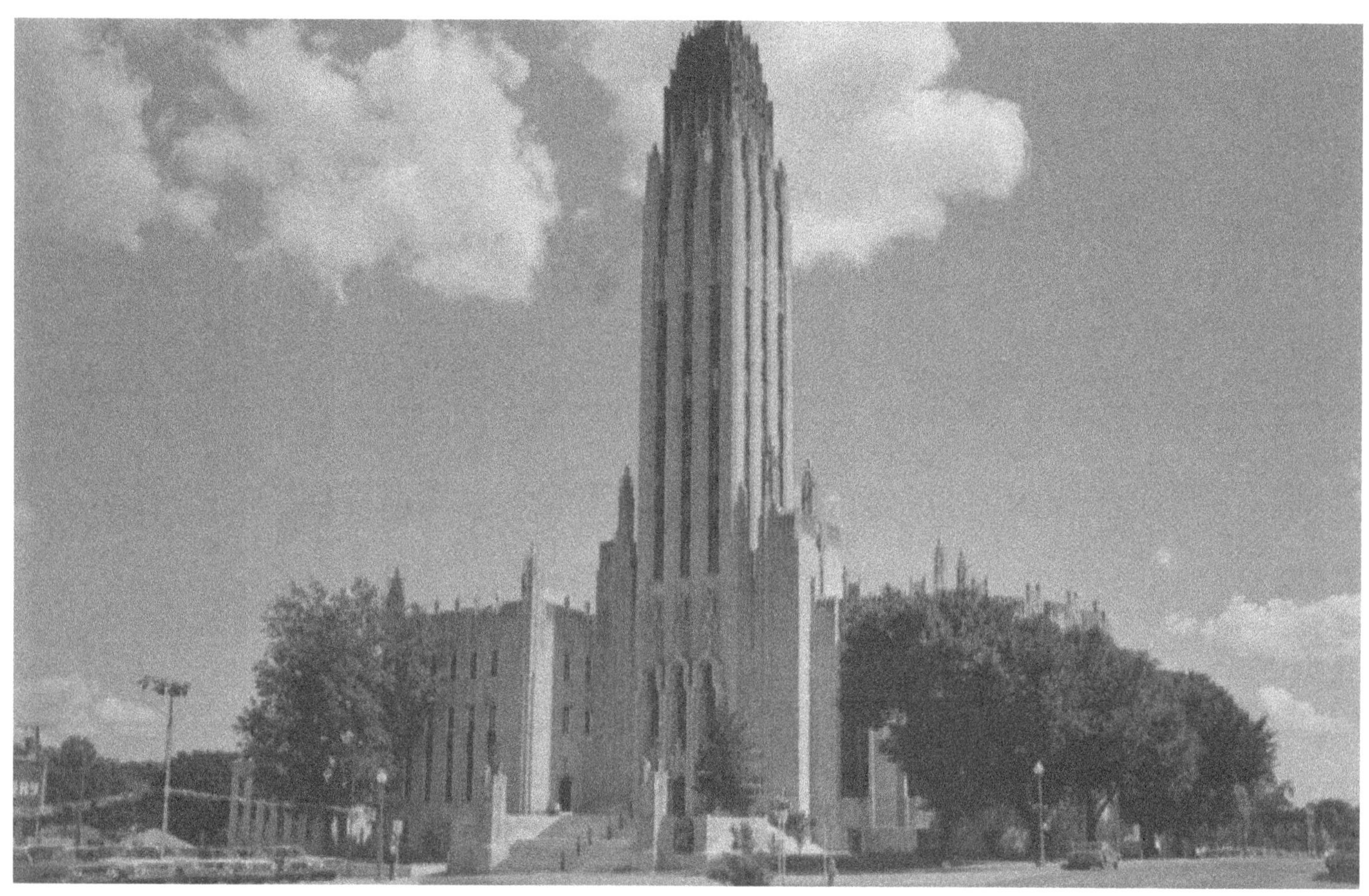

One of the state's most enduring architectural landmarks is Tulsa's Boston Avenue Methodist Church. Seen here in the 1960s, the church was completed in 1929 and its design, attributed to Bruce Goff, is considered quintessential art deco. It was named a National Historic Landmark in 1999.

Notes on the Photographs

These notes, listed by page number, attempt to include all aspects known of the photographs. Each of the photographs is identified by the page number, photograph's title or description, photographer and collection, archive, and call or box number when applicable. Although every attempt was made to collect all data, in some cases complete data was unavailable due to the age and condition of some of the photographs and records.

II **Fourth of July Celebration**
Oklahoma Historical Society
3303

VI **Iowa Indians in Guthrie**
Oklahoma Historical Society
3431

X **Finley Bowen Family**
Oklahoma Historical Society
15175

1 **Chapter Title**
from "Oklahoma Hills"
by Leon Jerry Guthrie and
Woody Guthrie

2 **Officers' Housing**
Oklahoma Historical Society
23347

3 **Basil LeFlore Home**
Oklahoma Historical Society
6435

4 **Stone Church**
Oklahoma Historical Society
2553

5 **Armstrong Academy**
Oklahoma Historical Society
6410 A

6 **Comanche School**
Oklahoma Historical Society
3728

7 **Comanches Encamped Near Fort Sill**
Library of Congress
LC-USZ62-53778

8 **Indian Tribes' Representatives**
Oklahoma Historical Society
8828

9 **Students at Seminole School in Wewoka**
Oklahoma Historical Society
1459

10 **Cowboy Dinner**
Oklahoma Historical Society
5078

11 **No-Man's Land Ranch**
Oklahoma Historical Society
15008

12 **Family Crossing into the Unassigned Lands**
Oklahoma Historical Society
21412.BH772.2

13 **Federal Troops Watering Horses**
Oklahoma Historical Society
9273

14 **Crowds Gather in Purcell**
Oklahoma Historical Society
18633

15 **Oklahoma City's Second Post Office**
Oklahoma Historical Society
8204

16 **Settlers Trying to Claim Lots**
Oklahoma Historical Society
15731

17 **Resident Holding Down a Lot**
Oklahoma Historical Society
15727

18 **Scene in Guthrie After Destruction of Liquor Supply**
Oklahoma Historical Society
4574.96

19 **St. John the Baptist Church**
Oklahoma Historical Society
3402

20 **A. W. Bennett's Grocery**
Oklahoma Historical Society
8032

21 **Kiowa Scout Elk Tongue**
Library of Congress
LC-USZ62-126697

22 **Marshal Paden Tolbert's Posse**
Oklahoma Historical Society
4069

23 **Land Run**
Oklahoma Historical Society
8426

24 Crowd Waiting at Perry Land Office
Oklahoma Historical Society
8405 B

25 View from Sixth and C Streets in Perry
Oklahoma Historical Society
8397

26 East Side of Enid Town Square
Oklahoma Historical Society
20282-66-1-17-60

27 Blaine County Sod Schoolhouse
Oklahoma Historical Society
3875

28 Jefferson Bowen Farm
Oklahoma Historical Society
3882

29 Elk City on Cotton Auction Day
Oklahoma Historical Society
7268

30 Last Choctaw Execution
Library of Congress
LC-USZ6-1849

31 Disastrous Fire in Ardmore
Oklahoma Historical Society
5254

32 U.S. Geological Survey Crew
Oklahoma Historical Society
8084

33 Street Fair in Blackwell
Oklahoma Historical Society
7845

34 Cherokee Female Seminary
Oklahoma Historical Society
1740

36 Tornado Near Oklahoma City
Library of Congress
LC-USZ62-95937

37 Group of Girls in Augusta
Oklahoma Historical Society
867

38 Members of the Dawes Commission
Oklahoma Historical Society
15870

39 Ponca City
Oklahoma Historical Society
20577-96-34-2636

40 Grant Foreman
Oklahoma Historical Society
8470

41 Dedication Parade for Shawnee Waterworks
Oklahoma Historical Society
4365

42 Youthful Group in Sulphur Springs
Oklahoma Historical Society
8244

43 Truax & Hopkins Hardware and Furniture Store
Oklahoma Historical Society
16828

44 Buffalo Bill's Wild West Show
Oklahoma Historical Society
18803

45 Chapter Title
from "The Farmer and the Cowman"
by Oscar Hammerstein II and Richard Rodgers

46 Home of Chief Tawakoni Jim
Oklahoma Historical Society
14994

47 Wagon Crossing the Neosho River
Oklahoma Historical Society
14754 A

48 Land Lottery in El Reno
Oklahoma Historical Society
8674

49 Chartered Buses in El Reno
Oklahoma Historical Society
8676

50 El Reno Liquor Company
Oklahoma Historical Society
9222

51 Oil Well in Lawton
Oklahoma Historical Society
4564

52 Cotton Market in Downtown Ardmore
Oklahoma Historical Society
35-1

53 Coal Mine in Wilberton
Oklahoma Historical Society
12973

54 Wheat Harvest Near Geary
Oklahoma Historical Society
4737

55 Apache Leader Geronimo
Library of Congress
LC-USZ62-45822

56 Geronimo's Last Buffalo Hunt
Library of Congress
LC-USZ62-127717

57 Creek Orphans' Home Baseball Team
Oklahoma Historical Society
1580

58 Rope Trick
Library of Congress
LC-USZ62-56646

59 Choctaw Lumber Company
Oklahoma Historical Society
2425.8

60 Trolley Car
Oklahoma Historical Society
5452

61 Osage Camp
Library of Congress
LC-USZ62-118787

62 **Pitts-Wells Grain Elevator in Broken Arrow**
Oklahoma Historical Society
4492

63 **Chickasha's First Christian Church**
Oklahoma Historical Society
2253

64 **Pit-roasting Chickens**
Oklahoma Historical Society
20288.93.19.1

65 **Bartlesville Interurban Company Track Construction**
Oklahoma Historical Society
2216

66 **Pawnee Bill**
Library of Congress
LC-USZ62-118293

67 **Minnie Chips**
Library of Congress
LC-USZ62-106983

68 **Buffalo Herd**
Oklahoma Historical Society
15255

69 **Typical Dugout in Western Oklahoma**
Library of Congress
LC-USZ62-100337

70 **Lead and Zinc Mining**
Library of Congress
pan 6a08639

72 **Lucille Mulhall**
Library of Congress
LC-USZ62-126135

73 **Oklahoma State Prison East Gate**
Oklahoma Historical Society
5754

74 **Butcher Tom Murphy and Others**
Oklahoma Historical Society
20760-1

75 **Colored Agricultural and Normal School Band**
Oklahoma Historical Society
20819-10-9

76 **Steer Roping Contestants**
Library of Congress
pan 6a28898

78 **Stickball Players**
Oklahoma Historical Society
1058

79 **Labor Day Parade in Sapulpa**
Oklahoma Historical Society
14481

80 **Twister near Ponca City**
Library of Congress
LC-USZ62-95938

81 **First Passenger Train Arriving in Woodward**
Oklahoma Historical Society
5444

82 **Drumright**
Library of Congress
pan 6a08677

83 **Oklahoma City's Emanuel Synagogue Members**
Oklahoma Historical Society
9225

84 **Charlie Scott**
Library of Congress
LC-DIG-nclc-04027

85 **Workshop of Sanitary Ice Cream Cone Company**
Library of Congress
LC-DIG-nclc-05241

86 **Jefferson School in Muskogee**
Library of Congress
LC-DIG-nclc-00686

87 **Oklahoma School for Deaf Mutes**
Library of Congress
LC-DIG-nclc-05254

88 **Lawton Schoolchildren**
Library of Congress
LC-DIG-nclc-05209

89 **Pauls Valley Training School**
Library of Congress
LC-DIG-nclc-05248

90 **Castle on the Hill**
Oklahoma Historical Society
21330 B

91 **American Red Cross Workers in Muskogee**
Oklahoma Historical Society
11586

92 **Armistice Day Parade**
Oklahoma Historical Society
10208

93 **Oklahoma Military Academy Cadets**
Oklahoma Historical Society
739

94 **O.K. Bus & Baggage Company Buses**
Oklahoma Historical Society
21120-11

95 **Cherokee Orphan Asylum Girls**
Oklahoma Historical Society
533

96 **West Duncan Oil and Gas Field**
Oklahoma Historical Society
23139-IO-O-F-D-5-2

97 **Federal Agents Destroying Liquor**
Oklahoma Historical Society
13647

98 **Black Wall Street Burns**
Oklahoma Historical Society
16936

99 **National Guardsmen at Tulsa Police Station**
Oklahoma Historical Society
16937

100 **Jeff Beaty and Joe Kimbrough**
Oklahoma Historical Society
18248

101 **University of Oklahoma's Holmberg Hall**
Oklahoma Historical Society
19352-5

102 **Nollin and Plow Boy at the Dewey Roundup**
Oklahoma Historical Society
22024.1

103 **Chickasaws Stir Cauldrons of Pashofa**
Oklahoma Historical Society
19589-19-30

104 **Aerial View of the Mile-long Barbecue Pits at Walton Inauguration**
Oklahoma Historical Society
19580-1

105 **Camp Wolf at Fort Sill**
Oklahoma Historical Society
4795

106 **A Gusher at Okemah**
Library of Congress
LC-USZ6-1903

107 **First Oklahoma State Flag**
Library of Congress
LC-DIG-npcc-26030

108 **Medicine Park Near Lawton**
Oklahoma Historical Society
22547.3

109 **Downtown Ardmore**
Oklahoma Historical Society
19589-6-4

110 **Oklahoma State Capitol**
Oklahoma Historical Society
15283

111 **Captured Bank Robbers**
Oklahoma Historical Society
15068

112 **Passengers Waiting to Board a Ward Way Lines Bus**
Oklahoma Historical Society
20281.2

113 **Southwestern Lumbermen's Association Short Course for Builders**
Oklahoma Historical Society
23350-1

114 **Real Wild West Show at the 101 Ranch**
Libary of Congress
pan 6a27090

116 **Ponca City**
Library of Congress
pan 6a08630

117 **Orpheum Theatre**
Oklahoma Historical Society
21412.BH1788

118 **Ada High School Band**
Oklahoma Historical Society
10653

119 **Chapter Title**
from "Dust Storm Disaster"
by Woody Guthrie

120 **Laborers for the Federal Civil Works Administration**
Oklahoma Historical Society
21486.A.2

121 **Army Blimp Being Inflated at Sapulpa**
Oklahoma Historical Society
21201-45

122 **Aftermath of a Devastating Tornado**
Oklahoma Historical Society
21412.M276.18

123 **Men of the Civil Works Administration**
Oklahoma Historical Society
21486.A.3

124 **Oklahoma Airlines Shuttle**
Oklahoma Historical Society
21412.M181.2

125 **The Hazel-Atlas Glass Company**
Oklahoma Historical Society
23141-AL-I9-O

126 **The Elk Movie Palace**
Oklahoma Historical Society
20546-8-1

127 **Garfield County's New Courthouse**
Oklahoma Historical Society
18225

128 **Young Boy in Cimarron County**
Library of Congress
LC-DIG-fsa-8b38282

129 **Okie Family on the Road**
Oklahoma Historical Society
21160.371014.9

130 **View up Broadway in Oklahoma City During Dust Storm**
Oklahoma Historical Society
20218.1044

131 **Students in Classroom During Dust Storm**
Oklahoma Historical Society
21171.1

132 **Guthrie's City Hall**
Oklahoma Historical Society
16583

133 **Town of Hooker Before Dust Storm**
Oklahoma Historical Society
20790.ST.DU.1

134 **Downtown Caddo**
Library of Congress
LC-DIG-fsa-8b32354

135 **A Family Near Muskogee**
Library of Congress
LC-USF33-012312-M1

136 **Idle Farmers Loiter in Sallisaw**
Library of Congress
LC-DIG-fsa-8b29735

137 **Boys Headed for Fishing Hole Near Muskogee**
Oklahoma Historical Society
15523

138 Oklahoma State Highway Patrol
Oklahoma Historical Society
20696

140 Migrant Workers Camped Near Prague
Library of Congress
LC-DIG-fsa-8b38113

141 Revival in Tahlequah
Library of Congress
LC-DIG-fsa-8a26796

142 Route 66 Along Vinita's Wilson Street
Oklahoma Historical Society
20546-27-4

143 The Poncan Theatre
Oklahoma Historical Society
21500-182-1

144 Community Gathering in McIntosh County
Library of Congress
LC-USF34-035396-D

145 Dance Scene in McIntosh County
Library of Congress
LC-DIG-fsac-1a34092

146 African-American Students Near Tabor
Library of Congress
LC-USF34-035091-D

147 Bartlesville's College High
Oklahoma Historical Society
17956

148 Charlie Christian
Oklahoma Historical Society
20699-84-92-16

149 Worker in the Seminole Field
Library of Congress
LC-USF346-012396-M2-Q

150 Will Rogers Theatre in Tulsa
Oklahoma Historical Society
21500-231-3

151 Great Lakes Pipeline Mechanic
Library of Congress
LC-USW33-000718-C

152 Great Dane Mascot
Library of Congress
LC-USW33-000376-ZC

153 Pack Mules Training with Artillerymen at Fort Sill
Library of Congress
LC-USW33-000275-ZC

154 Soldiers by the Roxy Theatre in Muskogee
Library of Congress
LC-USW33-000275-ZC-1

155 Workers at the Mid-Continent Refinery in Tulsa
Library of Congress
LC-DIG-fsac-1a35444

156 Moffett Homes in Flood
Library of Congress
LC-USW33-029189-C

157 Oil Derrick
Library of Congress
LC-USW4-029546

158 Wildcatters Working to Bring in a Well
Library of Congress
LC-USW4-029548

159 Chapter Title
from "Never Been to Spain"
by Hoyt Axton

160 Children of St. Joseph Industrial School
Oklahoma Historical Society
21412.M502.2

161 Hornbeck Theatre in Downtown Shawnee
Oklahoma Historical Society
21565-17

162 Strike at Oklahoma National Stock Yards
Oklahoma Historical Society
21040.4

163 Will Rogers Memorial in Claremore
Oklahoma Historical Society
21412.M62.14

164 President Harry S. Truman at Ardmore
Oklahoma Historical Society
23139.G174

165 Oklahoma City's Main Street with Christmas Decorations
Oklahoma Historical Society
21412.M92.14

166 Capitol Hill High School
Oklahoma Historical Society
21412.M267.4

167 Robinson Canyon
Oklahoma Historical Society
21412.B54.17.2

168 Wilson's Grocery Store
Oklahoma Historical Society
20978-109

169 Oklahoma City's Main Street at Night
Oklahoma Historical Society
22055.5509

170 Quanah Parker Lake Dam
Oklahoma Historical Society
21412.M108.27

171 Stillwater Airport
Oklahoma Historical Society
21810-1114

172 Tony's Grill
Oklahoma Historical Society
21412.M244.3

173 Biltmore Hotel
Oklahoma Historical Society
22055.7371

174 Aerial View of Downtown Oklahoma City
Oklahoma Historical Society
21412.B54.21.1

175 Aerial View of Downtown Tulsa
Oklahoma Historical Society
21412.M376.12

176 Catoosa Indian Trading Post
Oklahoma Historical Society
21160.0002502.9

177 The Gold Star Memorial
Oklahoma Historical Society
9130

178 Library at Oklahoma A&M University
Oklahoma Historical Society
21412.B124.2

179 African-American Riders Board Bus
Oklahoma Historical Society
21412.M413.20

180 Students at Chilocco Indian School
Oklahoma Historical Society
19055f

181 Mechanics of a Mobile Gas Station
Oklahoma Historical Society
21412.M137.7

182 Church Avenue in Harrah
Oklahoma Historical Society
19445-19-8

183 Operation Small Fry
Oklahoma Historical Society
23245-2

184 Semi-Centennial Celebration
Oklahoma Historical Society
23177-10

185 Hugo-based Blitz Popcorn Protest
Oklahoma Historical Society
21112-117

186 Semi-Centennial Celebration Parade
Oklahoma Historical Society
19599-1

187 Atkins Music Company
Oklahoma Historical Society
21412-M1680-2

188 Park Avenue
Oklahoma Historical Society
21412.M223.30

189 Members of the NAACP Youth Council
Oklahoma Historical Society
20246.38.395.T

190 Persian Room of the Skirvin Tower
Oklahoma Historical Society
22055-18565-7

191 Sit-inners
Oklahoma Historical Society
20246-38-407-2

192 Arnold Palmer
Oklahoma Historical Society
22055-20964-1

193 President John F. Kennedy
Oklahoma Historical Society
23139.G314

194 Guthrie Central Elementary School
Oklahoma Historical Society
21912-9

195 The Diana Theatre
Oklahoma Historical Society
21500-117-1

196 Members of the Teamsters Union on Strike
Oklahoma Historical Society
22055.23939

197 Richard Nixon
Oklahoma Historical Society
20246.38.352.6

198 Huckins Hotel
Oklahoma Historical Society
22055.26771

199 Camelot Hotel
Oklahoma Historical Society
10937

200 Boston Avenue Methodist Church
Oklahoma Historical Society
21175.238

HISTORIC PHOTOS OF
OKLAHOMA

Oklahoma has an excellent photographic record, largely because the twin territories developed along the same general timeline as modern photography itself. *Historic Photos of Oklahoma* is not an illustrated history of Oklahoma, nor is it an attempt at a visual chronology of the state. Rather, the photographs included here tell the story of this diverse group of people called Oklahomans as witnessed in their faces, the homes they cherished, and the streets they traveled.

Just as viewing a succession of school photos reveals the periods of beauty and awkwardness, innocence and maturity, and hardship and joy in a child's life, the reader of this book will see the tragedy of Indian removal, the exuberance of land runs, the shame of segregation, the anguish of the Depression, and the optimism for the future in Oklahoma. In between are glimpses of how we used to live, work, and play in the forty-sixth state of the Union.

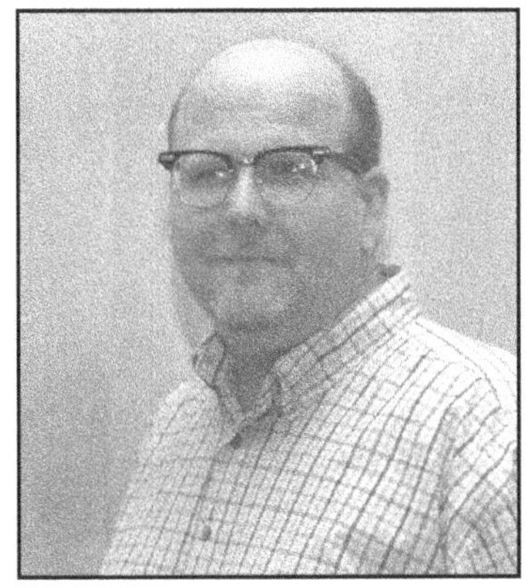

Larry Johnson holds a degree in history from Southern Nazarene University, a library degree from the University of Oklahoma, and a cherished certificate in Nuclear Disaster Preparedness from FEMA.

He is a reference librarian for Oklahoma City's Metropolitan Library System, for which he maintains the Oklahoma Room and the Oklahoma Images database. He is a frequent contributor to *Info* magazine and has written *Historic Photos of Oklahoma City* and *Historic Photos of Harry S. Truman*, both available from Turner Publishing.

He lives with his wife in Oklahoma City, where they share their home with a Jack Russell terrier named Mojo and a poodle named Cheez Whiz.

WWW.TURNERPUBLISHING.COM

www.ingramcontent.com/pod-product-compliance
Lightning Source LLC
LaVergne TN
LVHW060612110826
845154LV00003B/74
9781684420711